TOLERATION
and the
CONSTITUTION

TOLERATION
and the
CONSTITUTION

David A. J. Richards

OXFORD UNIVERSITY PRESS
New York   Oxford

Oxford University Press

Oxford   New York   Toronto
Delhi   Bombay   Calcutta   Madras   Karachi
Petaling Jaya   Singapore   Hong Kong   Tokyo
Nairobi   Dar es Salaam   Cape Town
Melbourne   Auckland

and associated companies in
Berlin   Ibadan

Copyright © 1986 by Oxford University Press, Inc.

First published in 1986 by Oxford University Press, Inc.,
200 Madison Avenue, New York, New York 10016

First issued as an Oxford University Press paperback, 1989

Oxford is a registered trademark of Oxford University Press

Library of Congress Cataloging-in-Publication Data

Richards, David A. J.
Toleration and the Constitution.

Bibliography: p.
1. United States—Constitutional law—Interpretation and construction.
2. Religious liberty—United States.
3. Freedom of speech—United States.
4. Privacy, Right of—United States.   I. Title.
KF4550.R48   1986   342.73'085   86-2358
ISBN 0-19-504018-X   347.30285
ISBN 0-19-505947-6 (PBK)

2 4 6 8 10 9 7 5 3

Printed in the United States of America

For Mother
and
For Diane,

Who Keep Faith

Absolute liberty, just and true liberty, equal and impartial liberty, is the thing that we stand in need of.

—JOHN LOCKE, *A Letter Concerning Toleration*

Preface

The personal and political identity of Americans is profoundly influenced by a written constitution in terms of which they define their basic liberties and responsibilities as a free people. Accordingly, the interpretation of that constitution is a just preoccupation not only of judges and lawyers, but of all American citizens. Paradoxically, this topic which should be of absorbing interest to all Americans—constitutional interpretation—has received little critical attention from students of constitutional law. But recent interest in the question of interpretation—among philosophers, literary critics, cultural historians and anthropologists, and others—suggests that the time may be ripe for constitutional law to rediscover its central and most absorbing topic. This book presents constitutional interpretation as vital to the needs of constitutional government in the United States, and proposes an approach to its study that calls for a new kind of critical synthesis of historiographical, legal, and philosophical methodologies.

Theoretical reflection on American constitutional law is in a period of creative ferment: certain traditional conceptions of the theory and practice of constitutional law are under sharp criticism and new alternatives are under construction. This book questions the sterile academic specialization that has isolated the discourse of the American law school from the wider discourse of political philosophy, moral theory, and history. It questions the segregation of thought from action which

The epigraph to this volume appears in the preface to Locke's *Letter Concerning Toleration*, p. 4. The statement is not by Locke but was inserted by his translator William Popple. See pp. 74, 91 n. 1, J. W. Yolton, *Locke: An Introduction* (Oxford: Basil Blackwell, 1985).

hinders Americans from thinking about their constitutional traditions
with the necessary intellectual rigor. If we are to heal these dangerous
rifts between our intellectual and political lives, we must, I argue, ask
deeper questions about the nature of constitutional interpretation and
its internal connections both to history and political theory. We must
be, at once, more philosophical as lawyers and as citizens, and, as philosophers, more political.

Because the issues of constitutional interpretation concern all Americans, I have written this book for both the general reader and for specialists in law, philosophy, or history, as the case may be. Consistent
with this objective, I have included some discussions largely to orient
the general reader to the state of the art in legal theory; thus, chapter
1 is a purely introductory review of the current state of constitutional
theory and might be lightly passed over by those already familiar with
this literature. On the other hand, in order to make clear the possible
uses of my interpretive perspective for specialized areas of constitutional interpretation, I have included some fairly detailed discussion of
constitutional doctrine. A specialist in free speech issues might therefore take an interest in chapter 7 of this book, while a more general
reader might find the general discussion in chapter 6 quite enough to
satisfy his interest in the law of free speech. That reader might skim or
omit chapter 7.

The structure of the argument of this book moves from criticism of
current positions on interpretation in general and constitutional interpretation in particular (chapters 1–3) to the construction of an alternative approach applied, *seriatim*, to religious liberty (chapters 4–5),
free speech (chapters 6–7), and constitutional privacy (chapters 8–9).
I conclude with a methodological assessment of the explanatory and
critical achievement and promise of the interpretive approach here
urged (chapter 10).

The novelty of the interpretive approach (chapters 1–3) lies in its
attempt to integrate a critical political theory of our constitutional law
with a self-understanding of our historical constitutional traditions, and
the larger moral, religious, and political ideals that they reflect. My
constructive methodological position is developed in chapters 2 and 3.
Here, the attempt to combine a sense of history with political theory
may enable us to deepen our understanding not only of constitutional
interpretation, but of the humane activity of interpretation more generally, which pervades every aspect of our cultural life. The interpretive activities of judges and lawyers serve, I argue, as extremely complex means of making both the best historical and philosophical sense
of our legal and political traditions. We can only do justice to such
interpretive complexity when we learn to bring to bear on it the tools
of historical understanding and political theory inseparable from such
interpretive activity. If we do this, however, both philosophers and
lawyers may begin to understand the historical truth behind Ralph Bar-

ton Perry's insistence[1] that American constitutional law is intrinsically philosophical and the interpretation of it clarified by more critical appreciation of its philosophical premises.

As part of the current state of intellectual discourse, made possible by Rawls's pathbreaking work,[2] political philosophers today acknowledge that arguments of political theory are, if anything, sharpened when considered in the context of our historical traditions of constitutional argument. But many legal scholars would not acknowledge the converse utility: that both our law and our history are better understood and more critically evaluated when arguments of political theory are brought to bear on legal argument.[3]

One aim of this book is to make the case for this latter point in a way that lawyers, legal theorists, and citizens generally cannot ignore, to demonstrate that certain kinds of arguments of political theory do indeed advance our understanding of constitutional interpretation. Such arguments explicate not only larger interpretive structures but interpretive controversies in various specific areas of the law.

Another aim of this book is to show how such a use of political theory clarifies the place of historical understanding in legal interpretation generally and constitutional interpretation in particular. Thus, the argument draws extensively from the complex historical materials of the Western tradition both of religious toleration and persecution, European theorists of toleration, and the links of these traditions to the development of the remarkable American commitment to toleration in central constitutional ideals. On examination, these traditions are, I suggest, clarified by appeal to background political theory, both implicit and explicit. Indeed, such arguments of political theory clarify the place of historical understanding, interpretive traditions over time, and current constitutional jurisprudence in a way that advances our understanding of each in relation to the other. This historical perspective is, I believe, the necessary condition of understanding the complex strands of meaning essential to the serious study of constitutional interpretation.

This constructive interpretive argument elaborates a contractarian political theory of equal respect for conscience (chapter 4). Suitably developed, this theory illuminates a common thread of argument underlying constitutional rights of religious liberty (chapter 5), speech (chapters 6–7), and ways of life (chapters 8–9), all of which are well recognized in contemporary constitutional jurisprudence. The argument not only makes sense of the complex historical traditions that frame our self-understanding as a constitutional community committed to the inalienable right to conscience, but coordinates and explains a

1. Perry, *Puritanism and Democracy*, pp. 129, 590–91.
2. Rawls, *A Theory of Justice*; cf. Richards, *A Theory of Reasons for Action*.
3. See, e.g., Ely, *Democracy and Distrust*, pp. 43–72.

remarkable range of strands of our contemporary constitutional jurisprudence of the religion clauses, free speech and press, and constitutional privacy. In the light of such critical arguments, areas of our law,
which are often discussed in unconnected isolation from one another,
appear as the coherent elaboration of common principles and background political ideals and conceptions. We thus gain a wider understanding not only of abstract unifying structures, but of quite detailed
tests and rules; we understand our law better both abstractly and con-
cretely. In short, such political theory makes possible a deeper, more
probing, and more analytically rigorous constitutional interpretation.
These are gains that no interpreter of the United States Constitution
can or should ignore. If constitutional interpretation is the duty that is
the condition of the liberty of all citizens, such a perspective on interpretation may deepen our understanding of citizenship itself in a free
society.

Toleration is, I argue, the central constitutional ideal. The respect for
our self-determining moral powers of conscience gives a meaning to the
state neutrality demanded by the constitutional command of toleration,
and dignifies the ideal of the moral sovereignty of the people over
themselves and the state. Substantive and procedural constitutional
guarantees are, I argue, ways in which we express and preserve the
moral force of this ideal of equal respect in our political life. Toleration,
thus understood, is at the very moral heart of the dignity of constitutional law, and is thus the central or paradigm case of the rights that
constitutionalism protects.

Accordingly, current political controversy over the role of religion in
American public life reflects, I believe, controversy over the meaning
and application of moral ideals at the core of the American constitutional tradition. We need, as a people, more critically to understand
these moral ideals, which so inextricably link the freedom of religion to
the vitality of constitutionalism itself. Such critical understanding must
embrace both a better historical understanding of the traditions of religious toleration American constitutionalism reflects, consolidates, and
extends, and a philosophical articulation of the underlying conceptions
and principles which that history expresses. This book is meant as a
contribution to such critical understanding of the linkages among our
religious, ethical, and political ideals. It reminds us of an inward spiritual unity among a religion of prophetic challenge, an ethics of moral
independence, and a politics of constitutional liberties. We can keep
faith with these interlocking traditions only if we cultivate in ourselves
the intellectual and moral powers that the moral ideals, internal to
these traditions, dignify. This book is one exercise in articulating a critical vision of our selves and our constitutional community adequate to
this end.

New York
October 1985   D.A.J.R.

Acknowledgments

This book was written during my sabbatical year leave, 1983–84, from New York University School of Law. That full-year leave and the summer researches that anticipated it were made possible by generous research grants from the New York University School of Law Filomen D'Agostino and Max E. Greenberg Faculty Research Fund. Dean Norman Redlich and the successive chairpersons of the Research Committee (Professors John Costonis and John Johnston) were essential to this support. I am deeply in their debt and the debt of my colleagues in general for making possible at the law school the kind of commitment to learning, scholarship, and writing that gave me the opportunity to come to terms with the subject of this book.

My work on this book profited from criticism of earlier drafts of parts of this book by many good people. My colleagues Anthony Amsterdam and Ronald Dworkin were each enormously helpful through their written and oral criticisms, comments, and support; and another colleague, Sylvia Law, challenged and stimulated me to think more deeply about privacy and abortion. Participants in the N.Y.U. Law and Philosophy Group were equally helpful. Thomas Nagel and Frances Myrna Kamm of the N.Y.U. Philosophy Department were especially supportive. Several participants from Columbia Law School in the N.Y.U. Law and Philosophy Group stimulated reflection at crucial points, in particular, Professors Louis Henkin, Kent Greenawalt, and Bruce Ackerman. The two fine historians on the N.Y.U. law faculty, my colleagues John Reid and William Nelson, at various points guided my historical researches, and I am grateful to them both. The visit of Professor Harold Hyman of Rice University, as the Meyer Visiting Professor at the law school (1982–

83), stimulated my interest in historiographical interpretation. Visits to the law school of John Rawls and Thomas Scanlon also stimulated my thinking at crucial points in my composition of the argument of this book; John Rawls generously made available to me his unpublished lectures on Kant, and supplied other helpful material.

My good friend Professor Donald Levy of Brooklyn College (Philosophy) generously criticized and discussed with me many of the crucial arguments in this book, and reviewed parts of it with characteristically probing critical acumen.

The general structure of the argument of the book was first developed in the course of preparing the series of three lectures (entitled "Conscience, Human Rights, and Constitutional Law") I gave in the 1983–84 Perspectives Series on the Philosophy of Law in the Department of Philosophy, University of Notre Dame, during the week of November 7, 1983. The generous invitation to be a lecturer in that distinguished series gave me the unusual opportunity to develop my views on the issues of this book with the most receptive, sympathetic, and philosophically challenging audience for this kind of work and the issues discussed herein. Both the members of that distinguished department and its fine graduate students gave me the benefit of many illuminating discussions and comments. I am particularly grateful for illuminating discussion with Professors Cornelius Delaney, Richard Foley, Gary Gutting, Alvin Plantinga, John Robinson, Kenneth Sayre, David Solomon, and James P. Sterba.

Revisions of the argument of the book were much assisted by the critical comments of publishers' anonymous readers; they alone will know the full extent of my debt. Similar assistance was graciously given by Professor Kenneth Winston and the Boston group of the Austinian Society, who devoted several sessions to discussion of the manuscript. In particular, I must thank Professor Judith DeCew for her detailed written comments and advice on the constitutional privacy discussion. Conversations with my colleagues Paul Chevigny and Lawrence Sager also assisted revision. Finally, I acknowledge with thanks the service above and beyond the call of editorial duty of Cynthia Read of Oxford University Press; her advice on stylistic revision illuminated and guided my task.

At various points over the last several years, a number of N.Y.U. law students have ably acted as research assistants on this project. They included Eric Doppstadt, Alan Emdin, Paul Herzfeld, and Warren Ingber. I am grateful to them all for the ways in which they assisted the wide-ranging research investigations that underlie this book, and gave me the benefit of argument and exchange on the issues discussed.

The kinds of research underlying this book were invaluably assisted by the law library of the N.Y.U. Law School, and I am grateful for the many assistances of Professor Julius Marke and his successor, Professor Diana Vincent-Daviss.

My former secretary, Ms. Mirta Yurnet, also ably helped me track down sources and assisted research during my sabbatical leave, and I am most grateful to her.

Some parts of this book have been adapted and elaborated from previous publications. Part of the argument of chapter 1 appears as "The Aims of Constitutional Theory," 8 *U. Day. L. Rev.* 723 (1983). My views on interpretation in chapters 2 and 3 were developed in criticism of papers of Michael Moore and Frederick Schauer given at the interpretation symposium sponsored by the *Southern California Law Review* on February 25, 1984, and appear in my "Interpretation and Historiography," 58 *So. Calif. L. Rev.* 490 (1985). Parts of the historiographical argument in chapter 2 appear in my "Constitutional Interpretation, History, and the Death Penalty," 71 *Calif. L. Rev.* 1372 (1983). Some of the argument in chapter 9 relating to abortion was initially presented at a conference on abortion at Hampshire College held on January 22, 1983, subsequently revised and delivered to the Philosophy Department at Tufts University, and published as "Constitutional Privacy, Religious Disestablishment, and the Abortion Decisions," in a volume of essays, *Abortion: Moral and Legal Perspectives* (Jay Garfield and Patricia Hennessey, eds., Amherst: University of Massachusetts Press, 1984). Another part of the argument in chapter 9, on the application of constitutional privacy to consensual sex acts, was developed in the brief, *amici curiae,* which I wrote on behalf of the American Association for Personal Privacy et al. in the case of *State of New York v. Uplinger,* No. 82–1724, Supreme Court of the United States, October Term, 1983. My work on that brief profited from the advice of Barbara Whitney, Executive Director of the Sex Information and Education Council of the United States, one of the groups on whose behalf I wrote that brief. Melvin L. Wulf, Esq. also gave helpful advice.

Contents

PART II. RELIGIOUS LIBERTY

PART III. FREE SPEECH

I / Interpretation
&
The Constitution

1 · The Aims of Constitutional Theory: A Comparative Analysis

This book takes constitutional interpretation to be the central topic of constitutional theory, and offers a certain constructive approach to this topic. The general reader will understandably want to know the kinds of questions that theories of constitutional law have traditionally posed and answered. It is, perhaps, a general truth that the construction of theory, whether in science or ethics or law, is comparative: we judge the adequacy and power of our theories against the comparable theories in the field, whether the comparison is between Ptolemaic and Copernican celestial mechanics[1] or between utilitarian and autonomy-based theories of ethics.[2] Accordingly, any new construction of constitutional theory must take as its benchmark the reigning theories of constitutional law.

The traditional terms of theoretical discussion are framed by controversies over the legitimate scope and limits of judicial review, that is, the ultimate power of the judiciary to declare laws unconstitutional, and thus invalid as law. The terms of the controversy are defined by

---

1. See, e.g., Lakatos, "Falsification and the Methodology of Scientific Research Programmes"; Laudan, *Progress and Its Problems.*
2. See Rawls, *A Theory of Justice;* Daniels, "Wide Reflective Equilibrium and Theory Acceptance in Ethics."

two kinds of skeptical theories: court-skeptical and rights-skeptical theories.[3]

COURT-SKEPTICAL THEORY

In order to explore these two kinds of theories, let us begin with the classic exemplar of a court-skeptical theorist, namely, James B. Thayer's 1893 article "The Origin and Scope of the American Doctrine of Constitutional Law." Thayer's argument has three stages. First, he insists that the power of judicial review by the Supreme Court is inferential, not explicit. Second, judicial review is clearly limited to judicial contexts. A court must be able to formulate and apply a justiciable standard of constitutionality to a case or controversy, whose just disposition requires that the constitutional issue be decided. Third, even assuming the requisite case or controversy and justiciable standard of decision, the standard of review should be deferential. Thayer's first two arguments make historical points about the origins and limits of the doctrine of judicial review established by Chief Justice John Marshall in *Marbury v. Madison.*[4]

Thayer's third argument is not historical at all. Here, Thayer invokes general considerations of democratic political theory in support of his deferential standard of review. The standard is Thayer's rule of clear mistake: a court should exercise its power of declaring a law unconstitutional only if the relevant legislative body has clearly made a mistake. The judiciary is only to exercise its power of judicial invalidation in the most extreme cases of blatant legislative disregard of constitutional constraints. As long as any constitutional basis for the legislature's action can be found, the legislation is to be sustained.

Thayer's argument in support of this deferential standard of review does not rest on rights skepticism. There is no indication that he does not believe in the existence of rights, or that he believes that rights are unimportant as constitutional constraints on legislative power in the United States. Thayer argues in the Jeffersonian tradition, a tradition that has no doubts about the status and force of rights as constraints on legislative power; thus, Jefferson spiritedly opposes the Alien and Sedition Act as a violation of the First Amendment.[5] Rather, on this view, judicial review is the wrong way to enforce rights. The Jeffersonian tradition is, after all, also that of Rousseau and French democratic constitutions, for which the historic norm was that a bill of rights was not enforceable by the courts, but was instead binding on the legislature directly. The legislature, then, is the ultimate judge of the compliance

---

3. Cf. Sager, "Rights Skepticism and Process-Based Responses."
4. *Marbury v. Madison,* 5 U.S. (1 Cranch) 137 (1803).
5. See, e.g., Koch, *Jefferson and Madison: The Great Collaboration,* pp. 174–211.

of proposed legislation with constitutional guarantees.[6] Thayer is not, however, a radical Jeffersonian; he concedes the place of judicial review in egregious cases, which Jefferson and the French tradition might not. Thayer's modified court skepticism is grounded in what he takes to be the basic postulate of democratic constitutionalism, popular sovereignty. Since popular sovereignty is the fount of constitutional legitimacy, those agencies of government that are more in tune with the popular will should enjoy a preeminent role in the elaboration of constitutional guarantees.

The conclusion of the argument can then be readily drawn. Courts, because they are remote from the popular will, are not the main enforcers of constitutional constraints. The main enforcers are both the legislators, who are closer to the people, and the people themselves, who exercise the franchise to enforce their own rights (for example, by driving the unconstitutional Federalists from office when they violated the First Amendment), and who, as Jefferson believed, regularly revolt (every nineteen years).[7] The rule of clear mistake rests not on skepticism about rights, but rather on a skepticism about courts as the preeminent enforcers of those rights. Thayer argues that aggressive judicial review has resulted in the greatest loss a republic may suffer—the enervation of the spirit of constitutional democracy, the republican virtue of a vigilant citizenry aggressive in the defense of basic human rights. A citizenry accustomed to aggressive judicial review by courts is rendered torpid, no longer alive to their duties of republican citizenship but merely passive and besotted consumers of interest-group politics. The rule of clear mistake would preserve a narrow role for the judiciary in the areas of gravest constitutional abuse; otherwise, it would return the role of constitutional monitor to the people, to whom, Thayer argues, it properly belongs.

Thayer's is an argument from democratic political theory, but it begs the very question it so urgently raises. For, surely, if so much weight is given to the normative force of popular sovereignty as the ground for democratic legitimacy, a theory of popular sovereignty is a fundamental requirement. The constitutional concept expressed by "We, the People" is not self-evidently a populist claim. The Founders appear to have been acutely conscious of the abuses of power worked by majority factions,[8] and meant the constitutional structure (federalism, separation of powers, and judicial review) as a complex design of interlocking institutions which could limit such abuses by appropriate constraints. And if, following Rousseau,[9] popular sovereignty is explained in terms

6. See Vile, *Constitutionalism and the Separation of Powers*, pp. 176–211.
7. See Koch, *Jefferson and Madison*, pp. 62–96. See also Boorstin, *The Lost World of Thomas Jefferson*, pp. 204–13.
8. See, e.g., *The Federalist* No. 10.
9. Rousseau, *The Social Contract*, in *The Social Contract and Discourses*.

of some idealized conception of freedom, rationality, and equality, then again it is hardly clear that the Founders thought of these values as best realized by direct popular democracy (indeed, they expressly disavow this way of institutionalizing democratic values,[10] a point to which we shall return in the next chapter). Perhaps there are other forms of court-skeptical argument that can more plausibly sustain Thayer's position. For example, judicial deference may be called for when constitutional values do not require aggressive judicial scrutiny, as in the commerce clause[11] and substantive economic due process.[12] But Thayer's general argument will not do.

RIGHTS-SKEPTICAL THEORY

The classic statement of a rights-skeptical argument against judicial review is Learned Hand's *Bill of Rights* (1968). Hand's argument is in two parts: first, a historical argument that judicial review of acts of Congress (as in *Marbury v. Madison*) is necessarily a usurpation; and second, an argument from political theory to the effect that rights are anachronistic forms of superstition, and that judicial review premised on them must therefore be abandoned. Let us focus here on Hand's second argument, for the first argument is very probably false[13] and, even if true, not one that even Hand, after so much history elaborating *Marbury*, regards as decisive. The real force of Hand's argument is this: the moral ideals of human rights, which constitutional guarantees assume, are roughly as intellectually defensible as the witchcraft beliefs of the Azande.[14] Since these superstitions are necessary to the elaboration of the meaning of these constitutional guarantees, a modern political theory must, in good moral and intellectual conscience, either abandon the whole enterprise, or, at the least, circumscribe it narrowly.

Hand argues under two influences. One is the Benthamite claim that rights are "nonsense on stilts," for they substitute empty a priori intuitions for the careful calculations required by the utilitarian principle of maximizing the greatest happiness of the greatest number.[15] The other influence is the uniquely twentieth-century moral philosophy, emotivism, which holds that ethical language has no propositional con-

10. See *The Federalist* No. 10 (expressly repudiating such a democracy in favor of a conception of a republic).
11. See, e.g., *United States v. Darby*, 312 U.S. 100 (1941).
12. See, e.g., *West Coast Hotel Co. v. Parrish*, 300 U.S. 379 (1937).
13. See, e.g., Beard, *The Supreme Court and the Constitution*; Berger, *Congress v. the Supreme Court*. But cf. Boudin, *Government by Judiciary*; Crosskey, *Politics and the Constitution in the History of the United States*.
14. Evans-Pritchard, *Witchcraft, Oracles and Magic Among the Azande*.
15. See Bentham, "Anarchical Fallacies," in *The Works of Jeremy Bentham*, Book II, p. 501.

tent and that its logical status is roughly equivalent to expressions of taste as governed by the maxim *de gustibus non disputandum*.[16] The value-skeptical element in Hand's argument is strong: moral values are irreducibly subjective and can hardly constitute the kind of objective standard that judicial impartiality requires. Hand concedes that strong substantive values of human rights were assumed by the great founding documents—the Declaration of Independence, the Constitution, the Bill of Rights. But, following Oliver Wendell Holmes,[17] he argues that a sound jurisprudence (legal positivism) requires that law be washed in the acid of cynicism to remove all traces of such ideals. When we do so (given the dependence of judicial review on such values), judicial review is left without content. We cannot, as judges or lawyers or citizens, give expression in our work to anachronistic conceptions of natural law for which we are unable to give any rational basis.

Hand concludes his general attack on judicial review with the argument of a third legislative chamber. The federal Constitution calls, Hand argues, for two legislative chambers and expressly limits the judiciary's role as constitutional monitor to cases of judicial necessity. But, if, as earlier argued, the mandated judicial role is grounded on baseless superstition, the judiciary's actual performance was simply a form of policymaking essentially no different from that of the two houses of Congress. In this case the power of judicial review, in effect, makes of the judiciary a third legislative chamber. The judiciary, however, has no special competence in policy matters superior to that of Congress; and since its other role is empty, judicial review merely indulges the subjective and incompetent policymaking of persons who lack the minimal accountability of electoral responsibility. Thus, modern political theory reveals judicial review as, in effect, a third legislative chamber, and fidelity to the residual spirit of rationality in the Constitution requires us to retain the legislative bodies that make sense and to lop off this moral monstrosity, judicial supremacy.

THE THEORY OF NEUTRAL PRINCIPLES

Response to Hand's rights-skeptical argument has focused on his claim that, on analysis, judicial review is seen to function as a constitutionally illegitimate third legislative chamber. The classic response was articulated by Herbert Wechsler in his "Toward Neutral Principles of Constitutional Law." Wechsler answers both Hand's historical and his political theoretic arguments. Since Hand himself did not regard the historical argument as decisive, it need not detain us here. The

16. See, e.g., Ayer, *Language, Truth and Logic.*
17. Holmes, "The Path of the Law," in *Collected Legal Papers.*

response to Hand's political theory involves the difference in the kinds of justification required of the judiciary as distinguished from legislatures, in particular, the requirement that courts justify their decisions in terms of neutral principles.

Wechsler's argument for neutral principles bypasses Hand's claims about the status of moral values in general and rights in particular and focuses instead on juristic method. The judiciary, consistent with *Marbury v. Madison,* does not in fact exercise policymaking discretion in deciding when, whether, or how to rule on cases, as Thayer suggests when he offers reasons for taking some but not other cases, or in the way Hand supposes all judicial decisions to be policy-based. Rather, both the place of the judiciary in the constitutional scheme and the due process of law demanded by the Fifth and Fourteenth Amendments[18] require that aggrieved parties have access to courts to hear their claims. If it is necessary to do justice between the parties, the courts should consider whether the law relevant to the rights and duties in dispute is consistent with the supreme law of the Constitution. In this latter constitutionally necessary role, the judiciary must decide in terms of general principles applicable to the case at hand and consistent with comparable cases that have arisen in the past.

This characteristic judicial methodology is distinct from the familiar processes of legislative reasoning. Legislatures are not required to justify their actions in any way analogous to the judicial method of following the authority of accepted precedents expressed in intricate written opinions which are subject not only to appellate review but to open and critical scrutiny by the profession in general, including the academic legal world of the American law school. Because of the distinctions between legislative and judicial decision making, courts do not function as a third legislative chamber.

Wechsler assumes that it is not necessary to address Hand's assertions about the moral vacuity of the values implicit in constitutional guarantees; indeed, Wechsler's argument almost glories in the purely legal, as opposed to ethical, aspect of the search for neutral principles. It is no accident that Wechsler chooses to demonstrate the demands of the requirement of neutral principles with a test of the legitimacy, on neutral principles grounds, of *Brown v. Board of Education.*[19] The reasoning of the Supreme Court in *Brown* and subsequent similar cases does not satisfy the requirement of neutral principles, for the cases cannot be squared with a general principle of acceptable form. The antidiscrimination principle stated in *Brown* appears to focus on the peculiar importance of a fundamental right, in this case education. But in later antidiscrimination cases, without explanation, the principle is extended

---

18. Cf. Hart, "The Power of Congress to Limit the Jurisdiction of Federal Courts: An Exercise in Dialectic."

19. *Brown v. Board of Education,* 347 U.S. 483 (1954)(segregated education invalid).

to areas (public swimming pools, golf courses, and the like) which cannot reasonably be supposed to concern fundamental rights.[20] If the neutral principle in question turns on the presence of racist motive actuating the law or policy in question, how is the judiciary reasonably to
infer such a motive? If racial motive is unconstitutional, is sexist motive
as well? Finally, if the Court has in mind as a neutral principle a simple
prohibition of any state-sponsored use of racial classifications, then how
can it permit what surely will reasonably be required in the future, the
use of racial classifications in affirmative action programs designed to
undo the effects of the now unconstitutional racial discrimination?[21]
Wechsler concludes that the available cases have not answered these
questions and thus they stand accused of lacking a neutral principle.
Wechsler proposes, tentatively, the principle that the state cannot stop
the associational rights of black and white parents to send their children
to school together, but since this associational liberty should also be
extended to parents who do not want their children to attend integrated schools, it would not yield the result in *Brown*.

Wechsler appears to concede that *Brown* is a *morally* right, a just
decision. His argument is that it is not *legally* acceptable because it
lacks the requisite form of publicly articulated and tested neutral principle. By contrast, Wechsler suggests that *Plessy v. Ferguson*,[22] the separate but equal decision that *Brown* overrules, does have a neutral principle, namely, that all whites will be segregated to one state facility, all
blacks to another, if the facilities are equal in quality. This principle
(separate but equal) is neutral because, given its stated terms and content, it may be applied impartially on the basis of its content, without
reference to particular characteristics of people irrelevant to the content or purpose of the principle. In short, cases similar in relevant
respects from the point of view of the content or purposes of the legal
rule are decided similarly; like cases are treated alike. *Brown* and its
progeny, however, lack any such stated content that courts would apply
in all similar cases. The consequence is that a putatively just decision,
Brown, is not legally acceptable, lacking a neutral principle, while a
clearly unjust decision, *Plessy*, is legally acceptable because a neutral
principle supports it.

Wechsler sidesteps Hand's accusation of moral vacuity by propound-
ing a method that can be elaborated independent of moral values; it
may legally validate the unjust and invalidate the just. The test of neutral principles is, for Wechsler, a formal one, what Lon Fuller called

---

20. E.g., *Gayle v. Browder*, 352 U.S. 903 (1956) (buses); *Holmes v. City of Atlanta*, 350
U.S. 879 (1955) (golf course); *Mayor of Baltimore v. Dawson*, 350 U.S. 877 (1955) (swimming pools).
21. See, e.g., *Fullilove v. Klutznick*, 448 U.S. 448 (1980); *United Steelworkers v. Weber*,
443 U.S. 193 (1979); *University of California Regents v. Bakke*, 438 U.S. 265 (1978).
22. *Plessy v. Ferguson*, 163 U.S. 537 (1896).

the "internal morality of law,"[23] but that is precisely its problem. If Hand's accusation of moral vacuity goes unanswered, then the method of neutral principles can be dismissed as simply consistent superstition, all the more outrageous because judges and lawyers are bound by it, even if it means validating what they know to be unjust, or invalidating what they know to be just. If the method has no internal moral justification other than consistency and if it throttles democratic politics in an illegitimate way (Wechsler fails even to address the democratic objection), then Hand clearly goes unanswered.

On these issues, there appears to be little advance in Alexander Bickel's book *The Least Dangerous Branch*. On all essential points, Bickel retains Wechsler's theory of neutral principles as a test of the legitimacy of judicial decisions on the merits, modifying the full rigor of Wechsler's demanding principles only at the stage of deciding whether to decide. At this stage, Bickel suggests, the Court may correctly entertain reasons of policy, using the devices of standing, mootness, ripeness, political questions, and the like, to avoid taking cases not wisely decided on grounds of principle. Thus, of the variant possible neutral principles for *Brown v. Board of Education*, Bickel opts for prohibition of state-sponsored racial classifications. He deals with the putative unconstitutionality of affirmative action programs under this principle by calling for the Court to exercise the "passive virtues," using various of the avoidance devices not to take such cases, at least until such time as the political goods from these programs have been adequately worked out.[24] Bickel's attempt to qualify the force of neutral principles in this way does not appear to be well supported by the law. It is also morally objectionable in that it would allow the Court always to avoid precisely the hardest and most controversial cases in which the constitutional order may most demand a principled disposition by the Court.[25]

Bickel does make one important addition to Wechsler's rather positivistic interpretation of the procedure of the search for neutral principles. Whereas Wechsler glories in the separability of law and morals that the search for neutral principles calls for (thus his criticism of *Brown*, a just decision, on neutral principles grounds), Bickel places the search for neutral principles in a larger ethical context, the product of background moral traditions of Western civilization.[26] The nature of this search is not elaborated. In his later books, however, the remark is

---

23. See Fuller, "Positivism and Fidelity to Law—A Reply to Professor Hart"; cf. Fuller, *The Morality of Law*.
24. Bickel was hoist with his own petard in *DeFunis v. Odegaard*, 416 U.S. 312 (1974), when he urged the Court to invalidate affirmative action programs, and the Court invoked the "passive virtues," here mootness, not to decide.
25. See Gunther, "The Subtle Vices of the 'Passive Virtues.'"
26. See Bickel, *The Least Dangerous Branch*, pp. 236–37.

amplified in terms of a vague conception of populist acceptance[27] or Burkean tradition,[28] neither of which advances much beyond Thayer's invocation of popular sovereignty.

On balance, despite his promising early appeal to background ethical traditions, Bickel's account does not address the rights-skeptical argument any more successfully than Wechsler's. To the extent that Bickel continues to depend on neutral principles, such principles remain, unless Hand is answered, merely consistent superstitions. To the extent that Bickel urges the utility of the "passive virtues" to free courts from the constraints of neutral principles, he compromises the whole functional theory of the judicial versus the legislative role. And to the extent that the substantive values of the judicial role are rooted in populism or tradition, it is unclear in what way the Court better expresses populism and how it discriminates valued and disvalued parts of tradition and yet facilitates just social change. In short, we need some appropriate methodology for identifying and elaborating those parts of our traditions that proper constitutional interpretation justly reflects. Bickel has pointed us in the right direction, but gives us no critical tools for making the required distinctions.

RIGHTS-BASED THEORY

These forms of constitutional theory set the stage for Ronald Dworkin's appeal for a new departure in constitutional theory, a theory that takes account of the "better philosophy . . . now available"[29] and takes rights seriously. Dworkin argues that skeptical theories of judicial review and the attempts to answer them lack any sophistication in the discussion of political theories of human rights. He concludes:

> Constitutional law can make no genuine advance until it isolates the problem of rights against the state and makes that problem part of its own agenda. That argues for a fusion of constitutional law and moral theory, a connection that, incredibly, has yet to take place.[30]

The great virtue of this new departure is that it takes seriously the basic arguments of political theory which underlie both the court-skeptical and rights-skeptical arguments. Neither Thayer nor Hand, the leading exponents of the two positions, rests his argument, at bottom, on history. Rather, they rely on certain propositions of political theory against which they test judicial review and find it wanting. One of

27. Bickel, *The Supreme Court and the Idea of Progress.*
28. Bickel, *The Morality of Consent.*
29. Dworkin, *Taking Rights Seriously*, p. 149.
30. Ibid.

them, Hand, expressly grants that the Founders believed that rights exist and intended that constitutional guarantees were to be elaborated as consistent with their normative requirements. He argues, however, that modern political theory compels the rejection of such superstition and prescribes the concomitant reconstruction of constitutionalism on rational grounds. We see, then, the primacy of political theory over constitutional theory; the power of the one controls, modifies, rearranges the other. But are the political theories of Thayer or Hand defensible? Is Thayer's view of popular sovereignty the soundest interpretation? Are rights so indefensible as normative constraints that the Constitution must be washed of them in cynical acid?

Dworkin's argument suggests that these questions, fundamental to the soundness of constitutionalism, can now be considered in the light of the rebirth of rights-based political theory, marked by the publication in 1971 of John Rawls's *A Theory of Justice*.[31] Rawls's argument has initiated this rebirth because his contractarian political theory plausibly defends principles of justice (for example, a principle of equal liberty) which give weight to distributive constraints of equal distribution (including certain equal rights) in a way that classical utilitarianism, with its focus on aggregates, does not. (The structure of such a contractarian argument will preoccupy us in later chapters.)

Rawls's book has prompted an outpouring of critical literature of enormous complexity which cannot be fully canvassed here.[32] Some accept the antiutilitarian paradigm of rights that Rawls formulates, but argue that his principles of economic justice do not properly respect people's rights in their natural abilities.[33] Others question whether the contractarian construction could not yield some form of utilitarian principle which, suitably interpreted, would capture many of the important intuitions of justice contained in Rawls's principles.[34] But, it is clear to all serious students of normative theory that, as H. L. A. Hart has said,[35] Rawls's book initiated a paradigm shift in political theory, replacing the long dominant utilitarianism (with its skepticism, at least in its Benthamite formulation, about rights) with a rights-based or rights-sensitive political theory. Rawls's principle of justice of equal liberty, for example, establishes certain basic equal rights of the person which cannot be sacrificed to the demands of the utilitarian principle.

Thus, to the extent that Hand's criticism of rights rests on the utili-

---

31. See Rawls, *A Theory of Justice*. See also Richards, *A Theory of Reasons for Action;* Rawls, "Kantian Constructivism in Moral Theory." For Dworkin's appeal to Rawls in this connection, see *Taking Rights Seriously*, p. 149.
32. See, e.g., Daniels, ed., *Reading Rawls;* Barry, *The Liberal Theory of Justice;* Wolff, *Understanding Rawls;* and Sandel, *Liberalism and the Limits of Justice.*
33. Nozick, *Anarchy, State, and Utopia.*
34. Hare, *Moral Thinking: Its Levels, Method and Point.*
35. Hart, "Between Utility and Rights," p. 77.

tarian paradigm in its crude Benthamite form, its assumptions are now discredited. To the extent that Hand's position rests on a form of value skepticism,[36] that position today hardly seems the dominant paradigm that Hand assumes it to be. To the contrary, reflective contemporary moral relativists like Harman[37] and Williams[38] reject crude forms of value skepticism and, if anything, see themselves as arguing against the dominant current of opinion in ethics today, which is both nonrelativist and nonskeptical.[39]

But how, precisely, can the proliferation of rights-based or rights-sensitive theories invigorate constitutional theory? Here it is useful to remind ourselves of certain distinctions used by Dworkin in his theory of adjudication—the most sophisticated and accurate theory of adjudication currently available.[40] Dworkin suggests that judges, whether involved in statutory law, common law, or constitutional interpretation, use a method of principle (opposed to policy) whereby they excavate from previous case law the applicable principle of law and apply it to the novel, hard case. This method has two tests; the first is one of "fit." The principle used in the hard case must fit the data of the other cases, explaining their holdings as well as the holding arrived at in the hard case. Moreover, in many hard cases the available precedents are inconsistent or in tension or ambiguous; therefore, the "fit" criterion will not always work. The judge must then appeal to background rights, more general rights which both explain and organize many more particular rights throughout the legal system and which have normative appeal as good arguments of rights. In the light of such rights, the previous case law may be reinterpreted, realigned, trimmed, and sometimes overruled in the interest of a deeper theory of law which the judge has been able to construct. Dworkin associates the capacity adeptly to excavate background rights with the sometimes great historians (Holmes), social theorists and men of letters (Benjamin Cardozo), and moral philosophers (Louis Brandeis) who are, in the American legal culture, great judges,[41] oracles of the law, people, in Dworkin's phrase, of Herculean capacity. Examples of such Herculean achievements are Cardozo in

---

36. American theorists since Holmes have been utilitarians in their considered critical ethics, but value skeptics about conventional nonutilitarian morality. For a useful treatment of the positivist thesis of separability of law and morals, see Hart, "Positivism and the Separation of Law and Morals."
37. Harman, *The Nature of Morality.*
38. Williams, "The Truth in Relativism," *Moral Luck,* pp. 132–43. But cf. pp. 156–73, in Williams, *Ethics and the Limits of Philosophy.*
39. See, e.g., Gewirth, *Reason and Morality;* Brandt, *A Theory of the Good and the Right;* and Lovibond, *Realism and Imagination in Ethics.*
40. Dworkin, *Taking Rights Seriously,* pp. 81–130.
41. See generally Richards, "The Theory of Adjudication and the Task of the Great Judge."

MacPherson v. Buick,[42] and Brandeis as the architect of the right to privacy first as a tort right[43] and then as a Fourth Amendment right.[44]

Dworkin holds that the legal positivist canon of the analytical separability of legal and moral concepts is inadequate as an account of the adjudication of hard cases. Often the disposition of a particular hard case will require the judge or other interpreter to analyze and elaborate a background right rooted in a substantive ethical concept; the legal task in question will require elaboration of substantive moral values as well. Dworkin is not, of course, a strong natural law theorist. Evil laws can, for him, be laws. If fit is satisfied, the judge must apply a principle, regardless of her view of background rights. Even background rights, to be judicially cognizable, must be implicit in legal practice as general values that organize bodies of law.[45]

New rights-based and rights-sensitive theories, which *A Theory of Justice* initiated, can, Dworkin suggests, be used in constitutional law whenever they fit or, when fit fails, to articulate background rights. The demise of the heretofore dominant utilitarian paradigm frees lawyers to take account, in a way that Holmes and Hand could not, of the historically intended premises of constitutionalism without finding themselves, as did Hand, at war with contemporary political theory. Instead, the tasks of historical reconstruction and political theory can be mutually fertilizing and illuminating, perhaps even in synthesis. Perhaps it is now possible to accept constitutional interpretation itself as the central topic of constitutional theory, or so I shall argue shortly.

THE ROLES OF POLITICAL AND MORAL THEORY

The above remarks are merely methodologically suggestive. It remains to be shown that one of the rights-based or rights-sensitive theories is better suited than another for the interpretive task. However, in the context of the essentially comparative concerns of this chapter, we may usefully mark and briefly anatomize one striking failure to integrate new forms of political theory into constitutional theory, namely, John

42. *MacPherson v. Buick Motor Company,* 217 N.Y. 382, 111 N.E. 1050 (1916). See also Richards, "The Theory of Adjudication and the Task of the Great Judge," pp. 200–202.
43. Warren and Brandeis, "The Right to Privacy."
44. Here, Brandeis invokes the "right to be let alone," *Olmstead v. United States,* 277 U.S. 438, 478 (1928) (Brandeis, dissenting).
45. Thus, Cardozo's invocation of the duty of reasonable care, in *MacPherson,* which Cardozo finds inconsistent with the privity rule, is a general principle underlying much of the law of unintentional torts and crimes. Or consider Brandeis's excavation of the right to privacy, as underlying various extant rights of property, tort, copyright, unfair competition, and thus resonating to an independent right of tort and, eventually, constitutional law. For further elaboration of these points, see Richards, "The Theory of Adjudication and the Task of the Great Judge," pp. 200–205.

Hart Ely's repudiation of such forms of moral and political theory on the grounds that they are controversial.[46]

Ely's theory has two ill-fitting parts.[47] He offers the interpretivist theory, in which he outlines the full range of rights protected by constitutional texts illuminated by reasonable historical inferences about the intentions expressed by those texts. These rights would include the expansive elaboration by our law of the constitutional right to privacy. Next, Ely proposes a noninterpretivist theory, in which he denies, on grounds of sound democratic theory, that the interpretivist model can reasonably be pursued. Thus, the full elaboration of the constitutional protection of privacy (to abortion, for example), however much consistent with text and history, was a blunder. In chapter 10, we shall have occasion to question whether Ely's noninterpretivist theory is consistent with much else in American constitutional law, including the equal protection doctrines that Ely himself takes to be at the core of the constitutional legitimacy of judicial review. For present purposes, however, we may assume, following Ely, that his noninterpretivist political theory delegitimates some constitutional doctrines, and legitimates others.

Ely's appeal to political theory is a familiar move in constitutional theory, which often leads to much more radical skepticism. But, as lawyers and students of law, it is not enough merely to acknowledge the traditional primacy of political theory in controlling constitutional theory; we must be able to do political theory. The question then is, are Ely's arguments of political theory sound?

The argument is this: the only sound way to reconstruct the aims of democratic politics is in terms of ideal democratic procedure, in which all the interests of the persons affected by the democratic polity are fairly represented and given weight in the democratic process. Constitutional law is valid as long as it is representation-reinforcing; that is, to the extent that judicial review is necessary to ensure that democratic politics gives weight to and represents interests. For example, laws that use racial classifications, giving racist stereotypes the force of law, are the paradigm case of Ely's representational unfairness. The imposition of such racial classifications not only does not represent the blacks affected, but is inimical to the giving of proper weight to their interests.[48] Accordingly, such racial classifications are the just object of condemnation under the equal protection clause, which denies validity to laws that rest on such a representationally unfair process. The use of racial classifications in affirmative action programs, however, is not subject to such constitutional invalidation. This is because the process that

46. Ely, *Democracy and Distrust*, ch. 3. See Richards, "Moral Philosophy and the Search for Fundamental Values in Constitutional Law."
47. See Laycock, "Taking Constitutions Seriously: A Theory of Judicial Review."
48. See Ely, *Democracy and Distrust*, pp. 135–70.

leads to the use of such classifications does give proper representational weight to the interests of blacks. Affirmative action programs are not being used to inflict injury on blacks, but rather to give them a benefit consistent with undoing the long heritage of unfair treatment dealt them in the past.[49] Ely objects to certain elaborations of constitutional privacy because the laws invalidated on this ground neither protect privacy interests in the home nor are they the product of representational unfairness, but rest on a substantive ground independent of such interests or procedural defects. Indeed, one of these cases[50] clearly fails to accord representational fairness to a relevant group.[51] But judicial review has, Ely suggests, in such cases no proper role besides judging the fairness of the underlying process of representation leading to legislation—a task in which courts are uniquely competent. Ely's argument about the proper form of constitututional interpretation is thus very much wedded to his highly traditional conception of the aims of constitutional theory, namely, determining the proper scope of judicial review.

The entire weight of Ely's argument rests on the accuracy of his representation of his noninterpretive theory as a *procedural* theory of fair democratic process. The proper judicial role is to rectify unfair procedures; an improper judicial role is one grounded in substantive values. Yet Ely's appeal to procedure itself actually masks a highly controversial appeal to substantive values.

Thus, one plausible criticism of Ely's arguments asks exactly how we know that a democratic process has been, in Ely's sense, unfair. The underlying premise, against which the fairness of the process is tested, is, on this interpretation, some form of utilitarianism.[52] A process is unfair to the degree to which certain *interests* are not given weight or are actively prejudiced. If democratic politics fails to advance these interests or actively frustrates them, it fails to maximize the aggregate of satisfaction over frustration of interests, and judicial review assures that the interests are given their proper utilitarian weight. Once one sees that utilitarianism is the guiding premise of Ely's political theory, the theory cannot be represented as process-based at all: the judgment of representational fairness rests on a judgment of substance, namely, the utilitarian principle. If utilitarianism is the basic political theory,

---

49. Ibid., pp. 170–72.
50. *Roe v. Wade*, 410 U.S. 113 (1973).
51. See Ely, "The Wages of Crying Wolf: A Comment on *Roe v. Wade.*" For a fuller discussion of Ely's argument, see chapters 8 and 9.
52. Ely has, in fact, denied this utilitarian interpretation of his views. See Ely, "Professor Dworkin's External/Personal Preference Distinction." It is, however, a quite natural interpretation of his argument—see, e.g., Brest, "The Fundamental Rights Controversy: The Essential Contradictions of Normative Constitutional Scholarship", pp. 979–81. Certainly Ely affords no careful examination of the underlying conception of political theory he assumes, which would make clear what political theory he does assume.

one surely needs some extensive defense of it against the many forms of rights-based theories current in the philosophical field. Ely, however, simply dismisses all such theories because there is controversy about relative adequacy.[53] However, nothing can be more certain than that controversy also exists about the inadequacy of utilitarianism, especially in its classical forms, as a moral theory.[54] Ely's account, like the accounts of Thayer and Hand, rests on premises of political theory that prove, on examination, to be inadequately defended.

A related analysis of Ely's argument might note that utilitarianism can hardly do justice to the judicial decisions Ely regards as paradigmatically just, particularly cases in which despised minorities are subjected to prejudice through the political process. If the minority is sufficiently small and despised and the majority sufficiently large and cohesive, the pleasures of group solidarity and domination gained by the majority may be much greater than the frustrations inflicted on the minority. Such political action would, then, on utilitarian grounds, be justified. If the intuitive spirit of Ely's argument would still condemn the procedural unfairness of such actions, some underlying substantive argument of justice must explain why they are unacceptable. The very concept of procedural unfairness requires an underlying nonutilitarian, perhaps rights-based substantive political conception. Yet it is precisely such conceptions that Ely earlier dismissed. Again, the controlling issues of political theory are not adequately examined and defended.

The force of Ely's noninterpretive political theory, as a critical theory of American constitutional law, must be that it best captures the core values of the American democratic tradition. There is reason to doubt whether the pluralist model of democracy, which Ely assumes, is the best such theory. The pluralist model assumes that groups have interests exogenous to the political process, and that the democratic political process satisfies or aggregates those interests in an acceptable way. There is, however, an alternative understanding of American democratic traditions that construes government as properly responsive not only or essentially to private interests as such, but to a conception of the public good and basic rights articulated through public argument and debate. Constitutional guarantees serve, in part, to define principles and structures of public argument which delimit the force of purely private interests as the fundamentally legitimating force of democratic politics.[55] On this view, Ely's noninterpretive political theory not only does not understand its own premises, but is not the best critical theory of the enduring values of constitutional government as such.

53. See Richards, "Moral Philosophy and the Search for Fundamental Values in Constitutional Law."
54. Cf. Brest, "The Fundamental Rights Controversy: The Essential Contradictions of Normative Constitutional Scholarship," pp. 1102–4.
55. See Sunstein, "Naked Preferences and the Constitution."

Yet Ely would use this political theory to limit the scope of many doctrines of constitutional law. How is it, to echo Dworkin's similar question,[56] that lawyers of considerable intellectual capacity can deliver constitutional theories with such defective premises? There are, I believe, two plausible explanations, each of which suggests critical defects in the traditional understanding of the aims of constitutional theory.

In the first place, part of the problem appears to be the "lawyer's disease," deeply entrenched in American legal education, with its bias against cross-disciplinary inquiry. Lawyers fail to examine the philosophical and political theories they readily take for granted, thus distancing themselves from valuable discourse that could bring them to a better sense of the complementary aims of constitutional and political theory.[57] Whenever a theorist denies the relevance of philosophy in doing law, one can be reasonably sure that the theory itself rests on a philosophy (hidden under such labels as popular sovereignty, value skepticism, neutral principles, representational fairness) which the author is unprepared to examine philosophically.

Further, the focus on judicial review has, I believe, misdirected constitutional theory away from its central topic, constitutional interpretation, to a narrower preoccupation. This reverses the proper order of discussion, to the detriment of an understanding of both constitutional interpretation and judicial review. We can, for example, only understand the proper scope for judicial review under the Constitution when we understand the prior question of how the substantive and procedural constraints of the Constitution are to be interpreted and, derivatively, the appropriate role of the judiciary in this interpretive task.[58] We must, therefore, abandon the futile search for procedural neutrality as the aim of constitutional theory, and focus on the underlying issues of substantive political theory, which control the interpretive issues central to understanding constitutional government.

Ely's theory incoherently dismisses and assumes controversial political theory, coincident with his invocation and then dismissal of history in sound constitutional interpretation. Our examination suggests a diagnosis for both these incoherent elements. The practice of constitutional theory, if it denies political theory, will in fact assume a political theory, and typically one not critically examined and defended. The problem arises whenever constitutional theory denies the conditions of its own intelligibility and coherence as a historical practice constitutive of our moral and political identity as a community. We require a new per-

56. "Why has a sophisticated and learned profession posed a complex issue in this simple and misleading way?" Dworkin, *Taking Rights Seriously*, p. 148.
57. Cf. Dworkin, "The Forum of Principle."
58. Cf. Agresto, *The Supreme Court and Constitutional Democracy*.

spective that will enable us to use and understand our history more deeply, while deploying a more critically defensible form of democratic political theory. We need, in short, to ask more fundamental, more philosophical questions about the nature of interpretation in general, and legal and constitutional interpretation in particular.

2 · Legal Interpretation & Historiography

The theories of constitutional interpretation examined in chapter 1 are based on political theory, which is often sharply critical of the history and practice of constitutional interpretation in the United States. This tension between history and political theory pervades current constitutional theory. At one extreme are theorists who, like Raoul Berger, regard a certain conception of history or convention as essential to legitimate constitutional interpretion, and deny that contemporary political theory has any proper role therein.[1] The opposite extreme is occupied by theorists who, like Ely, appeal to a certain political theory to edit out historical doctrines inconsistent with the theory.[2] Both positions are, I believe, fraught with difficulties. The appeal of the first position to history or convention often rests on an undefended and indeed indefensible way of understanding the role of history or convention in interpretive practices. The second position invokes political theories, which also prove, on examination, to be inadequately defended. We

1. See Berger, *Government by Judiciary*; Berger, *Death Penalties*. See also Monaghan, "Our Perfect Constitution."
2. Ely, *Democracy and Distrust*. See also Perry, *The Constitution, the Courts, and Human Rights*. Perry argues that Berger is correct in arguing that constitutional *interpretation* can only track Berger's denotative exemplars, but then argues that constitutional decision making is legitimate, even if noninterpretivist, because it appeals to the best moral argument articulated by moral prophecy. In effect, constitutional law should, for Perry, track the best moral and political theory.

need to rethink what interpretation is, to find an approach that yields at once a fidelity to our history and a more critically defensible political theory.

Since all sound theoretical work depends on comparisons of alternative perspectives on the subject under discussion,[3] I will develop my own alternative constructive theory of interpretation by way of criticism of such views. This chapter will examine forms of both of the polar positions: first, the claim that constitutional law should ignore history and simply track the best moral and political theory we have; and second, Raoul Berger's claim that constitutional interpretation must track the denotative exemplars identified by his view of the Founders' intent.

It is not difficult to understand or appreciate the motives underlying the insistence of recent advocates of the natural law position that legal interpretation should ignore history or convention in the service of critical morality:[4] history or convention is often substantively unjust, and interpretive theories of law resting on history or convention must, accordingly, improperly trammel law in its task of doing justice. But this argument depends on two mistakes. One is the implicit disengagement of meaning in law from history and convention, suitably understood; the other is the false supposition that a theory of law that takes seriously the place of history and convention in legal interpretation must blind lawyers to their roles of doing the work of justice. We may best rebut the first mistake by asking more probing questions about interpretation in general and legal interpretation in particular. Chapter 3 will then be able to undo the second mistaken premise by doing what that premise claims cannot be done: defining a perspective on constitutional interpretation that is both rooted in history and convention and adequate to the moral mission of law.

INTERPRETATION AND WESTERN CULTURE

Interpretation of human action takes a characteristic form. As a simple example, consider the interpretation of the act of walking down the

3. See, e.g., Daniels, "Wide Reflective Equilibrium and Theory Acceptance in Ethics." For a comparable approach to scientific theory, see Lakatos, "Falsification and the Methodology of Scientific Research Programmes"; and Laudan, *Progress and Its Problems.*
4. In constitutional theory, Michael Perry has most notably taken this line; see Perry, *The Constitution, the Courts, and Human Rights.* For an articulation of a general legal theory of this kind, see Moore's "The Semantics of Judging"; "Moral Reality"; and "A Natural Law Theory of Interpretation." Ely's theory, because it limits legitimate constitutional law to the assessment of just procedures not just outcomes, does not adopt a general view of the primacy of critical morality to constitutional law, as such. See Ely, *Democracy and Distrust.* Ely does, of course, appeal to what he takes to be the best political theory in defining just procedures, but he recognizes such procedures often fall short of outcomes consistent with critical morality. For a sketch of the traditional contrast between legal positivism and natural law, see Richards, *The Moral Criticism of Law,* ch. 2.

street. Our interpretation of this action rests on a form of holistic, that is, nonreductive explanation in which such factors as the person's rationality, beliefs, desires, capacities, and the like appear as mutually interdependent variables.[5] Our imputation of a desire to a person (say, wanting food to allay hunger, or desiring companionship and entertainment, or desiring to exercise competence at one's vocation) will depend on the background beliefs we assume the person has (stores sell food, the theater provides entertainment, or getting to the office enables one to do one's work). In turn, our analysis of the person's beliefs will depend on the desires we assume he has. We are therefore led to characterize the act as going to the store, to the theater, or to work.

The conventional modes of discourse by which we communicate our beliefs, aims, and desires are also those in which we tend to think. The public conventions of language thus frame our understanding of the beliefs, aims, and desires that actions reflect, and therefore influence our interpretation of such actions. The role of language in interpretation is most salient in communicative actions (for example, speaking), but it also affects the understanding of all forms of action.

As other publicly acknowledged and regulated social conventions (such as language) frame the interpretation of human actions, so does law. People make wills and contracts, marry, respect property and personal rights, pay taxes, and the like, or they fail to do so; we interpret their actions, in part, in terms of the legal principles or rules that their conduct reflects or flouts. The interpretation of human action often requires a background theory of the cultural conventions that shape our consciousness, including law and, of course, language.

The interpretation of such cultural conventions requires, in turn, holistic explanation of the standard beliefs, desires, and purposes underlying these conventions, a kind of interpretive explanation aptly compared by philosophers and interpretive social scientists to the hermeneutic methodologies of textual interpretation.[6] In the familiar hermeneutic circle,[7] the interpretation of one text requires a certain kind of reading of others, and success depends upon making sense of the earlier text. Similarly, understanding the purposes of individuals in the culture requires an understanding of the cultural conventions that these individuals' purposes reflect.[8] Understanding these conventions is not, however, the same interpretive task as understanding an individ-

---

5. See Richards, *A Theory of Reasons for Action*, pp. 31–36, 54–59. For similar more recent accounts, see Hollis, *Models of Man*; Hookway and Pettit, eds., *Action and Interpretation*; Peacocke, *Holistic Explanation*.
6. See generally Rabinow and Sullivan, eds., *Interpretive Social Science*; Bernstein, *Beyond Objectivism and Relativism*.
7. See Hoy, *The Critical Circle*.
8. See Taylor, "Interpretation and the Sciences of Man," pp. 25–71.

ual's purposes. The difference is marked, I believe, by the more hypothetical and idealized use of rationality in the interpretation of cultural conventions. A cultural interpreter can arrive at a coherent sense of such community norms or ideals or standards of a kind that the interpretation of any individual's action does not either require or indeed permit. For example, the idealized community norms of the proper role of a parent or child may be only imperfectly reflected in the lives and attitudes of individual parents and children; or, in language use, the meaning that a speaker gives to a word (speaker's meaning) may depart from the standard and acceptable uses of those words in the language community in question (word or sentence meaning). Individuals in their pursuit of complex individual ends may both depart from and yet reflect the underlying cultural norm; indeed, the sense of departure from a norm is derived from the norms themselves. It is a now banal but nevertheless profound Wittgensteinian truth that more radical departures from such norms violate the basic conditions of community which make humans intelligible to one another.[9]

In order to make sense of cultural conventions of this kind, we must investigate the ways in which the conventions might reasonably be understood to reflect sensible human purposes in the community in question, including the common, perhaps idealized purposes that persons in the community would impute to their traditions as a whole.[10] In short, we make sense of such conventions as ways in which communities of rational agents might achieve and structure their individual and collective ends.

With unfamiliar cultures and peoples, this task of interpretation may require enormous intelligence, empathic identification, and imagination to understand how, in such communities, both purposes are achieved and experience explained.[11] Philosophers since Quine have puzzled over the translation problem posed by the "language" of a radically unfamiliar people with whom the translator shares no common ground.[12] Plausible reflections on the problem emphasize the significant place that the translator must give to principles of charity (maximizing agreement between the translator and translatee),[13] or, even more plausibly, principles of humanity (assuming that the translatee is

9. For an illuminating statement of this truth, see Cavell, "The Availability of Wittgenstein's Later Philosophy."
10. As an interpretive matter, this tends to express itself by inquiring into the larger purposes of traditions and institutions themselves. On the nature of this interpretive move, which is a kind of hypothetical interpretive personification of institutions, see Ronald Dworkin, *Law's Empire*. Cf. Gadamer, *Truth and Method*.
11. See, e.g., Geertz, *The Interpretation of Cultures*.
12. See Quine, *Word and Object*, esp. ch. 2, "Translation and Meaning," pp. 26–79.
13. See, e.g., Davidson, "Belief and the Basis of Meaning."

minimally rational, like the translator, and observing the same pattern of connections among evidence, belief, desires, capacities, and so on).[14] The translation practices of good cultural anthropologists solve a translation problem much less extreme than the radical unfamiliarity that interests philosophers. Their interpretive practices show how, once diverse circumstances and historical traditions of explaining experience are given weight, unfamiliar and superficially inexplicable behavior is found to reflect, in fact, a community's intelligible and rational pursuit of ends.[15] Often, such anthropologists use the distinction between "experience-near" and "experience-distant" concepts in their interpretation of such cultures. Explanatory concepts are "experience-near" if they would be used by individual members of the culture themselves in describing behavior; concepts are "experience-distant" if they are used by specialists, whether inside or outside the culture, to articulate larger or deeper interpretive patterns of thought and behavior in the culture.[16] The use of both kinds of concepts may be necessary in order to interpret an alien culture in an intelligible and accurate way. With familiar cultures and peoples, interpretation may be intuitive; nonetheless it can sometimes be equally demanding in precisely similar ways.

Concededly, in purely oral cultures, the interpretation of one's own culture may be uncontroversial. The central values and conceptions of the culture will be imparted through the cultural authorities who embody its oral tradition, and who transmit it in sometimes complex artistic forms suitably structured to enable the speaker and audience to retain the material in oral memory (the poetic structure of the *Iliad* and *Odyssey* may embody such structures, as a remnant of the oral prehistory of Greece).[17] Controversy over the interpretation of the meaning of the oral culture will be unthinkable at least in the terms typical of literate culture.

Culture is transformed, in ways we are only beginning to understand,[18] by the emergence of literacy and written texts: the very capacity to think of oneself as part of a culture is now delimited not by the

14. See, e.g., Lewis, "Radical Interpretation"; Grandy, "Reference, Meaning, and Belief."
15. See Horton, "African Traditional Thought and Western Science"; Horton, "Tradition and Modernity Revisited." See also Horton and Finnegan, eds., *Modes of Thought;* Benn and Mortimore, eds., *Rationality and the Social Sciences;* and other readings in *Rationality and Relativism.*
16. See Geertz, "From the Native's Point of View: On the Nature of Anthropological Understanding." See esp., pp. 226–27 (for example, love is an "experience-near" concept; object-cathexis an "experience-distant" concept). Specialists in "experience-distant" concepts include "an analyst, an experimenter, an ethnographer, even a priest or an ideologist," thus forwarding "their scientific, philosophical, or practical aims," p. 227.
17. See Lord, *The Singer of Tales;* Havelock, *Preface to Plato.*
18. For a recent overview of the burgeoning literature, see Ong, *Orality and Literacy.* For a seminal article, see Goody and Watt, "The Consequences of Literacy," pp. 27–68. For a seminal book, see Havelock, *Preface to Plato.*

exigencies of oral memory, but by the written texts that today preserve the content of the culture. Cultural homogeneity may still be very great, indeed greater than in the oral period, for a small and exclusive literate elite may, as in ancient Babylonia and Egypt, now be capable of a theocratic hierarchy which enforces forms of economic and political domination that were previously impossible.[19] But the presence of a written tradition introduces the possibility of divisive cultural controversy over the meaning of the written texts that convey the tradition. In favorable historical circumstances, such controversy is unleashed with cultural consequences as transformational as those associated with the emergence of literacy itself.

The culture of the West, the culture that we associate with the philosophical genius of ancient Greece and the religious genius of Judaism and Christianity, unleashed these controversies in a way not seen in such comparable high cultures as China.[20] The culture of the West has been decisively shaped by two historical moments, one integrative, the other divisive, both of which permanently established forms of interpretive controversy as part of the very foundations of that culture.

The first such moment grew out of the decision to build Christian culture on two kinds of synthesis: Old Testament prophecy, as fulfilled by the New Testament elaborating the uniquely Jewish conception of a personal and ethical God who acts in and through history;[21] and the assimilation of intellectual achievements of the pagan culture that the new culture supplanted.[22] Thus, for example, in both his *Confessions* and *The City of God*, Saint Augustine uses typological Bible criticism to interpret and integrate the meanings of the Old and New Testaments, and then applies this synthesis to interpret God's will acting through history.[23] And, in *The Trinity*, he discusses central theological questions in the context of interpretations of the integrated meanings of biblical texts and the great texts of pagan philosophy—in particular, the Neoplatonism of Plotinus.[24] This remarkable interpretive synthesis of complex texts, interpretive techniques (biblical typology), and background

19. See, in general, Goody, *The Domestication of the Savage Mind*. For a recent important study of the interaction of oral and written cultures, see Todorov, *The Conquest of America*.

20. See Plumb, *The Death of the Past*, pp. 62–101.

21. See, e.g., Jacobson, *The Story of the Stories*; Alter, *The Art of Biblical Narrative*.

22. See Cochrane, *Christianity and Classical Culture*; Santayana, *The Life of Reason*, vol. 3: *Reason in Religion*, pp. 69–177; Blumenberg, *The Legitimacy of the Modern Age*; Gilson, *God and Philosophy*. On the transition from pagan to Christian culture in late antiquity, see Dodds, *Pagan and Christian in an Age of Anxiety*; Brown, *The Making of Late Antiquity*.

23. Augustine, *Confessions*, Books XI–XII; Augustine, *City of God*. See Bonner, "Augustine as Biblical Scholar."

24. Augustine, *The Trinity*, in *Augustine: Later Works*, pp. 37–181. For general commentary on Augustine, his thought and period, see Brown, *Augustine of Hippo*; Brown, *Religion and Society in the Age of Saint Augustine*.

philosophical doctrines reveals a distinctively Western style of complex interpretive synthesis, wedded to a linear historical self-consciousness. Thus, in cultural historical perspective, Marxism, for example, appears to be very much a Western religion, or rather antireligion, in the long and vitally important Western heretical tradition.[25]

The second great moment arises in the Reformation in divisive disagreements within Christianity over the terms and content of the interpretive integration of its authoritative texts. Luther and Calvin, whose movements are fueled by the more widespread literacy made possible by the printing press,[26] propose alternative interpretive models for the exegesis of authoritative biblical and philosophical texts.[27] A new Erasmian philosophy, humanist in inspiration,[28] calls for the text of the Bible to be read in light of historical views of authentic primitive Christianity before it was corrupted by an unbiblical Church.[29] The domination of Christian philosophy by Aristotle is gradually eroded, giving way to a self-consciously more voluntarist, nominalist theology and a more Augustinian integration of Christian and pagan texts.[30] The earlier Christian interpretive integration provides the context for continuing discussion of the coherent meanings of diverse texts; the Reformation introduces a new kind of discussion of metainterpretive questions concerning how such texts should be interpreted.[31] These debates, in turn, energize new forms of interest in and cultivation of the nature of belief and knowledge, including the authenticity of different sources of knowledge and the proper ways of acquiring knowledge of the past, the present, and the future.[32] Indeed, it is these Reformation debates which vitalize the modern philosophy that we conveniently but misleadingly date from Descartes;[33] they significantly shape as well the development of the methods of knowledge acquisition

25. See Needham, *Science in Traditional China*, pp. 122–31.
26. For a brilliant general treatment, see Eisenstein, *The Printing Press as an Agent of Change*.
27. See Bainton, "The Bible in the Reformation." See also Sykes, "The Religion of Protestants."
28. See Bouyer, "Erasmus in Relation to the Medieval Biblical Tradition."
29. See Eisenstein, *The Printing Press as an Agent of Change*, vol. 1, pp. 163–450.
30. See P. Miller, *The New England Mind: The Seventeenth Century*, pp. 3–34. On the influence of nominalist theology, see Lovejoy, *The Great Chain of Being*, pp. 163, 332–33.
31. See Bainton, "The Bible in the Reformation"; and Sykes, "The Religion of Protestants."
32. See, e.g., Shapiro, *Probability and Certainty in Seventeenth-Century England;* Van Leeuwen, *The Problem of Certainty in English Thought, 1630–1690.*
33. See Popkin, *The History of Scepticism from Erasmus to Spinoza;* and the earlier version, Popkin, *The History of Scepticism from Erasmus to Descartes.* Also see Popkin, *The High Road to Pyrrhonism.* For a brilliant set of background readings, see Burnyeat, ed., *The Skeptical Tradition.*

(scientific method, historiography, and so on) characteristic of the modern mind.[34]

Within a literate culture such as the West, the task of interpretation even of one's own culture, completely familiar and intuitive as it is, may evidently make interpretive demands at least as difficult as the more obvious demands of understanding an alien and unfamiliar culture. Some aspects of the culture will be understandable only in light of a familiar authoritative text whose meaning in some respects is, nonetheless, controversial in the way that is structurally characteristic of Western culture as a whole. Here interpretation may call for metainterpretive inquiry. In some areas, notably religion, such metainterpretive controversy has naturally led to the development of independent moral and political norms of respect for the integrity of interpretive conscience and to the gradual elaboration of concomitant political and civil rights which express a similar respect for the person as free, rational, and equal. In effect, the authoritative interpretive tradition of no church may enjoy the force of law; each person is, as it were, a church unto herself, free to adopt, on terms of equal respect, metainterpretive principles in matters of basic conscience consistent with one's moral powers of rationality and reasonableness (see chapters 4 and 5). In other areas, an interpretive community is authoritative, but the task of interpretation within that community is often difficult and controversial.

LEGAL INTERPRETATION

Legal interpretation in Western legal systems exemplifies the authoritative situation, in which the conventions in question are intuitively familiar, but the interpretation of them often extremely difficult and, when addressed at all, often controversial.[35] For example, in the United States, the social conventions called law are embodied in complex written forms, including the written Constitution. Often, however, in hard cases, the proper interpretation of the legal conventions is extremely controversial: precedents conflict or are ambiguous, relevant historical materials are unclear or disputed, and the like. Here, legal interpretation is necessary, leading to controversy, which in turn calls into question the approach to legal interpretation as well. Legal interpretation, itself a convention directed at the understanding and elaboration of conventions (laws), must also be interpreted. The goal of such interpre-

34. See works of Shapiro and Eisenstein, cited in notes 32 and 26, respectively. See also Merton, *Science, Technology and Society in Seventeenth Century England;* Hill, *Intellectual Origins of the English Revolution.*
35. On the unique features of the Western legal tradition, see Berman, *Law and Revolution.*

tation, as in the interpretation of unfamiliar cultures, should be to
determine which approach to legal interpretation most rationally
advances the beliefs, desires, and aims of the legal community in a
coherent and sensible way. This, of course, is a metainterpretive
inquiry.

For the purposes of this inquiry, there can, a priori, be no reasonable
endorsement of any one style of interpretation. A style and method of
interpretation appropriate to one system of legal conventions may be
wildly inappropriate to another. All will depend on which form of legal
interpretation appears more rationally explanatory of the beliefs,
desires, and aims that the system reflects.

This casts doubt upon any abstract characterization of what *legal*
interpretation, as such, must be, in terms stronger than the normatively
weak requirements of Fuller's "internal morality of law".[36] Perhaps a
legal system, in order to count as a legal system, must, as Fuller proposed, satisfy certain criteria by which it may be identified as a public
system of rules through which people in the community may regulate
their conduct and which provides a stable basis of legitimate expectations. Derivatively, any characterization of legal interpretation must be
coherent with these weak normative criteria. Positivist and natural law
accounts of legal interpretation, however, often characterize such
interpretation in stronger ways. For example, a positivist like Raoul
Berger assumes that interpretation must track the denotative exemplars
contemplated by those who established the legal standard; advocates of
natural law claim that the legal process tracks moral reality. If such positivist accounts rest, as I shall shortly argue, on unsound theories of
what interpretation must be, natural law theories appear no less
unsound.

We should remind ourselves that legal theories are theories of law,
the norms that define in the relevant community the institutions of final
and ultimate authority in governance, including the use and application
of the legitimate coercive power over which the modern state maintains a monopoly.[37] The theory of the law of a particular legal system
must, accordingly, give an account of the way in which a particular
community defines and understands its final and ultimate authorities in
governance. In the legal systems expressive of the cultural tradition of
the West, as earlier described, the sense of how the community understands and defines such basic authorities will often focus on certain
written texts, many of which are arranged in a temporal sequence,
often in a self-conscious conception of authoritative interrelationship
(thus elaborating a continuous tradition). The interpretation of the law
of such communities is, accordingly, profoundly historical, often in illu-

36. Fuller, *The Morality of Law.*
37. See Hart, *The Concept of Law.*

minating analogy to the ways in which its religious and moral traditions are rooted in a deeply historical self-consciousness. Legal interpretation must therefore, as part of its interpretive task, utilize historical reconstruction of traditions of the community. Such a reconstruction may best define the community's sense of what its traditions now mean or should mean.

There have been various historiographic conceptions of method and purpose: cyclical conceptions of recurrent growth and decay, religious and eventually secular theories of a providential order of progressive meaning in history, mythical conceptions of an idealized past against which present religious or political corruption is critically assessed, and critical historiography based on rigorous standards of authentication of records against which hypotheses of historical description and explanation of human action in history are self-critically assessed.[38] Historical reconstruction in legal interpretation has as often been associated with providential theories of meaning in history (for example, the Whig theory of history)[39] and mythical conceptions of an ideal past (the primitive English Constitution)[40] as it has been with critical historiography. This should signal to us that historical reconstruction in legal interpretation serves purposes different from those of critical history as such. The task of legal interpretation is faithfully to account for a community's self-conscious historical understanding of itself as a legal tradition. The use of history in reconstructing this understanding must faithfully account for the normative values that necessarily explicate the structure of that historical tradition. Legal interpretation has often, however, tended to idealized conceptions of value in history, in a way that critical historiography must debunk.

On this view, a natural law theory of legal interpretation is open to decisive objection: it appeals to moral reality without an account of a community's self-understanding of legitimate power. If legal theory is a theory of anything, it is a theory of a central political practice of the most profoundly significant, shaping, and intrusive kind in the life of the community. But the natural law account appeals directly to moral reality bypassing the necessary intermediating account that a theory of law requires, namely, an explanation of why the appeal to moral reality is (as it often is) an illuminating way of reconstructing the historic meaning of legal tradition. Rather, history and convention are implausibly dismissed on the assumption, often unexamined, that the preservation of the integrity of moral reality so requires. As such, the theory diminishes the very basis of moral theory as an interpretive tool, which

---

38. For studies of these different approaches to history, see Plumb, *The Death of the Past;* Butterfield, *The Origins of History;* Collingwood, *The Idea of History.*
39. See Butterfield, *The Whig Interpretation of History.*
40. See Pocock, *The Ancient Constitution and the Feudal Law;* Pocock, *Politics, Language and Time.*

appears precisely in its utility in clarifying historical self-understanding. It is therefore subject to the decisive objection positivists have always made to strong natural law theories: law is often clearly immoral, and theories of law should sharpen our sense of this and not deny its ugly and recurrent reality.[41]

But why, in fact, is critical moral and political theory often useful as an interpretive tool of political self-understanding? How are its claims connected to critical historiography? Legal interpretation, as a form of historical reconstruction, does not merely call for a critical historiography of the facts of legal history. It requires as well that those facts, or rather the facts that bear on the centrally relevant texts of the legal tradition, all authenticated and clarified by critical history, be interpreted in a normative way, so as to provide the best theory of the values of the tradition. The best moral and political theory, precisely the theory that critical moralists use to discern moral reality, may, suitably developed and understood, be a primary tool in explicating the basic values of the historic legal traditions as well.

This thought is easily misunderstood, even summarily dismissed as another Pickwickian daydream of an idealizing moralist with no sense of history. But in fact this appears to be the thought of the best contemporary historians of political theory, who first debunk the ahistorical way in which the great works of political theory have been understood and then suggest that the best contemporary political theory may serve to illuminate the inchoate sense of past works of political theory.[42] The interpretation of the sense and historical influence of John Locke's political theory, for example, has been sharply reassessed by critical historians, who note that Locke's thought appears to have played a different and more complex role in the political traditions of England and America than many Whig historians have represented.[43] Such critical historical assessment of the meaning of Locke's work brings out features salient for American political tradition. The arguments for religious toleration appear not only central to Locke's own essentially religious conception of political justice,[44] but also highly relevant to the remarkable American legal tradition of commitment to religious freedom.[45] These arguments of critical historiography converge with some of the most powerful contemporary political theories (that of Rawls, for

---

41. See Hart, "Positivism and the Separation of Law and Morals."
42. See Pocock, *Politics, Language and Time*, pp. 30–31; Skinner, "Meaning and Understanding in the History of Ideas"; Dunn, "The Identity of the History of Ideas," in *Political Obligation in its Historical Context*, pp. 13–28.
43. Dunn, "The Politics of Locke in England and America in the Eighteenth Century," in *Political Obligation in its Historical Context*, pp. 53–77. Cf. Kramnick, "Republican Revisionism Revisited."
44. See Dunn, *The Political Thought of John Locke*.
45. See Dunn, "The Politics of Locke in England and America in the Eighteenth Century"; Mead, *The Lively Experiment*; Howe, *The Garden and the Wilderness*.

example), which argue for the priority of civil liberties using the central model of religious toleration.[46] A good political theory of this kind may illuminate the deep structure of Locke's (or Rousseau's or Kant's) political theory, and indeed their historic significance, in a way that clarifies, and certainly does not distort, the historical record.

I believe that Dworkin is thinking along these lines when he proposes and elaborates his much misunderstood interpretive theory of law. Dworkin argues, as we saw in chapter 1, that a theory of legal interpretation must satisfy two criteria: fit and background rights.[47] In the event that the criterion of fit does not suffice (when cases are irreconcilable or ambiguous among several possible interpretive principles), the interpreter must appeal to background rights, more abstract considerations that underlie and organize a body of law, and which, suitably understood, enable us to resolve conflicts or ambiguities in case law in a satisfactory way. Thus, a great judge like Cardozo appeals to the abstract background right of persons to reasonable care by others in avoiding injury to them when he overturns the privity rule, because this rule (limiting the scope of liability to the immediate buyer) does not reflect a sensible interpretation of the scope of reasonable care in contemporary circumstances.[48] Similarly, a great theorist like Brandeis appeals to a background right of privacy (underlying a great body of disparate property and personal law) when he argues that this right to privacy should in contemporary circumstances be extended to encompass a legal right of persons against novel forms of privacy intrusion by communications media (mass circulation newspapers).[49] Later, as a justice of the Supreme Court of the United States, Brandeis appeals to the same background right of inviolable personality in defending the extension of Fourth Amendment guarantees to novel forms of bugging on the ground that such bugging is as much an intrusion into the background right of privacy, central to the values of the Fourth Amendment, as those intrusions more historically familiar.[50] Such appeals to background rights are, Dworkin suggests, forms of theoretical reflection on basic values in law continuous with and often clarified by more abstract forms of reflection by political theory on basic political values. This kind of interpretive reflection on background rights is, I believe, an instance of the specialist use of "experience-distant" concepts that anthropologists apply to the interpretation of alien cultures. The discovery of such concepts in use in legal theory marks them as a form of interpretation continuous with the historic traditions of Western political theory. An abstract political theory of human rights, which gives

46. Rawls, *A Theory of Justice*, pp. 195–257.
47. Dworkin, *Taking Rights Seriously*, pp. 81–130.
48. See *MacPherson v. Buick Motor Company* 217 N.Y. 382, 111 N.E. 1050 (1916).
49. Warren and Brandeis, "The Right to Privacy."
50. See *Olmstead v. United States*, 277 U.S. 438, 478 (1928).

central place to the right to privacy among fundamental rights of the person, may, for example, converge with and further elucidate the kinds of background rights implicit, as Brandeis sees, in a great deal of property, personal, and constitutional law in the United States.[51] The aims of legal theory, historically conceived, here converge with the aims of political and moral theory.

More recently, Dworkin has given his interpretive theory a more expressly historical dimension.[52] Interpretation in law is conceived as intrinsically historical: the interpreter of law is seen as in the position of a novelist who inherits an unfinished novel to which he must coherently add and pass on to the next novelist in a continuing chain. The interpreter cannot continue the novel in *any* direction: he must continue the novel in a way consistent with previous text. But, if the criterion of fit cannot be met without conflict or ambiguity, the interpreter must bring to bear on his continuation a theory of the best value in the previous text. This he must deploy both to resolve the conflicts and ambiguities in the previous text and to continue the novel as the best work it can, in the circumstances, be. The best theory of law, Dworkin argues, is a theory of the basic political values embodied in law. The legal interpreter, by analogy to the chain novelist, must bring abstract political theory, to the extent useful in the way suggested, to bear on his work. Political theory is to historical reconstruction in legal interpretation what a theory of literary aesthetics is to the chain novelist.

Dworkin's analogy is useful for explaining the role that moral and political theory can properly play in legal interpretation. Interpretation, on this view, is the coherent articulation and elaboration of the traditions of a community—the attempt by the interpreter to make the most reasonable sense of the strands of history and value that collectively constitute a community's identity. Legal interpretation is the often specialized attempt coherently to articulate and develop a community's conception of its legitimate exercise of power. Political and moral theory plays a central role in this conception in Western legal systems, functioning as an interpretive tool. It is not, as critical moralists insist, an ahistorical organon to moral reality; it is the very condition of the most profound understanding of what one's legal tradition is. The historiography required in legal theory is not the false history of progressivists or lovers of a mythic past; it is a critical history wedded to a normative reflection that clarifies the self-understanding of our com-

---

51. For a more extended treatment of the examples discussed in this paragraph along these lines, see D. Richards. "The Theory of Adjudication and the Task of the Great Judge." For a recent proposal of the central role of political theory in law, see Soper, *A Theory of Law.*

52. Dworkin, "Law as Interpretation." On the general rule of narrative in historical explanation as such, of which Dworkin's theory might be a special case, see Porter, *The Emergence of the Past.*

munity as to what our law is. Any other use of history in legal interpretation is distorting and can often be unacceptably ideological. This point bears more extended examination in the context of constitutional theory, where such abusive use of history is, I believe, currently rampant.

CONSTITUTIONAL INTERPRETATION

The American constitutional tradition embodies the unique process characterizing the formation of the literate culture of the West, that is, the historically self-conscious integration of diverse texts and, after the Reformation, the even more historically self-conscious and divisive metainterpretation of how such texts should be understood. Constitutionalism is an expression of this latter historical movement, which culminated—in the republican ferment of England's abortive Puritan Revolution—in the political ideal of the interpretive equality of all persons in understanding and applying the culture's authoritative texts. Commitment to this ideal naturally calls for protection of basic rights of the person to conscience and religious toleration and, inchoately, to associated civil and even political rights.[53] Constitutionalism, emerging in this context of the equality of all persons as increasingly literate interpreters of basic texts, itself offers a text, a kind of metatext which expressly constrains state power to procedural and substantive limits that respect basic equal rights of the person, on the model, as we shall see in chapter 3, of covenant. The legal interpretation of constitutional law thus itself requires prior inquiry into the modes of interpretation that best express the complex historical traditions of respect for metainterpretive diversity and the correlative political and moral theories of human rights expressive of these traditions. Such a self-understanding must surely itself be a form of political theory, as I earlier suggested. Conventional self-understanding and political theory here are one.

We may better understand the force of this conception of constitutional theory and its consequences for the historical reconstruction of legal interpretation by considering an alternative conception of constitutional interpretation that also uses history but to different interpretive ends (Raoul Berger's strict constructionism). If this alternative is demonstrated to be intellectually inadequate to the explication of the historical self-understanding of American constitutional law, we may then be en route to an understanding of how and why political and

---

53. See, in general, Jordan, *The Development of Religious Toleration in England*. See also Walzer, *The Revolution of the Saints;* Woodhouse, *Puritanism and Liberty;* Hill, *The World Turned Upside Down;* and Hill, *Milton and the English Revolution.* For the related American developments, the classic study remains Miller, *The New England Mind: The Seventeenth Century;* and *The New England Mind: From Colony to Province;* also, Miller, *Orthodoxy in Massachusetts 1630–1650.* See also Cobb, *The Rise of Religious Liberty in America.*

moral theory have a central role to play in constitutional interpretation qua interpretation, not as noninterpretivist moral prophecy.[54]

Berger on History and Constitutional Interpretation

Berger combines legal history and constitutional interpretation in the following way: legal history shows that those who drafted and approved the language of some constitutional text clearly contemplated that the language would apply to X and would not apply to Y; therefore, the failure to apply the language to X or its application to Y is a wrong and abusive interpretation of the meaning of the constitutional text. The fundamental premise of Berger's theory is Founders' intent: the meaning of constitutional text is Founders' intent.[55]

In order to free ourselves from the intellectual inevitability that this model of interpretation entails, we should recall that legal interpretation, as a convention directed at the understanding and elaboration of conventions (laws), is not primarily about persons. The characteristic fallacy of Berger's strict constructionist model is the assimilation of legal interpretation to the explanation of the subjective purposes of the Founders, or legislators, or whomever. In fact, however, the subjective purposes of legislators should play only the role that legal conventions place upon their purposes, given the governing political theory of the society.

For example, in the United States it is a familiar principle of statutory interpretation to impute to the often conflicting and sometimes incoherent data of legislative language, context, and history the purpose of a hypothetical reasonable legislator.[56] Courts impute a hypothetical rationality to the legislative process because fundamental principles of due process of law require that both courts and legislatures pursue constitutionally reasonable purposes in rational ways. Courts must therefore frame their interpretive task accordingly. It is not true that these features of legal interpretation wholly disengage the process from any contact with persons' intentions. Rather, the intentions of legislators are themselves shaped by such conventions.[57]

Legal standards are often formulated in the understanding that tough questions about ambiguities and tensions in purpose have not been set-

54. Michael Perry, accepting Berger's conception of history and of constitutional interpretation, appeals to moral theory in this way because he sees no other way to express the conviction that much contemporary constitutional law, which cannot be squared with Berger's picture, is legitimate. See Perry, *The Constitution, the Courts, and Human Rights.* If, as I believe, Berger's interpretive picture is indefensible, Perry's moral prophecy is the solution to a false dilemma. See Richards, "The Aims of Constitutional Theory."
55. Berger, *Government by Judiciary;* Berger, *Death Penalties.*
56. See Hart and Sacks, *The Legal Process,* pp. 1414–15; see also Dickerson, *The Interpretation and Application of Statutes,* ch. 12; Moore, "The Semantics of Judging, pp. 246–70." Cf. Hurst, *Dealing with Statutes,* pp. 31–65.
57. Cf. Dworkin, "Law as Interpretation."

tled, but have rather been left to courts to resolve as consistent with sound principles of legal interpretation. The normative assumptions of rationality or reasonableness that courts bring to such a task are stronger than those found in other forms of holistic explanation, for they impute a hypothetical ideal of reasonableness to a subjective process often politically haphazard and sometimes incoherent. But this is simply to mark an important truth about the metainterpretation of legal interpretation; as we have just seen in the case of statutory interpretation and shall shortly see regarding constitutional interpretation, legal interpretation is embedded in larger moral and political ideals of just and good government.

The strict constructionist model of constitutional interpretation appeals to a philosophical picture of what legal interpretation must be (indeed, it does not even acknowledge an alternative conception); but it rests on bad philosophy. The model assumes there is no other plausible theory of constitutional interpretation, but this assumption is simply false.

An alternative model of interpretation of the general normative clauses of the Constitution focuses on the more abstract intentions expressed by the clauses: namely, principles concerning freedom of expression (First Amendment), prohibitions on unnecessary harshness in criminal sanctions (Eighth Amendment), and general requirements of equal dignity (Fourteenth Amendment). Which style of constitutional interpretation is, in fact, more consistent with the imputation of reasonable and coherent purposes to the historical self-understanding of the American Constitution? As I have suggested elsewhere,[58] at least five convergent and interdependent considerations tend to the conclusion that the relevant constitutional clauses should be construed in terms of abstract intentions.

First, the language of the clauses ("cruel and unusual punishment," "equal protection of the laws") is itself abstract. The clauses certainly do not use denoting or referring expressions that would confine meaning to some class of historic objects. This claim could plausibly be made regarding "an impartial jury,"[59] considering the relatively high degree of specificity that the concept of an impartial jury had acquired at the time of the Founders, and the relatively low degree of generalization that the subject matter of the phrase permits. On the other hand, the claim appears less plausible when applied to "bill of attainder,"[60] because the subject matter here is capable of more general application. If "bill of attainder" is not specific enough to confine interpretation, it

58. The following analysis of Berger's position is adapted from Richards, "Constitutional Interpretation, History, and the Death Penalty: A Book Review."
59. See *Williams v. Florida*, 399 U.S. 78, 117 (1970) (Harlan, concurring).
60. See *Lovett v. United States*, 328 U.S. 303 (1946); *United States v. Brown*, 381 U.S. 437 (1965).

is hard to see how "equal protection" or "cruel and unusual punishments" could possibly be. In any event, it is not reasonable to impute to the Founders an intent to bind later interpretation by their applications of the language when the language used does not do so; when the range of such applications is often enormously controversial historically (the general language may have been purposely chosen to gloss over disagreements in application); and when available conceptions of the judicial role at the time included the common law model of case-by-case elaboration of general concepts and abstract principles.[61]

Second, no matter what the common meanings were of what was included or excluded when the constitutional language was approved, it is not reasonable, in view of the abstract language employed, to limit the language forever to its historic denotations. Matters of constitutionally relevant and controlling fact and value may evolve so that applications unimaginable earlier may become reasonable, and earlier applications may become unreasonable. To bind interpretation to historic referents would impute to the constitutional design the unreasonable intent to apply abstract language counterfactually, ignoring changes in relevant factors that would lead reasonable persons to apply the relevant language differently.

Chief Justice Charles Hughes made precisely this point in *Home Building & Loan Association v. Blaisdell.*[62] Justice George Sutherland had set forth a historical argument that the contract clause was intended precisely to invalidate stay laws of the kind that Hughes, writing for the majority, upheld.[63] Hughes suggested that the denotative exemplar of state stay laws in the 1780s, which Sutherland's theory of interpretation supposed controlling, could not reasonably control when the Founders would not, hypothetically, thus have construed the contract clause in modern circumstances.[64] Hughes's point may be glossed as follows. The interpretation of cultural conventions such as law requires that we construe them as reasonable systems for advancing individual and collective purposes. One must thus hesitate to impute an irrational or self-defeating purpose, as the counterfactual application of constitutional language may demand, unless clear evidence so requires. In the case of the American Constitution with its aspirations to long-term stability ("a constitution intended to endure for ages to come"),[65] there is no such evidence. Indeed, few legal systems have been so

---

61. See *The Federalist* No. 78 (Hamilton) For relevant historical material further supporting this interpretation of the Founders' intent, see Powell, "The Original Understanding of Original Intent."
62. *Home Building & Loan Association v. Blaisdell*, 290 U.S. 398 (1934).
63. For relevant history of the 1780s, see Wood, *The Creation of the American Republic, 1776–1787*, pp. 393–467; Miller, *The Supreme Court and the Uses of History*, pp. 39–51.
64. *Home Building & Loan*, 290 U.S. at 427–28 (1934).
65. *McCulloch v. Maryland*, 17 U.S. (4 Wheat.) 316, 415 (1819).

clearly the product of rational and reflectively self-conscious design in light of the best available political theories and political science of republican government, or so acutely sensitive to the fact (basic to Enlightenment thought) that human institutions change as circumstances change and that good government must accommodate to new experience.[66]

Third, the general normative clauses derive their force and meaning from a larger political and moral culture which perceived the human rights embodied in these clauses as grounded in enduring and inviolable principles of justice. General enforcement of these clauses, as abstract principles accommodated to the circumstances of evolving historic situations, would ensure a basic framework of just institutions over time.[67] The interpretation of these clauses as incorporating abstract intentions is more consistent with these moral norms.

The fourth reason to construe constitutional language in terms of abstract intentions is that judicial elaboration of constitutional doctrine over time coheres only with the broader interpretive approach. The interpretation of American constitutional law requires, I have suggested (embedding the account in fundamental characteristics of Western culture), a historically self-conscious understanding both of the Founders' self-conception of their place in the history of republican thought, and of the interpretive development of constitutional doctrine over time. Interpretation of the constitutional design must make sense not only of language, historical evidence of Founders' intent, and surrounding conventions and norms, but of the interpretive traditions that have construed constitutional language over time.[68] These traditions are reflected, in part, in conventions of judicial interpretation, identification, and application of law. One should hesitate to use one kind of data (Founders' intent, for example) to undercut the legitimacy of another kind of data (traditions of judicial review over time) unless there is the strongest evidence of inconsistency and there are good reasons to believe that one kind of data represents the more authoritative purposes of the system. However, aside from a question-begging appeal to one interpretation of Founders' intent (denotative exemplars) which does not even acknowledge an alternative interpretive approach, there

---

66. See Adair, *Fame and the Founding Fathers*, pp. 3–26, 93–140.
67. See generally, Wood, *The Creation of the American Republic*; Bailyn, *The Ideological Origins of the American Republic*; White, *The Philosophy of the American Revolution*; Commager, *The Empire of Reason*, pp. 176–235; May, *The Enlightenment in America*, pp. 88–101, 153–76, 197–251.
68. See Brest, "The Misconceived Quest for the Original Understanding"; Fiss, "Objectivity and Interpretation." But cf. Brest, "Interpretation and Interest," in which he takes a more skeptical view of his earlier position; Brest, "The Fundamental Rights Controversy."

are no such weighty reasons. Indeed, if we are to take Founders' intent as central, other indications of that intent—language, reasonable purpose, cultural norms—support the abstract intention approach.[69] Even. if they did not support this approach, it is difficult to see why such intent should embody more authoritative purposes than those reflected in traditions of judicial review when, in fact, the self-understanding of constitutional law—the subject matter of constitutional interpretation—is historically self-conscious of its nature as a developing tradition, a development reflected, in part, in judicial traditions.

The fifth consideration is the great appeal of strict constructionism derived from an undefended and indefensible positivistic conception of popular sovereignty. Berger frequently invokes popular sovereignty in criticizing traditions of judicial interpretation that betray the Founders' intent (that is, the Founders' applications of constitutional language).[70] According to this view, the people, the fount of constitutional legitimacy, imposed constitutional limits on the state in the form of the Founders' sense of the application of constitutional language, and any subsequent judicial deviance from this sense, no matter how entrenched the judicial tradition it reflects, is thus fundamentally illegitimate (Founders' intent must always prevail). But this argument cannot withstand critical examination either as a matter of jurisprudence or of political theory.

As jurisprudence, positivism, which Berger's argument assumes, has always had problems in explaining how there can be any legal limits on the sovereign. Bentham, probably the most profound of the early proponents of positivism, struggled unsuccessfully to accommodate the existence of such legal constraints (exemplified, for example, by the enforceable constitutional guarantees of the American republic) with the requirement of his positivistic command theory that there be a sovereign who is habitually obeyed, but who habitually obeys no one.[71] The natural move, within positivistic command theory, is to fictionalize a kind of sovereign that imposes limits on the state, but is itself illimitable, namely, the people, or popular sovereignty. But, as the more perceptive positivists have always recognized,[72] such a reading of the facts of American constitutional government is strained indeed, a far cry from the European centralized bureaucracy[73] and British parliamen-

---

69. Indeed, if anything, historical data from the founding period supports the abstract intention reading of Founders' intent. See Powell, "The Original Understanding of Original Intent." See, for discussion of Berger's question-begging theory of interpretation, Brest, "The Fundamental Rights Controversy," pp. 1080–105.
70. See Berger, *Death Penalties*, p. 66.
71. See Hart, *Essays on Bentham*, pp. 220–42.
72. See Hart, *The Concept of Law*, pp. 49–76; Hart, *Essays on Bentham*, pp. 220–68. Cf. Raz, *Practical Reason and Norms*.
73. See Kelsen, *The Pure Theory of Law*; Kelsen, *General Theory of Law and State*.

tary supremacy,[74] which positivist theories have more naturally explained.

How in the American context is the sovereign to be understood? If understood as the historical persons who approved the original Constitution, why should they bind a later generation long removed in time? If understood as the current generation, how do we know who they are or what they approve when most of them in fact do not understand, let alone reflectively approve, constitutional institutions? Precisely because of such problems, the most plausible contemporary forms of positivism have abandoned the kind of command theory that requires such a futile and disfiguring search for or invention of a fictionalized sovereign.[75] Indeed, these forms of positivism tend to identify valid law with the critical attitudes reflected in conventions of judicial interpretation, identification, and application of law (traditions of judicial review), not with the Founders or some other sovereign.[76] Under this contemporary view, in conflicts between judicial convention and Founders' intent, it is the former, not the latter, which should govern, so that, even conceding Berger's argument that Founders' intent and judicial convention are in clear conflict, his conclusion would not follow. But, in fact, as earlier noted, there is good reason to reject Berger's stark picture of conflict: the more reasonable construction of relevant data (language, reasonable purpose, moral conventions, and so on) yields the broader interpretive approach in any event.

As political theory, popular sovereignty has long enjoyed and justly continues to enjoy a central place in intuitive moral conceptions of constitutional legitimacy. Thayer, for example, appealed to it, as we saw in chapter 1, not in Berger's sense (Founder's intent) but in the sense of populist approval. It is important to understand that popular sovereignty is, if any concept in constitutional discourse is, essentially contestable—subject to a range of reasonable interpretations among which good political argument must reflectively choose.[77] Accordingly, we should resist simplistic interpretations of popular sovereignty, which are no more than persuasive definitions[78] and certainly do not deal in a

---

74. See Austin, *The Province of Jurisprudence Determined;* Bentham, *The Limits of Jurisprudence Defined.*
75. See Hart, *The Concept of Law;* Raz, *The Concept of a Legal System;* Raz, *Practical Reason and Norms;* Raz, *The Authority of Law;* MacCormick, *Legal Reasoning and Legal Theory.*
76. See sources in preceding note. See also Hart, *Essays on Bentham,* pp. 243–68.
77. See Gallie, "Essentially Contested Concepts," in *Philosophy and the Historical Understanding,* ch. 8.
78. Cf. Stevenson, *Ethics and Language,* pp. 206–26 (vague, ethical terms must be understood by use of mode of analysis which incorporates meanings not intended by the speaker but nonetheless suggested by the terms).

principled way with the arguments supporting alternative conceptions; indeed, they do not even acknowledge the fact of reasonable controversy. Berger's use of popular sovereignty is, like Thayer's, fatally flawed in precisely this way, for he uses his explanation of it—the Founders' common sense of the application of constitutional language—to dismiss alternative conceptions without addressing the basic questions of democratic political theory which his conception of popular sovereignty raises. For example, why, as previously suggested, should a contemporary generation be bound in this way to the will of a generation long dead?

Surely, there is much in the history of American constitutionalism, at least since Madison's *The Federalist* No. 10, to suggest that any purely populist interpretation of popular sovereignty, understood either as some historical moment or some continuing acclamation, is not what the most reflective explication of the values of constitutional government would suggest. Madison's idea of a republic, in contrast to popular direct democracy, suggests that the institutions of constitutional democracy (federalism, separation of powers, judicial supremacy) express a complex moral ideal resting not on populism, but on a conception of principles of justice in which democratic self-rule appears as one constitutional value among others. These other values restrain the untrammeled exercise of the popular will by means of both procedural and substantive constraints. For example, Madison's proposal for a procedure of representation in a federal system argues that such representation will minimize the tendency for democratic politics in a free republic to polarize around factions, which ignore both the common interest and the rights of minorities.[79] Elsewhere, Madison (following Jefferson) defends substantive constraints of equal liberty of religious conscience restricting the power of intolerant religious factions to oppress outsiders through law.[80] From this perspective, the very foundation of constitutional legitimacy—the people—is naturally construed in terms of the basic rights of the person which the contractarian

79. For a range of commentary on Madison's argument, widely diverging in perspective, see, for example, Adair, *Fame and the Founding Fathers*, pp. 75–140 (way of securing moral impartiality in political leaders); Wills, *Explaining America: The Federalist*, pp. 179–264 (following Adair); Dahl, *A Preface to Democratic Theory* (defense of polyarchy); Beard, *An Economic Interpretation of the Constitution of the United States*, v–vii, 14–16, 152–88 (reduction to economic interests).

80. See Madison, *Memorial and Remonstrance*, in Meyers, ed., *The Mind of the Founder: Sources of the Political Thought of James Madison*, pp. 8–16. In addition to his role in the history of religious freedom in Virginia, Madison was, of course, the central figure in both the drafting and approval of the free exercise and antiestablishment clauses of the first amendment. For a discussion of the pertinent historical records, see Stokes, *Church and State in the United States*, pp. 538–52.

state exists to defend, strengthen, and vindicate and cannot, therefore, constitutionally transgress.[81]

The institutions of democratic self-rule—the separation of powers with its controlling conception of the rule of law, federalism, and judicial supremacy to enforce such basic rights as religious toleration—are the result, perhaps, of an attempt to design a complex system of institutions to realize a form of enduring and stable justice in government. That conception of justice (sometimes called popular sovereignty) aims to protect an idealized moral conception of persons as free, rational, and equal.[82] The institutions of constitutional government thus preserve a substantive moral conception of the relation of the person to other persons and to the state, one in which the equality and liberty of persons are guaranteed and maintained. If this alternative interpretation of popular sovereignty is, as the cumulative argument of this book aims to show, much more sensible as a theory of constitutional government than any variant of populism (including Berger's),[83] the appeal of Berger's argument as political theory evaporates.

Berger's use of history as a tool for unearthing the denotative exemplars of Founders' intent is a metainterpretively unsound theory of what constitutional interpretation in the United States properly is: his theory, by Dworkin's criteria, neither fits the relevant data, nor corresponds to a defensible background political theory. The consequences of such a theory for constitutional interpretation are not only abuse of constitutional law, but abuse of critical historiography as an intellectual and humane discipline of central importance in legal interpretation. Berger's use of history distorts the historian's task in assisting legal interpretation, by asking the wrong questions in ways that disable the historian in assisting the legal interpreter in understanding the meaning of the legal tradition.

In both Berger's *Government by Judiciary* and his *Death Penalties* the use of history is extremely confined and narrow. *Government by Judiciary* concentrates, for example, on the congressional debates over the

---

81. Consistent with this conception, leading Founders argued in state ratifying conventions that a Bill of Rights was not needed because any rights not expressly surrendered remained beyond constitutional power. See, e.g., James Wilson of Pennsylvania, Jonathan Elliot, *Debates in the Several State Conventions*, vol. 2, pp. 434–437; James Madison of Virginia, *id.*, vol. 3., pp. 620, 626–7. Cf. No. 84, *The Federalist* (Hamilton). In the Virginia ratifying convention, Patrick Henry resists adoption of the Constitution on the ground that it undercuts the natural right of majority rule, Jonathan Elliot, *Debates in the Several State Conventions*, vol. 3, pp. 50–51. Madison's reply is in terms of a deeper moral conception of "the rights of the minority" which cabins the appropriate scope of majority rule, Jonathan Elliot, *id.*, p. 87.
82. See generally Rawls, *A Theory of Justice*.
83. See Richards, *The Moral Criticism of Law*, pp. 39–56. See also Cohen and Rogers, *On Democracy: Toward a Transformation of American Society*, ch. 6.

proposed Fourteenth Amendment, with occasional allusions to second-ary accounts of the history of Reconstruction. By contrast, Harold Hyman, an American historian not bound by an interpretive theory like Berger's, supplements his examination of the debates with clarifying, detailed analyses of the political and social history of Reconstruction.[84] In more recent work, Hyman insists that the Fourteenth Amendment must be understood in the context of the egalitarianism of the Thir-teenth Amendment and the larger moral aspirations of the abolitionist movement.[85]

Berger's interpretive theory directs him away from such inquiries. Because he limits the scope of the Fourteenth Amendment to the appli-cations contemplated by the Reconstruction Congress that approved the amendment, he examines only evidence that bears on that issue. This historiographical decision causes him to ignore larger historical and cultural contexts that clarify the abstract ideals of equal respect for human dignity which the Fourteenth Amendment decisively contrib-utes to the substantive values of American constitutional law. Berger's narrow use of history may also lead to serious interpretive distortions of the limited data he does consider. Plausible inferences about the commonsense applications of "equal protection of the law" in 1868 may in fact confuse abstract arguments of principle with historically contingent and shifting conceptions of application and thus lead to mis-taken judgments. Similarly, by focusing on the application at the time of adoption it is possible to constitutionalize what is really only one among several historically competing views of application, whereas the abstract language was chosen precisely to enable independent judicial elaboration of abstract arguments of principle.

The historiographical distortion created by Berger's approach is readily seen when we compare *Death Penalties*, and the kind of under-standing it affords concerning our legal traditions surrounding the injustice of punishment condemned as cruel and unusual by the Eighth Amendment, with the insight afforded by a book not about American legal history at all, John McManners's *Death and the Enlightenment*, a study of changing attitudes toward death (including natural deaths, exe-cutions, and suicides) in eighteenth-century France.[86] For Berger, the focus of historiographical research is simply whether, for example, the

---

84. Hyman, *A More Perfect Union*. Compare the similar observation about the compara-tive value of constitutional historiography in Tushnet, "Following the Rules Laid Down," pp. 781, 795 n.39.
85. See Hyman and Wiecek, *Equal Justice Under Law: Constitutional Development, 1835–1875*, pp. 386–438. Hyman's interpretive approach converges with that of my colleague William E. Nelson, *The Roots of American Bureaucracy, 1830–1900*, and his general work in progress on the Fourteenth Amendment. See also Cover, *Justice Accused: Antislavery and the Judicial Process*, pp. 154–55.
86. McManners, *Death and the Enlightenment*. See also Aries, *The Hour of Our Death*; Stannard, *The Puritan Way of Death*.

Founders thought the death penalty violated the Eighth Amendment. Once the question is resolved negatively, the matter is forever closed, and any Supreme Court opinions to the contrary are dead wrong. Berger considers a narrow range of legal materials for the strictly limited purpose of establishing the required negative. For McManners, the historiography of death in eighteenth-century France requires the broadest integration of diverse sources and perspectives bearing on major shifts in moral and human sensibilities. The consequence is remarkable: McManners, writing about France with no particular focus on legal issues, enables us to understand the moral norms implicit in the Eighth Amendment in a way that Berger, the American legal historian, does not even approach.

McManners enables us to understand complex historical features of eighteenth-century Enlightenment thought about just punishment in general and the death penalty in particular.[87] Among these complex features are the following: major shifts in moral norms (Beccaria's criticisms of the extent and forms of use of the death penalty);[88] the egalitarian criticism of the use of terroristic punishments to maintain status hierarchies against subjugated groups;[89] pertinent social realities relating to the perceived need for or acceptability of the death penalty (undeveloped police work; the commonness of premature death, which devalued the taking of human life); and how ideas of just punishment were associated with background theological concepts.[90] When these factors are considered, we see why Berger's emphasis on the fact that everyone (even Beccaria) accepted the appropriateness of the death

87. See Richards, "Constitutional Interpretation, History, and the Death Penalty," pp. 1389–93.
88. Beccaria, *On Crimes and Punishments.* For commentary, see McManners, *Death and the Enlightenment*, pp. 392– 408. For the many American readers of Beccaria in the historical period leading to the Constitution and Bill of Rights, see May, *The Enlightenment in America*, p. 118. For the continuities between the European and American Enlightenment, see also May; Commager, *The Empire of Reason*; Wood, *The Creation of the American Republic*; Bailyn, *The Ideological Origins of the American Revolution*, pp. 22– 93; White, *The Philosophy of the American Revolution.*
89. The grotesque forms of the death penalty (see Foucault, *Discipline and Punish*, pp. 3–6), against which Enlightenment figures reacted so violently, were associated with a self-consciously elaborated drama of terror inflicted on outrageous violations of the majesty of the hierarchical order, whose patterns of deference needed to be enforced by dramatic outward shows, McManners, *Death and the Enlightenment*, p. 130. The natural inference is that a more egalitarian, less hierarchical conception of political justice must question such uses of terror, or analogous actions. Cf. Hay, "Property, Authority and the Criminal Law," in Hay et al., eds., *Albion's Fatal Tree* (arguing that in eighteenth-century England the wealthy ruling class could afford to be benevolent and oppose the imposition of the death penalty on humanitarian grounds, since the possibility of the death penalty as a threat of unpredictable terror for a broad range of offenses was in the grace of the ruling class and thus reinforced the social and political hierarchy).
90. McManners, *Death and the Enlightenment*, pp. 376–79; 374; 130, 133, 134, 176– 79.

penalty in some cases not only distorts our understanding of the history of this period (we learn none of the above) but misreads the meaning of the American legal traditions established in that period. For Berger, the meaning of these traditions simply is that the death penalty was, as such, acceptable; this is the core organizing principle of the Eighth Amendment which must forever freeze constitutional thought regarding the death penalty. Yet this is to constitutionalize a historically contingent fact without reading the background principles, understandings, and context that explain that fact and, indeed, even in its own historical period, sharply qualified its meaning. True, the Enlightenment thought the death penalty acceptable in certain cases. It was, however, more historically remarkable in its skepticism about the extent and forms of its use and in its special concern with the abuse of the death penalty for terroristic degradation.[91] So Berger's "meaning" of the Eighth Amendment is not the eighteenth century's meaning; indeed, even his account of centrally important episodes of legal history (the Titus Oates affair)[92] appears to miss its salient historical feature for the age, the use of freakish terror. Why, then, should Berger's meaning be our meaning on the issue of the death penalty? In fact, many of the eighteenth century's grounds for skepticism, implicit in the principles of the Eighth Amendment, suitably adjusted to contemporary circumstances (alternative ways of securing deterrence, the greater value of life, and so on), might dictate a complete repudiation of the death penalty.[93]

Surely, a better metainterpretation of our interpretive practices would focus on the abstract intention of normative clauses such as the Eighth and Fourteenth Amendments. Original understandings of application are just that: the way in which one age, in its context and by its lights, construed these abstract intentions. We can get a better sense of these original understandings of earlier generations when we see how

91. Certainly, the preoccupation of Enlightenment thought with limiting both the crimes for which death was a legal penalty and the ways in which the death penalty was carried out (see McManners, *Death and the Enlightenment,* pp. 392–408) suggests a principled continuity with the ways in which the Supreme Court has limited the forms, procedures, and scope of the death penalty, see, e.g., *Furman v. Georgia,* 408 U.S. 238 (1972); *Gregg v. Georgia,* 428 U.S. 153 (1976); *Coker v. Georgia,* 433 U.S. 584 (1977).

92. For a good statement of this position on the Titus Oates case, see *Brief for Petitioner* at 26–45, *Fowler v. North Carolina,* 428 U.S. 904 (1976)(No. 73–7031). Titus Oates was a minister of the Church of England, whose perjured testimony about a Catholic plot to assassinate the king led to the execution of fifteen Catholics for treason. In 1685, Oates was convicted of perjury and sentenced to a fine, life imprisonment, whipping, pillorying four times a year, and defrocking, The House of Lords rejected Oates's petition to be released from the judgment; the dissenting members emphasized that defrocking by a temporal court was "unusual" because that was the function of an ecclesiastical court, and the punishment of life imprisonment and whipping were without precedent for the crime of perjury.

93. See Richards, "Constitutional Interpretation, History, and the Death Penalty," pp. 1391–93, 1395–98.

and why abstract principles were applied by them in the way they were, as my comparison of Berger and McManners shows. We better understand our traditions and ourselves when we make the most civilized sense we can of the actuating principles of the tradition in our circumstances. If we come to see the death penalty as unnecessary (because it is not a marginal deterrent) and terroristic (because of its tendency to subjugate certain groups who bear the brunt of it), then as a coherent elaboration of our legal traditions we fairly read the Eighth and Fourteenth Amendments to condemn it.

We should, I believe, be struck by the way in which a sounder history of the Founders' attitude to the death penalty and the Eighth Amendment converges with a more abstract understanding of the values that guide our use of history in the reconstruction of a historically self-conscious legal tradition, in this case American constitutional law. This view resembles the point of those critical historians who find that a better historical reading of Locke, say, converges with better political theories developing Lockean ideas: a great political theorist like Locke can be better understood historically when we better understand political theory. The corresponding point in constitutional theory is, I believe, that abstract political theory of constitutional democracy may deepen our understanding both of original understandings and of the elaboration of tradition. The common point is one earlier touched on: American constitutional law was one of the most remarkable exercises in the use of the best political theory and political science of an enlightened age to make a lasting republic in a large territory. It should, therefore, be no surprise that a republic so shaped by political theory should be illuminated by political theory, and that we read it better historically to the extent that we better read political theory. Has constitutional theory been adequate to this task?

3 · Constitutional Interpretation

An adequate understanding of constitutional interpretation requires a more critically reflective use of political theory to explain the historical traditions of American constitutional law. The easiest way to resist this task is to question its necessity. In fact, because of the very structure of American legal education—with its inbred professional traditions of isolation from the larger intellectual discourse of the university—such resistance is the natural common sense of many academic lawyers. A positivistic theory of law expresses this sense: law is neutrally given to us by legal authority independent of any larger historical or political inquiry. If Berger's version of historical positivism (the meaning of law is given by a certain conception of the Founders' applications) must be rejected because of its inadequate and indefensible theory of interpretation, the natural alternative positivistic move is an appeal to ongoing tradition, at least tradition suitably isolated in some way from larger political, moral, and social inquiry.

I do not take issue with the claim that understanding tradition is central to constitutional interpretation, but rather with the positivistic interpretation of what tradition is. Such positivism does not do justice to the complexity of our interpretive practices as a constitutional community. In this chapter, I offer both critical and constructive arguments in support of this latter notion.

AGAINST POSITIVISTIC CONVENTIONALISM

Positivistic conventionalism, in contrast to interpretive theories of constitutional law, is absorbed by the easy, not the hard, cases of constitutional interpretation.[1] These positivistic conventions are, as it were, traditions so clear that they are never the subject of controversy in case law. The theory has the virtue of capturing the common sense of constitutional law as a living tradition, not bound by the unalterable Founders' intent of Berger's mythology. The tradition is sufficiently independent of nonlegal inquiries to entitle academic constitutional lawyers to think of themselves as the masters of the independent expertise of constitutional lawyering. Essentially, the conventions are lawyerly traditions of law identification and application.

The attraction of positivistic conventionalism is not only its sense of a living constitution and its emphasis on the unique role of lawyers as the carriers and exegetes of legal conventions. It also offers a not implausible theory of interpretation in general, one rooted in a theory of language as an expression of a public community of well-understood conventions of meaning and use.[2] This view of language, however, a form of which I defended in the preceding chapter, is consistent with many different accounts of interpretation, some less plausible than others. Positivistic conventionalism offers an account of constitutional interpretation that is, I believe, clearly wrong as a substantive account of the meaning (or, the conventions, if you will) of American constitutional law.

Positivistic conventionalism identifies the task of constitutional interpretation as the lawyerly explication of the conventions of constitutional law, that is, as the ways those conventions are identified, applied, and elaborated by relevant legal officials. The task of constitutional interpretation may proceed with no need for any larger moral, social, or political inquiry. However, it has repeatedly been seen, in American constitutional experience, that current legal conventions, positivistically understood, do not correctly explicate the meaning of the Constitution. Such conventions may, for example, fail to grasp and apply the abstract principles of government implicit in original historical understandings; or they may fail to give appropriate weight to the settled and often brilliantly articulated case law and other authoritative constructions of how these principles should be understood; or they may not do justice to the deeper political theory of constitutional democracy that organizes or explicates these principles.

Felix Frankfurter's criticisms of the Supreme Court's abuse of the commerce clause incorporate all of these points.[3] The Court's invali-

---

1. Monaghan, "Our Perfect Constitution"; Schauer, "Easy Cases."
2. See Schauer, "Easy Cases."
3. See Frankfurter, *The Commerce Clause Under Marshall, Taney, and Waite.*

dation of federal legislation on commerce clause grounds misconceived the federalist principles underlying the original understanding. These principles were directed not against the power of Congress, but against that of the states; if anything, Congress's power over interstate commerce was conceived as a representationally fair embodiment of the national interest.[4] In addition, the Court flouts brilliantly articulated and settled case law which clarifies the principles of representational fairness underlying the commerce clause and the preeminent role of Congress (not the judiciary) as the appropriate institution to weigh and apply them.[5] Moreover, an abstract political theory of representation secures fairness in commerce clause matters through the representational design of the federal legislative branch, and leaves the fair disposition of these matters to the Congress so structured to handle them fairly.[6] Associated arguments against substantive economic due process illustrate similar claims: the Spencerian ideology of natural property rights does not conform to the Lockean theory of the Constitution either as a matter of original understanding, judicial or other construction, or abstract political theory.[7]

These criticisms must not be limited to current majorities of the Supreme Court of the United States (lest it be said that the Court in these cases diverges from some other positivistic legal convention). The Court, Congress, the executive, indeed the nation may all concur on some practice of constitutional interpretation for which there is good interpretive ground to reject as dead wrong. The long national acquiescence in the executive usurpation of the war powers was and is arguably wrong, wrong in terms of original intent, long periods of practical construction, and the political theory of separation of powers.[8] Objections of these and other kinds are meaningful and often valid. Any theory of constitutional intent that renders such objections meaningless or

4. See Stern, "That Commerce Which Concerns More States Than One."
5. Chief Justice Marshall's most brilliant interpretive exegesis is, in my jugment, his commentary on the appropriately deferential judicial approach to the construction of the clauses conferring powers on Congress: *McCulloch v. Maryland*, 17 U.S. (4 Wheat.) 316 (1819). For his application of this approach to the commerce clause, see *Gibbons v. Ogden*, 22 U.S. (9 Wheat.) 1 (1824).
6. See Wechsler, "The Political Safeguards of Federalism: The Role of the States in the Composition and Selection of the National Government." On the relevant historical background for the ideas of representation implicit in the Constitution, see Pole, *Political Representation in England and the Origins of the American Republic*.
7. See *Lochner v. New York*, 198 U.S. 45, 65, 74 (1905) (Harlan and Holmes, dissenting).
8. For historical understanding, see *Records of the Federal Convention*, vol. 2, Farrand, ed., pp. 318–19. For supportive political theory, see Madison, writing as Helvidius, *Gazette of the United States* (Aug. 24,1793), answering Hamilton, writing as Pacificus, *Gazette of the United States* (June 29, 1793), reprinted in Hirschfield, ed., *The Power of the Presidency*, pp. 55–59 and pp. 49–54, respectively. For judicial construction, see *Prize Cases*, 67 U.S. (2 Black) 635 (1863). See generally Henkin, *Foreign Affairs and the Constitution*, chs. 2–4.

false fails to capture the substantive sense of our interpretive practices as a political community.[9] Contrary to the common sense of the American law school, the interpretation of constitutional law cannot be identified with positivistic conventions of the living Constitution. Rather, constitutional interpretation engages in a complex historical reconstruction of our constitutional traditions guided by precisely the kind of larger inquiry into political, moral, and social theory with which the American law school is so understandably uncomfortable.

A CONVENTIONALIST ARGUMENT AGAINST POLITICAL THEORY IN CONSTITUTIONAL INTERPRETATION

Frederick Schauer, who defends a form of conventionalist approach to constitutional interpretation,[10] has raised thoughtful questions about the utility of general moral and political theory in constitutional interpretation.[11] Schauer concedes the utility of such theory in the interpretation of particular constitutional clauses (for example, in his own interpretation of free speech).[12] But he contrasts such fruitful horizontal clause-bound interpretation with what he considers the distorting use of general political theory, by myself and others,[13] to explicate larger interpretive patterns common to vertically disjoint constitutional texts (for example, free speech and equal protection). The limitation of political theory to horizontally clause-bound interpretation of discrete constitutional texts recognizes,

> as more free-wheeling theories do not, that the values specified in the text are more or less discrete, and that they have a textual preeminence over values not so specified.[14]

These more "free-wheeling theories," mine included, are wrong for three reasons. First, these general theories fail to see that the relevant data of constitutional law underdetermine any theory: the data are consistent with many different theories, and thus it is wrong to urge on judges the exclusive claims of one such theory.[15] Second, these theories mistakenly assume that theory and data can be separated, failing to see that our selection of data is itself theory-laden.[16] And third, there is suf-

9. Cf. Barber, *On What the Constitution Means.*
10. Schauer, "Easy Cases."
11. Schauer, "An Essay on Constitutional Language."
12. Schauer, *Free Speech: A Philosophical Inquiry.*
13. See Richards, *The Moral Criticism of Law;* Dworkin, *Taking Rights Seriously.*
14. Schauer, "An Essay on Constitutional Language," p. 830.
15. Ibid., pp. 816–18.
16. Ibid., pp. 818–19.

ficient reason to doubt that any general theory of morality is true, and therefore we should resist such theories in favor of irreducibly plural-istic first principles.[17]

If these objections were decisive against general theories as such, as Schauer appears to believe, they would, of course, be decisive against Schauer's horizontally clause-bound theories as well. These theories, including Schauer's own theory of free speech, rest on the same mis-takes and wrong assumption. They commit the mistake, if it is a mis-take, of offering a theory underdetermined by the data, and the further mistake of picking examples laden with theory; and they wrongly assume a unified theory as their aim when pluralistic first principles may be more plausible. The claim that a theory of free speech that is horizontally clause-bound is less objectionable than more general the-ories is purely illusory. The relevant texts of the First Amendment are quite general; they are consistent, as text, with a number of alternative theories; and any theory of them will be controversial in precisely the ways Schauer finds objectionable in more general theories. Since all theories, clause-bound or not, will be objectionable in these ways, the issue is not whether we abandon theory (interpretively impossible, in any event), but how we distinguish between better and worse theories.

Since Schauer draws inspiration for his "mistakes" from the philos-ophy of science, we should look with care at the philosophy he assumes. Neither of Schauer's alleged two flaws of general theories in law (underdetermination and theory-ladenness of data) is supposed by post-positivistic philosophies of science to prevent practitioners from distin-guishing between better and worse theories in science. Data may underdetermine scientific theory, but those theories are more ratio-nally acceptable when they explain more diverse kinds of data in sim-pler ways, and when they are fruitful in guiding research and solving problems.[18] And, data may be theory-laden, but conflicting scientific theories usually agree on many kinds of data for which any adequate theory must account.[19] Both judgments apply to theory construction in law. Theories of constitutional law, for example, are better when they explain in simpler and more explanatory ways a wider range of diverse aspects of the law on which all agree, and when they are fruitful in guiding further research and solving problems, including clarification of the proper disposition of hard cases. From this perspective, general

17. Ibid., pp. 820–21.
18. See, e.g., Kuhn, "Objectivity, Value Judgment, and Theory Choice," in *The Essential Tension*, pp. 320–339; Newton-Smith, *The Rationality of Science*; Lakatos, "Falsification and the Methodology of Scientific Research Programmes"; Laudan, *Progress and Its Prob-lems*; Laudan, *Science and Values*; Hesse, *The Structure of Scientific Inference*.
19. See, e.g., Newton-Smith, *The Rationality of Science*, pp. 148–82; Scheffler, *Science and Subjectivity*; Hacking, *Representing and Intervening*, pp. 65–74; Shapere, "Meaning and Scientific Change"; Laudan, *Science and Values*.

theories appear, other things being equal, to be theoretically superior to clause-bound theories: general theories have explanatory power and coherence, while clause-bound theories are ad hoc and unsystematic. For Schauer, other things are not equal, because he views general theories as somehow nontextual: thus, his earlier-cited remark that clause-bound theories are superior to "free-wheeling" ones because "values specified in the text are more or less discrete."[20] But this begs the question in favor of Schauer's theory—it must be shown that a particular general theory does not, in fact, account for text. Schauer's abstract arguments against general theories do not show this. They make general points about all theories, Schauer's included. No argument could show that general theories, as such, must betray text, because the claim is false. For Schauer to make his point, what is required is not a bad abstract argument of the kind he, in fact, offers, but a detailed intertheoretical comparison of the relative adequacy of theories. Since he offers no such account, his argument fails.

Schauer's appeal here, and in his focus on easy cases,[21] is to text, which allegedly cabins argument in ways that general theories disfigure. But the appeal either assumes positivistic conventionalism, which is clearly false, or assumes that only clause-bound theories preserve text, which begs the question. In order to defend his position successfully, he must abandon this sterile and question-begging textualism and engage in discussion concerning better and worse political theories of constitutional law, which is the only issue really in dispute between him and the general theorists.

There remains Schauer's claim that general theories, mine included, rest on the unfounded assumption that there exists a unified theory of ethics, which these theorists unwarrantably foist on the complexity of constitutional law. The argument, again, is altogether abstract and programmatic, could as well be directed against a unified clause-bound theory, and does not give the kind of intertheoretical comparison that would show wherein such unified theories distort the complexity of law. Suppose some such theory fully preserves, indeed better explicates, the complexity of legal doctrine, but does so in a way that shows that diverse clauses and doctrines connect in illuminating ways to coherent political principles and deeper ethical conceptions and ideals (in chapter 10, I make a claim of this kind about the general interpretive theory proposed in this book). Such a theory would clearly be a better theory than one that perceives constitutional texts as discrete and isolated ones, for it would enable us, consistent with sound interpretive principles of imputing hypothetical reasonable purposes to community norms (see chapter 2), to see the community's self-under-

20. Schauer, "An Essay on Constitutional Language," p. 830.
21. Schauer, "Easy Cases."

standing as reflective of a more coherently explanatory set of principles and conceptions. In the case of the American Constitution, critical historiography supplies especially cogent reasons, as we shall see, to believe that such a project may be both practicable and true. Thus, there are the soundest reasons both of general interpretive practice and of specific background history to explore the construction of such theories before we yield to narrower kinds of interpretation that may, in fact, distort more than they clarify. There are no good a priori arguments against such interpretive projects, only bad ones, not least Schauer's misleading appeal to ethical pluralism, which confuses a kind of ethical ideal (which many general theorists also defend) with an explanatory one. The failure of legal theory to identify such simplifying conceptions, because of a programmatic commitment to clause-bound interpretation, may itself distort and disfigure the coherent sense which constitutional law may have. This is, I believe, the fundamental point: which view is more clarifying and least distorting of the complex interpretive structure of American constitutional law? In fact, Schauer's program distorts the interpretive practices of American constitutional law and, in one case, that of constitutional privacy, it violates text, history, and political theory.[22] In contrast, a program using general political theory promises to advance interpretive understanding of a wide range of issues of constitutional interpretation. I sketch in the next sections some of this interpretive promise, and present the analytic program of the following chapters.

HISTORY AND CONTRACTARIAN POLITICAL THEORY IN CONSTITUTIONAL INTERPRETATION

In order to see why Schauer's interpretive program (horizontal clause-bound interpretation and positivistic conventionalism) is unsound as a general methodology for interpreting the American Constitution, we should more closely examine the postpositivistic philosophy of science to which Schauer appeals. My concern here is to remedy Schauer's failure to use this philosophy in a way that would be fertile of discussions of interpretation in general and legal and constitutional interpretation in particular. The most arresting feature of such philosophy of science is its redirection away from a timeless scientific method neutrally operating on simple facts to a historically self-conscious understanding of scientific practice. Such understanding is evidenced both in Polanyi's emphasis on the intuitive practices of scientific communities[23] and the

22. In "Easy Cases," Schauer questions the interpretive legitimacy of the constitutional right to privacy, at n. 82. For Ely's analogous attack, see chapter 1. For further criticisms of both Ely's and Schauer's attacks on constitutional privacy, see discussions in chapters 9 and 10.
23. Polanyi, *Personal Knowledge*.

sometimes radical shifts in scientific practice as noted by Kuhn,[24] Lakatos,[25] Laudan,[26] and others.[27] When philosophy of science takes seriously actual scientific practice and changes therein, the nature of science is no longer self-evident (as it was, perhaps, to philosophy of science before the breakdown of the Newtonian synthesis).[28] Rather, the nature of science itself requires interpretation, a historically self-conscious interpretation of the practices of scientific communities[29] which cannot be sharply demarcated from the larger cultural communities of art, philosophy, and religion in which they are embedded.[30] The positivist idea of a timeless accumulation of neutral facts appears, on historical reflection, grossly to undervalue the role of theory in science, including both philosophical reflection on theory and the crucial presence of competitor theories, which give fact finding its significance and point.[31]

We may be surprised that an activity like science requires interpretation, but it does not surprise, once we acknowledge this need, to find that it gives rise to the cultivation of historical self-consciousness. Interpretation in the arts, for example, familiarly requires a sense of the history of the art, for example, performance practices in Mozart's time or the conventions of Handelian opera seria. If the historical conventions are sufficiently remote and discontinuous with current practice (Handelian opera seria), the work may be interpretively inaccessible; performance will, at best, abuse the work, in some sense failing, as we may say, to interpret the work.[32] If we believe that works in the remote style are works of the highest musical and dramatic genius (Handel's "Tamerlano," say), we may struggle to revive the lost conventions, to develop in the public an understanding of their nature and power. Consider, for example, the development in opera lovers of a taste and relish for Monteverdi's three extant masterpieces.

Interpretation in law typically involves a continuous legal tradition, and it is natural to suppose, once one rejects as interpretively unsound

24. Kuhn, *The Structure of Scientific Revolutions.*
25. Lakatos, "Falsification and the Methodology of Scientific Research Programmes."
26. Laudan, *Progress and Its Problems;* Laudan, *Science and Values.*
27. See, e.g., Nickles, ed., *Scientific Discovery, Logic, and Rationality;* and Cohen, *The Newtonian Revolution.*
28. The importance of this breakdown, in shattering the complacency of the philosophy of science, and the need, nonetheless, to account reasonably for the sense of progress in science are much emphasized by Newton-Smith in his *The Rationality of Science.*
29. See, e.g., Shapere, "The Character of Scientific Change"; Glymour, *Theory and Evidence;* Hacking, *Representing and Intervening;* Cartwright, *How the Laws of Physics Lie;* van Fraassen, *The Scientific Image.*
30. The importance of these larger connections is underscored by Laudan, *Progress and Its Problems.*
31. See ibid.; Lakatos, "Falsification and the Methodology of Scientific Research Programmes."
32. See, e.g., Dean, *Handel and the Opera Seria,* pp. 200–214.

an appeal to Founders' applications, that such interpretation tracks current conventions: thus, the attraction of positivistic conventionalism. But the example of science strikes home the conviction that ahistorical consideration of current practices may distort their interpretive complexity, indeed, disfigure the reality and sense of these practices and their connections to broader cultural ideas. Interpretation in law is not only interpretively complex in this way, often it is also, in a way science is not, about or directed at some historical text or set of texts. We are poised, then, between two unacceptable alternatives: the appeal to history in Berger's myth of Founders' intent or the ahistorical appeal to positivistic conventionalism. We need some acceptable account of how history may be part of our interpretive practices.

We have already sketched the outlines of such an account in chapter 2, both in response to the natural law appeal outside history and practice to moral reality and as an alternative to Berger's approach to history. American constitutionalism is, I then suggested, itself an expression, indeed an exemplar, of certain unique features of the Western cultural tradition: the integration of self-consciously diverse texts into a coherent tradition, the diffusion of literacy[33] and consequent metainterpretive divisions over reading these texts, and the political legitimation of metainterpretive dissent by recognition of the inalienable right of conscience and inchoate political and civil rights.[34] When the idea of a written constitution appears in the period of the English Puritan Revolution, it is thought of as the political analogue of the covenant of theology:[35] in the same way that the absolute God binds Himself to the terms of a predictable and reliable covenant that enjoys and dignifies the free and rational consent of His people, the self-limitation of state power by a written constitution binds the state to substantive and procedural terms that secure and express the nature of persons as free, rational, and equal moral individuals who are assured, as a political community, of the dignity of their human and natural rights.

The idea of a written constitution does not arise in a historical and cultural vacuum. It flows out of deep currents in Western political and religious thought, and the moral ideal to which both political and religious thought points is contractarian. When the greatest political theorist of this culture and period, John Locke, gives clear expression to the underlying moral ideal of religious and political community, his highly abstract political theory, whose actual political recommendations are quite unspecific and even inchoate, is clearly contractarian.[36]

33. Protestantism appears to have been a central motive force in the diffusion of literacy; see Lockridge, *Literacy in Colonial New England*, pp. 5, 45–46, 97–101.
34. See sources at note 53, chapter 2.
35. See Miller, *The New England Mind: The Seventeenth Century*, pp. 365–462; Miller, *Errand into the Wilderness*, pp. 48–98.
36. See Locke, *The Second Treatise of Government*, in *Locke's Two Treatises of Government*, pp. 285–446.

The interpretation of Locke's political theory and its historical influence on American political culture are complex matters. Critical historians of political theory increasingly are uncovering the religious roots of Locke's thought.[37] The influence of contractarian thought on America may have been mediated primarily by Francis Hutcheson and other moral-sense theorists who nevertheless incorporated and developed Locke's political ideas;[38] the Lockean texts that had most influence in the early eighteenth century in America appear to be his general epistemology and his arguments for religious toleration.[39] Moreover, the text of Locke's political theory (that is, *The Second Treatise of Government*) appears as a major vehicle of American political thought only in the revolutionary period.[40] Nonetheless, the critical historiography of this period confirms the pervasive contractarian flavor of political thought, which though not always tied to specifically Lockean political texts, is implicit in other texts that *were* read, including Lockean texts and works of others that assume and elaborate Locke's thought.

To understand the self-conception of the American Constitution as a written constitution, legal interpreters must take seriously the contractarian moral ideal of community that actuates it, for the republican ideals and concepts of the abortive Puritan Revolution, which never took root in Britain, received in America a remarkable opportunity of self-conscious political elaboration.[41] The American Constitution, as suggested in chapter 2, represents a historically unique attempt to use the best political theory and political science of the age, combined with a diverse practical experience of democratic self-rule, to create a written text of constraints on state power that would achieve in America what

37. See Dunn, *The Political Theory of John Locke;* Tully, *A Discourse on Property.*
38. See, e.g., Shaftesbury, *An Inquiry Concerning Virtue and Merit;* Hutcheson, *An Inquiry Concerning the Original of Our Ideas of Virtue or Moral Good;* Hutcheson, *Illustrations on the Moral Sense;* Hutcheson, *A System of Moral Philosophy.* A useful discussion of Hutcheson's incorporation of Lockean ideas in his political philosophy is Campbell, "Francis Hutcheson: 'Father' of the Scottish Enlightenment." For other pertinent writings of the relevant historical period, illustrating the emerging philosophical conflict between emotional and intellectual interpretations of the "moral sense", see vols. 1 and 2, Selby-Bigge, ed., *British Moralists.* For later developments in Scottish thought, also influential on American thought, see Reid, *Essays on the Active Powers of the Human Mind;* Stewart, *The Philosophy of the Active and Moral Powers of Man.* For specific influences of early and later "moral sense" theory on Jefferson, for example, see Koch, *The Philosophy of Thomas Jefferson,* pp. 15–22, 44–53. For an example of the influence on Madison, see Witherspoon, *Lectures on Moral Philosophy.* See also Ahlstrom, "The Scottish Philosophy and American Theology."
39. See Dunn, "The Politics of Locke in England and America in the Eighteenth Century," in *Political Obligation in its Historical Context,* pp. 53–77.
40. Ibid.
41. See Hanson, *From Kingdom to Commonwealth;* Walzer, *Exodus and Revolution,* pp. 73–98.

had never been achieved elsewhere: enduring republican government in a large territory.[42] The Constitution, followed shortly by the Bill of Rights, is the product of self-conscious reflection on past republican experiments (Greece, Rome, the Florentine and Venetian republics, the Cromwellian commonwealth) and the republican political theory and science of their emergence, stability, and decline (Polybius, Machiavelli, Guicciardini, Giannotti, Sarpi, Harrington, Locke, Sidney);[43] on various federal systems and their comparative success;[44] on both explanatory and normative theories of federalism, separation of powers, a mixed or balanced constitution, and the British Constitution (Aristotle, Hume, Montesquieu);[45] on historical traditions of respect for metainterpretive diversity and the correlative political, moral, and religious theories calling for an institutional expression of respect for basic rights of the person, including the rights of conscience and free speech (Locke, Milton);[46] on the practical political experience of colonial self-government, the struggles with Britain centering on concepts of political representation, and the republican experiments in the states after the American Revolution;[47] and on much else besides. The expression of such self-conscious reflection in the form of a written constitution grows out of a larger cultural and moral tradition that conceives political legitimacy on a contractarian model calling for observance by the state of predictable and orderly constraints that acknowledge and express the dignity of persons and citizens as free, rational, and equal. The written form of the constraints takes its moral life from a culture of widespread textual literacy which recognized in the written terms of the constitution the acknowledgment of one's interpretive dignity as a

---

42. See Adair, *Fame and the Founding Fathers*, pp. 107–23.

43. See ibid.; Pocock, *The Machiavellian Moment*; Bouwsma, *Venice and the Defense of Republican Liberty*.

44. For relevant textual evidence of Madison's use of comparative political science in the analysis of America's need for a certain form of federal system, see Meyers, ed., *The Mind of the Founder: Sources of the Political Thought of James Madison*, pp. 47–69. For useful perspective on the history of the federal idea, see Davis, *The Federal Principle*.

45. See Adair, *Fame and the Founding Fathers*, pp. 75–123; Wood, *The Creation of the American Republic, 1776–1787*; Bailyn, *The Ideological Origins of the American Revolution*; Pocock, *The Machiavellian Moment*, pp. 333–552.

46. See, e.g., Locke's letters on toleration, in vol. 6 of *The Works of John Locke*. For Milton on free speech, see *Areopagitica* in *The Prose of John Milton*, pp. 247–334; for Milton on religious freedom, see pp. 443–518. For a striking and influential American use of Lockean arguments in defense of religious toleration, see Williams, "The Essential Rights and Liberties of Protestants." For Jefferson's express use of both Locke and Milton in drafting the Virginia Bill for Religious Freedom, clearly central to Madison's later work on the religion clauses of the first amendment, see *The Papers of Thomas Jefferson*, vol. 1, pp. 544–50 (Locke), pp. 551–53 (Milton). On the influence of American religious thought on revolutionary ideals, see Heimert, *Religion and the American Mind*. See also the relevant sources at note 53, chapter 2.

47. The best synthetic treatment remains Wood, *The Creation of the American Republic, 1776–1787*. For a useful study focusing on the issues of representation alone, see Pole, *Political Representation in England and the Origins of the American Republic*.

free and rational person: thus, the focal significance in constitutional thought and practice of the inalienable right to conscience.

CONTRACTARIAN THEORY AND THE INALIENABLE RIGHT TO CONSCIENCE

My attempt to use contemporary political theory of an explicitly contractarian kind in constitutional interpretation is said by Schauer[48] to be underdetermined by the data and by Perry[49] to be without historical warrant or defense. These remarks arise from positivistic conventionalism on the one hand (Schauer) or an appeal to moral reality on the other (Perry). Neither takes seriously the task of constitutional interpretation as an interpretive reconstruction of the historical traditions of American constitutional law. Only the belief that a constitutional theorist need not look at history can explain Schauer's and Perry's positions, for the historical investigation of the formation of our constitutional tradition uncovers, as earlier suggested, a profoundly contractarian style of thought. Contractarian theory is not introduced into constitutional interpretation extrinsically in the manner of Perry's appeal to moral prophecy; it is introduced as an explanation of one dominant strain in the motivating political theory of the Founding period, which was characterized by a remarkably self-conscious use of political theory, a political theory that shapes the sense of much of the constitutional text and also its elaboration over time by amendment and by interpretation. Constitutional interpretation, when understood as the imputation of reasonable purposes to the text and history of the Constitution, finds a certain political theory, suitably developed and understood, to be simply the most reasonable explanation of its task, because, on interpretive examination, a form of the theory is seen implicitly to guide the historical self-conception of constitutional government.

The utility of contemporary political theory of a contractarian kind in constitutional interpretation should not be understood as woodenly descriptive, in the way Schauer construes my views as calling for a certain organization of atheoretical particulars. Just as a better contemporary contractarian theory may illuminate the structure of Locke's (or Rousseau's or Kant's) argument, so, I believe, a deeper contemporary contractarian political theory may transform and broaden our interpretation of our historically contractarian ideas of government, and thus constitutional interpretation.

Lockean contractarian theories of the state have, for example, been rejected since Hume as ahistorical.[50] Locke's theory of natural "prop-

---

48. Schauer, "An Essay on Constitutional Language," pp. 816–18.
49. Perry, *The Constitution, the Courts, and Human Rights*, pp. 107–8.
50. See Hume, "Of the Original Contract."

erty rights" associated contractarian theory with economic privilege.[51] Contractarian theory in Rousseau has been rejected as totalitarian.[52] The suggestion of contractarian ideas in Kant has been supposed to be wedded to an unacceptably antiempirical metaphysics and an ultimately incoherent moral theory, whose only sense could be (so J. S. Mill argued) proto-utilitarianism.[53] If contractarian theory is rootedly antiredistributive, antiegalitarian, antiliberal, metaphysical, and, at bottom, proto-utilitarian, a thoroughly empirical utilitarianism would be the natural alternative paradigm for critical political thought; the contractarian structures of American constitutional law must be, at best, reinterpreted in acceptably utilitarian terms (Ely),[54] at worst, condemned as based on rights, "nonsense on stilts"[55] (Hand).[56]

A contemporary contractarian theory of some depth and sophistication, like Rawls's, not only makes possible a revival of nonutilitarian political philosophy, but enables us to read past contractarian political theory in a more critical and truer way, to find a distinctive approach to political legitimacy, which is neither inevitably antiredistributive, antiegalitarian, illiberal, metaphysical, or proto-utilitarian. We may thus come better to understand the history of political theory and our intellectual history as a culture. In political theory, for example, we may better grasp continuities and discontinuities between Locke's constitutional liberalism and the classical republican tradition culminating in Rousseau.[57] On the one hand, both theories express often similar ideals of a moral community of free, rational, and equal persons under the rule of law; on the other, they offer quite different institutional designs to achieve many common ends. In intellectual history, we may better grasp the complex and unexamined tensions in the eighteenth-century political thought that shaped the American political mind, and thus our constitutional tradition.

If constitutional interpretation is an investigation into historical self-

---

51. See MacPherson, *The Political Theory of Possessive Individualism.* But cf. Ryan, "Locke and the Dictatorship of the Bourgeoisie"; Tully, *A Discourse on Property.* See, however, Wood, *John Locke and Agrarian Capitalism.*
52. See Taine, *L'Ancien Regime.* But cf. Cassirer, *The Question of Jean Jacques Rousseau.*
53. See, e.g., Mill, *Utilitarianism,* pp. 6, 65.
54. See, e.g., Ely, *Democracy and Distrust.* See discussion in chapter 1.
55. See ibid., pp. 43–72. The phrase, of course, is Bentham's; see Bentham, "Anarchical Fallacies" in *The Works of Jeremy Bentham,* Book II, p. 501.
56. Hand, *Bill of Rights.* See discussion in chapter 1.
57. For a form of mistaken contrast, see Pocock, *The Machiavellian Moment,* pp. 545–46; see also Sullivan, *Reconstructing Public Philosophy;* Barber, *Strong Democracy.* I do not, of course, deny important contrasts between the classical civic republican tradition and the Lockean tradition of republican government. See, e.g., Kramnick, "Republican Revisionism Revisited." Indeed, at the state conventions ratifying the Constitution, leading founders argued that the classical republican tradition should not be followed, because it led to tyranny and faction. See Hamilton of New York, Jonathan Elliot, *Debates in Several State Conventions,* vol. 2, pp. 253–4; Madison of Virginia, *id.,* vol. 3, p. 87.

understanding, better readings of our intellectual history may be of signal interpretive importance. For example, the recent reexamination of Locke's influence on American thought has led one analyst to focus on the influence on Jefferson's political thought of Hutcheson and the moral-sense theorists in general. Because Hutcheson was a utilitarian, the inference is made to a more communitarian, less individualistic (less Lockean) strain in American thought.[58] But, of course, the sharp contemporary analytic distinctions between utilitarian and deontological argument were not available in this period;[59] and it is an ahistorical blunder to impute to the political or moral theories of a particular historical period a clarity and coherence which that period demonstrably lacked. Such misreadings of history disfigure the intellectual landscape of an age, missing, for example, the Lockean roots of Jefferson's commitment to religious toleration and associated ideals of human rights, with which Hutcheson concurred.[60] Hutcheson, for example, combined contractarian and rights-based thought in his political theory with a crude utilitarianism in his moral philosophy. He clearly did not think of himself as challenging Locke (who had not published an ethical theory,[61] a lacuna Hutcheson was clearly attempting to fill on terms shaped by Lockean epistemology).[62] Rather, Hutcheson assumed and elabo-

58. See Wills, *Inventing America.*
59. Sensitive moral theorists of this period did recognize that the deliverances of the "moral sense" often did not obviously square with the utilitarian principle; see, e.g., Butler, *Fifteen Sermons*, pp. 199–200, 254–55; Kames, *Essays on the Principles of Morality and Natural Religion*, pp. 42–91. But, these deliverances were not regarded as resting on nonutilitarian moral foundations, for a just God—as a kind of rule-utilitarian lawgiver— designed these pluralistic moral principles in a way that, when acted on, would result in a utilitarian optimum. See, e.g., Butler, *Fifteen Sermons*, pp. 253–55; Kames, *Essays*, pp. 90–91. The notable exception is, I believe, Richard Price, who appears clearly to have seen the moral depth of the distinction between moral constraints and utilitarian aggregation. See Price, *A Review of the Principal Questions in Morals*, p. 160.
60. See, in general, Hamowy, "Jefferson and the Scottish Enlightenment: A Critique of Gary Wills's *Inventing America: Jefferson's Declaration of Independence.*" For related arguments emphasizing the Lockean roots of American republican thought in general and of Jefferson's thought in particular, see Kramnick, "Republican Revisionism Revisited"; Appleby, "What Is Still American in the Political Philosophy of Thomas Jefferson?"; Appleby, "Commercial Farming and the 'Agrarian Myth' in the Early Republic."
61. Locke's most sustained effort in ethics is a form of normative ethics and Bible criticism; see Locke, *The Reasonableness of Christianity*. For a striking evidence of specific Lockean influence on American political thought, see Jefferson's comparably Lockean effort at normative ethics through Bible criticism: Adams, ed., *Jefferson's Extracts from the Gospels*. Insofar as Locke's conception of normative ethics can be inferred from his published and unpublished writings, it appears to be some form of rule-utilitarianism, which again indicates how little contrasts between rights-based and utilitarian argument were drawn in this period, for Locke's political theory is rights-based. See, in general, Colman, *John Locke's Moral Philosophy.*
62. See, e.g., Hutcheson's main work on moral epistemology, *Illustrations on the Moral Sense.*

rated Locke's political theory,[63] and, of course, appears quite unaware of any sharp distinction between rights-based and utilitarian argument. Such a distinction, though developed later by Bentham and Kant,[64] has probably achieved real clarity of statement only in contemporary political theory.[65] The very idea of moral community in the thought of the eighteenth century, as expressed by Jonathan Edwards, for example, may be more consistent with a Kantian, rather than a utilitarian, interpretation;[66] but since Kant had not yet written,[67] the ambiguity could hardly be identified, let alone critically discussed. Contemporary political theory makes these underlying tensions in thought clearer, allowing us to read the thinkers of this period less ahistorically, and critically to decide which of their underlying conceptions are justly supportive of the constitutional traditions shaped by their thought.[68] In constitutional theory, contemporary political theory may enable us to improve and even transform our understanding of the moral structures that compose our constitutional traditions, to understand the enduring meanings of our constitutional history.

This utility of political theory, wedded to a critical historiography, for constitutional interpretation may be strikingly demonstrated in a way that also brings out the promise of an approach to constitutional interpretation that is not clause-bound. The American constitutional guarantees of religious freedom (the free exercise and antiestablishment clauses of the First Amendment) provide a useful case study for this kind of approach.

The form of these guarantees in the First Amendment is a distinctively American contribution to constitutional practice. Its political fathers and architects were Jefferson and Madison: Jefferson who authors the Virginia Bill for Religious Freedom; Madison who secures

63. See the clarifying discussion on this point in Campbell, "Francis Hutcheson: 'Father' of the Scottish Enlightenment."
64. Even then, of course, the notorious difficulties in Kantian exegesis led even those sympathetic to Kant's autonomy-based ethics not to appreciate its possibility of a defensibly nonutilitarian ethical theory. See, e.g., Mill, *Utilitarianism*, pp. 6, 65.
65. For evidence that contemporary political theory now recognizes the distinctively antiutilitarian nature of rights-based arguments in political theory, see Hart, "Between Utility and Rights."
66. I have in mind Edwards's extraordinary emphasis in his moral philosophy on the voluntarism of a good will and its characterization in terms of "consent and good will to Being in general," p. 262, Edwards, *Dissertation on the Nature of Virtue*, and his use throughout that work, pp. 261–304, of an intuitive form of universalized consent criterion for the properly ethical; see, e.g., his contrast between "*cordial* agreement" and "*natural* union or agreement," p. 273. For the roots of Edwards's ethical and religious thought, see Fiering, *Jonathan Edwards's Moral Thought and Its British Context*.
67. But see note 64, above.
68. A comparable critical argument can, I believe, be made about the attempt to impute to Jefferson and others a non-Lockean commitment to the civic republican tradition. See, for example, the articles by Kramnick and Appleby, note 60, above. See also Diggins, *The Lost Soul of American Politics*.

the bill's enactment, and then authors the religious freedom guarantees of the First Amendment.[69] The focal significance that Jefferson and Madison give to the right to conscience is a reflection of the similar weight given this right in the political culture of Cromwellian England (Milton et al.)[70] and America (Roger Williams)[71] and draws inspiration both from the Lockean epistemology of experience and from Locke's *Letters Concerning Toleration.*[72] These works by Locke were widely read and disseminated in the American political and religious culture of the Great Awakening,[73] legitimating a personal and experimental religion of the heart, which centered on cultivation of Edwards's "religious affections."[74]

Contractarian political theory may advance our understanding of these political traditions and the constitutional guarantees shaped by these traditions. In view of the primacy that the right to conscience has enjoyed in constitutional history, it is significant that Rawls gives central place to the case for religious toleration in his argument for his first principle of justice (the principle of equal liberty). The argument for religious toleration is, Rawls contends, a paradigm case, which can be suitably generalized to cover the other rights and liberties protected by the first principle.[75] The priority given to this argument is neither

69. See, for this remarkable collaboration, Koch, *Jefferson and Madison*, pp. 3–61. For documentary material, see Stokes, *Church and State in the United States*, pp. 333–50, 366–97, 519–52.

70. See note 53, chapter 2; and note 46, chapter 3, and accompanying text.

71. See Williams, *The Bloudy Tenent of Persecution*. See also Miller, *Roger Williams;* Morgan, *Roger Williams*. For discussion of comparable arguments for toleration, importantly influential in America, see Dunn, *William Penn: Politics and Conscience*. Williams was self-consciously invoked by Isaac Backus, the Baptist defender of toleration during the revolutionary and early constitutional period. See, e.g., McLoughlin, *Isaac Backus and the American Pietistic Tradition*, p. 229. See also Backus's influential "An Appeal to the Public for Religious Liberty," Boston, 1773, reprinted in McLoughlin, ed., *Isaac Backus on Church, State and Calvinism*, pp. 306–43 (Williams cited at p. 322–23). Locke was also frequently cited by Backus; see McLoughlin, *Isaac Backus and the American Pietistic Tradition*, pp. 31–32, 122, 131, 141, 191. For an important general study of the influence on dissenters like the Baptists on American political thought, see McLoughlin, *New England Dissent, 1630–1833*. See also McLoughlin, "Isaac Backus and the Separation of Church and State in America."

72. See Locke, *An Essay Concerning Human Understanding;* and Locke's *Letters Concerning Toleration*.

73. See notes 39 and 46, above, and accompanying text. On the cultural importance of the Great Awakening, see McLoughlin, *Revivals, Awakenings, and Reform;* Ahlstrom, *A Religious History of the American People*, pp. 261–384; Heimert, *Religion and the American Mind;* Isaac, *The Transformation of Virginia, 1740–1790*. See also Marty, *Righteous Empire;* Mead, *The Lively Experiment*.

74. See Edwards, *Religious Affections*, a piercing psychological portrait of the religion of the heart. Cf. James, *The Varieties of Religious Experience*.

75. Rawls, *A Theory of Justice*, pp. 195–257. Cf. Rawls, "Fairness to Goodness," pp. 536, 542–45; Rawls, "Reply to Alexander and Musgrave," pp. 633, 636–37.

an expository convenience nor is it merely accidentally connected to the structure of the underlying contractarian moral concept, as it might be in a comparable utilitarian argument. On a contractarian model, as we shall see in the next chapter, the terms of the basic regulative constitutional principles agreed to must dignify the nature of persons as free, rational, and equal. These principles and the constitutional guarantees that embody them must therefore protect the inalienable right to conscience, for this right is the very condition of the freedom and rationality of the person. Thus, contractarian theory clarifies the moral significance of the centrality of the right to conscience in the historical elaboration of constitutional thought and practice; the recognition of this right to interpretive independence in basic questions of life's meaning is uncovered as at the core of the concept of persons as free, rational, and equal, which constitutional government dignifies, and progressively elaborates.

This illuminating convergence of political theory and constitutional interpretation has the remarkable interpretive consequence so characteristic of American constitutional discourse: quite abstract philosophical reflection on relevant issues of justice in government shapes the terms of constitutional discourse. With respect to the religion guarantees of the First Amendment, for example, such philosophical inquiry can clarify the way in which freedom and rationality of the person are best understood, and thus can help to determine the scope and meaning of the right to conscience. Such an inquiry would be both an exercise in moral and political philosophy and a searching investigation of values and concepts implicit in our larger cultural and political history. As abstract normative philosophy, the agenda would include a philosophical psychology of the relations among will, desires, belief, and knowledge; a naturalized epistemology of cognitive rationality; a theory of practical rationality and its connections to epistemic rationality; an analysis of concepts of freedom; and an account of moral ideals of the person and the unity of the self.[76] As political and cultural history, the same account would clarify and be clarified by the examination of broad, interactive changes in the direction of Western thought—metaphysical (the impact of voluntarist theology), epistemological (the reintroduction and development of skeptical thought), and moral (the defense of the right to conscience as a moral and political ideal). Thus, voluntarist theology hastened the decline of metaphysical beliefs in the centrality to our personhood of contemplation of and regulation by "the great chain of being,"[77] and legitimated active scientific curiosity.[78] Skeptical thought attacked Aristotelian certainty and stimulated

76. See, e.g., the elements of some aspects of this analysis in Richards, *A Theory of Reasons for Action.* I draw on and elaborate this account in chapter 4.
77. Lovejoy, *The Great Chain of Being,* pp. 163, 332–33.
78. Blumenberg, *The Legitimacy of the Modern Age.*

scientific and philosophical interest in ways of knowing.[79] And the political and religious defense of toleration, as in Bayle[80] and Locke,[81] was premised on both the new epistemology of experience (and the universally accessible theory of commonsense rationality that it made possible) and a moral ideal of respect for the uncompromisable demands of one's own conscience.

Such a political theory would illuminate the connection of constitutional traditions to the larger cultural traditions that they reflect, and would reveal the rich common discourse existing between philosophy and law. For example, such an abstract exercise in political philosophy and historical understanding would make possible a plausible theory of background rights, in Dworkin's sense. This would improve understanding of the right to conscience as an abstract background right, thereby empowering constitutional theory to clarify how the religion clauses (free exercise and antiestablishment) should be understood and coordinated. We might thus advance the discussion of the meaning of the underlying constitutional conception of neutrality, pervasive throughout the jurisprudence of the First Amendment. Controversy over the proper historiography of the religion clauses might then be resolved,[82] and intractable contemporary controversy over church-state relations might be clarified by bringing out the crucial significance of the antiestablishment principle as an expression of respect for the dignity of a free mind and person.[83]

INTERPRETATION AND JUDICIAL REVIEW

Much constitutional theory is preoccupied with the scope and justification of judicial review. The strategy of this book is to develop an appropriately rich and plausible theory of constitutional interpretation, and to take the tradition of judicial review as part of this theory. This approach may bear both descriptive and normative fruit.

79. See Popkin, *The History of Scepticism from Erasmus to Descartes;* and his revised version, *The History of Scepticism from Erasmus to Spinoza;* Van Leeuwen, *The Problem of Certainty in English Thought, 1630–1690;* Shapiro, *Probability and Certainty in Seventeenth-Century England.*
80. Bayle, *Philosophique Commentaire.*
81. Locke, *The Works of John Locke,* vol. 6. For a useful integration of Locke's epistemological, moral, and political views, see Yolton, *Locke: An Introduction.*
82. The leading works of accommodationist historiography are Howe, *The Garden and the Wilderness;* O'Neill, *Religion and Education Under the Constitution;* Antieau, Downey, and Roberts, *Freedom from Federal Establishment;* see also Cover, "Foreword: Nomos and Narrative." Leading statements of separationist historiography are Levy, *Judgments: Essays on American Constitutional History,* pp. 169–233; Dargo, *Roots of the Republic,* pp. 77–107; Pfeffer, *Church, State and Freedom;* Curry, *The First Freedoms.*
83. See, e.g., Konvitz, *Religious Liberty and Conscience.*

A theory of constitutional interpretation in the United States must give weight to our interpretive practices over time, among which, inter alia, is judicial review. Accordingly, one of the tests for a theory of constitutional interpretation is whether it can clarify interpretive patterns of judicial review. A better theory of constitutional interpretation may thus promote more insightful understanding of judicial review if it can show how, when, and why such review secures better constitutional interpretation over all.

On the other hand, patterns of judicial review are, in the United States, recurringly controversial, and any plausible theory of constitutional law must address the normative question of how, when, and why judicial review is, as it has often been, constitutionally in error. Positivistic theories of constitutional law are inadequate precisely because they do not do justice to normative claims of interpretive mistake. In contrast, an interpretive approach, of the kind here taken, enables us to give sense to and even to assess such claims.

The course of the argument of the chapters to follow will include both descriptive and normative components. Often, the interpretive practices of judicial review will be explained by the kind of interpretive arguments that are, on my view, most defensible. To the extent that my arguments better explain the law, that will be to their credit as explanatory theories of law. Sometimes, however, I shall argue to the effect that a judicial construction of a constitutional issue is an interpretive mistake. If the argument is a sound criticism of the constitutional interpretation judicially imposed, that will be to its credit as part of the normative component of constitutional interpretation.

The largest questions of the legitimacy of judicial review must thus be postponed until the end of the constructive interpretive argument. Then we can ask what any good theory of constitutional law must be able to answer: what role does judicial review properly play in our constitutional law? This, the traditional first question of constitutional theory will, in my account, be answered last (chapter 10).

II / Religious Liberty

4 · The Inalienable Right to Conscience

The opening language of the First Amendment to the United States Constitution reads:

> Congress shall make no law respecting an establishment of religion, or prohibiting the free exercise thereof.

The very place of the religion clauses—the first clauses of the First Amendment—suggests the kind of primacy that religious toleration in fact enjoys in our constitutional history and interpretive practices. Madison and Jefferson, for example, clearly saw the underlying right to conscience as central to the justice of republican government and to the rights such government would protect. As early as the Virginia debates over the Declaration of Rights and Virginia Constitution of 1776, Madison insisted that mere toleration of sects outside the established church was not enough, for republican justice required full respect for conscience, associated by him and Jefferson with disestablishment itself.[1] Toleration, understood not in the narrow sense Madi-

---

1. During these debates, Madison objected to both the wording and substance of George Mason's article on religion: to the wording because it used "fullest toleration in the exercise of religion, according to the dictates of conscience," whereas Madison's first substitute used "full and free exercise of it [religion] according to the dictates of conscience";

son condemned but in the full sense of protection for conscience he intended, was the central paradigm of the kind of respect for rights that actuates the form and substance of constitutional government.

Consistent with this vision, the cumulative weight of the argument of this book is that the rights characteristic of liberal constitutionalism converge in a certain way on a distinctive moral conception of toleration of thought, speech, and action. We begin with religious toleration itself, turning, in later chapters, to free speech and constitutional privacy. In all these areas, a historically self-conscious political theory will identify a common structure of motivating conceptions, which I call the primacy of religious toleration.

In this and the next chapter, I elaborate this constructive approach in the interpretation of the religion clauses of the First Amendment. I start with a form of abstract moral and political theory of the inalienable right to conscience. Constitutional theory, at this point, uses abstract moral and political philosophy to organize and explicate a distinctive structure of thought, and shows, at crucial points, how the account clarifies our understanding of the most historically influential philosophical arguments (by Locke and Bayle) for toleration. In the next chapter, this political theory of the inalienable right to conscience is used to explain a background constitutional right, in Dworkin's sense, a right implicit in the history and practice of our constitutional traditions. Here, constitutional theory uses the political theory, earlier abstractly developed, to advance understanding and critical assessment of the primacy of religious toleration in our historical traditions and current interpretive practices (including often highly controversial case law centering on the proper interpretation of the idea of constitutional neutrality).

COVENANT AND RIGHTS OF THE PERSON

Historically, conceptions of constitutional government expressed larger religious and moral ideals of covenant (as noted in chapters 2 and 3). Ethical and religious covenant with God, who limits His power on con-

---

to the substance, because it prohibited only coercion of religious worship not disturbing the peace, whereas Madison found the free exercise limitation too narrow, and called for disestablishment provisions as well. See Brant, *James Madison: The Virginia Revolutionist*, pp. 244–45. The article adopted did not contain Madison's desired antiestablishment provisions, but the free exercise guarantee was broader, as Madison wished, not containing Mason's language of "toleration" but "all men are equally entitled to the free exercise of religion, according to the dictates of conscience"; see ibid., p. 247. Jefferson's Bill for Religious Freedom (which he drew in 1777, abortively proposed in 1779, and Madison saw adopted—with the assistance of Madison's crucial *Memorial and Remonstrance Against Religious Assessment*, reprinted in Meyer, ed., *The Mind of the Founder*, pp. 5–13.—in 1786) called, crucially, for disestablishment. See Boyd, ed., *The Papers of Thomas Jefferson, 1777–1779*, pp. 545–53; Malone, *Jefferson the Virginian*, pp. 274–80.

dition of free consent to the terms of an ethical life, is mirrored in the state's covenant to limit its power constitutionally as the condition of voluntary consent. But, contractarian political thought is a metaphor capable of benign and malign interpretations: the Lockean contract of limited government and respect for rights of conscience is hardly the same conception as the Hobbesian contract of autocratic, indeed total-itarian submission. In order to understand the sense of contract central to our constitutional traditions, we must penetrate beneath the con-tractarian metaphor, and examine the moral conceptions that motivate it. The Lockean contract is, I shall suggest, a way of expressing a deeper moral thought about treating persons as equals: equal respect for per-sons calls for constitutional constraints which a legitimate government and community must observe.[2] Respect for the right to conscience is, for Locke, such a constitutional constraint, because it expresses an underlying notion of treating persons as equals.

The nature and force of the inalienable right to conscience may be usefully situated in a general discussion of the rights perspective on politics and law. If it is sensible to speak or think of any basic human right, whose demands are incumbent on all rational agents as such, the inalienable right to conscience is one such demand. The nature and force of such demands reflect a certain interpretation of the basic moral imperative of treating persons as equals, in contrast, for example, to the utilitarian interpretation of treating persons as equals.

UTILITARIAN EQUALITY

The notion of treating persons in the way one would oneself want to be treated is a conception of the nature of ethics or morality familiar to many moral traditions.[3] Ethical conduct, on this view, treats persons as equals, for the ultimate moral imperative to treat others in the way one would oneself want to be treated presupposes that we are, in some sense, equals. However, the notion of treating persons as equals is ambiguous. For example, John Stuart Mill, following Bentham, argued that utilitarianism treated persons as equals: the pleasures and pains of everyone stand equal before the utilitarian calculus, which calls for the neutral maximization of the aggregate of pleasure over pain.[4] An impor-tant recent literature has made clear that the traditional utilitarian interpretation of treating persons as equals is a weighting principle con-

---

2. Cf. Dworkin, *Taking Rights Seriously*, ch. 6.
3. For a fuller development of this analysis, see Richards, "Rights and Autonomy." This chapter's analysis and criticism of utilitarian theory is highly incomplete and schematic, intended only as a useful foil for the introduction of my theory of the right to conscience.
4. Mill, *Utilitarianism*, ch. 5, pp. 76–79.

sistent with grossly unjust forms of unequal treatment.[5] It suffices, on the utilitarian theory of equality, that all pleasures and pains are impartially registered by the hedonic calculus. But the aggregation of them (maximizing pleasure over pain overall) may call for plowing under the interests of some persons in ways naturally regarded as unjust or indecent, namely, failing to treat them as persons.

The nerve of the problem is the utilitarian way of interpreting equality—as a certain conception of pleasures or pains. To treat persons in the way, for example, required by Bentham's utilitarianism is to treat pleasures, not persons, as equals.[6] But pleasures and pains, identical on a utilitarian metric, have different sorts of evaluative significance: some may be grounds for claims of basic rights, others may have no comparable force at all.[7] Compare, for example, the normative force of claims to a basic subsistence diet with claims to exquisitely cultivated tastes, acquired over years of sophisticated exploration of the subtle tastes and textures in food and drink. From the perspective of our consistently neutral Benthamite utilitarian view (undistorted by nonutilitarian moral premises[8] or dubious empirical assumptions),[9] the pains of malnutrition for the poor may be the same as the pains of deprivation of Beluga caviar for the food aesthete; indeed, the overall pains of the aesthete may be greater. For example, the investment of the cultivated palate in comparative superiority of consumption may give rise to special pains of social humiliation from relative deprivation that are empir-

5. See, in general, Hart, "Between Utility and Rights," p. 77. Cf. Williams, "A Critique of Utilitarianism," p. 77; Rawls, A Theory of Justice.
6. Contemporary advocates of utilitarianism standardly do not use a conception of pleasure and pain of this kind, but the rather different idea of rational preferences and avoidances. See, e.g., Hare, Moral Thinking. Such accounts are, I believe, still susceptible to criticisms related to those here offerred. See, e.g., Richards, "Prescriptivism, Constructivism, and Rights."
7. See Scanlon, "Preference and Urgency"; Rawls, "Social Unity and Primary Goods."
8. Mill's theory of higher and lower pleasures (see Mill, Utilitarianism, ch. 2, pp. 9–33) introduces a weighting of pleasures into the utilitarian metric, which does not appear to be utilitarian, but controlled by nonutilitarian values of dignity or autonomy. See Richards, Sex, Drugs, Death and the Law, pp. 2–20.
9. See Richards, A Theory of Reasons for Action, p. 115. The inegalitarian conclusions implicit in aggregative utilitarianism are traditionally ameliorated by appeal to the empirical premise of diminishing marginal utility: since more pleasure, aggregatively conceived, can be secured by distributing a good to another once the utility declines for the person who would otherwise get the good, the pursuit of the aggregate will have an equalizing tendency in distribution. But, if diminishing marginal utility is empirically false (to the contrary, people with more may want even more, experiencing greater pain than those used to less, see Veblen, The Theory of the Leisure Class), it may, in fact, be a nonutilitarian moral judgment: the wealthy do not deserve more, and their pain at deprivation of their expensive tastes is morally contemptible. Of course, this is true. But the judgment is nonutilitarian, which suggests that the plausibility of utilitarianism depends on empirical premises concealing nonutilitarian moral assumptions.

ically greater, now and in the long run, than the pains of the simpler palate of the poor person.[10] Not implausibly, poor people, already indurated to such deprivations, have scaled down their desires (and thus their pleasures and pains) congruent with the harsh realities of their lives.[11] The dull pain of the poor is, on neutral hedonic grounds, outweighed by the intense suffering of the aesthete. Nevertheless, malnutrition, in and of itself, gives rise to normative claims; those of the cultivated aesthete do not. A natural utilitarian interpretation of treating persons as equals appears to do violence in some fundamental way to the pattern of moral discourse, in this case to the salient moral distinction between basic needs and factitious tastes. Utilitarian thought does not naturally identify and give special weight to these or other kinds of claims; indeed, such special weight would violate its conception of equality, hedonic neutrality.

EQUAL RESPECT FOR PERSONS

The alternative, rights-based interpretation of treating persons as equals requires us to express in and through our action equal respect for persons. Accordingly, we must explore the theory of the person, taking into account both the natural capacities and the internal ideals for their competent exercise constitutive of the person, which is a central conception of our empirical and normative discourse. Since respect is the natural attitude appropriate to the exercise of competence,[12] the very sense of equal respect requires an investigation of the competences of the person, the grounds of respect for persons.

The theory of the person is both empirical and normative, in that it describes capacities that persons possess, and characterizes the ideals and principles to which the exercise of those capacities implicitly appeals. The relevant capacities are, I believe, those of freedom (or autonomy); the relevant principles are those of rationality and reasonableness. On analysis these capacities identify our powers to act on these principles (our twin moral powers of rationality and reasonableness).

Freedom and the Person

Freedom or autonomy identifies the capacity of persons to formulate and act on higher-order plans of action, which take as their self-critical

10. See Veblen, *The Theory of the Leisure Class.*
11. Cf. the similar point about preference adaptation and utilitarianism in Elster, *Sour Grapes*, pp. 133–40.
12. See White, *Ego and Reality in Psychoanalytic Theory.*

object one's life and the way it is lived, changing or not changing one's life, as the case may be. As Harry Frankfurt put it,

> No animal other than man . . . appears to have the capacity for reflective self-evaluation that is manifested in the formation of second-order desires.[13]

The description of this capacity is in part the description of the familiar human fact of our reflective wills, which make possible what Rawls calls the self-origination of claims and revisability thereof.[14]

Persons originate claims when they make claims and demands as an expression of their own internal capacities of personal judgment, reflection, and will. Such capacities are not in play when persons are thought of as having preassigned places or roles, irrespective of such capacities or their exercise. For example, persons are not thought of as having these capacities when they are defined solely by their functional utility in some larger design which alone specifies the status, place, and worth of the person (for example, their role in some political or social hierarchy or religious theocracy). Slavery, in which the slave is an extension of the master's will, denies, in principle, such a moral power in the slave.[15]

Revisability characterizes our actions when we exercise our powers of will and self-reflection, and change some destructive aspect of our lives or relationships: we stop smoking or drinking, or seek better friends or truer lovers.[16] The will is, of course, often stable and rooted, the expression of a character with certain outlines and foundations, itself unchanging in a way in which our corrigible bad habits are not. Persons do, of course, differ in the levels at which they exercise their capacities of revision, and some foundational levels (physical constitution) may constrain revisability altogether. Nevertheless, all persons exercise revisability in some areas of their lives, and some at quite deep levels of personality and character. Indeed, some of the most valued aspects of our culture (in art, religion, education, critical moral discourse, therapies of self-knowledge, and so on) derive their value from the contribution they make to our capacities for penetrating critical judgment on our lives and, sometimes, for the transformation of self.

Rationality

Our characterization of autonomy must naturally be complemented by investigation of the capacities for rationality and reasonableness in

13. Frankfurt, "Freedom of the Will and the Concept of a Person," p. 7.
14. Rawls, "Kantian Constructivism in Moral Theory." See also Richards, "Rights and Autonomy"; Benn, "Freedom, Autonomy and the Concept of a Person."
15. See, in general, Patterson, *Slavery and Social Death*.
16. See Richards, *A Theory of Reasons for Action*, pp. 40–43.

terms of which such claims and self-criticisms may be and are conducted. These capacities may be understood in terms of the principles of good reasoning to which they implicitly appeal, for the mark of the exercise of our rationality is that we make judgments on the basis of those good, better, or worse reasons associated with the aims of the inquiry in question. The aims of our practical rationality are inquiries into actions that achieve the good and realize the right; the aim of epistemic rationality is true belief. I begin with practical rationality, then examine epistemic rationality, and finally discuss the ways in which their integration characterizes the unity of the self.

Our practical rationality is, I believe, structured by the principles associated with its two aims: the good and the right. The good is the object of our prudential rationality; the right the object of our moral reasonableness.[17]

Our prudential rationality is exercised in terms of the principles of rational choice which specify the more satisfying, and less frustrating, ways to realize our ends coherently over time. We conduct our deliberations about our prudential good in terms of the good, better, and worse reasons associated with those principles.

Our moral reasonableness is shown in the ways we consider and weigh reasons associated with principles of conduct that persons as moral equals would offer and accept as the basic requirements of mutual respect incumbent on moral agents, as such. Our deliberations about right conduct reflect such principles, which, accordingly, constrain our pursuit of the good of prudential rationality.

Our epistemic rationality is, I believe, structured by our evolving conceptions of procedures of inquiry into true beliefs, reflected in the ways we reason about such beliefs. We reason, for example, about current beliefs, reflecting on their internal consistency or coherence, or the kind and weight of evidence that supports them; and we change them in ways that reflect the complex and often interactive force of such considerations.[18] A naturalized epistemology,[19] which takes as its task the description and explication of such procedures, must give place both to the role of experience in assessing the truth of beliefs, and the forms of argument and inquiry that guide such assessment, including, inter alia, deductive and inductive inference. Deductive inference allows us to extend truths already ascertained to those truths logically

---

17. See, in general, Richards, *A Theory of Reasons for Action*, where I formulate at some length both principles of practical rationality and moral reasonableness. My remarks here depend on that account.

18. See, e.g., Quine and Ullian, *The Web of Belief*. For a more foundationalist account, see Kenny, *Faith and Reason*.

19. See Quine, "Epistemology Naturalized"; Goldman, "Epistemics: The Regulative Theory of Cognition"; Cherniak, "Minimal Rationality"; Ellis, *Rational Belief Systems*.

implied, and to detect and eliminate inconsistencies in our beliefs.[20]
Inductive inference, subject to the probability calculus,[21] allows us to
infer, from propositions already known, hypotheses confirmed or made
probable by such propositions.

Epistemic rationality, understood in this way, is shown in the distinctive ways that humans use language in learning from experience,[22] and
assess competing theories as better or worse explanations of evidence.[23]
Such epistemic procedures evolve as the underlying methods of inquiry
become more powerful, including the development of new languages
of mathematics and the theory and experiment associated with the rise
of modern science.[24] Reflection on the history of these scientific methods (Kuhn,[25] Lakatos,[26] Laudan,[27] among others) reveals the pivotal
importance of intertheoretical comparisons in assessing competing theories. Such comparisons are based on theoretical or philosophical considerations about the degree to which competing theories minimize
conceptual problems, as well as their comparative merits in increasing
the range of explanatory problems that can be solved. The neopositivist
criterion of disconfirmability is not systematically crucial in the comparison of such theories at every stage; many successful theories,
including those of Galileo and Newton, were developed despite conflicting evidence.[28] Indeed, crucial empirical predictions of such theories only were confirmed much later (for example, the existence of
Neptune).[29]

The theory of rationality, as a part of the larger theory of the person,
must give an account of how our principles of practical and epistemic
rationality conflict with or complement one another, and must deter-

20. Affirmation of inconsistent beliefs would allow us, by logical implication, to believe
anything. See Newton-Smith, "Relativism and the Possibility of Interpretation," pp. 108–
10. Accordingly, the detection of inconsistency creates pressure to eliminate one of the
beliefs, or to reformulate our beliefs without the inconsistency. The pressure to such resolution often creates fruitful theoretical ferment when two empirically supported scientific hypotheses are inconsistent, yet, in their respective claims, both useful. See, e.g.,
Jammer, The Conceptual Development of Quantum Mechanics. Sometimes, no resolution
appears possible for long periods of time, but the pressure to resolution remains.
21. See, in general, Horwich, Probability and Evidence; also Hesse, The Structure of Scientific Inference. On the bad arguments against inductive inference, see Stove, Popper and
After. For an important exploration of inductive procedures, see Goodman, Fact, Fiction,
and Forecast, pp. 59–124; and Goodman, Problems and Projects, pp. 389–93.
22. See, e.g., Bennett, Rationality; cf. Bennett, Linguistic Behaviour.
23. See Harman, Thought.
24. See Shapere, "The Character of Scientific Change."
25. Kuhn, The Structure of Scientific Revolutions.
26. Lakatos, "Falsification and the Methodology of Scientific Research Programmes."
27. Laudan, Progress and Its Problems and Science and Values.
28. See Lakatos, "Falsification and the Methodology of Scientific Research Programmes";
and Laudan, Progress and Its Problems and Science and Values.
29. See Polanyi, Personal Knowledge, pp. 20, 30, 181–82.

mine the bearing of this relationship on the unity of the self. The complementariness of these principles is typically clear. Neither the aims nor the methods of practical and epistemic rationality can be sharply distinguished.[30] Statements about the good and the right are, in my judgment, true or false, and practical reasoning, thus, defines kinds of reasons for believing propositions true.[31] Certainly, procedures of epistemic rationality advance the aims of practical rationality. As I earlier noted, principles of epistemic rationality are implicit in the ways humans learn from experience, one's own and others, thus securing true belief relevant to avoiding evils and achieving practical goods. The technological and other revolutions worked by modern science extend this capacity for practical rationality in ways continuous with our basic capacities for intelligent learning from experience. The critical community of science has self-consciously elaborated such capacities through the careful assessment and checking of empirical and theoretical claims, and the cumulative preservation and further elaboration of its epistemic successes.[32]

Correspondingly, epistemic rationality is shaped by practical rationality. Our procedures of epistemic rationality do not blindly garner truths as such, but self-consciously search for that subclass of truths most relevant to our practical aims. For this reason, scientific procedures may either use false, simplifying assumptions[33] or risk falsity[34] in the interest of a greater probability of securing more explanatory beliefs that, overall, increase the scope of useful knowledge and probable belief.

Epistemic and practical rationality conflict only where their aims are clearly antagonistic. This, as we have seen, is usually not so. The supposition of such conflict is, often, based on misunderstandings of various kinds. Two pertinent examples of the "will to believe" illustrate these misunderstandings, which suggest, in turn, a larger theme about the unity of reason and the self.

In the first kind of case, a person allegedly believes something solely because he wants or wishes it to be true, irrespective of its epistemic rationality. The clearest case of conflict is thus believing something known, on epistemic grounds, to be false: I do something (believe X) because it advances my desires, having conclusive reasons to believe X false. But the unity of reason and the self is such that I and no person can intelligibly do anything of the kind.[35] The example, as stated, makes no sense. The object of belief is truth, and a person cannot sensibly

---

30. Cf. Putnam, *Reason, Truth and History.*
31. For an extended defense of this position, see Richards, *A Theory of Reasons for Action.*
32. See, in general, Polanyi, *Personal Knowledge.*
33. Cf. Goodman, *Ways of Worldmaking*, pp. 17–19.
34. See, e.g., Levi, *Gambling with Truth* and *The Enterprise of Knowledge.*
35. See, e.g., Williams, "Deciding to Believe," in *Problems of the Self*, pp. 136–51; Winters, "Believing at Will"; O'Shaughnessy, *The Will*, vol. 1, pp. 21–29.

"believe" something known to be false. Indeed, there could be no good practical reason to do anything of the kind, because the desire, known to embrace a false and therefore nonexistent object, must frustrate itself in a clearly irrational way. Accordingly, there can be no reason of any kind whatsoever to "believe" something in the case described. Neither practical nor epistemic rationality has any hold on this kind of case, which, properly understood, does not divide reason from reason, but reason and belief from desire in a way that disrupts, irrationally, the unity of the self.

But in my opinion these considerations do not apply to a second example of "the will to believe": the historically important and much misunderstood argument for fideistic religious belief. In his classic statement of this argument,[36] William James states quite general conditions for the reasonableness of believing what cannot be proved, applicable to both secular and nonsecular beliefs. These conditions are the following: (1) the belief is not susceptible to ordinary methods of scientific invalidation as false; (2) the consequence of believing something is momentous to advancing human interests; and (3) the issue of believing or not believing something cannot be avoided, but is forced on us by the needs of living. James argues that many forms of basic trust of others, or beliefs about being likable or lovable, satisfy these three conditions. The trustworthiness of a putative friend, one's own lovability, neither may be a clearly false belief—and the consequence of entertaining such beliefs is that friendship and love, central needs of living, are made real. The lack of such beliefs (mistrust of others, lack of self-confidence) undercuts, James suggests, our capacity to realize aims central to living well. The argument as stated by James is, I believe, valid. The belief in question is not an epistemically irrational belief known to be false, and thus is not ruled out by epistemic rationality. Entertaining such beliefs may, if anything, increase their epistemic warrant (the friend is trustworthy, one is loved). And action on such beliefs is practically rational, because such action secures essential aims of a life worth living.

James's argument is also a valid argument for religious beliefs that satisfy its three conditions. Like Jonathan Edwards,[37] James seeks to enrich a Lockean commitment to empiricism (including its rejection of religious enthusiasm)[38] with the demands of personal experience solidly

36. James, "The Will to Believe."

37. See White, *Science and Sentiment in America*. For the complexity of Edwards's thought, see Fiering, *Jonathan Edwards's Moral Thought and Its British Context*. Cf. Miller, *Jonathan Edwards*.

38. See Locke, "Of Enthusiasm," *An Essay Concerning Human Understanding*, vol. 2, Book 4, ch. 29, pp. 428–41. For pertinent historical background, see Knox, *Enthusiasm: A Chapter in the History of Religion*.

integrating our rational and reasonable powers. Like Pascal[39] and Kierkegaard,[40] James points out that beliefs in God are not epistemically ruled out by scientific theories that do not require the hypothesis.[41] To the contrary, the existence of God may be consistent with such theories; the idea certainly was an important motivating assumption of the natural theologians Boyle and Newton and Einstein who developed scientific theories as a way of better understanding God's mysterious will;[42] the belief may be no more unreasonable than many familiar assumptions of a coherent human life;[43] and the hypothesis is independently reasonable on at least weak inductive grounds.[44] Such beliefs may also make possible for persons the achievement of ends necessary to living well both personally and ethically. James points to the role of such beliefs in a sense of significance, love, and grace, all of which make possible more robust living. But another ground for their reasonableness is ethical. Certain such beliefs are not only consistent with our conceptions of natural morality, but may enhance our capacity to be alive to the internal ideals of morality, a point at the center of Edwards's complex moral theology,[45] Newman's vision of the converging probabilities of religious belief and a coherent moral will and integrity,[46] and Kant's moral argument for God as a postulate of practical reason.[47] If so, religious belief may advance not only personal ends, but important moral ends.

---

39. "Faith certainly tells us what the senses do not, but not the contrary of what they see; it is above, not against them," Pascal, *Pensees*, no. 185, p. 85. Pascal offers, in fact, arguments of practical reason for belief in God, for example, his famous wager; see no. 418, pp. 149–53. The argument, as James sees, does not uniquely prove the existence of the Christian God, but could prove any fanaticism with a comparably serious wager. See, in general, Hacking, "The Logic of Pascal's Wager."

40. For Kierkegaard, it is precisely that science neither requires nor excludes God's existence which makes religious faith possible: "Faith is precisely the contradiction between the infinite passion of the individual's inwardness and the objective uncertainty," Kierkegaard, *Concluding Unscientific Postscript*, p. 182.

41. This point is, I believe, lost in the standard criticism of James's argument, namely, that it allows us to believe anything at will. See, e.g., Miller, "'The Will to Believe' and the Duty to Doubt"; and Miller, "James's Doctrine of 'The Right to Believe.'"

42. For Boyle and Newton, see Merton, *Science, Technology and Society in Seventeenth Century England*; on Einstein, see Pais, *'Subtle is the Lord . . .': The Science and the Life of Albert Einstein*, for example, p. vi.

43. For example, the belief in other minds. See Plantinga, *God and Other Minds*.

44. See Swinburne, *The Existence of God*; but cf. Mackie, *The Miracle of Theism*; Gutting, *Religious Belief and Religious Skepticism*.

45. See Fiering, *Jonathan Edwards's Moral Thought and Its British Context*.

46. See Newman, *Grammar of Assent*; for useful commentary, see Ferreira, *Doubt and Religious Commitment*.

47. Kant, *Critique of Practical Reason*, pp. 128–36.

Unity of Reason and Nature of Freedom as a Moral and Political Ideal

James's argument also expresses an important truth about the unity of reason,[48] a point earlier made by Kant as the primacy of practical over theoretical reason.[49] This truth, once properly understood,[50] clarifies, as Kant seminally saw, the nature of freedom as a moral and political ideal.

The primacy of practical reason roots the unity of the person in our practical capacity rationally and reasonably to reflect on conceptions of how to live, and to be moved by and to act on such unifying conceptions. The unity of reason is the coherence of belief, desires, and action that practical and epistemic rationality make possible both for persons as individuals (rationality) and as moral persons in community (reasonableness). Ethical conduct supremely establishes this primacy, for Kant, because it is itself motivated by a conception of principles expressing a reasonable coherence among our universal ends, namely, our rational natures as ends in themselves.[51] In contrast, prudential rationality pursues contingent and variable desires; and theoretical reason establishes no conceptions that we pursue as ends in themselves, but serves whatever ends are given by our practical rationality.

We may understand the epistemological as well as the moral and political originality of this conception when we reflect on the conception of the person it rejects. Kant's theory of the person, like James's, rejects the Aristotelian ideal of the self-sufficient life of contemplation[52] or the Cartesian picture of the person as pure knower:[53] neither picture

---

48. See, e.g., James's "The Sentiment of Rationality."

49. Kant, *Critique of Practical Reason*, pp. 124–26.

50. For criticisms of Kant's arguments based on a different interpretation of those arguments than that here proposed, see Warnock, "The Primacy of Practical Reason," *Morality and Language*, pp. 179–91. Warnock criticizes Kant's argument as resting on two inadequate grounds: first, that practical reason is primary because we often reason morally contrary to our inclinations; and second, that practical reason establishes postulates (God, immortality) that theoretical reason does not itself support. But the first argument improperly distinguishes reasons for belief and reasons for action. The exercise of deliberating about reasons for belief is no more mechanistic than thinking about reasons for action: in both cases, we decide in the light of what we take to be reasons for so deciding; and in both cases, the weight of argument may carry belief or action against the drift of our inclinations. And, Warnock suggests, the second argument assumes it is a virtue that practical reason requires postulates not otherwise supported; but why should it not be a vice of practical reason that, in contrast to theoretical reason, it requires unsupported assumptions? The deeper truth in Kant's view, or James's, is not captured by this interpretation of these arguments, in my opinion.

51. Cf. Nell, *Acting on Principle*.

52. Kant appears to have been converted from this Aristotelian ideal by reading Rousseau. See Warnock, "The Primacy of Practical Reason," pp. 188–89.

53. See Williams, *Descartes: The Project of Pure Inquiry*.

takes seriously the practical roots of our rational and reasonable wills.[54] The epistemological upshot of this rejection is that the rationality of modern science is not construed on the model of Aristotelian certainty and cosmic attunement,[55] which modern science (under the influence of voluntarist theology) decisively rejects.[56] Rather, scentific rationality is interpreted as probabilistic reasoning shaped by our ends of explanatory coherence, simplicity, and usefulness.[57] The root of science in our nature is the unity of the person that reason makes possible. Santayana stated the point succinctly: "What enables men to perceive the unity of nature is the unification of their own wills."[58]

Correspondingly, the ethical imperative, treating persons as equals, expresses for Kant a constructivist moral ideal of the principles persons would reasonably impose on themselves as the expression of mutual respect for the like rational capacity of all to motivate themselves by practical conceptions of their ends.[59] The "fact of reason," on Kant's conception, makes possible the construction, expression, and revision of practical conceptions of the rational and reasonable will (associated with the principles of rationality and reasonableness).[60] It most fully realizes its transforming moral power in the shape moral reasonableness gives to moral and political ideals: equal respect centers on the capacity for such practical conceptions.

Kant's conception of the primacy of practical reason, thus interpreted, gives a sense and place to the related ideals of freedom earlier discussed. The respect for our capacity for practical rationality dignifies the self-determination by reason which Kant supposes to be the basis of our experience of moral freedom. Since reason is the capacity through which we unify our experience, aims, and ends in practical conceptions of a valued life, the equal respect for the exercise of this

54. See, e.g., Dewey, *The Quest for Certainty;* O'Shaughnessy, *The Will.* Cf. Rorty, *Philosophy and the Mirror of Nature.*
55. The classic statement of the force of this Platonic, as well as Aristotelian, ideal for Western thought is Lovejoy, *The Great Chain of Being.* For a recent exploration of the question, see Taylor, "Rationality."
56. See Lovejoy, *The Great Chain of Being,* pp. 163, 332–33; Blumenberg, *The Legitimacy of the Modern Age.*
57. For the pervasive importance of the criticism of Aristotelian scientific certainty for the rise of modern science, see, in general, Van Leeuwen, *The Problem of Certainty in English Thought, 1630–1690;* Shapiro, *Probability and Certainty in Seventeenth-Century England.* The great apologist for the new view of practical science was Francis Bacon; see, e.g., Hill, *Intellectual Origins of the English Revolution,* pp. 85–130. On the role of probability in contemporary scientific procedure, see Hesse, *The Structure of Scientific Inference.*
58. Santayana, *Reason in Common Sense,* p. 123; cf. pp. 203–4.
59. See Rawls, "Kantian Contructivism in Moral Theory."
60. The term "fact of reason" is Kant's; see *Critique of Practical Reason,* p. 31. My understanding of Kant's argument here was deepened by John Rawls's unpublished lectures on Kant, and by discussion with Thomas Nagel.

capacity enables us to express and realize the integrity of our moral powers independently as free persons.

The application of this moral conception to politics gives central significance, characteristic of democratic theory and practice, to the design of institutions that foster and express such mutual respect for the rational and reasonable will;[61] this naturally includes respect for the capacities of claim origination and revision to which we adverted earlier. The rejection of an epistemological ideal of attunement to an evident order of being is at one with a morally motivated political rejection of natural hierarchies of order and submission. Thus, Locke, who anticipates (albeit incompletely)[62] the Kantian conception of the primacy of practical reason, insists, like Milton:[63] "Our business here is not to know all things, but those which concern our conduct."[64] Naturally, he gives this conception the moral and political weight of an inalienable right to conscience. Failure to respect this right degrades, for Locke, Milton, and Kant, the moral powers of our rational and reasonable wills: it deprives us of the freedoms that respect for our reason requires.

What Autonomy Is Not

After we have examined in greater depth the classical arguments for an inalienable right to conscience and universal toleration, I shall, in the next chapter, use Kant's conception of practical reason to develop a philosophical interpretation of these arguments and the political traditions they decisively shaped. For our present philosophical purposes, we can show, by negative example, how this conception critically shapes the interpretation of autonomy as a defensible political ideal.[65]

Consider a person, objectively free from coercion but lacking the capacities of rational self-direction. The will is disordered, rationality disturbed, beliefs and appetites incoherent and in divisive and irremediable conflict.[66] Clearly, this is not a free person, for the minimal capacities of rationally reflective self-control are absent.

61. See, in general, Riley, *Will and Political Legitimacy.* Cf. Bourke, *Will in Western Thought,* pp. 151–89.
62. Locke does give a kind of Kantian primacy to the free reason organizing and interpreting experience, but he regards such reason not as itself establishing ethics, but as constructing ethics from natural facts of the world and God's existence and nature, and as leading to belief in the chain of being. See, in general, Colman, *John Locke's Moral Philosophy* (for the chain of being, see pp. 2–3). On the originality of Locke's theory of the person, see pp. 17–73, Yolton, *Locke: An Introduction;* on his constructivist view of normative ideas as mixed modes, see Tully, *A Discussion on Property,* pp. 3–34; cf. Jenkins, *Understanding Locke.*
63. See the advice to Adam that Raphael gives in Book 7 of Milton's *Paradise Lost,* 11. 115–30, pp. 390–91.
64. Locke, *An Essay Concerning Human Understanding,* vol. 1, introduction, sec. 6, p. 31.
65. My thought here was stimulated by a discussion in Gray's *Mill on Liberty: A Defence,* pp. 73–86.
66. Cf. Benn, "Freedom, Autonomy and the Concept of a Person," pp. 112–17.

Another interpretation, the converse of this example, may be dismissed equally easily. The slave, who exhibits Stoic equanimity and apathy, and whose powers of rational autonomy might be fully intact and expressed in an articulate Stoic philosophy, clearly lacks the freedom from coercion (negative freedom) fundamental to a free person. Indeed, slavery precisely fails to accord respect for the person as an originator of claims: the normative status of the slave is a kind of civil death, deriving essentially from the master's claims and uses.[67]

An interesting case is posed by the person who, enjoying the negative liberty of the absence of coercion or threat, also exercises all the normal capacities associated with rational self-direction of one's life, but has not done and cannot do so in a way independent of social convention. The form of enforceable law and social convention is, let us assume, aristocratically hierarchical or theocratic. It gives no weight, in principle, to the capacity of persons themselves to originate and assess claims. All such claims, rather, are defined by an externally imposed system of appropriate roles.

That defensible values are often rooted in certain traditions is a truism. But traditions, as such, are not aristocratic or theocratic in this sense, so long as the traditions do not deny the capacity of persons reasonably to originate and assess claims. All sides of the Reformation battles over authority, for example, may charitably be interpreted as nontheocratic in this sense.[68] Their differences are, as Popkin suggests,[69] over essentially philosophical questions of criteria for the reasonableness of assenting to beliefs (Calvin's inner persuasion of reasonableness is, thus, subjected to the skeptical doubts of Erasmus and Montaigne, who prefer the implicit reasonableness of tradition). Both Calvin, the Protestant Reformer, and Erasmus, the Catholic, might agree that religious faith must be reasonably and freely embraced by each person; but they would disagree, as Protestants and Catholics did, over the degree to which reason here legitimated the authority of certain interpretive traditions.

Suppose we have an aristocratic or theocratic system that clearly denies, in principle, this capacity of persons reasonably to originate and assess claims. Persons simply are their institutional roles, given by a metaphysically ordered caste hierarchy that denies the point, propriety, or even possibility that persons may assess, let alone reflect on, its aims. Such a system is contemptuous of the just liberties of a free per-

---

67. See Patterson, *Slavery and Social Death.*
68. For the idea that Catholic tradition, properly interpreted, articulates a weighty right to conscience, see D'Arcy, *Conscience and Its Right to Freedom.* For a charitable reading of the history, see Lecler, *Toleration and the Reformation.*
69. See Popkin, *The History of Scepticism from Erasmus to Descartes,* pp. 8–9, 70–75, 194–96, 205; see also the revised edition, Popkin, *The History of Scepticism from Erasmus to Spinoza.*

son because it denies, in principle, the place or weight of the capacities of persons for rational freedom. Indeed, in the crude self-fulfilling prophecies characteristic of such contempt, the very failure to respect such capacities is rationalized by a mythology of incapacity (for example, a dismembered human completeness),[70] on which its contempt feeds.

Mill's theory of the injustices to women, in *The Subjection of Women*, rests, I believe, on this perception: the deepest injustice to women is worked at the level of deprivation of basic privacy and education.[71] These deprivations disabled women from assessing their situation and lives independent of men or of sexist social convention, and thus restricted their rational freedom to originate and assess claims. This injustice remains even if free and rational women would choose to live as women then currently did, for Mill's point is that a life lived without the requisite respect for moral independence is a moral insult in and of itself. Such systematic contempt for rational freedom institutionalizes forms of preference adaptation[72] by entrenching in social ideology an orthodoxy of the natural order (for example, of women's roles, or famine).[73] The consequence is a subversion of rational freedom: we do not see corrigible evils of institutional design for the injustices they are. Such forms of moral degradation of the person's very self-conception of demands for respect[74] surely suggest a natural analogy to the degradation of slavery, an analogy fully used by Mill[75] and at the heart of the equal protection jurisprudence of gender discrimination today.[76] Certainly, there are important differences between the moral evils of racism and sexism, but a pervasive theme in our attempts in ethics and law to combat them is the sense of a common underlying contempt for the person's moral powers (see chapter 10).

A different case is posed by the person who is fully rational and free in the sense described above, but who is inauthentic. While the exercise of rational freedom is often a means to authenticity, the connection is not inevitable. Consider the kind of case contemplated by Michael Sandel.[77] A person, in the free exercise of his moral powers, has been led wholly to eschew certain deep early identifications (for example, with his ethnic group, or the like); his life, in consequence, is superficial, without the rooted depth in early experience of an authentic life. Sandel builds his case on a poignant dilemma of personal morality famil-

---

70. See, e.g., the Purusa Veda, in which the caste system is characterized in terms of the body parts of a dismembered person. See *The Rig Veda*, pp. 29–32.
71. See, especially, Mill, *The Subjection of Women*, ch. 2, 157–80.
72. See, in general, Elster, *Sour Grapes*.
73. See Sen, *Poverty and Famines*.
74. See Richards, "Rights, Resistance, and the Demands of Self-Respect."
75. See, e.g., Mill, *The Subjection of Women*, pp. 157–61.
76. See, e.g., *Frontiero v. Richardson*, 411 U.S. 677 (1973).
77. Sandel, *Liberalism and the Limits of Justice*; see also MacIntyre, *After Virtue*.

iar in an immigrant culture such as the United States, in which confor-
mist pressures of a dominant culture take their toll on ethnic variety
and pluralism. Sandel concludes that this dilemma brings out the moral
unreality and superficiality of equal respect for rational freedom as a
moral ideal, in other words, its abstraction from the prior community
identifications around which we organize our identities as moral persons. Accordingly, we should modify the theory of the person, as a
moral ideal, to include such constitutive community identifications.

Yet there is good reason to doubt whether authenticity, to the extent
it is an attractive humane value, is inconsistent with respect for the free
exercise of our moral powers. Rather, authenticity is a defensible value,
for political theory, only to the extent it is itself consistent with such
respect. Respect for rational freedom is, if anything, likely to foster
such authenticity. Such respect requires precisely the requisite kind of
independence in exploring and discovering the truth of one's nature;
and the moral conception of equal respect may give weight to the values of continuity in early bonding in significant ways, for example, in
terms of moral obligations of gratitude and even fidelity to one's family
and their better traditions.

In any event, authenticity, as such, is often unsound as a value of
either personal or political morality, which should caution us that Sandel's argument has force only within certain background normative
assumptions. Many kinds of authentic truths about our natures, including aspects born of early identifications, we reject and change (for
example, our competitiveness or sadism), and we esteem those of our
early identifications, which we retain, not because they are authenti-
cally us, but because they advance or at least do not retard values that
we find reasonably and humanely defensible. We do so, I believe,
because, not in spite of the fact that, background political values of
equal respect for freedom and rationality guarantee us the right thus to
examine our lives at their deepest levels. Group identifications, as such,
have value only as the implicit product of such judgments, which can
be so only if they have precisely stood the test of a free and rational
judgment not hostage to them. Surely, the truths of group identification
can be barbarous or atavistic. Indeed, the lesson of twentieth century
totalitarianism is that the appeal of our "authentic" group may be at
the heart of our moral darkness.[78] We ensure that such claims are not
the shabby rationalizations for group domination, which they have historically been, by our commitment to an ideal of the person that allows
us to define our selves and our attachment to our traditions as the
expression of a greater respect for the rational freedom of our moral

78. See, in general, Arendt, *The Origins of Totalitarianism*. In Western literature and
thought, authenticity is often linked to moral horror, as in Joseph Conrad. See Trilling,
Sincerity and Authenticity, pp. 106–11, 133. Thus, Heidegger's value of authenticity
appears to have been one of the values motivating his sympathy with the Nazi movement
in Germany. See Kimball, "Heidegger at Freiburg," p. 15.

powers. In contrast, Sandel compromises this deeper moral ideal precisely at the morally sensitive point of possible group domination.

Equal Respect for Persons

Let us now more explicitly connect this theory of the person to a rights-based interpretation of the basic moral imperative, treating persons as equals. We may interpret equal respect for persons in terms of the principles that could be justified to every person understood as capable of rational and reasonable freedom. It is no accident that this perspective justifies human rights that are not merely nonutilitarian but antiutilitarian. Respect for persons, thus interpreted, secures the essential distributive conditions of the self-respecting integrity of each and every person against utilitarian impersonality (the view, as we earlier say, of persons as the locus or container of impersonal, uninterpreted pleasures which may be manipulated and rearranged in whatever ways aggregate maximum utility overall). Thus, rights have a force in our moral and legal discourse which Dworkin characterizes as trumps over utilitarian calculations.[79]

Such claims of rights not only impose distributive constraints on utilitarian aggregation, but they distinguish, in a way utilitarianism does not, among agent preferences, explaining the different kinds of evaluative significance and weight that various preferences or pleasures or pains have in the moral life (the different significance, in my earlier example, of the pains of malnutrition and of a frustrated taste for Beluga caviar). Equal respect for persons engages not preferences, as such, or pleasures or pains, but the demands on their common, mutually cooperative lives that could be justified to the self-determining rational and reasonable powers of all persons living in community. It thus takes seriously, as utilitarian impersonality does not, the roots of human and moral goods in the interpretive dignity and common needs of our moral powers and agency as persons. Such a conception naturally gravitates to some conception of primary or general goods, those all-purpose goods given interpretive weight and point by all persons as conditions of the more ultimate ends and ambitions of their lives as rational and reasonable beings.[80] Thus, the demands for the food necessary to sustain life and a minimum diet, the necessary condition for any semblance of a life of self-respect, would engage such ethical concern in a way that factitious and dispensable tastes would not. A theory of equal respect for persons, suitably developed, might plausibly give an explanatory sense and point to these distinctions of intuitive moral thought in a way that utilitarianism cannot. It also, as I now aim to show, explains, in a

---

79. See Dworkin, *Taking Rights Seriously*, pp. 90–94, 188–92.
80. See Rawls, "Social Unity and Primary Goods;" cf. Taylor, "What Is Human Agency?," "Self-Interpreting Animals," "The Concept of a Person," and "The Diversity of Goods."

way utilitarianism cannot, the moral priority of claims for certain goods that ensure the very integrity of our rational freedom itself.

CONSCIENCE AS AN INALIENABLE HUMAN RIGHT

One kind of demand must, from the rights perspective on treating persons as equals, have priority of place, namely, the demand that the capacity itself for rational freedom must be respected. If we have any rights, we must have this right, the inalienable right to conscience.[81] Rawls puts the point well: the central case, both historically and philosophically, to be made on behalf of human rights is the argument for conscience, and many other claims of rights may be regarded as generalizations or elaborations of this focal argument.[82]

We may enrich philosophical understanding of this argument when we see it, in historical perspective, as a sharp departure from the Western political tradition. At the same time, we may enlarge historical understanding of the argument and the political tradition it shaped when we construe the history in light of the political theory of human rights implicit in it. Here, political theory and historical understanding are complementary and mutually fertilizing.

Conscience in Pre-Reformation Christianity

The idea of conscience long antedates the idea of an inalienable right to conscience in Western thought. The argument for the right to conscience is, therefore, better understood when we see the argument against the background of the tradition that it assumes, criticizes, and develops.

Conscience is usually distinguished into two kinds: judicial and legislative conscience, both of which are associated with moral judgment.[83] The older, pre-Christian idea of the judicial conscience assumes that moral principles are in place, and applies those principles to judgment on one's own past life. The legislative conscience is, in contrast, a way of knowing general moral principles applicable both in judgment

81. The inalienability of conscience is a familiar claim made by such eighteenth-century philosophers as Hutcheson and political leaders as Jefferson and Madison. See, e.g., Hutcheson, *A System of Moral Philosophy*, Book 2, ch. 5, sec. 3, pp. 295–96; Jefferson, *Notes on the State of Virginia*, pp. 157–161 (for Jefferson's Bill for Religious Freedom to similar effect, see pp. 223–25); James Madison, *Memorial and Remonstrance Against Religious Assessment*, in Meyers, ed., *The Mind of the Founder*, pp. 5–13. The important sense of inalienability is that an inalienable right is one that cannot ever be legitimately surrendered, thus cannot be justly given up in the Lockean social contract or under just constitutional government. Locke's assumption of such rights appears to be importantly connected to his conception that such powers are not ours to dispose, but those of the just God who made us. See, e.g., Simmons, "Inalienable Rights and Locke's *Treatises*."
82. See Rawls, *A Theory of Justice*, ch. 4; Rawls, "Kantian Constructivism in Moral Theory."
83. See D'Arcy, *Conscience and its Right to Freedom*, pp. 3–19.

on one's own past actions and prospectively to future actions. Saint Paul uses both the notions of judicial and legislative conscience; he is historically notable in giving prominence to legislative conscience, which he identifies with the freedom of Christian faith.[84] On the one hand, legislative conscience authoritatively announces applicable moral standards of conduct. On the other hand, conscience may err, which, for Saint Paul, calls for charity.[85]

Because conscience has such moral authority for Saint Paul and the Christian tradition he develops, the erring conscience is a central religious and ethical concern. The Pauline suggestion of charity is elaborated into doctrines of toleration during the patristic period by Tertullian, Lactantius, and Origen, among others,[86] all of whom interpret Christianity as a religion of freely given faith, inconsistent with religious coercion.

The Western cultural tradition was characterized by moments of interpretive controversy over the integration of various authoritative texts and traditions (see chapter 2). The Christian tradition dominant until the Reformation was a complex interpretive synthesis of Old Testament and New Testament Bible interpretation and pagan philosophy, developed against the historical background of establishing an orthodoxy against Gnosticism and other competing belief systems.[87] The issue of toleration, once a doctrine protecting Christians themselves from persecution, was cast in a very different light by relevant developments in Christian doctrine after Constantine elevated Christianity into the official state religion of the Roman Empire.[88] The central figure who mediates the transition from early Christian tolerance to intolerance is Saint Augustine.

Augustine's views on toleration are an unstable amalgam of conflicting tendencies in his best philosophical thought on philosophical psychology, his theory of history and approach to Bible interpretation, and the practical exigencies of his position as the bishop of Hippo confronted by Donatist insurrection.[89] Augustine's earlier views advocate toleration, which is the position most consistent with his trinitarian philosophical psychology.[90] In *The Trinity*, Augustine argues that we

84. See ibid., pp. 8–12; Lecler, *Toleration and the Reformation*, vol. 1, pp. 11–31. On Paul's complex relation to his religious heritage, see Sandmel, *The Genius of Paul*.
85. See 1 *Cor.* 8:9–13. For commentary, see Lecler, *Toleration and the Reformation*, vol. 1, pp. 16–18.
86. Lecler, *Toleration and the Reformation*, vol. 1, pp. 32–39.
87. See, e.g., Brown, *The Making of Late Antiquity*; cf. Dodds, *Pagan and Christian in an Age of Anxiety*; MacMullen, *Christianizing the Roman Empire*.
88. See Lecler, *Toleration and the Reformation*, vol. 1, pp. 39–64; MacMullen, *Christianizing the Roman Empire*.
89. See, in general, Brown, "St. Augustine's Attitude to Religious Coercion," *Religion and Society in the Age of Saint Augustine*, pp. 260–78; Brown, *Augustine of Hippo*, pp. 233–43.
90. Lecler, *Toleration and the Reformation*, vol. 1, p. 54.

should understand the nature of a triune God on the model of the soul, made, in the biblical phrase, in God's image.[91] The soul has three parts—understanding, memory, and will—each of which is, we may say, holistically linked with the others. The rational inquiries of understanding crucially require memory, in the same way that memory requires understanding if it is to have any coherent point or place in the structuring of our lives. And, both understanding and memory unify the life of the person over time only when they are guided by the higher-order desires of the person for a rationally coherent life over time; such desires have no rational ends without the use of understanding and memory. The consequence of this quite plausible theory of the unity of the person is that one part of the soul always draws on the others: understanding, memory, and will work, as it were, in tandem. No part is prior to any other, nor can one sensibly be isolated from another. The life of the person is guided by their integrated activity. The natural corollary of this theory is that an erring conscience is the integrated consequence of understanding, memory, and will, and thus expresses the integrity of one's moral powers as a person. Since Christian faith requires the free assent of the whole person, Christian premises require the toleration that will alone assure the requisite free assent. Pauline charity seems in order.

Augustine's tolerant philosophical premises were eroded, however, by his need to deal with and make sense of the schismatic Donatists in light of his deep commitment to a theory of history.[92] That theory required Augustine to give a reasonable sense to both biblical prophecy and recent catastrophic political events (the fall of Rome).[93] For Augustine, who associated Roman order with civilization, a redemptive meaning, compatible with the Bible, could be given to Rome's fall only if the spiritual ideals of civilization were transferred from the fallen corrupt world of politics to the institutions of the Catholic Church. If the Church alone civilizes, a concern to maintain the authority of the Church has a kind of world historical significance, especially for a working bishop. Accordingly, resistance to the authority of the Church by schismatic Christians, such as the Donatists, appeared to Augustine so irrational that he came to see the resistance of the Donatists as the product not of reasonable disagreement, but of the culpable and vin-

---

91. See *The Trinity, Augustine: Later Works*, pp. 17–181: *Gen.* 1:26.
92. The Donatists were creedally Catholic, separating from the Church largely over their belief that a duly ordained minister, once lapsed or otherwise morally unworthy, could not perform the sacraments. See, in general, Greenslade, "Heresy and Schism in the Later Roman Empire;" also, Markus, "Christianity and Dissent in Roman North Africa: Changing Perspectives in Recent Work."
93. See Lecler, *Toleration and the Reformation*, vol. 1, pp. 54–59. For historical context, see Brown, "St. Augustine's Attitude Toward Religious Coercion," cited in note 89, above.

cible ignorance of persons who know the truth but who wilfully deny it through a corruption of the will.[94] No respect is owed these persons because their views are the product not of the integrated moral powers of the person, but of a diabolic fault in the soul. Augustine's trinitarian psychology is, *pro tanto*, suspended; such persons so lack freedom and rationality that others may justly intervene, paternalistically, to protect them from themselves for the same reason that we protect the insane from their own self-destructive irrationalities. The analogy is, for Augustine, exact. Heresy reflects a corrupt will lacking rational capacities, and the self-destructiveness is of the worst kind—eternal damnation.[95] Indeed, the ground for coercive intervention is even stronger, since the destructiveness of the heretical madman inflicts damage on those he corrupts as well, from which society may justly be protected.[96]

While Augustine himself urged leniency in the treatment of heretics,[97] the Augustinian argument for intolerance was later elaborated by Saint Thomas Aquinas, among others, to justify capital punishment of heretics.[98] Thomas Aquinas proposes a faculty of moral knowledge, *synderesis*, the legislative conscience that authoritatively declares general moral principles, a faculty found in Christians and pagan alike.[99] Since faith is free, Thomas Aquinas resists the forced conversion of Jews and pagans.[100] But once a person has embraced the true faith of Catholicism, he cannot be permitted heretically to renege. Such ignorance is, following Augustine, vincible error, a moral corruption in the soul of the heretic, which (contagiously) corrupts others. A secular society that uses the death penalty to combat the evil of counterfeiting money may, Thomas Aquinas argues, justly use death to combat the greater evil of corrupting the soul.

Conscience in the Reformation

If the first great interpretive moment in Western culture was the Augustinian integrative synthesis, the second such moment was the divisive metainterpretive controversies of Renaissance humanism and Reformation Christianity (see chapter 2). Fueled by the printing press and the rediscovery of classical learning, European humanists naturally reexamined the terms of the Christian synthesis, including Bible interpretation and the truths of pagan philosophy, and submitted their findings to an increasingly literate world.[101] Metainterpretive controversies

94. See, e.g., Augustine, *The Political Writings of St. Augustine*, pp. 190–240.
95. See texts cited in Augustine, *The Political and Social Ideas of St. Augustine*, p. 205, which make this point exactly.
96. The damage is called by Augustine spiritual murder; see ibid.,p. 207.
97. Lecler, *Toleration and the Reformation*, vol. 1, p. 59.
98. Thomas Aquinas, *Summa Theologiae*, 2a2ae.11,3, pp. 89–91.
99. See D'Arcy, *Conscience and its Right to Freedom*, pp. 20–112.
100. Thomas Aquinas, *Summae Theologiae*, 2a2ae.10, 8, pp. 61–65.
101. See, in general, Eisenstein, *The Printing Press as an Agent of Change*.

over how to interpret the Bible naturally led, under the impact of the reintroduction of skeptical philosophy, to widespread philosophical controversies over the nature of knowledge.[102] Such controversies— scientific, historical, and ethical—shaped, in turn, the conception and practice of science, history, ethics, politics, and religion. Such inquiries led, for example, to surprising alignments on toleration within the competing Reformation schools of thought. The Catholics Erasmus and Montaigne defend toleration on the ground that doctrinal controversy cannot be reasonably resolved, that an ethical minimum of decency is of the essence in Christian ethics, and that the lesser evil is to allow people to follow their own native traditions of religious piety[103]. The Protestant Reformer Calvin appeals to the inner light of certitude in Bible interpretation, and follows the Augustinian tradition in condemning the heretic Michael Servetus to death.[104]

In reaction to such excesses, Protestant thinkers, for example Castellio[105] and Acontius,[106] articulate minimal conceptions of epistemic and moral reasonableness, which are consistent with a broad latitude of doctrinal variations among which they urge toleration. Conscience, long familiar in Western thought, is in process of being given a new moral interpretation and weight, a concept that shortly appears in Locke and Bayle as the inalienable right to conscience and universal toleration.

Locke and Bayle on Conscience

The argument of John Locke's four *Letters Concerning Toleration* is as classically authoritative for the Anglo-American democratic tradition as Pierre Bayle's contemporary defense in his *Philosophique Commentaire* is for the French and European democratic tradition.[107] While both

---

102. See, in general, Popkin, *The History of Scepticism from Erasmus to Descartes*; Van Leeuwen, *The Problem of Certainty in English Thought, 1630–1690*; Shapiro, *Probability and Certainty in Seventeenth-Century England*; Hill, *Intellectual Origins of the English Revolution*.
103. On Erasmus, see Lecler, *Toleration and the Reformation*, vol. 1, pp. 114–33; on Montaigne, vol. 2, pp. 168–77.
104. Ibid., vol. 1, pp. 325–32. See also Levy, *Treason Against God*, pp. 122–57; Bainton, *The Travail of Religious Liberty*, pp. 72–94.
105. See Castellio, *Concerning Heretics*. For useful commentary on Castellio's criticisms of Calvin's intolerance, see Lecler, *Toleration and the Reformation*, vol. 1, pp. 336–47, 350–60.
106. Acontius, *Darkness Discovered (Satan's Stratagems)*. For the powerful influence of this text on English thought, see Jordan, *The Development of Religious Toleration in England*, vol. 1, pp. 315–65. See also Lecler, *Toleration and the Reformation*, vol. 1, pp. 369–76.
107. *Commentaire Philosophique sur ces paroles de Jesus-Christ "Contrain-les d'entrer"* (hereinafter cited as *Commentaire Philosophique*). Remarkably, there is no currently available English translation of the complete work. Accordingly, my references are to the 1727 edition.

arguments were anticipated, sometimes to more radical effect (for example, by Roger Williams),[108] no other statements of the argument for toleration are more profound or more influential. Both thinkers worked within a Calvinist heritage, wrote in a common cultural environment of the Netherlands, knew one another, and shared many common philosophical premises.[109] We may, therefore, plausibly construe their arguments as reflective of common principles. At different points, the arguments differ in acuteness and depth. Accordingly, a discussion of the arguments together may elicit the best interpretation of their common principles. For example, Bayle's argument for an inalienable right to conscience is more philosophically profound and straightforward than Locke's.[110] However, Locke writes his argument in the context of the more general democratic theory of *The Second Treatise of Government:* the state's violation of basic human rights reserved from the social contract (for example, violation of the right to conscience) may justify disobedience and, in extremis, rebellion.[111] Bayle certainly argues that Louis XIV's revocation of the Edict of Nantes and the consequent persecution of the Huguenots (including the death of Bayle's brother) was morally, politically, and religiously wrong. But, unlike Jurieu and Locke, as a defender of the French absolute monarchy Bayle does not embrace any general republican theory of the social contract and the right to revolution.[112] Accordingly, the best interpretation of Locke's and Bayle's common principles should combine strands of Bayle's more probing philosophy of conscience with Locke's more articulate democratic theory.

Locke and Bayle give conscience a moral interpretation and weight associated with their conception of the proper respect due to the highest-order interest of persons in their freedom (the origination and revisability of claims) and rationality (practical and epistemic rationality).

108. See Williams, *The Bloudy Tenent of Persecution.* Williams, for example, appears to forbid any taxation to support an established church (see, e.g., pp. 297–302, 304–5), which neither Locke nor Bayle criticize. He also, remarkably, extends toleration to atheists, a position he shares only with the contemporary Dutch author Dirck Coornhert. See Lecler, *Toleration and the Reformation,* vol. 2, p. 486. Neither Locke nor Bayle extends toleration to atheists, as we shall shortly see.

109. The theorists appear, however, to have conceived their arguments independently of one another. See Labrousse, *Bayle,* p. 85.

110. Bayle's arguments exhibit, for example, a remarkable philosophical subtlety in the defense of the rights of the erring conscience; see *Philosophique Commentaire,* pp. 419–43. Locke, in contrast, assumes the point. See *Works of John Locke,* vol. 6, pp. 146–7, 330.

111. Locke, *The Second Treatise of Government,* in *Two Treatises of Government,* pp. 285–446.

112. In this, Bayle, the advocate of universal toleration and absolute monarchy, was diametrically opposed to his former teacher, Jurieu, who advocated both intolerance and a republican contract which justified the right of the Huguenots to resist Louis XIV. See Labrousse, *Bayle,* pp. 33–39.

We may say, plausibly, that Locke and Bayle assume the concept of the person of Augustinian philosophical psychology: the freedom, rationality, and unity of the person, which dignify the nature of persons made in the image of an ethical God. They reach the conclusion that Augustine and the later thinkers in the Christian tradition failed, tragically, to draw: that this conception of the person is inconsistent with the Augustinian theory of persecution.

Augustine's arguments center on the idea of the culpable and vincible ignorance of persons who know the truth but wilfully deny it through a corruption of the will, to which we owe nothing but the contempt and opposition due a diabolic fault in the soul. Thus, the heretic is owed no respect, because her freedom is enslaved by her will and her rationality is at war with itself.

Neither Locke nor Bayle denies the existence of the erring conscience, that is, people may believe false religious propositions on inadequate grounds.[113] They deny, however, the moral and political interpretation given to the erring conscience by Augustine and those using Augustinian arguments in England and France to justify persecution of dissenters from the established Anglican or Catholic churches, respectively.[114] They deny, in particular, that the nature of religious questions and the ways in which people believe them allow any ground for repression that does not itself rest on contempt for the freedom and rationality of the person. Bayle classically anatomizes Augustine's arguments in the *Philosophique Commentaire* as follows: there is no impartial criterion for culpably false religious belief; obstinacy cannot be distinguished from sincere consistency of principle; the heart cannot in any event be discerned by human law; and the criteria of rationality may be perceived and applied to these questions in irreconcilable ways.[115] Strikingly, Bayle's theory of the person accords with Augustinian trinitarian philosophical psychology: persons form conscientious beliefs in a holistic integration of intellect, memory, and will.[116] He

---

113. See Locke, *Works of John Locke*, vol. 6, p. 95; Bayle, *Philosophique Commentaire*, pp. 395–96.

114. A form of the Augustinian argument was urged in criticism of Locke's first *Letter Concerning Toleration*, namely, that coercion is imposed only to the extent required to make wilfull believers of the false reconsider their beliefs, an argument that Locke identifies as of Augustinian provenance (*Works of John Locke*, vol. 6, pp. 292, 529). Locke's response preoccupies the three subsequent letters in a point by point response: see *Works of John Locke*, vol. 6, pp. 59–574. Bayle writes in express response to the use of Augustine's arguments to justify Louis XIV's revocation of the Edict of Nantes, which had guaranteed limited toleration to Huguenots in France. See Lecler, *Toleration and the Reformation*, vol. 2, pp. 140–156.

115. See, e.g., Bayle, *Philosophique Commentaire*, at pp. 393–97, 433–43.

116. On the origins of Bayle's views in previous Calvinist thought, see, in general, Rex, *Essays on Pierre Bayle and Religious Controversy.* Cf. Sandberg, *At the Crossroads of Faith and Reason.*

draws, however, from this theory the natural inference that Augustine failed to draw. Our best efforts at forming reasonable beliefs arise from our personal experience as embodied creatures, including powerful memories of parental and cultural training; accordingly, such diverse experience leads to quite different ways of reasonably forming religious beliefs.[117] The erroneous conscience is as much the product of an integrated freedom and rationality as the correct conscience.

The crux of the problem with the Augustinian argument, Locke and Bayle both note, is its conception of a politically just criterion for the erring conscience. Both criticize this conception in light of the procedures of epistemic rationality which, in their view, direct our practical rationality and reasonableness. In particular, probabilistic rationality, not Aristotelian certainty, guides such inquiries. Since religious questions fall in the area of probabilistic reasoning for which there is no certain criterion of truth,[118] any political criterion for an erring conscience will rest on an assumed conviction of truth. Everyone, however, has such a conviction of the truth of her or his beliefs. The argument will justify universal persecution, which neither a just God nor the law of nature could have intended.[119] Any such theory of persecution itself expresses, Locke emphasizes, contempt for the equal rationality of persons in using such probabilistic reasoning in diverse ways consistent with experience equally available to all and with free conscience.[120] At bottom, one theological system, among others equally reasonable, is made the measure of rationality. This, of course, fails to accord the respect due free and rational persons.

Both Locke and Bayle condemn illegitimate state coercion of religion as an unwarranted imposition of standards of rationality by the state. Locke, for example, continually interprets such an imposition as an assumption of infallibility,[121] the essence, for him, of Catholic intolerance. Bayle concedes the justice of the Catholic criticism of Protestant appeals to the inner light; such appeals must, as Locke also noted in the *Essay*,[122] independently satisfy criteria of rationality in order to be credited. But Bayle goes on to observe that the Catholic appeal to tradition is in no better position: traditions are only to be credited when they

117. See Bayle, *Philosophique Commentaire*, pp. 433–43.
118. For Bayle, see ibid., pp. 396–7, 433–43; for Locke, see *Works of John Locke*, vol. 6, pp. 143–45, 297–300, 333–34, 418–20, 434–35, 536–37, 558–74.
119. Thus, Bayle points out that the Augustinian argument would require all pagans to persecute Christianity (*Philosophique Commentaire*, pp. 376–80, 388–91); Locke insists that such universal persecution would do so much more harm than good that it violates the law of nature (*Works of John Locke*, vol. 6, pp. 61–137).
120. See, e.g., *Works of John Locke*, vol. 6 pp. 333–34.
121. See, e.g., Ibid., pp. 26, 145, 194, 366 (expressly compared to the Pope's infallibility), 401, 407, 411, 412, 517, 531, 532.
122. Locke, *An Essay Concerning Human Understanding*, vol. 2, pp. 415–41.

also satisfy such criteria.[123] Equal respect for rational conscience requires that the state adopt neither inner light nor tradition as the criterion of rational belief, but that it use a conception of rational capacity that does not illegitimately confuse beliefs in truth with standards of reasonableness.

Bayle, who is not a social contractarian in his general political theory, finds it useful to put this point in terms of a hypothetical contract. Ask yourself, Bayle suggests, not what your beliefs are, but whether some controversial belief, not currently accepted in a country, could reasonably be accepted there "after a free and critical examination."[124] If the belief passes the test, political persecution of it stands condemned as the illegitimate confusion of one's own beliefs with reasonable beliefs as such. In short, respect for conscience is only assured by political principles that do not distort judgments of freedom and rationality by sectarian judgments.

Such a biased conception of rationality corrupts, in turn, the conception of freedom of the person. The putatively irrational person is supposed, for that reason, to be unfree, marred by a disordered will. Such a judgment of unfreedom, here the ground of coercive persecution, itself degrades the freedom that, for Locke and Bayle, is the natural right of conscience: conscience is made hostage to the judgments of others. The moral nerve of the argument for the right to conscience is that persons are independent originators of claims, and that the demands of ethics and of an ethical God are only both known and practically effective in our lives when persons' right to conscience is appropriately respected. Otherwise, the demands of ethics are confused with public opinion or popular taste.

The association of religious conscience with ethical imperatives is, of course, pervasively characteristic of the Judeo-Christian tradition and its conception of an ethical God acting through history.[125] Locke and Bayle are religious Christians in this tradition. They regard themselves as returning Christianity to its ethical foundations (reminding Christians, for example, of the toleration of the early patristic period).[126] Both support their arguments, in part, by Bible interpretation.[127] Dis-

123. Bayle, *Philosophique Commentaire*, p. 438. Bayle also invokes the condemnation of assumptions of infallibility, p. 438.
124. Ibid., pp. 368–69. I take the translation from the short excerpt of this passage in Sandberg, *The Great Contest of Faith and Reason*, pp. 45–46.
125. For the distinctive force of this conception in the Old Testament's narrative style and sharp repudiation of different conceptions of the divinity in surrounding cultures, see Schneidau, *Sacred Discontent: The Bible and Western Tradition*; Jacobson, *The Story of the Stories*; Alter, *The Art of Biblical Narrative*.
126. See, e.g., Bayle, *Philosophique Commentaire*, pp. 387–88.
127. Ibid., pp. 367–92; Locke, *Works of John Locke*, vol. 6, pp. 37–38.

agreements in speculative theology, which had grounded Augustinian persecutions for heresy, were, for them, patent betrayals of essential Christianity; they disabled people from regulating their lives by the simple and elevated ethical imperatives of Christian charity.

Thus, the deepest motivation of Locke's and Bayle's arguments for the inalienable right to conscience is a new interpretation of what ethics is, and how it connects to religion and politics. To be precise, Locke connected a free conscience to the capacity of persons to reason about the nature and content of the ethical obligations imposed on persons by a just God,[128] and thought of these obligations as centering on a core of minimal ethical standards reflected in the Gospels.[129] Bayle regarded independent conscience both as the mode of knowledge of ethical principles and as the agency by which persons incorporated them in the intentional structure of their ends (later called by Kant a good will).[130] Ethics, for Bayle (as for Kant), is only a vital force in one's life when one independently acknowledges its principles oneself and imposes them on one's life. Respect for the right to conscience ensures, for Bayle and Locke, that speculative theological disagreements do not distort the central place of this conception of ethics in what both regarded as true religion. Bayle, who rejoiced in paradox, put the point bluntly. Beliefs in speculative religious truths did not ensure salvation.[131] Such beliefs were often brigaded with the greatest irreligion, that is, barbarous failures of ethical obligation and Christian charity (religious persecution); moreover, disbelief in such truths, even atheism, was consistent with decent conduct.[132] Respect for conscience, which ensures that such corrupting theological conceptions are not enforced by law, thus yields both a purer religion and a truer and more practical ethics.

This conception—that ethical independence and the right to conscience are mutually supportive—leads to the most radical departure of this argument from other political traditions, namely, Locke's principle that religious ends are not a legitimate state concern.[133] This argu-

128. See, in general, Colman, *John Locke's Moral Philosophy*. On Locke's theocentrism and ethics of moral independence, see Dunn, "From Applied Theology to Social Analysis."

129. Locke, *The Reasonableness of Christianity*.

130. Bayle, *Philosophique Commentaire*, pp. 367–72, 422–33.

131. As Bayle stated in his *Pensees Diverses sur la Comete*, "L'homme n'agit pas selon ses principles"; see Rex, *Essays on Pierre Bayle and Religious Controversy*, p. 55.

132. Bayle set forth this point in the provocative paradox that mere belief in speculative truths does not lead to ethics, and may, if idolatrous (lacking in true faith), be worse than atheism. See ibid., pp. 51–60. Human nature is so complex, for Bayle, that though atheistic beliefs may mandate immorality, atheists do not always act that way; ibid., pp. 62–65. Conversely, though religious beliefs may mandate morality, believers may act immorally.

133. The statement of this principle is the subject of the first *Letter Concerning Toleration, Works of John Locke*, vol. 6, pp. 5–58.

ment was naturally opposed as undermining public morality and political stability, especially when it was later elaborated to encompass disestablishment (in Virginia and under the First Amendment of the United States Constitution).[134] Political experience theretofore had associated religion with state coercive and other support, so that many wondered how a state could be stable when all religions were independent of it. Both Locke and Bayle argue, in response, that a peaceful civility can be restored only when Augustinian persecution is abandoned; persecution itself creates the instabilities of intractable sectarian conflict.[135] Past political experience was, for Locke and Bayle, a poor guide once the metainterpretive diversity of religious thought was unleashed by the Reformation. Indeed, for them, such political experience was itself based on an unsound theory of intolerance and on a corrupt conception of public morality. The warning drawn from past political experience proved, of course, wrong. The argument for the right to conscience did not undermine public morality; it led to a new conception of what ethics is, made possible by the ethical independence that respect for conscience fosters. That was, I believe, exactly Locke's and Bayle's prophetic point.

The Scope of Universal Toleration

The natural consequence of the argument for an inalienable right to conscience is universal toleration. Locke and Bayle draw this conclusion, with two notable qualifications to the scope of such toleration. First, they exclude Catholics and atheists from such toleration.[136] Second, they deny that such toleration includes conscientiously motivated immoral acts.[137] The first exclusion may be inconsistent with respect for conscience; the second limitation is not.

The exclusion of Catholics from universal toleration is directed not against their worship (Bayle condemns such coercion, and much else),[138] but against what Locke and Bayle took to be their commitment to intolerance and their seditious advocacy of the overthrow of legitimate Protestant governments. The argument did not properly apply to

---

134. For example, opposition to total disestablishment of the Anglican Church in Virginia, led by Patrick Henry and Richard Henry Lee, centered on the idea that some form of multiple establishment was necessary to preserve public morality in the state. See Eckenrode, *Separation of Church and State in Virginia*, p. 74.

135. For Locke, see, e.g., *Works of John Locke*, vol. 6, pp. 7–9; for Bayle, see *Philosophique Commentaire*, pp. 415–19.

136. For Locke, see *Works of John Locke*, vol. 6, pp. 45–47 (Catholics); p. 47 (atheists). For Bayle, see *Philosophique Commentaire*, pp. 410–15 (Catholics); p. 431 (atheists).

137. Locke, *Works of John Locke*, vol. 6, pp. 7–9; Bayle, *Philosophique Commentaire*, pp. 415–19.

138. For example, Bayle insists that Catholics should not be subject to stigma, nor should their possessions be threatened, nor should their right to bring up their children according to their beliefs be disturbed. See Bayle, *Philosophique Commentaire*, p. 412.

all Catholics even when Locke and Bayle wrote. Catholics (in the tradition of Erasmus and Montaigne)[139] advocated toleration, and many Protestants (including Calvin and the Massachusetts theocrats)[140] advocated Augustinian intolerance of heresy. If some group of Catholics was seditious and treasonous, appropriate laws could be directed against them for such acts, not against their Catholicism as such.

The deeper issue of principle is this: should the scope of toleration extend to those who advocate intolerance? The structure of the argument for universal toleration expresses respect for the right to conscience, the capacity of persons to originate and assess claims. The argument requires respect for the capacity as such. As Bayle sees in his examples of moral atheists and immoral theists (though not to the effect here urged), persons are not propositions; and it is a vicious fallacy of both the political left and the right to infer, as Augustine did, from one's contempt for a proposition believed by a person that one contemptuously may deprive that person of the free exercise of judgment in believing or saying it. The argument applies fully to beliefs in intolerance, whether entertained on militantly theocratic or atheistic grounds. Such toleration of the intolerant, as Rawls has argued,[141] gives priority of place to the inalienable right to conscience among human rights, namely, the protection of the highest-order interest of persons in their very freedom and rationality. Accordingly, the line of legitimate intervention cannot be drawn at speculative fears (itself often reflective of fear, stereotypical misunderstanding, and unjust contempt), but only at the point of imminent action ("clear and present" dangers are discussed further in chapters 6 and 7). Otherwise, rebuttal and education, including state support of education in the values of toleration, are the just responses.

The exclusion of atheists from universal toleration is, I believe, more structurally connected to the moral motivations of the right to conscience. The weight accorded conscience by both Bayle and Locke reflects their conceptions of its link to ethical independence. Such independence, for them, makes possible experience of the uncompromisable demands of an ethical God, who reveals Himself in the ethical demands through which we experience His Augustinian image, the dignity of our moral powers. The absoluteness of conscience, which requires that all other voices be stilled, is the voice of God under whose judgment we experience our natures as free, rational, and equal. Bayle is not, therefore, inconsistent when, on the one hand, he paradoxically insists that atheists lead decent moral lives and theists lead immoral

139. The argument was often put as a natural extension of Thomas Aquinas's toleration of pagans and Jews grounded not in inviolable conscience, but in the lesser evil. See Lecler, *Toleration and the Reformation* vol. 2, pp. 79, 222, 231–32, 449.
140 See, in general, Miller, *Orthodoxy in Massachusetts 1630–1650.*
141. J. Rawls, *A Theory of Justice*, pp. 216–21.

lives, and, on the other, excludes atheists from full toleration (he constrains their advocacy, not their quiet living according to their beliefs).[142] Toleration turns, for Bayle, on the right to conscience, on the independence uncompromisably demanded by an ethical God. The moral lives of some atheists, the immoral lives of some theists—neither are to the point if full toleration requires conscience, through which both our inward and outward lives are ethically transformed under the demands of Absolute goodness and justice. Atheists, on this view, may mimic the outward show of a moral life, but they lack the inward attitude (belief in God) necessary to ethical motivation.

Locke and Bayle may be wrong, however, in linking ethical independence to theism. If so, the moral motivation of the right to conscience would require an enlarged understanding of the scope of the right to conscience and of universal toleration. Since Locke and Bayle wrote, reflection on ethics and religion (including eighteenth-century moral philosophy influential in the American Enlightenment)[143] has increasingly reinterpreted these issues in this way. Today, this position is so reasonably entertained that the narrower theistic definition of conscience would almost certainly unjustly narrow the underlying conception of freedom and rationality in the way that Locke and Bayle condemned (sectarian views of the falsity of things believed would imply that they are irrationally and unfreely believed). Accordingly, as we shall further explore in chapter 5, the Supreme Court has extended toleration well beyond theism.

Both Locke and Bayle argue, also, that respect for conscience and universal toleration does not encompass conscientiously motivated immoral acts, to the extent such acts exist.[144] To the contrary, both thinkers insist that immoral acts should, in general, be the subject of state penalty, and that there is no exemption of conscience for such acts. The very idea that conscience could be the motivation of immorality is one that Bayle, for example, questions.[145] We should remind ourselves that, for both thinkers, the argument for conscience pivots on the ethical independence it allows and fosters. A conscience, which makes possible a purer and more practical ethics, is not easily thought of as motivating immorality.

There is an ambiguity in the argument at this point. The right to conscience could be limited to beliefs, never to acts; or, the right could

142. Bayle, *Philosophique Commentaire*, p. 431.
143. See, e.g., Shaftesbury, *An Inquiry Concerning Virtue or Merit*, pp. 15–22, 45–47; Hutcheson, *An Inquiry Concerning the Original of Our Ideas of Virtue or Moral Good*, pp. 71–72, 79, 85–86, 90–92, 122–23, 125.
144. See Locke, *Works of John Locke*, vol. 6, pp. 7–9, 241–42; Bayle, *Philosophique Commentaire*, pp. 415–9. Locke does, however, note that not all immoralities are condemned by law, *Works of John Locke*, vol. 6, pp. 36–37, 295, 535.
145. Bayle, *Philosophique Commentaire*, pp. 415–19.

extend to not immoral acts. Locke writes of the scope of toleration in this ambiguous way when he argues that religious beliefs and exercises do no injury to anyone, and thus do not fall under the jurisdiction of the secular state.[146] The argument could be taken to limit the right to conscience solely to beliefs and rituals, or, more generally, to include as well all expressions of conscience (including conscientious actions) which injure no one. The only thing the argument cannot mean is that uncontroversially immoral acts (those, for example, which injure others, like murder) are exempt from secular law on grounds of conscience.

The resolution of the ambiguity will turn here on how we understand the concept of immorality, its connections to harm, and Locke's working criterion of religious versus secular ends. Both Locke and Bayle assume an uncontroversial consensus on the notion of immorality, and thus fully support the standard Calvinist idea of legally enforceable immorality.[147] Yet their argument contains the seeds of a different view, examined further in chapter 5 and in Part IV on constitutional privacy.

CONTRACTARIAN THOUGHT AND THE MORAL SOVEREIGNTY OF THE PEOPLE

Our extended examination of the inalienable right to conscience enables us also to show how Locke, in contrast to Bayle, integrates a democratic theory of the social contract with the right to conscience. Both conscience and the social contract rest, I shall argue, on an underlying political ideal of the moral sovereignty of the people.

We may recall that the central concerns of Locke's *Second Treatise of Government* are twofold: circumstances that release citizens from the moral obligation to obey the law and further circumstances that justify the right to rebel.[148] Locke understands release from the moral obligation to obey the law to be the necessary, but not sufficient, condition of the right to rebel; the right to rebel arises when moral obligations are released, but also demands that independent requirements of respect for rights of innocent third parties and feasibility must be met. The historical novelty of Locke's argument should not be underestimated. Certainly, earlier political theory and practice recognized the legitimate power of resistance to tyrannous monarchs. But Locke, following George Lawson,[149] localizes such power not in the other

146. Locke, *Works of John Locke*, vol. 6, pp. 34, 36–37, 40, 51.
147. Locke does, however, note that not all immoralities are condemned by law; see ibid., pp. 36–37, 295, 535.
148. See the discussion of Locke's argument in Richards, *A Theory of Reasons for Action*, pp. 152–157.
149. See Franklin, *John Locke and the Theory of Sovereignty* (1978). See also Tierney, *Religion and the Growth of Constitutional Thought, 1150–1650*, pp. 97–102.

ordained institutions of government (for example, parliament) but directly in the people themselves. The violation of their rights justifies both release from moral obligations of fidelity to law and the right to rebel. The conception of the sovereignty of the people and their rights is expressed by Locke through the idea of a social contract understood both historically and hypothetically. The hypothetical formulation is the one of continuing historical interest; it is the Lockean idea further interpreted and deepened by Rousseau,[150] Kant,[151] and Rawls.[152] Locke's form of the hypothetical contract is a criterion of justice: the justice of government, one of the necessary conditions for the moral obligation to obey law, is interpreted against the benchmark of whether all persons subject to the government would, consistent with their inalienable human rights, find the government more acceptable than a state of nature. Locke regards the inalienable right to conscience as one of the central rights, whose violation by the state is unjust by the test of the hypothetical contract. The inalienability of the right follows, for Locke, from its protection of the highest-order interests of persons in the freedom and rationality by which they come to know themselves as ethical beings—a control over integrity that persons cannot ethically surrender to anyone, including the state.[153]

The arguments of the *Second Treatise* and the *Letters Concerning Toleration* are, thus, intimately linked. The violation of the right to conscience is, by the test of the hypothetical contract, unjust, with necessary implications for both moral release from fidelity to law and the justification of rebellion. The intimacy of the linkage can be understood in terms of the way Locke, in contrast to Bayle, connects the inalienable right to conscience (a value both Locke and Bayle share) to the moral sovereignty of the people over legal and political community. Locke, the deeper political theorist, conceives protection of the right to conscience as central to justice in politics and law because it preserves the moral sovereignty of the people. That moral sovereignty—the very benchmark of justice in government—is secure only if each and every person subject to the government retains what Locke supposed constitutive of each person's moral sovereignty, the independent control of the formation, expression, and revision of personal conscience. Since the moral sovereignty of each and all is the necessary condition of any

150. Rousseau, *The Social Contract*, in *The Social Contract and Discourses*.
151. Kant, "Concerning the Common Saying: 'This May be True in Theory, but It Does Not Apply in Practice.'"
152. Rawls, *A Theory of Justice*.
153. For the central importance of the experience that religious toleration made possible in Locke's political theory, see Dunn, *The Political Thought of John Locke*. The connection of conscience to ethical constraints, which constrain the surrender of conscience, gives a sense to inalienability in Locke not, I believe, given appropriate weight by Simmons, "Inalienable Rights and Locke's *Treatises*."

political legitimacy at all, the coercion of conscience was, for Locke, a central political injustice.

We may have some sense of the startling historical originality of Locke's conception when we contrast it with the familiar idea of previous political theory and practice, namely, that political legitimacy is achieved when all play their proper and ordained institutional and other roles on the model of cosmic order. As Shakespeare's Ulysses puts it, all

> Observe degree, priority, and place,
> Insisture, course, proportion, season, form,
> Office, and custom, in all line of order.[154]

Deviation from such an order, as by a tyrannous monarch, could, as we earlier saw, justify the place of other ordained institutions in combating tyranny and restoring the proper order of things. Locke's conception of revolution is not linked to the restoration of ordained order in this way, because, for him, political legitimacy arises in a radically different way—from the sovereignty of the people. Ideas of natural orders of governance and hierarchy enjoy, from this perspective, no ultimate political or other authority. To the contrary, the claims of citizens on legitimate government are not given sense by the natural order of ordained roles, but by the originating claims expressive of their free conscience. Indeed, the whole sense of Locke's alternative conception of politics, as I earlier suggested, arises from a larger repudiation, rooted in medieval nominalism, of the Platonic and Aristotelian epistemology of the chain of being, attunement to which, prior to empirical investigation, gives order to individual and political life.[155] Locke's politics of conscience is continuous with his epistemology of probabilistic experience:[156] the legitimacy of all belief must now be tested against the inquiries and investigations of a rational mind, free to assent to those beliefs and theories that best bear reasonable personal examination. The imposition of ideas of cosmic order, in defiance of reasonable personal investigation, was, for Locke, as bad science as it was unjust politics and corrupt religion.[157] Conscience is, thus, naturally central to his political theory, because the right to it is the very condition of giving a personal sense to life and experience as a free and rational being.

154. Shakespeare, *Troilus and Cressida*, act I, scene III, 11. 85–88, in *Shakespeare: Complete Works*, p. 672
155. See Lovejoy, *The Great Chain of Being*; Blumenberg, *The Legitimacy of the Modern Age*.
156. See, in general, Locke, *An Essay Concerning Human Understanding*; Van Leeuwen, *The Problem of Certainty in English Thought, 1630–1690*; Shapiro, *Probability and Certainty in Seventeenth-Century England*; Wood, *The Politics of Locke's Philosophy*.
157. Of course, one could come to believe in such a chain of being as the consequence of such an investigation. In fact, Locke accepted some such argument. See John Colman, *John Locke's Moral Philosophy*, pp. 2–3.

Contractarian theory is a natural way to express the underlying political conception of the moral sovereignty of the people, which links democratic theory with a larger moral conception of respect for persons, a link assumed by both Locke and Bayle. Scanlon has recently characterized this larger contractualist moral view in a similar way: ethical principles of conduct are standards regulative of our relations to one another, which could be justified to and not reasonably rejected by each person.[158] As I earlier suggested, the utilitarian principle would fail this test, because persons would reasonably reject the kinds of deprivations and inequalities that the principle requires. Indeed, the underlying utilitarian idea of pleasure or preference satisfaction, as the primary ethical good, would not satisfy the contractualist criterion: persons would reasonably reject it in favor of minimal all-purpose goods immune from the impersonality of utilitarian aggregation and manipulation.

The political social contract, as used by Locke, Rousseau, Kant, and Rawls, is an application of this larger moral conception to political life. The contractarian idea is, again, a useful way of elaborating the underlying moral concept of free, rational, and equal persons, for the free and rational consent of each person to regulative political principles expresses this moral concept. One such principle is the guarantee of the inalienable right to conscience, which each person would reasonably demand as a protection of freedom and rationality, the highest-order good, in terms of which all other goods in life are interpreted and given weight. If there is any human right, there must be the inalienable right to conscience. This priority is shown, I believe, by the structure of political principles that respect for this right requires, in other words, by the primacy of toleration among democratic values.

Respect for conscience precisely ensures the contractarian ideal of the moral sovereignty of the people, for it requires that persons retain the right independently to form, express, and change the structure of their highest-order interests in freedom and rationality. The historical connection of the emergence of this right to ideas of covenant is no accident, but integral to its moral structure as a substantive political right. Our covenant with a just God, who limits His power on terms of our free and rational consent, dignifies the moral powers that are God's Augustinian image in us; our covenant with the state, which limits its power by political and/or constitutional constraints of respect for our rights, dignifies our moral powers as a sovereign people. Ethics, religion, and politics are here integrally linked through contractarian ideas of the consenting expression of the freedom and rationality of moral personality in a community of equals.

American constitutional law is contractarian to the extent that its

158. Scanlon, "Contractualism and Utilitarianism."

principles of a written constitution reflect these conceptions, principles
that give a sense to constitutional interpretation itself as a way in which
people express and realize their dignity as free and rational persons in
a community of equals. The clearest evidence that constitutional law is
contractarian would be the salient weight of the inalienable right to
conscience as a background constitutional right, in Dworkin's sense, for
this right, more than any other, expresses the interpretive moral dignity
central to contractarian political theory. In fact, American constitutional law reflects this background right, so that our examination of an
abstract right of political theory may, *pari passu*, deepen constitutional
theory as well.

5 · The Primacy of Religious Toleration

American constitutional law has contractarian moral foundations if, I have suggested, it gives the kind of place and weight to the inalienable right to conscience characteristic of contractarian theory. The remaining chapters of this book aim to show that the right to conscience, so far discussed as an abstract moral right of democratic political theory, is, in fact, a background constitutional right, in Dworkin's sense. That right, properly understood, provides the best interpretive explication of central principles of American constitutional law, namely, those of religious liberty, free speech, constitutional privacy, and much else. The initial move in this larger intellectual strategy must be the examination of constitutional guarantees of religious toleration: the religion clauses of the First Amendment of the United States Constitution.

Our interpretive task here must be the most sensible imputation of reasonable purposes to the relevant data to be interpreted. In the American constitutional tradition, such interpretation must give sense and weight to the history of the enactment of the religion clauses (including their language and their structural links to other parts of the constitutional design), the larger moral and political traditions to which that history implicitly appeals, and the way in which those clauses have been understood, elaborated, and applied over time both by the community in general and by the judiciary. I earlier argued (chapter 2) that constitutional interpretation must resist interpretive positions that, without good argument, tendentiously emphasize one kind of data at the expense of another—for example, a historical appeal to original intent which ignores later interpretive traditions, or later interpretive conventions which give no weight to history, or political theory unlinked to either history or interpretive conventions. We need, I suggested, an interpretive approach that avoids such sterile positions.

Contemporary controversy over the meaning of the religion clauses exemplifies these larger interpretive sterilities; often, interpretive advocacy sharply isolates subsidiary inquiries into history, interpretive traditions, and political theory in a way that distorts each. (Examples of interpretive distortions of these kinds will be the subject of criticism throughout this chapter.) We need better to understand how the isolation of political theory from the historiography of the religion clauses disfigures both the interpretation of our history and the interpretation of our law. When we have come to grips with this problem, our interpretive analysis can more articulately use the arguments of abstract political theory, introduced in the previous chapter, to understand both our history and our contemporary interpretive traditions of religious liberty.

HISTORIOGRAPHY OF THE RELIGION CLAUSES

Chapter 4 elaborated a political theory of the inalienable right to conscience in light of the great historical texts of Locke and Bayle, which gave the right its seminal political and philosophical expression. A constitutional theory cannot, of course, use the insights of such a political theory unless those texts are at the core of the historical self-understanding of the interpretive community. The historiography of the religion clauses is centrally fractured by divisions over the interpretive significance and weight of these texts. The examination of these divisions will, I believe, repair the distortion of historical understanding by inadequate conceptions of political theory, and lay the groundwork for a richer and truer historical understanding of the remarkable American commitment to religious liberty.

It is not difficult to make the case for the place of Locke's argument for universal toleration in the history of the religion clauses—both in the general normative assumptions that the clauses reflect and in the specific arguments urged by the leading political figures who shaped, wrote, and secured approval of these clauses. In both areas, Lockean argument was the fulcrum for understanding, analysis, and reform, often in directions well beyond Locke's own limited political ambitions. In order to comprehend how and why this was so, we must put Locke's argument for the inalienable right to conscience in an Anglo-American historical perspective.

Locke's Impact on American Thought

The American tradition of religious liberty is best understood as the natural political elaboration of the inchoate republicanism of the abortive English Civil War. The metainterpretive controversies—unleashed by humanism, the Reformation, and the diffusion of literacy through printing—gave rise to a powerful moral and political ideal of the egalitarian interpretive independence of each person, which motivated the idea of protection of the inalienable right to conscience by a written constitution (see chapters 2 and 3). The ferment in English political theory and practice during this period was interactively continuous with comparable ferment in America. Roger Williams, for example, published in England his criticisms of the intolerance of the Massachusetts theocrats. His English audience included English independents, like Milton, who were increasingly critical of the intolerant form independency took in New England.[1] The Lockean theory of toleration in the *Letters* justified the Toleration Act of 1689, to which the American colonies reluctantly conformed.[2] These crosscurrents of argument and influence not only created pressures toward greater religious toleration in America, but fed into an internal American dynamic.[3] Under the stimulus of the remarkable religious diversity of the colonies, that dynamic gave Lockean ideas a radical turn, placing the very idea of an established church, an institution Locke does not question, in a new critical light.

In eighteenth-century prerevolutionary and postrevolutionary America, Lockean principles expressed and stimulated this dynamic because Americans found these principles consistent with the best moral and political thought of the age, the religious principles of the people, and the political needs of a religiously diverse people to constitute themselves, after revolution, as a republic.[4] For example, Puritan moral

---

1. See Williams, *The Bloudy Tenent of Persecution.* For commentary, see Miller, "Roger Williams: An Essay in Interpretation"; Miller, *Roger Williams: His Contribution to American Thought;* Morgan, *Roger Williams: The Church and the State.* On the widening rift between the doctrinal intolerance of New England's nonseparating congregationalism and the increasing tolerance of England's separating congregationalists (or independents), see Miller, *The New England Mind: From Colony to Province*, pp. 8–9, 78, 119–29; Miller, *Orthodoxy in Massachusetts 1630–1650*, pp. 53–101, 148–211; Miller, *Errand into the Wilderness*, pp. 12–14, 144–45. For Milton's views on religious freedom, see Milton, *A Treatise of Civil Power in Ecclesiastical Causes;* also his *Considerations Touching the Likeliest Means to Remove Hirelings from the Church.* For commentary, see Hill, *Milton and the English Revolution*, pp. 102–3, 198–99.
2. See Miller, *The New England Mind: From Colony to Province*, pp. 141–42, 165–69, 373–78. On the British history leading to the act, see Seaton, *The Theory of Toleration under the Later Stuarts.*
3. See, in general, Mead, *The Lively Experiment.*
4. See *ibid.*, pp. 1–71; Cobb, *The Rise of Religious Liberty in America.*

thought of the seventeenth century took a view of the light of natural moral reason culpably darkened and corrupted by a religiously unregerate will;[5] this view supported (however dubiously)[6] the intolerance of the Massachusetts theocracy,[7] justifed on the Augustinian ground of correcting culpable and vincible ignorance. But the moral theology of covenant, so central to Puritan religious and political thought,[8] gave weight as well to conscience, understood, consistent with Augustinian voluntarism, as the rational and reasonable will.[9] Once the premises of Augustinian intolerance became increasingly suspect,[10] such moral thought would naturally gravitate to Lockean contractarian thought, the natural vehicle for both retaining its basic ideals and disincumbering itself of suspect premises.[11]

This natural transition was facilitated by the eighteenth-century moral philosophy of the moral sense so influential on American religious and moral thought.[12] Locke had maintained that ethics was demonstrable, but had not published any such demonstration; rather, in accord with his general commitment to theological ethics, he argued that the Gospels sufficed as a practical guide to conduct.[13] The theory of the moral sense, consistent with a Lockean epistemology, filled this gap with a distinctive kind of experience available to everyone's moral

5. On this moral thought, see Fiering, *Moral Philosophy at Seventeenth-Century Harvard*, pp. 52–62, 120–27.
6. In fact, the Puritans' theory of persecution was in tension with their doctrinal predestinarianism: for, if faith was not chosen, how could one be culpable for not having faith? See Jordan, *The Development of Religious Toleration in England*, vol. 3, pp. 296, 308–9.
7. See Miller, *Orthodoxy in Massachusetts 1630–1650*, pp. 148–200.
8. The best study of this thought remains Miller, *The New England Mind: The Seventeenth Century*, pp. 365– 462; also, Miller, *Errand into the Wilderness*, pp. 48–98.
9. On the Puritan conception of conscience, reason, and the will, see, in general, Miller, *The New England Mind: The Seventeenth Century*, pp. 3–299; and Fiering, *Moral Philosophy at Seventeenth-Century Harvard*, pp. 10–206. See also Bercovitch, *The Puritan Origins of the American Self*, pp. 1–34.
10. On the continuity of the transition trom seventeenth-century to eighteenth-century moral thought, reflecting shifts in such assumptions, see Fiering, *Moral Philosophy at Seventeenth-Century Harvard;* and Fiering, *Jonathan Edwards's Moral Thought and Its British Context*. Fiering puts great emphasis on the importance of the sharper distinction of religion and ethics.
11. See, e.g., Miller, *The New England Mind: From Colony to Province*, pp. 367–84.
12. For the impact of such thinking on a central figure in American thought, Jonathan Edwards, see Fiering, *Jonathan Edwards's Moral Thought and Its British Context*. For the transitional links to Edwards, see also Fiering, *Moral Philosophy at Seventeenth-Century Harvard*.
13. See, in general, Colman, *John Locke's Moral Philosophy*. For Locke's central work of normative ethics, see Locke, *The Reasonableness of Christianity*. Locke's attempt to extract essential ethics from a form of Bible criticism of the Gospels appears to have been immensely influential. See, for a notable example of such influence, Adams, ed., *Jefferson's Extracts from the Gospels*.

sense. However, in contrast to Locke,[14] the theory of the moral sense
was not conceptually linked to theistic premises of God's will, let alone
particular religious conceptions of that will.[15] If Puritan intolerance
crucially assumed that the corrupt will had little natural knowledge of
ethics apart from a particular conception of biblical revelation,[16] moral-
sense theory starkly eroded that premise more than Locke's conception
of ethics allowed.[17] Indeed, the theory of the moral sense gave a more
potent sense to Locke's and Bayle's argument that Augustinian intolerance corrupted both religion and ethics. The violation of the right to
conscience was now construed, by Jefferson among others, as a corruption of the moral sense itself.[18]

The reassessment of Locke's impact on American political thought of
the early eighteenth century has underscored the significance of both
Locke's epistemology of experience and theory of toleration for the

14. On the relevant views of William Perkins and William Ames, immensely influential
on Puritan thought, see Fiering, *Moral Philosophy at Seventeenth-Century Harvard*, pp.
55–62, 120–37.
15. For Locke, ethical experience, as such, depended on the concept of an omnipotent
and ethical creator God. See Colman, *John Locke's Moral Philosophy.* Accordingly, any
inference to the content of ethics required, for Locke, such an operative concept of divine
will.
16. Both Shaftesbury and Hutcheson, who shape the moral-sense theory of the age, specifically deny that the concept of ethics depends either on God's will or on divine punishment. See, e.g., Shaftesbury, *An Inquiry Concerning Virtue*, pp. 15–16, 23–24, 45–47;
Hutcheson, *An Inquiry Concerning the Original of our Ideas of Virtue or Moral Good*, pp.
71–72, 79, 85–86, 90–92, 122–23, 125. Since the experience of ethics is defined by an
independent moral sense, the very content of such ethics depends on the exercise of this
natural sense, in terms of which, in fact, we define our concept of a good and just God,
not conversely. For both Shaftesbury and Hutcheson, the concept of ethics as linked to
divine will and punishment degrades the intrinsic appeal and power both of ethical reasoning and motivation, and thus degrades the concept of an ethical God.
17. Since, for Locke, knowledge of ethics requires knowledge of God's will, respect for
conscience is, at bottom, respect for religious conscience. When a broader view of ethics
is taken by later thinkers, respect for conscience cannot be limited even in this (for
Locke's and Bayle's time) latitudinarian way.
18. The corruptibility of the moral sense by factual and other misbeliefs was a point made
by Kames; see *Essays on the Principles of Morality and Natural Religion*, pp. 136–49. For
Bolingbroke, the history of intolerance exemplified such corruption of ethics, including
the ethics of the Gospels, by speculative theology. See *The Works of Lord Bolingbroke*,
pp. 373–535. Jefferson was deeply influenced by these interconnected views of Kames
and Bolingbroke, which he linked to the importance of religious liberty. See Koch, *The
Philosophy of Thomas Jefferson*, pp. 9–39. For Jefferson's own linkage of religious persecution with moral and religious corruption, see Jefferson, *Notes on the State of Virginia*,
pp. 159–61; and the preface to his Bill for Religious Freedom, Boyd, ed., *The Papers of
Thomas Jefferson, 1777–1779*, vol. 2, pp. 545–46. In his later life, Jefferson subscribed to
Joseph Priestley's views on the corruption of true Christianity. See, in general, Adams,
ed., *Jefferson's Extracts from the Gospels*, pp. 14–30; Jefferson's own attempts at Bible
criticism were actuated by the attempt to distinguish the gold from the dross.

shape and direction of American thought and experience.[19] In a historical period when the *Second Treatise* was itself not widely circulated (though derivative works to the same effect were), both the *Letter Concerning Toleration* and the *Essay Concerning Human Understanding* were widely read and absorbed into American thought and experience.[20] For example, seminal American religious thinkers, for example Jonathan Edwards, assumed the Lockean epistemology of experience and the theory of the moral sense, and linked them, consistent with the spirit of Locke's argument,[21] to the idea that only each person's own inward reflection and experience could make possible the integrity and purity of both religion and practical ethics.[22] Edwards thus gave powerful philosophical support to the Great Awakening,[23] which so threatened the authority of an established religious order of habituated submission to religious authority. Edwards found virtue precisely in the major threat to the established order and its apologists, namely, access to itinerant ministers outside the established order. Such ministerial diversity advanced, for Edwards, the kind of choice, expression, and change of religious conscience which alone dignified its religious and moral integrity.[24] For Edwards, as for Locke and Bayle, it was such independence from the conventional order or from the judgment of others that facilitated the ethical dignity of the values thus affirmed. The ethical impartiality of one's moral sense, which Edwards assumes, is deepened by a kind of choice of values in reflective detachment from early attachments and experience and the narcissistic preoccupations

19. See, in general, Dunn, "The Politics of Locke in England and America in the Eighteenth Century," in *Political Obligation in its Historical Context*, pp. 53–77.

20. Much of Locke's substantive political theory was, for example, assumed and circulated by Hutcheson; see, in general, Hutcheson, *A System of Moral Philosophy*. See Dunn, "The Politics of Locke in England and America in the Eighteenth Century," in *Political Obligation in its Historical Context*.

21. For Edwards's profound intellectual roots in Lockean epistemology, see Miller, *Jonathan Edwards*, pp. 52–68. For his commitment to and critical elaboration of moral sense theory, see Norman Fiering, *Jonathan Edwards's Moral Thought and Its British Context*.

22. Fiering makes clear that Edwards well recognizes that people may be externally ethical without true religion, though he believes a living religious faith works an internal ethical transformation in the believer. See Fiering, *Jonathan Edwards's Moral Thought and its British Context*. To this extent, he accepts the commonplace of the moral philosophy of the age, that ethics and religion are separable. See note 16, above.

23. For Edwards's most brilliant defense, see his *Religious Affections*. For commentary, see Miller, *Errand into the Wilderness*, pp. 153–66.

24. Thus, Edwards insists that true religious affections must be "a reasonable persuasion or conviction," "a conviction based on real evidence, or upon that which is a good reason, or just ground ground of conviction," and distinguishes such reasonable persuasion from mere persuasion: "Men may have a strong persuasion that the Christian religion is true, when their persuasion is not at all built on evidence, but altogether on education, and the opinion of others." Edwards, *Religious Affections*, p. 295.

that imprison the self.[25] Indeed, such reflective independence enables us to regenerate our moral freedom. In place of the parochial partialities borne of particular attachments of family or nation, we experience a universal equal respect for the Augustinian image of God in us and all persons.[26] Thus, Jonathan Edwards, who stands in the great tradition of Puritan intellectuals, defends the Great Awakening's celebration of "experimental religion," one of whose authenticating marks is a practical ethics that transforms personal relationships.[27] Respect for religious liberty is linked to a conception of reflective conscience and ethical impartiality, which it makes possible.

Edwards is, of course, essentially a religious and ethical, not a political, thinker.[28] But his influence is rightly perceived as part of the American political dynamic of religious liberty,[29] a central expression of the interaction of American religious and political thought.[30] Certainly, his deeply Lockean assumptions express a kind of politics, and were so understood and interpreted by others. Thus, Elisha Williams (Edwards's kinsman) makes on this basis expressly Lockean arguments (including appeal to the *Second Treatise*).[31] Coercion in religion, Williams argues, is wrong; it makes one's religion dependent on the judgment of another, which

> may pass for Religion in the Synagogue of *Satan*, whose Tenet is that Ignorance is the Mother of Devotion; but with no understanding Protestant will it pass for any Religion at all. No Action is a religious Action without Under-

---

25. Edwards's distinction between the virtue of natural ethics and "true virtue," which he grants to be often coextensive in the things done, rests on the more impartial release of the latter from the preoccupations of self-love or self-love universalized. See Edwards, *Dissertation on the Nature of True Virtue*, esp. pp. 285–91. It is this release from narcissistic preoccupation that explains Edwards's concept of evangelical humiliation in *Religious Affections*, pp. 311–40, a humiliation of introspection that releases the aim of true religion, love: "A truly Christian love, either to God or man, is a humble broken-hearted love," p. 339. For useful commentary on Edwards's distinction between natural and true virtue, see Fiering, *Jonathan Edwards's Moral Thought and its British Context*, pp. 257–60, 322–61.
26. For Edwards the release from particular affections, into a sense of universal obligations, was a mark of true virtue. See Edwards, *Dissertation on the Nature of True Virtue*, pp. 292–93, 296. For Edwards, only through heightened critical awareness of our own nature can we know God; see pp. 286–87.
27. The phrase is Edwards's, *Religious Affections*, e.g., pp. 303, 452. The transformation of personal relationships is Edwards's twelfth sign of authentic religion; see pp. 383–461.
28. For Williams's general social and political conservatism, see Alexis, "Jonathan Edwards and the Theocratic Ideal."
29. See Cobb, *The Rise of Religious Liberty in America*, pp. 484–89.
30. See, in general, Heimert, *Religion and the American Mind*; Philip Greven, *The Protestant Temperament*. For the story carried beyond the revolutionary period, see Marty, *Righteous Empire*; Ahlstrom, *A Religious History of the American People*.
31. See Fiering, *Jonathan Edwards's Moral Thought and its British Context*. pp. 25–28.

standing and Choice in the Agent. Whence it follows, the Rights of Conscience are sacred and equal in all, and strictly speaking unalienable.[32]

Man may alienate some parts of his property,

but he cannot transfer the *Rights of Conscience*, unless he could destroy his rational and moral Powers, or substitute some other to be judged for him at the Tribunal of God.[33]

Indeed, Elisha Williams's implicit criticism of the established religious order reflects, as well as motivates, a radical turn in the use of Lockean argument against establishments themselves.[34] These radical tendencies, inherent in American religious thought, naturally express themselves in the peculiarly American hostility to established churches. The hostility starts with opposition to the establishment of one religion (leading to multiple establishments); it grows into attacks on even multiple establishments and, above all, the imposition on the colonies of an Anglican establishment, one of the great fears of the pre-revolutionary period.[35] Various factors fostered these tendencies: the example of several colonies that lacked even multiple establishments (Roger Williams's Rhode Island and William Penn's Pennsylvania, for example),[36] the diversity and mobility of American religious groups,[37] and the widespread perception of religious and moral corruption in some of the established colonial churches (most notably, Virginia's).[38] The revolutionary break with Britain, with its antipatriarchal imagery, of course, accelerated these tendencies.[39] The Anglican establishment of Virginia was, naturally, in quite bad revolutionary odor, and the commitment of Americans to republican self-rule led to a search for the institutionalization of a republican ethics of the moral independence of free citizens. The Virginia Bill for Religious Freedom and the religion clauses of the First Amendment are natural experiments in this latter direction.

32. Williams, *The Essential Rights and Liberties of Protestants*, p. 8.
33. *Ibid.*
34. For the use of such arguments against established churches, see Heimert, *Religion and the American Mind*, pp. 121–22. 162–63, 200–208, 386–91, 524 ff. I refer here to the elaboration of Lockean-style arguments for toleration, not to other uses of Lockean argument sometimes, during this period, to more conservative effect. See *ibid.*, pp. 253–66.
35. See, for a general study of these events, Cobb, *The Rise of Religious Liberty in America;* Curry, *The First Freedoms.*
36. See *ibid.*, pp. 422–52.
37. See Mead, *The Lively Experiment*, pp. 1–54.
38. See, in general, Isaac, *The Transformation of Virginia, 1740–1790.*
39. See, in general, Fliegelman, *Prodigals and Pilgrims.*

Jefferson and Madison on Religious Toleration

Lockean argument for toleration actuates not only general patterns of religious and political thought in the community in question, but it is also self-consciously assumed by the central political figures who shaped, wrote, and secured approval of the religion clauses to an effect well beyond Locke's own ambitions. Thus, the language of the relevant constitutional text has two prongs, the antiestablishment clause and the free exercise clause:

> Congress shall make no law respecting an establishment of religion, or pro-
> hibiting the free exercise thereof.

The free exercise clause, of the two, has the longer political history. It dates at least from the debates about religious toleration unleashed in the wake of the English Civil War, and was implicit in the limited toleration extended by the English Toleration Act of 1689 and philosophically justified by Locke's *Letter Concerning Toleration*.[40] The concern here is, on the basis of certain stipulated conditions of allegiance, to remove state coercion from religious worship, coercion either to attend religious services of one religion or not to attend services of another. These limited guarantees (excluding, for Locke, Catholics and atheists, as we have seen) operated within the unquestioned assumption of an established church, a national church supported by the state by tax monies. The antiestablishment clause is, in contrast, more historically original to American political experience, constitutive of a distinctively American pattern of civil religion.[41] An understanding of its motivating assumptions requires that attention be paid to the arguments of its two most powerful political advocates, Jefferson and Madison.

The arguments against an established church crystallized in Jefferson's 1779 Virginia Bill for Religious Freedom, approved in Virginia in 1786 in the wake of Madison's famous *Remonstrance*. The focal concern of Jefferson's bill was to guarantee not only religious free exercise, but to disallow state taxation for the support of any church or number of churches, including the multiple establishment that Patrick Henry, among others, urged. For Jefferson, to the contrary;

> even the forcing him to support this or that teacher of his own religious per-
> suasion, is depriving him of the comfortable liberty of giving his contribu-
> tions to the particular pastor whose morals he would make his pattern and
> whose powers he feels most persuasive to righteousness.[42]

40. See, in general, Jordan, *The Development of Religious Toleration in England*, vols. 1–4; Seaton, *The Theory of Toleration under the Later Stuarts.*
41. For useful comparisons with other political traditions, see Bellah and Hammond, *Varieties of Civil Religion.*
42. See Boyd, ed., *The Papers of Thomas Jefferson, 1777–1779*, p. 545.

In the long preface to the bill as originally written by Jefferson, its theory is starkly Lockean in its epistemology,[43] its conception of Bible interpretation,[44] its linkage of toleration to religious and ethical integrity,[45] and its clear statement that the test for religious liberty cannot be corrupted by sectarian judgments of true religious belief (as he puts it, "setting up their own opinions as the only true and infallible" ones).[46] Indeed, Jefferson appears to have drafted the statute after a close study of Locke (both on toleration and on normative ethics)[47] and related texts of Shaftesbury and Milton.[48] His corresponding arguments for religious freedom in his *Notes on the State of Virginia* are similarly Lockean.[49]

These Lockean principles are, of course, independently elaborated by Jefferson congruent with his reasoned conception of their proper form and scope. Three advances on Locke are crucial for later American constitutional practice. First, the bill makes no exception for Catholics or atheists, and Jefferson's notes on Locke make clear that the omission is intended. Pointing to the Lockean exceptions, Jefferson states: "but where he stopped short, we may go on."[50] Second, Jefferson, in contrast to Locke, expressly elaborates the underlying moral ideal of respect for conscience to include not only free exercise, but any form of religious qualification for civil rights or any compulsion of tax money for support of religious beliefs, even one's own. Since Jefferson believes that the rights of conscience are inalienable rights reserved from the Lockean social contract, he regards any state financial or other support for the propagation of religious belief as tyranny (a usurpation of an inalienable right). Third, Jefferson clearly echoes Locke's conception that conscience must be free because it harms no

43. "Well aware that the opinions and beliefs of men depend not on their own will, but follow involuntarily the evidence proposed to their minds", *ibid.* Some of the more philosophical of these passages were excised by the Virginia legislature, e.g., that belief is involuntary, and moved by reason alone.
44. It states that "the holy author of our religion . . . chose . . . to extend it by its influence on reason alone,"*ibid.*
45. Ibid., pp. 545–6.
46. Ibid., p. 545. Thus, the "ill tendency" of beliefs is rejected, as a criterion for abridgment, "because he being of course judge of that tendency will make his opinions the rule of judgment," *ibid.*, p. 546.
47. See Boyd, ed., *The Papers of Thomas Jefferson, 1760–1776*, vol. 1, pp. 544–48 (Locke's *Letter Concerning Toleration*), pp. 549–50 (Locke's *The Reasonableness of Christianity*).
48. See *ibid.*, pp. 548–49 (Shaftesbury's "A Letter concerning Enthusiasm," in Shaftesbury, *Characteristics of Men, Manners, Opinions, Times*, vol. 1 [1711]; pp. 551–53, Milton's "The Reason of Church-Government Urg'd against Prelaty" and "Of the Reformation in England," in Milton, *Works*, vol. 1, [1698].
49. See Jefferson, *Notes on the State of Virginia*, pp. 157–61.
50. See Boyd, ed., *The Papers of Thomas Jefferson*, vol. 1, p. 548.

one:

> it does me no injury for my neighbor to say there are twenty gods, or no
> god. It neither picks my pocket nor breaks my leg.[51]

But he more clearly articulates a limiting principle with two subparts:
"that it is time enough for the rightful purposes of civil government for
its officers to interfere when principles break out into overt acts against
peace and good order," and that the normal course for rebuttal of noxious belief, consistent with respect for the right to conscience, is "free
argument and debate."[52]

When Patrick Henry and other advocates of a multiple establishment
in Virginia appeared close to victory, Madison reversed the tide in their
favor, and secured enactment of Jefferson's bill, in part, by publication
of his remarkably Lockean *Remonstrance*.[53] The language and thought
of the *Remonstrance* is notably contractarian, with conscience as the
central inalienable right:

> This right is in its nature an unalienable right. It is unalienable, because the
> opinions of men, depending only on the evidence contemplated by their own
> minds, cannot follow the dictates of other men: It is unalienable also,
> because what is here a right toward men, is a duty towards the Creator.[54]

The violation of this right is, by definition, tyranny, for the people,
whose rights are thus violated, are no longer governed by themselves,
"and are slaves."[55] This conception of the inalienable moral sovereignty
of the people is expressed by Madison through a striking elaboration of
Locke's idea of equal respect for the rational freedom of persons in
forming conscience:

> Whilst we assert for ourselves a freedom to embrace, profess and to observe
> the Religion which we believe to be of divine origin, we cannot deny an
> equal freedom to those whose minds have not yielded to the evidence which
> has convinced us.[56]

---

51. Jefferson, *Notes on the State of Virginia*, p. 159.
52. Boyd, ed., *The Papers of Thomas Jefferson*, vol. 2, p. 546.
53. *Memorial and Remonstrance Against Religious Assessment*, in Meyers, ed., *The Mind
of the Founder*, pp. 5–13.
54. *Ibid.*, p. 7.
55. *Ibid.*, p. 8.
56. *Ibid.*, pp. 8–9. For speculation that Madison actually consulted Locke's *A Letter Concerning Toleration* in drafting the *Remonstrance*, see Hutchinson and Rachal, eds. *Papers
of Madison*, vol. 1, p. 297. Writing in 1792, Madison used Lockean terminology in regarding rights of conscience and free speech as central property rights. See Stokes, *Church
and State in the United States*, vol. 1, p.551.

The argument echoes Locke's and Bayle's central claim that respect for
a rational and reasonable freedom of conscience cannot, given the
nature of the issue in question, be confused with respect for true religious belief. Indeed, Madison expressly condemns the false and "arro-
gant pretension" "that the Civil Magistrate is a competent Judge of
Religious truth."[57] Thus, Madison's condemnation of the multiple
establishment is that it is, in principle, indistinguishable from the doctrine of Augustinian intolerance (which associates false religious belief
with irrationality and, in turn, with a corrupt will). In short, it makes
claims that express the same kind of moral contempt for equal freedom
of rational and reasonable conscience:

> It degrades from the equal rank of Citizens all those whose opinions in Reli-
> gion do not bend to those of the Legislative authority.[58]

Such violation of the right to conscience has corrupted Christianity into
a servile "dependence on the powers of this world," and has subverted
the ethical independence of republican virtue that respect for conscience makes possible. Madison thus echoes the claim familiar from
Locke and Bayle: respect for independent conscience makes possible a
purer Christianity and a more practical (Madison adds a republican)
ethics.[59]

Madison is, of course, a central architect both of the Constitution and
the Bill of Rights, and there is no question that he brought to both tasks
the philosophical commitments he had forged in the crucible of Virginia politics.[60] Accordingly, the Constitution itself is remarkably free
of any invocation of God and contains one express prohibition on any
religious test in Article VI, which is quite consistent with the kind of
equal respect for conscience that Madison advocated. In addition, Madison's own justification of two great structural innovations of the federal
system, federalism and the separation of powers, defended the legitimacy of such divisions of political power on the same model as respect
for religious liberty:

> In a free government the security for civil rights must be the same as that
> for religious rights. It consists in the one case in the multiplicity of interests,
> and in the other in the multiplicity of sects.[61]

---

57. *Memorial and Remonstrance Against Religious Assessment,* in Meyers, ed., *The Mind
of the Founder,* p. 9.
58. *Ibid.,* pp. 10–11.
59. *Ibid.,* pp. 9; 7–8.
60. See, e.g., Koch, *Jefferson and Madison,* p. 30 (Madison incorporates Virginia Bill for
Religious Freedom into First Amendment). Cf. Curry, *The First Freedoms,* pp. 193–222.
61. See Rossiter, ed., *The Federalist Papers,* Nos. 10 and 51 (Madison); and p. 324.

Madison's substantive views on religious liberty are more evidently in play when, in the House of Representatives on June 8, 1789, he proposes a series of amendments to the Constitution, including an early form of the religion clauses.

> The civil rights of none shall be abridged on account of religious belief or worship, nor shall any national religion be established, nor shall the full and equal rights of conscience be in any manner, or on any pretext, infringed.[62]

A select committee of the House, in which Madison was the dominating figure, later changed the proposed amendment to read,

> No religion shall be established by law, nor shall the equal rights of conscience be infringed.[63]

An inconclusive House debate on this form of the amendment voiced concern that the language, aimed at forbidding the federal government to establish a church, would forbid the enforcement in federal courts of the bona fide rights and duties of state-established churches. Accordingly, the final House wording was

> Congress shall make no law establishing religion, or to prevent the free exercise thereof, or to infringe the rights of conscience.[64]

The Senate apparently considered and rejected several proposals to narrow the antiestablishment clause to forbid establishing one religious group over another, and finally modified the House proposal in the following way:

> Congress shall make no law establishing articles of faith or a mode of worship, or prohibiting the free exercise of religion.[65]

The sense of the proposal clearly is limited to the established preference of one sect over others.

The House conferees, with Madison as chair, flatly refused to accede to the Senate version, making clear that the House would not accept the prohibition ostensibly of an established preference for one sect

62. Levy, "No Establishment of Religion: The Original Understanding," in Levy, *Judgments*, p. 179. Madison's next recommended amendment would have extended such protection to the states: "No State shall violate the equal rights of conscience, or the freedom of the press, or the trial by jury in criminal cases," *ibid.*

63. *Ibid.*, p. 180.

64. *Ibid.*; for the previous debate, see pp. 180–85.

65. *Ibid.*, p. 185.

over others. The Senate conferees abandoned the Senate proposal, and the present language of the First Amendment was adopted:

> Congress shall make no law respecting an establishment of religion, or preventing the free exercise thereof.[66]

The natural inference from these facts, not contradicted by the ratification debates in the states,[67] is that the antiestablishment and free exercise clauses are centrally actuated by Lockean principles, at least in the way those principles were interpreted by Jefferson and Madison. The principles of toleration, which Jefferson and Madison had secured in Virginia, were here secured against the federal government. When the mandates of the First Amendment were incorporated against the states under one or another of the pertinent clauses of the Fourteenth Amendment, this conception of toleration is applied as well,[68] where—for Jefferson and Madison—the arguments were focally developed in the first place. The excision of the clause "or to infringe the rights of conscience" is not inconsistent with this reading if the clause is redundant, as it would appear to be on Jefferson's and Madison's conception that the right to conscience is the background right actuating principles of anti-establishment and free exercise.[69]

Revisionist Historiography

The plausible inference that Lockean principles are the moral conceptions actuating the religion clauses has, however, been resisted on the basis of a revisionist historiography. We should, initially, put aside those forms of this revisionist historiography that appear blatantly to distort the historical record. One such argument, for example, claims that an antiestablishment prohibition, which in Europe applies to the preferential establishment of one preferred sect, cannot forbid nonpreferential support for religion.[70] But this claim, of course, ignores American colonial and postrevolutionary experience, in which such preferential establishments were, if anything, uncommon.[71] Indeed, at the time of the framing of the Bill of Rights, all state establishments that still existed in America were multiple establishments of all churches,

---

66. See *ibid.*, pp. 185–86.
67. The maneuverings of the anti-Federalists in Virginia, opposing the religion clauses or allowing a preferential establishment, represent an interpretive tactic not representative of considered opinion. See *ibid.*, pp. 188–90; Curry, *The First Freedoms*, pp. 207–22.
68. See, e.g., *Everson v. Board of Education*, 330 U.S. 1 (1947).
69. Cf. Freeman, "A Remonstrance for Conscience"; Konvitz, *Religious Liberty and Conscience*; Marshall, "Solving the Free Exercise Dilemma."
70. See O'Neill, *Religion and Education under the Constitution.*
71. See, Cobb, *The Rise of Religious Liberty in America*; Curry, *The First Freedoms*

something unknown in European experience.[72] Accordingly, an antiestablishment provision would, in American experience, sensibly forbid both preferential and nonpreferential religious establishments. The Virginia debates are precisely over this issue, and the congressional consideration of the religion clauses is to similar effect.

Another unsound historical argument rests on construing Madison as opposed only to preferential establishments, or on dismissing Madison and Jefferson as simply one opinion among others,[73] or as Lockean ideologues foreign to the American tradition.[74] The first point makes no sense of Madison's support of Jefferson's Bill for Religious Freedom or the arguments of the *Remonstrance*.[75] The second and third points fail to give appropriate weight to the ways the political principles of Jefferson and Madison best explicate the form and substance of the institutions in whose design they seminally participated. Surely, Jefferson's and Madison's views of how these principles should be applied cannot always be decisive: the principles of religious liberty they espoused are sufficiently abstract that their conceptions of application may err and certainly cannot bind later generations. We rejected, in chapter 2, Berger's myth of Founders' intent and there is no reason to revive the myth here. The fact of controversy over application, including the Founders' conceptions of application, gives us, however, no reason whatsoever to dismiss more abstract statements by Jefferson and Madison of principles of toleration if these articulations profoundly clarify our constitutional practices. For example, such views may best consolidate and elaborate the prior conceptions of universal toleration drawn on in drafting the constitutional guarantees, and clarify later interpretive practice, including contemporary constitutional jurisprudence.

A better argument of revisionist historiography does not dispute the nature or weight of Jefferson's and Madison's Lockean arguments for the shape of our constitutional culture, but points to an implicit tension in the political support for their position on toleration.[76] Jefferson and Madison, on this view, created a political coalition for religious tolera-

72. See, in general, *ibid.*, esp. pp. 193–22; Levy, "No Establishment of Religion: The Original Understanding," in Levy, *Judgments*, p. 191.
73. See Antieau, Downey and Roberts, *Freedom from Federal Establishment*, pp. 196–98, 207–8. But see Curry, *The First Freedoms*.
74. See Murray, "Law or Prepossessions?"
75. Madison's concern about one sect seeking preeminence at the expense of others does not exclude a concern about all sects seeking such preeminence. Cf. Levy, "No Establishment of Religion: The Original Understandings," in Levy, *Judgments*, pp. 183–84; Curry, *The First Freedoms*, pp. 207–22. Indeed, the *Remonstrance* precisely links the two concerns. See *Memorial and Remonstrance Against Religious Assessments*, in Meyers, ed., *The Mind of the Founder*, pp. 8–9.
76. See, e.g., McLoughlin, "Isaac Backus and the Separation of Church and State in America"; McLoughlin, *Isaac Backus and the American Pietistic Tradition*; McLoughlin, *New England Dissent, 1630–1833*.

tion consisting of two disparate groups: secular humanists like themselves, and anti-establishment religious groups like the Baptists of Isaac Backus.[77] If Locke articulated the claims for toleration of the former (protect civil society from sectarian strife), Roger Williams stated the view of the latter (protect the purity of religion—the garden—from the wilderness of civil society). On this view, Williams anticipated both Jefferson's "wall of separation"[78] and associated antiestablishment principles,[79] but on a different interpretive basis. Accordingly, the secularism of the Lockean tradition may conflict with the separatist religiosity of the Williams tradition if what the former construes as a legitimate secular purpose is construed by the latter as actively hostile to religious integrity (for example, teaching Darwin or forbidding prayer in public schools, or toleration of blasphemous expressions of unbelief, or not supporting religious schools, or not giving tax exemptions to religious organizations, and so on). The religious sectarians are one powerful constituency for church-state separation in the United States; but their view argues for a de facto establishment of Christianity, of the kind envisioned by Justice Joseph Story in the nineteenth century, not for an enforced secularism.[80]

This reading of the history of the religion clauses is marred, I believe, by an unexamined conception of what the Lockean political theory of toleration is, thus disfiguring our historical understanding of why the tradition enjoyed the cumulative political support reflected not only in the religion clauses of the First Amendment but in comparable movements to disestablishment in the states.[81] Such historical misunderstanding distorts, in turn, our conception of later constitutional controversy.

Neither Locke nor Bayle was a secular humanist in the sense intended by revisionist historiography. Both were deeply religious Christians, who argued for universal toleration as the expression of a respect for the inalienable right to conscience; that respect was, in their

---

77. The leading statement of this position is Howe, *The Garden and the Wilderness.* For recent endorsement of it, see Cover, "Foreword: Nomos and Narrative."
78. Thus, in Williams's *Mr. Cottons Letter Lately Examined and Answered,* Williams appeals for a "wall of separation between the garden of the church and the wilderness of the world," Miller, *Roger Williams,* p. 98. Jefferson uses "a wall of separation," to characterize the religion clauses of the First Amendment, in his letter of January 1, 1802, to the Danbury Baptists. See Stokes, *Church and State in the United States,* vol. 1, p. 335.
79. For Williams's opposition to any form of compulsory support of a religion not believed in, see Williams, *The Bloudy Tenent of Persecution,* pp. 297–305.
80. See excerpt from Story, *Commentaries on the Constitution of the United States.*
81. See, for the prerevolutionary period, Cobb, *The Rise of Religious Liberty in America;* Curry, *The First Freedoms.* For the movement to disestablishment in the states after this period, culminating in the end of the last state establishment in Massachusetts in 1833, see Stokes, *Church and State in the United States,* vol. 1, pp. 358–446.

view, necessary to purify religious belief of its corruption by the state coercion of established churches and, at the same time, to make possible an independent and practical sense of ethics. Locke and Bayle, like Roger Williams, do not defend the inalienable right to conscience as a proxy for secularism. Rather, they argue precisely to the contrary: respect for conscience secures the interpretive independence of religious conscience from secular incentives, which makes possible the only kind of religious and moral integrity expressive of an ethical God's image in us.

Jefferson's Bill for Religious Freedom, his associated commentary in *Notes on the State of Virginia*, and Madison's *Remonstrance* develop exactly this form of Lockean argument; and they were so understood by the Baptists, such as Isaac Backus, who supported them. For Backus, the arguments of Locke and Roger Williams were to the same effect: respect for the inalienable right to conscience alone enables religion to realize its transforming ethical dignity.[82] Jefferson, Madison, and Backus entertained widely different views of religious truth, but the essence of their common Lockean principles was that their disparate views of religious truth could not, mindful of respect for rational and reasonable conscience, be the measure of civil rights and obligations, benefits and burdens.

The confusion of revisionist historiography is a philosophical confusion of basic political theory. It infers, fallaciously, from the conclusion of the Lockean argument (views of religious truth cannot be the measure of civil rights) that the argument must be motivated by secular ambitions. But this confuses means with ends. Lockean contractarian argument tends to gravitate, as we saw in chapter 4, to a set of all-purpose general goods, what Locke in the first *Letter Concerning Toleration* calls the

[c]ivil interest . . . life, liberty, health, and indolency of body; and the possession of outward things, such as money, lands, houses, furniture, and the like.[83]

---

82. See, e.g., Isaac Backus, "An Appeal to the Public for Religious Liberty," in McLoughlin, *Isaac Backus on Church, State and Calvinism: Pamphlets, 1754–1789*, pp. 306–43, which combines Lockean arguments appealing to the equal liberty of "[e]ach rational soul" (p. 309) with Williams's arguments that religious persecution corrupts the church (pp. 321–22). Cf. Isaac, *The Transformation of Virginia, 1740–1790*, pp. 291–92, 310–11. At the Massachusetts ratification debates of the Constitution, Backus defends the Constitution's exclusion of religious tests in strikingly Lockean terms: "nothing is more evident, both in reason and the Holy Scriptures, than that religion is ever a matter between God and individuals; and, therefore, no man or men can impose any religious test, without invading the essential prerogatives of our Lord Jesus Christ", Jonathan Elliot, *Debates in the Several State Conventions*, vol. 2, p. 148.
83. *Letter Concerning Toleration, Works of John Locke*, vol. 6, p. 10.

Roger Williams offers a similar list, expressly grounded in the same motivating contractarian conception.[84]

Yet, the conception of contractarian political theory that legitimate political power must be limited to the pursuit of general goods of such kinds is not motivated by any idea that such goods define what makes a life ultimately meaningful and of value. The idea, rather, is quite the opposite. The pursuit of such goods defines the limits of legitimate state power precisely because they do not themselves define such ultimate questions, but are the all-purpose goods consistent with the kind of interpretive independence on such questions that respect for the inalienable right to conscience requires. We may interpret, weight, and order such goods in a manner consistent with however we define our highest-order interests in freedom and rationality. For Williams, as for Kierkegaard, such freedom alone makes possible the ethical independence that gives life and vitality to prophetic religious conscience.[85]

There is a sense, then, in which the familiar assumption that Lockean principles require state laws to reflect secular, not religious, purposes is seriously misleading. It misdescribes not only, as we have seen, the historical understanding of the religion clauses but the deeper political principles that understanding reflects.[86] It wrongly suggests some dichotomous division between forms of our religious and our secular lives, when, in fact, on historical examination, the patterns of secularization in Western culture, fueled by our Lockean principles, themselves make possible a distinctive kind of religious concern, namely, what I have called respect for persons. The motivating idea of Lockean principles is the underlying conception of ethical independence that respect for the inalienable right to conscience makes possible—a conception of ethics crucially linked, for Locke, Bayle, Jefferson, Madison, and Backus, to our experience of equal respect for the moral powers that are an ethical God's image in us. The distinctive vision of God in the Judaeo-Christian tradition—God as personal and as supremely ethical—profoundly motivates this conception.[87] Respect for conscience

84. Williams's repeated ground of objection to religious persecution is that such persecutors wrongfully apply sanctions against those who "neither wronged them in *body* or *goods*, and therefore should not be punished in their *goods* or persons," Williams, *The Bloudy Tenent of Persecution*, p. 95; see also pp. 159, 197, 202, 228, 252, 254, 371–75, 388–89. Williams expressly grounds his views in a contractarian conception of a right to conscience that cannot be surrendered to the state. See pp. 249–50, 355–56, 398.

85. See Kierkegaard, *Attack Upon "Christendom."* Cf. pp. 83–84, Newman, *Foundations of Religious Tolerance.*

86. For amplification of the historical distortions of revisionist historiography, see Dargo, *Roots of the Republic*, pp. 77–107. Cf. Curry, *The First Freedoms.*

87. On the importance of this conception in shaping Old Testament narrative and revulsion against surrounding religions, see Schneidau, *Sacred Discontent;* Jacobson, *The Story of Stories.* On the impersonality of India's concept of the divine, see pp. 40–41, Danto, *Mysticism and Morality.* On the personality of the Western conception of the divine and its broader cultural significance for Western ethics, politics, and science, see de Rougemont, *Man's Western Quest.*

enables us more purely to know this personal God and thus to realize our ethical nature in relation to Him and all persons. The secularization, which this respect for conscience requires, is thus intimately linked to what Van Leeuwen calls peculiarly Western anti-ontocratic religious concerns.[88] Religion, on this view, does not embed us in ontological hierarchies characteristic of many of the world's cultural traditions, but makes possible a respect for persons expressive of our rational and reasonable freedom.

If revisionist historiography fails in such ways to understand the underlying Lockean principles that united the architects and supporters of religious liberty in the United States, we need an alternative understanding of the nature of historical controversy over the meaning of these principles.

Political Theory and Historiography

In chapters 2 and 3, I argued that constitutional interpretation in the United States must resist exclusive dependence on Founders' denotations or current interpretive conventions or abstract moral and political philosophy *simpliciter*. Rather, a full understanding of constitutional interpretation requires a coherent integration of all these modes of inquiry. We only understand, thus, the weight that Founders' applications should be given when we ourselves interpret those applications in a way not isolable from either later interpretive conventions or the political theory often implicit in both history and interpretive conventions. Berger's mistake, on this view, is to beg the question of what Founders' intent means in favor of the things the Founders included or excluded from constitutional language. This way of construing intent does justice neither to the general language used, nor to abstract political principles implicit therein, nor to democratic political theory, nor to later interpretive conventions. Reading our history in this way interpretively distorts that history, imputing to it a sense that it lacks.

This interpretive methodology should liberate us from the following three kinds of interpretive dogmas, all of which distort the jurisprudence of the religion clauses. First, moments of historical understanding may be, as it were, counted up, and the better interpretive account is the one, put starkly, with the better score card. Second, certain interpretive moments are obviously more authoritative than others, and these are to prevail. Third, American culture has changed so radically over time that we may blankly ignore all such historical moments, and attend only to some vague current populist consensus as the measure of contemporary constitutional meaning. There is some kernel of sense in each position; otherwise, reasonable people would not have

---

88. See, in general, van Leeuwen, *Christianity in World History*. Cf. Albright, *From the Stone Age to Christianity*.

defended them. But each of them fails to do the kind of justice to constitutional interpretation that our interpretive methodology calls for.

The first kind of interpretive methodology is exemplified by accounts that focus exclusively on historically given interpretive moments of the following kinds.[89] On the basis of their readings of the religion clauses, Jefferson and/or Madison took a certain view of excluding religion from schools, were reluctant as presidents to sponsor religious thanksgivings, resisted the placement of chaplains in the armed services, vetoed attempts to incorporate religious groups, and resisted tax exemptions for churches as such. Certain historical practices have been longstanding in the United States, for example, chaplains in the armed services and in Congress, or prayers and Bible reading in public schools, or tax exemptions for religious groups. Such historical litanies are then toted up: Jefferson and Madison accepted for one purpose, rejected for another. This kind of account is, I believe, not an interpretation at all; it lacks the kind of coherent articulation of arguments of principle that constitutional argument requires. It gives us no criterion of what makes something an interpretive moment, or what weight different moments should enjoy, or how they are to be cumulated and critically assessed. It supplies, in short, no context of argument which could clarify for us how each historical moment is interpreted as elaborating constitutional principles in a continuous tradition. Only an examination of their context and principles would enable us to assess these interpretive moments, their weight, and their cumulative force. Any argument lacking these criteria must be viciously circular, since its intelligibility depends on an implicit interpretive framework, which it refuses to examine critically.

The second interpretive strategy errs for a similar reason. It gives weight to one interpretive moment (for example, Jefferson's and Madison's opinions on religious education in public schools) as more decisive than others.[90] It does not explain why this interpretive moment is more authoritative than others, or why it is authoritative here but not elsewhere (for example, tax exemptions for religious groups).[91] The natural justification for this strategy is the kind of positivist jurisprudence which we saw to be implicit in Berger's conception of authoritative Founders' intent. But this rationale is, as we also saw, badly argued interpretation, jurisprudence, and political theory. Such arguments often enjoy selective appeal for those engaged in conscientious constitutional interpretation. Justice Hugo Black, for example, appealed to such historical understandings when they supported his convictions about correct interpretation of the liberal clauses of the First Amend-

89. See, e.g., Antieau, Downey, Roberts, *Freedom from Federal Establishment* (1964); Cord, *Separation of Church and State.* Cf. Stokes, *Church and State in the United States.*
90. See, e.g., *Everson v. Board of Education,* 330 U.S. 1 (1947).
91. See *Walz v. Tax Commission of the City of New York,* 397 U.S. 664 (1970).

ment, including the religion clauses;[92] but he and the Court abandoned such history in other areas when it did not similarly support their views.[93] The motivating criteria of such selectivity are principled arguments of political theory, which shape the interpretive sense of how history is properly read. The appeal to the greater weight of one historical interpretive moment is, as such, question-begging: it assumes a framework of political theory that it does not examine.

The third interpretive strategy, ignoring history for contemporary consensus, is doubly defective.[94] On the one hand, it abandons constitutional interpretation as an inquiry into historical self-understanding, and, on the other, negates what is most valuable in the elaboration of arguments of constitutional principle. It thus partakes of the vices, without any of the countervailing virtues, of constitutional interpretation understood exclusively as the appeal to history or as the appeal to political and moral philosophy. Both of these approaches, at their best, respect constraints on democratic majorities which ensure protection of those inalienable rights of the person, necessary for democratic self-rule to correspond to its internal ideals of the moral sovereignty of the people. But the appeal to contemporary consensus precisely dilutes the force of such constraints of constitutional argument, perversely, on the very ground of consensus which such constraints justly cabin and regulate.

This third strategy should not be confused with the entirely legitimate claim that historical circumstances may so change that constitutional principles apply differently. This claim does not, contra Berger, abandon history. Rather, it interprets history in a way more coherently revelatory of the abstract principles which may, though applied differently in various historical contexts, unite a constitutional community over time. We shall have occasion to examine several such arguments later.

We may, however, usefully examine here one abstract issue of moral and political theory that directly bears on a range of interpretive questions. The issue is the central importance to religion clause jurisprudence of background conceptions of the nature of ethics. For example, I earlier noted that background assumptions about the nature of ethics—Locke's theological ethics versus moral-sense theory—are an important source of interpretive disagreement over Lockean principles

92. See *Everson v. Board of Education*, 330 U.S. 1 (1947).
93. See *Brown v. Board of Education*, 347 U.S. 483 (1954). On the historical arguments supporting the constitutionality of state-endorsed racial segregation, see Berger, *Government by Judiciary*, pp. 117–33. Cf. Bickel, "The Original Understanding and the Segregation Decision."
94. See, e.g., Morgan, *The Supreme Court and Religion*, pp. 183–202; Kauper, *Religion and the Constitution*, pp. 67–79. Cf. Freeman, "The Misguided Search for the Constitutional Definition of 'Religion'"; Greenawalt, "Religion as a Concept in Constitutional Law."

of toleration, and thus over the meaning of the religion clauses. Jefferson's refusal to follow Locke in excluding Catholics and atheists from the protection of the Bill for Religious Freedom reflects, I believe, such assumptions, and many later historical shifts in the interpretation of these clauses pivot on similar changes in thought. When Justice Story, for example, dubbed Protestant Christianity the de facto established church of the United States, he assumed that Protestantism was a just proxy for ethics itself. Accordingly, Story found no violation of constitutional neutrality in state imposition of prayers or Bible reading in the public schools, or prosecutions for blasphemy, or exclusion of atheists from public office.[95] If we today take constitutional objection to such practices, this must pivot on background shifts in our ideas of whether Protestant Christianity can any longer justly be regarded as a proxy for ethics as such.

Such disagreements do correspond to the moral motivations of the argument for universal toleration in Locke and Bayle. Thus, Bayle, as we saw in the previous chapter, rejoices in the paradox that those who believe true religious doctrines can be immoral, and atheists can be moral; but he nonetheless does not extend his principles of universal toleration to atheists.[96] For Bayle, the motivating point of respect for conscience is that one should be inwardly ethically transformed by the uncompromisable demands of an ethical God, an experience which, by definition, an atheist cannot have. For Bayle, as for Locke, the right to conscience can have no application where its moral motivations are idle.

Accordingly, the sense of the political theory of toleration is linked to a cognate moral philosophy of ethics by the very structure of the argument for toleration. Interpretive questions of religion clause jurisprudence (including the scope of toleration) will turn on how these background questions of political theory and moral philosophy are resolved.

We may, indeed, map a range of alternative positions on the scope of religious liberty onto their associated theories of ethics—for example, the Massachusetts theocrats, Locke and Bayle, moral sense theorists, and contemporary moral philosophers. Thus, the Massachusetts theocrats supposed natural knowledge of ethics to be corrupted by the Fall and thus associated ethical knowledge with reading the Bible in a certain way. Locke and Bayle believed that we may come to know ethics by our natural reason inferring God's existence and His will for us; they

95. For a revealing statement of the governing assumptions of this period and the consequent view of legitimate state power, see, in general, Schaff, *Church and State in the United States*. On Bible reading in public schools, see McCloskey, ed., *The Bible in the Public Schools*. On blasphemy, see, in general, Levy, *Treason Against God*.
96. Bayle does, however, sharply narrow the scope of legitimate blasphemy prosecutions. See Bayle, *Philosophique Commentaire*, p. 421.

believed that the Bible is both assisted by and assists such inquiry into ethical knowledge. Moral sense theorists argued that we know what is ethically right by our uncorrupted moral sense independent of God's will (a sense confirmed, however, by a proper reading of the Bible and reenforced by a belief in an afterlife). Contemporary moral theory— whether deontological, utilitarian, or intuitionist—analyzes ethical reasoning independently of religious reasoning or belief in an after-life.[97] Presumably, all these ethical theories, in the order roughly arranged, will dictate a correspondingly broader ambit for universal toleration: from belief in God and reading the Bible in a certain way, to belief in God and reading the Bible, to belief in God, to agnosticism and atheism.

Attitudes about Bible interpretation are a useful historical guide to the enlarging ambit of toleration, and an important background issue in controversies over religion clause jurisprudence in the United States. We should put these controversies in the context of the historical tra-dition they often reflect and elaborate. Both Locke and Bayle, for exam-ple, are religious Christians in the Protestant tradition, a tradition in search of a pure Christianity of the Bible, to which one alone looked for guidance, *sola scriptura*.[98] But the metainterpretive diversity encouraged by humanism and the Reformation also unleashed diversity in styles of Bible interpretation. Erasmus undertook scholarly exami-nation of Biblical texts,[99] and La Peyrère, Richard Simon, and Spinoza originated modern approaches to biblical exegesis and criticism.[100] Both Locke and Bayle took seriously the wide range of disagreements over Bible interpretation that reasonable persons could, in view of this metainterpretive diversity, entertain; indeed, they conceived of respect for the right to conscience (the ground of universal toleration) as allowing persons to exercise such reasonable judgment, including both epistemic and practical rationality. Bayle, for example, quite clearly brings to Bible interpretation standards of moral reasonableness which he will not allow that an ethical God could have violated,[101] and Locke brings to the Bible as much as he finds in the Gospels the mini-mum of ethical reasonableness.[102] Thus understood, the essence of their argument for toleration is that the state may not itself dictate standards of Bible interpretation (as both supposed that Catholic intolerance did), but must allow the exercise of the independent epistemic and practical

97. Among deontological theories, see Gewirth, *Reason and Morality*; Rawls, *A Theory of Justice*; Richards, *A Theory of Reasons for Action*. Among utilitarian theories, see Hare, *Moral Thinking*; Brandt, *A Theory of the Good and the Right*. Among intuitionist theories, see Ross, *The Right and the Good*; Prichard, *Moral Obligation*.
98. See Sykes, "The Religion of Protestants."
99. See, e.g., Bouyer, "Erasmus in Relation to the Medieval Biblical Tradition."
100. See, e.g., Popkin, *The History of Scepticism from Erasmus to Spinoza*, pp. 214–48.
101. See Bayle, *Philosophique Commentaire*, pp. 367–72.
102. See Locke, *The Reasonableness of Christianity*.

rationality of persons in adopting, expressing, and revising such standards on their own. All reasonable people, once afforded opportunity to study the Bible, must believe in God and must believe that the Bible is the word of God; but they must be allowed rationally and reasonably to determine by their own standards what that truth is. This freedom alone ensures a pure religion and a practical ethics. Elisha Williams makes precisely this point in the defense of conscience and toleration earlier mentioned.[103]

Locke and Bayle, as well as Elisha Williams, implicitly concede that universal toleration must extend much further if rational and reasonable judgment, guaranteed the right to conscience, thus achieves their underlying ethical aims. While Catholic standards of Bible interpretation cannot be enforced by law, the reasonable adoption of such standards must be respected if it is consistent, as it certainly is, with realizing one's ethical dignity. Once conceptions of moral reasonableness are, under the impact of moral-sense theory, not linked to God's will, respect for independent rational and reasonable judgment may not require either belief in God in general or in the Bible in particular. Jefferson, for example, believed in a deist God, in an afterlife, and, like Locke, in the essential ethical wisdom of the Gospels, suitably edited (see the Jefferson Bible).[104] But apparently his lifelong study of and interest in pagan ethics led him to doubt that moral reasonableness required such beliefs.[105] An acute sensitivity to issues of reasonable metainterpretive diversity about ethics and its sources led Jefferson to believe that the argument that Christian ethics was superior to pagan ethics was an argument with which reasonable persons might disagree.[106] The implicit premise of the argument is that rational and reasonable persons might realize their ethical dignity through beliefs other than Christian ones focusing on the Bible, religious beliefs, or beliefs in an afterlife.[107] If rational and reasonable persons could realize their ethical dignity through other kinds of beliefs and other texts

103. Williams summarizes his argument as follows: "that the sacred *Scriptures* are the alone Rule of Faith and Practice in Religion to a Christian; that the Right of private Judgment, what the Christian is to believe and do in Religion according to that Rule, in his natural and unalienable right; so that he neither really may nor can give up his Soul, his Conscience in these Matters to the Controul of human Laws," p. 33, *The Essential Rights and Liberties of Protestants.*
104. See Adams, ed., *Jefferson's Extracts from the Gospels.*
105. On Jefferson's religious and ethical views, see ibid., "Introduction," pp. 3–42. Cf. Koch, *The Philosophy of Thomas Jefferson*, pp. 1–43.
106. See Adams, ed., *Jefferson's Extracts from the Gospels;* pp. 3–42. Jefferson's attempt to integrate the study of classical moralists with the enlightened ethics of the Gospels reflects the tension between classical and Christian sources characteristic of the metainterpretive diversity of the Reformation and the Enlightenment. See, in general, Gay, *The Enlightenment: An Interpretation*, pp. 207–419.
107. For historical background on the seventeenth century debates over an afterlife, see, in general, Walker, *The Decline of Hell.*

besides the Bible, respect for conscience must be accorded them. The conception of the scope of universal toleration expands accordingly.

If this was so in Jefferson's historical context, contemporary notions of universal toleration can hardly be less generous. Undoubtedly, the nineteenth-century American consensus on religion clause jurisprudence reflected an understanding of ethics closer to Locke's than to Jefferson's. This is the consensus that Justice Story articulated when he appealed to the de facto establishment of Protestant Christianity in the United States. But the nineteenth and twentieth centuries saw a number of developments in Bible criticism and in science, sharper demarcation of religious and ethical claims, and even criticism of religion on ethical grounds. These developments have, I believe, irretrievably undermined Justice Story's conception.

Developments in historiography and Bible criticism have permanently fractured any monolithic conception of the essential beliefs and sources of Protestant Christianity. Indeed, these developments have accelerated the metainterpretive diversity of Bible interpretation in ways that have eroded clear-cut distinctions between believers and unbelievers, and sharpened distinctions among believers themselves.[108]

Developments in science have further expanded such metainterpretive diversity, for example, over how to reconcile the epistemic claims of science (such as evolution) with traditional Bible interpretation.[109] The various ways in which these claims are reconciled further erode traditional distinctions between belief and unbelief, as science affords a common basis of explanation for both believers and unbelievers.

Correlative with the radical metainterpretive diversity regarding essential religious beliefs and sources, a more critical appreciation is accorded the autonomy of ethics from religion.[110] This appreciation is, as we earlier saw, implicit in the arguments for universal toleration of Locke and Bayle; they appeal, for example, to independent ethical values in determining what an ethical God could have meant in the Bible, and they criticize religious intolerance precisely for its distortion of essential ethical truths by speculative theology. Our sense of the auton-

108. See, e.g., Brown, *The Rise of Bible Criticism in America, 1800–1870;* Neill, *The Interpretation of the New Testament 1861–1961;* Hatch and Noll, *The Bible in America;* Barr, *The Bible in the Modern World.* On the resulting divisions within Protestantism, see Hutchison, *The Modernist Impulse in American Protestantism;* Marty, *Righteous Empire;* Sandeen, *The Roots of Fundamentalism;* Marsden, *Fundamentalism and American Culture.* On the erosion of distinctions between believers and unbelievers, see Marty, *Varieties of Unbelief;* also, his *The Infidel: Freethought and American Religion.* Cf. Cox, *The Secular City;* also his *Religion in the Secular City.*
109. See, in general, Gillispie, *Genesis and Geology;* Greene, *The Death of Adam.* On the response to Darwin by American religion, see Ahlstrom, *A Religious History of the American People,* pp. 766–772.
110. See, in general, Outka and Reeder, *Religion and Morality;* Helm, ed., *Divine Commands and Morality.* Cf. Quinn, *Divine Commands and Moral Requirements;* Mitchell, *Morality: Religious and Secular.*

omy of ethical and religious religious argument has been sharpened by our need for a common ethical basis in the face of radical metainterpretive diversity, that is, for an ethics of equal respect centering on all-purpose general goods. Indeed, such an autonomous ethics may be required from an internally religious perspective if it better expresses, as it may, the deepest ethical motivations of a religion in which our free and rational moral powers dignify and integrate the Augustinian image of God in us and all persons.[111] From this perspective, the ethical independence of an unbeliever may more truly express the spirit of ethically prophetic religion than a conventional religious group who mirrors, and does not ethically examine, the callous inhumanity of its culture's values.[112]

Furthermore, some influential contemporary perspectives criticize religion itself as ethically repressive, and claim that alternative nontheistic, or even atheistic, views are more expressive of realizing a community of equal respect.[113] Such a conception would, if true, turn the traditional exclusion of atheists from universal toleration on its head: advocacy of religion, not atheism, would be excluded from universal toleration.

None of these developments requires us to say that belief in God or in the truth of the Bible is false, or that any of the alternative propositions claimed is true. But they do establish Jefferson's general concept: persons may realize their ethical dignity, expressing their moral powers of rationality and reasonableness, through belief in any of these propositions. Our conception of reasonable metainterpretive diversity, in the exercise of our freedom of conscience, has, if anything, widened beyond Jefferson's conception of reasonable arguments and sources. The scope of universal toleration must be correspondingly larger.

THE JURISPRUDENCE OF THE RELIGION CLAUSES

If political theory assists us in the interpretation of our historical traditions of religious liberty, it clarifies, at the same time, current controversies over the interpretation of the religion clauses. The natural focus of interpretive attention is the corpus, the jurisprudence of the religion clauses offerred by the Supreme Court of the United States, a highly articulate and elaborate body of interpretive reflection on these issues. A preliminary introduction to the topography of such religion clause jurisprudence will set the stage of contemporary interpretive controversy, to which the political theory of the right to conscience may then be addressed.

111. Cf. Allport, *The Individual and His Religion.*
112. See, in general, Marty, *Varieties of Unbelief.*
113. See, e.g., Nielsen, *Ethics Without God.* Cf. Muzzey, *Ethics as a Religion.*

The Supreme Court and Controversy over the Religion Clauses

The judicial opinions (or case law) interpreting the religion clauses repeatedly emphasize the central constitutional value of state neutrality regarding religion, both neutrality among systems of religious belief and neutrality between religion and irreligion.[114] The value of neutrality is invoked in the interpretation of each of the two distinct prongs of the constitutional imperative of religious liberty: the antiestablishment clause and the free exercise clause.

The free exercise clause has the longer political history. The central historical exemplar of a free exercise violation is state coercion of the expression of religious belief and worship, for example, compulsory attendance at the services of one religion or a prohibition on attending services of another. Such coercion is, of course, nonneutral in the sense that it compels a form of religious worship, nonneutrally compelling or forbidding one form of religious worship over another, or compelling religious worship at all. At one point in the last century, when confronted with the Mormon claim that the criminal prohibition of its religiously based practice of polygamy violated the free exercise clause, the Supreme Court, citing Jefferson, narrowed the scope of free exercise protection solely to the expression of religious belief and worship.[115] On this view, coercion of religious belief or worship violated religious free exercise, but the prohibition of any action (such as polygamy or conscientious objection to military service), motivated by religious conviction, was not protected at all. More recently, the Supreme Court has retreated from this interpretation, extending free exercise protection to actions motivated by religious convictions.[116] Coercion of belief or worship is absolutely forbidden; coercion of or burden on religiously motivated action is conditionally forbidden if there is no compelling secular state purpose. Religious polygamy might, thus, still be properly prohibited by the state, but not because it is action; the state prohibition, if constitutionally valid, must advance a compelling secular state purpose. Such coercion, if unjustified by such a purpose, violates constitutional neutrality because the religious practices of one group are compromised for inadequate secular reasons.

In contrast, the jurisprudence of the antiestablishment clause centers not on coercion of religious belief, worship, or action, but on the historical preoccupations of the antiestablishment clause, namely, state financial and other support of religious teaching, even the religion of the person's choice. Jefferson made this latter point, as earlier noted,

114. The best general studies are Giannella, "Religious Liberty, Nonestablishment, and Doctrinal Development: Part I and Part II."
115. *Reynolds v. United States*, 98 U.S. 145 (1878). The Court cites Jefferson's letter to the Danbury Baptists at 98 U.S. 164.
116. *Sherbert v. Verner*, 374 U.S. 398 (1963); *Wisconsin v. Yoder*, 406 U.S. 205 (1972); *Thomas v. Review Board*, 450 U.S. 707 (1981). But cf. *United States v. Lee*, 102 U.S. 1051 (1982).

in terms of each person's "comfortable liberty" of choosing "the particular pastor whose morals he would make his pattern."[117] Accordingly, antiestablishment clause jurisprudence condemns state support of religious education in public schools (release time for religious education,[118] school prayer,[119] bans on teaching Darwin[120] or requirements to teach creationism),[121] and aid to parochical schools.[122] Such state support violates constitutional neutrality because, as the Court puts it, it has a religious, not a secular, purpose. The Court makes this point by a three-pronged test: to be free of an establishment clause violation, state action must (1) have a secular state purpose, (2) have as a primary purpose neither to aid nor inhibit religion, and (3) must be free of excessive entanglement of the secular state with religious interests.[123]

There are two salient, interconnected controversies about the interpretation of the religion clauses. What counts or should count as a religion either univocally for both clauses or divergently given their different purposes? Which forms of state activity bearing on religion, properly understood, run afoul of the mandates of either or both of the clauses? Both controversies touch on a larger question: how, if at all, is the pursuit of one clause to be coordinated with the pursuit of the other?

The text of the First Amendment appears to use one concept of religion, which has suggested to some interpreters that constitutionally protectable religion must be coextensivefor both the anti-establishment and free exercise clauses.[124] This view appears to lead to doctrinal incoherence, however. The expansive ambit given protected religion for free exercise purposes would, if applied to the antiestablishment clause, invalidate much unexceptional secular legislation.

The problem arises from the expansive elaboration of the concept of religion under the free exercise clause. The Supreme Court has tended, in the interest of reasonably developing the basic value of content-based neutrality, to expand the constitutional concept of religion to protect conscience as such from coercion or undue burdens. There are three familiar constitutional landmarks of this development. In the first, *United States v. Ballard,* the Court, speaking through Justice William

---

117. Boyd, ed., *Papers of Thomas Jefferson, 1777–1779,* vol. 2, p. 545.
118. *McCollum v. Board of Education,* 333 U.S. 203 (1948); cf. *Zorach v. Clauson,* 343 U.S. 306 (1952).
119. *Engel v. Vitale,* 370 U.S. 421 (1962); *Abington School Dist. v. Schempp,* 374 U.S. 203 (1963).
120. *Epperson v. Arkansas,* 393 U.S. 97 (1968).
121. *McLean v. Arkansas Board of Education,* 529 F. Supp. 1255 (E. D. Ark. 1982).
122. See, e.g., *Lemon v. Kurtzman,* 403 U.S. 602 (1971).
123. See *ibid.,* pp. 612–13.
124. See, e.g., Choper, "Defining 'Religion' in the First Amendment." Cf. Greenawalt, "Religion as a Concept in Constitutional Law."

O. Douglas, forbade any inquiry into the truth or falsity of beliefs in a mail fraud action against the bizarre "I am" movement of Guy Ballard (alias "Saint Germain, Jesus, George Washington, and Godfre Ray King").[125] In the second, *Torcaso v. Watkins,* Justice Black, speaking for the Court, declared unconstitutional a state requirement that state officials must swear belief in God, on the ground that the constitutional conception of religious neutrality covered belief systems without a God (in footnote 11, the Court gives as examples "Buddhism, Taoism, Ethical Culture, Secular Humanism and others").[126] And in the third case, undoubtedly to avoid background questions of religion clause constitutional neutrality, the Supreme Court interpreted a quite clear congressional statutory exemption from military service—limited to religiously motivated conscientious objectors to all wars—as extending more broadly: to all who conscientiously object to all wars.[127] Such cases suggest that the guarantee of religious free exercise might encompass freedom of conscience as such. While the Supreme Court has drawn back from embracing any such clear statement of principle,[128] the gravitational pull to this principle in the case law is obvious, and it may be the most just interpretation of underlying constitutional principles.

But if the constitutional concept of religion, for free exercise purposes, embraces conscience as such, then the application of the same concept to the antiestablishment clause undermines the kind of constitutionally neutral distinction between secular and religious purposes that antiestablishment clause jurisprudence requires. For example, if any form of conscience is religious (including "Secular Humanism"), then state support of that form of conscience is a forbidden establishment of religion. If so, there would be great force in the criticism of the decisions banning school prayers and scientific creationism from the public schools; such decisions establish the religion of secular humanism in clear violation of constitutional neutrality.[129] On this analysis, much unexceptional secular legislation raises establishment clause questions (any putatively secular purpose advances conscientiously

125. *United States v. Ballard,* 322 U.S. 78, 79 (1944).
126. *Torcaso v. Watkins,* 367 U.S. 488, 495 (1960).
127. *United States v. Seeger,* 380 U.S. 163 (1965); *Welsh v. United States,* 398 U.S. 333 (1970). But cf. *Gillette v. United States,* 401 U.S. 437 (1970) (failure to exempt selective conscientious objectors supported by adequate secular purpose).
128. See *Wisconsin v. Yoder,* 406 U.S. 205 (1972).
129. See, e.g., Bird, "Freedom of Religion and Science Instruction in Public Schools"; also his "Freedom from Establishment and Unneutrality in Public School Instruction and Religious School Regulation"; also his "Creation-Science and Evolution-Science in Public Schools." See also Whitehead and Conlan, "The Establishment of the Religion of Secular Humanism and Its First Amendment Implications"; McCarthy, Oppewal, Peterson, and Spykman, *Society, State, and Schools.*

held values). In effect, the free exercise clause would dilute the kind of distinctive force that the antiestablishment clause has traditionally been supposed to have.

Some commentators would accept this consequence in the following way.[130] For them, the free exercise clause should enjoy constitutional priority, and the traditional understanding of the antiestablishment clause should give way whenever it seriously compromises free exercise values. For example, if antiestablishment prohibitions on state funding of parochial school education compromise the free exercise rights of parents, such prohibitions should give way. The free exercise clause would dominate the antiestablishment clause whenever they are in conflict or in tension.

The implicit tension between the two religion clauses has been resolved in the converse direction by those interpreters who, in the spirit of the argument of Locke's first *Letter Concerning Toleration*, propose one overarching principle for both religion clauses: the principle that the state may never support purely religious purposes.[131] Kurland, the leading exponent of this view, reduces all religion clause jurisprudence to one antiestablishment clause, understood as an equal protection clause for religion.[132] Classic cases of coercion of religious belief and worship would violate this principle (their purpose is religious uniformity), but any coercion of or burden on religion incidental to the pursuit of a secular purpose does not. The Supreme Court's opinions to the contrary (exempting religious groups from unemployment compensation requirements,[133] or compulsory education requirements,[134] or service in the military)[135] are, for Kurland, wrong. The underlying statutes advance secular purposes, and any exemption from them for religion is itself a violation of the constitutional mandate that all religions stand equal before secular purposes. In effect, the antiestablishment clause would dilute any independent force of the free exercise clause.

These interpretive controversies over religion clause jurisprudence raise questions of constitutional principle. They invite probing philo-

---

130. See Choper, "The Establishment Clause and Aid to Parochial Schools"; also his "The Religion Clauses of the First Amendment: Reconciling the Conflict." Choper does, however, defend the school prayer decisions. See his "Religion in the Public Schools."
131. Locke states the principle thus: "The commonwealth seems to me to be a society of men constituted only for the procuring, preserving, and advancing their own civil interests," *A Letter Concerning Toleration, Works of John Locke*, vol. 6., p. 9.
132. See Kurland, "Of Church and State and the Supreme Court"; see also his "The Supreme Court, Compulsory Education, and the First Amendment's Religion Clauses"; also his "The Irrelevance of the Constitution." Cf. Merel, "The Protection of Individual Choice."
133. *Sherbert v. Verner*, 374 U.S. 398 (1963); *Thomas v. Review Board*, 450 U.S. 707 (1981).
134. *Wisconsin v. Yoder*, 406 U.S. 205 (1972).
135. *United States v. Seeger*, 380 U.S. 163 (1965); *Welsh v. United States*, 398 U.S. 333 (1970).

sophical inquiry into the moral foundations of the nature and place of religious toleration among constitutional values.

Respect for Freedom and Rationality as a Background Constitutional Right

Our earlier historical argument suggested that the religion clauses rest on a radical understanding of the primacy of religious toleration, elaborating the linkage of respect for conscience to universal toleration in the tradition of Locke and Bayle. The American conception is radical in that it calls for more than toleration in Locke's sense, requiring, as Madison early insisted,[136] a respect for the rights of conscience protected by political principles of antiestablishment as well as free exercise. The respect for conscience, which actuates these principles, is motivated, in turn, by an ethics of equal respect, which such radical toleration both expresses and makes possible.

We need an account of how equal respect for conscience organizes the political principles of the religion clauses. The challenge to interpretation offerred by the religion clauses is, thus, implicitly philosophical: it turns on controversies that ask how we may understand and delineate the ideal of free conscience in a way that properly expresses the regulative moral conception of equal respect. We need an account of equal respect that expresses such respect in an acceptably content-neutral way, one that does not prejudge the substance of beliefs that free and rational people may entertain. Otherwise, as we saw in the preceding chapter's discussion of Bayle's criticism of Augustine, the interpretation of equal respect will be skewed in question-begging ways by assumptions of irrationality and unfreedom which degrade the moral powers they claim to protect.

The political theory of freedom and rationality in chapter 4 is, I believe, acceptable in the required way. Our interpretation of freedom, for example, identified aspects of freedom that are broadly neutral among diverse ends and ways of life. These included negative liberty, the normal capacities of rational choice associated with self-direction of one's life, and the capacity to originate claims and assess one's goals as an expression of one's moral powers independent of social convention and other people. Freedom as independence plays a crucial role in implementing this conception: others should not exercise illegitimate control over or compromise the ultimate responsibility of the person for forming, expressing, and revising personal conscience. Such independence lays the foundation of an integrity of personal experience and critical reflection grounded in one's nature as a rational being.

136. Thus, in the 1776 Virginia debates over the Virginia Bill of Rights, Madison resists George Mason's language of "toleration" in favor of a direct appeal to the "dictates of conscience," which he associates with antiestablishment as well as Mason's Lockean focus on free exercise. See Brant, *James Madison: The Virginia Revolutionist, 1751–1780*, pp. 243–50.

The account of rationality, epistemic and practical (rationality and reasonableness), is neutral in the sense that it is procedural.[137] It specifies certain weak principles of inquiry and choice which guide persons in the integrating assessment of the beliefs, desires, and actions of the rational and reasonable will. As we saw in that earlier discussion, epistemic and practical rationality mutually support one another in complex ways. The good reasons for belief guided by deductive and inductive inference advance our rationality in pursuing and achieving ends. And the ends of our practical rationality (both prudential rationality and moral reasonableness) shape the ends and ambitions of our epistemic inquiries. Epistemic strategies are structured by reference to the practical fruits of explanation, prediction, and control they make possible. Subject to an epistemic minimum, we act on beliefs that advance either rational ends of a robust and fulfilled life or the reasonable coherence of our moral integrity (James's conception of the "will to believe").

The discussion of the primacy of practical reason brought into focus the basis of the ideal of freedom as independence. An understanding of the value placed on practical rationality will also give life and sense to the inalienable right to conscience as a background constitutional right.

The deeper truth in Kant's view of the primacy of practical reason is, as suggested in chapter 4, that the basis of the unity of the person is our practical capacity rationally and reasonably to reflect on conceptions of how to live, to be moved by, and to act on such unifying conceptions. Ethical conduct supremely establishes this primacy, for Kant, because it is itself motivated by a conception of principles expressing a reasonable coherence among our universal ends, our rational natures as ends in themselves.[138] Accordingly, the ethical imperative, treating persons as equals, is given a constructivist interpretation by Kant, namely, those principles persons would impose on themselves as the reasonable expression of mutual respect for the like rational capacity of all to motivate themselves by practical conceptions of their ends.[139] The "fact of reason" is, for Kant, shown in the way we construct, express, and revise our practical conceptions of the rational and reasonable will.[140]

This conception of the primacy of practical reason gives sense and place to the ideals of freedom. Respect for the capacity of practical rationality makes possible the self-determination by reason which Kant supposes to be the basis of our experience of moral freedom, the exercise of our twin moral powers (rationality and reasonableness) indepen-

---

137. Cf. Habermas's conception of procedural norms of rationality, at pp. 227–28 of his "Reply to My Critics," in Thompson and Held, *Habermas: Critical Debates.*
138. Cf. Nell, *Acting on Principle.*
139. See Rawls, "Kantian Constructivism in Moral Theory."
140. Kant, *Critique of Practical Reason,* p. 31.

dently as free persons. In contrast, Kant regards other models of practical moral reasoning, such as utilitarianism and related theories of a moral sense, as unreasonably subjecting our moral freedom to heteronomous natural facts.[141] For example, the maximization of desires is heteronomous because it may justify the degradation of the human person to serve manipulative ends of an impersonal utilitarian aggregate.

Kant's conception of practical reason makes possible, I believe, an illuminating philosophical interpretation of the classical arguments for an inalienable right to conscience and universal toleration. On the one hand, his conception of practical reason enhances understanding of two central claims of Locke, Bayle, and Milton: first, that reason is crucially practical; second, that respect for conscience and universal toleration permits a truer and purer practical ethics.[142] On the other hand, Kant's criticism of utilitarian and moral-sense reasoning affords a critical perspective on the inessential, indeed incongruous, place of such arguments among the classic arguments for such toleration. Utilitarian argument in Locke and both utilitarian and moral-sense arguments by Hutcheson may, on critical examination, mischaracterize the essential character of conscience as what Locke and Hutcheson believed it to be, an inalienable human right.[143] Utilitarian argument gives this claim no special normative salience, and the contemplative epistemology of moral-sense theory betrays the practical basis of the right. In contrast, a Kantian conception enables us to understand the place and weight that this right was accorded, and allows interpretation of the antiutilitarian themes in the moral thought of others (for example, Jonathan Edwards) who also advanced its elaboration.[144] A philosophical interpretation of practical reason thus enables us to understand the distinctive arguments essential to a humane political tradition, and to excise inessential and even corrupting elements.[145] In this way, moral and

141. See, e.g., Kant, *Foundations of the Metaphysics of Morals*, pp. 60–64.

142. Milton's arguments for toleration include arguments for both free exercise and disestablishment. See his *A Treatise of Civil Power in Ecclesiastical Causes*, and *Considerations Touching the Likeliest Means to Remove Hirelings Out of the Church*.

143. See, in general, Colman, *John Locke's Moral Philosophy*; Hutcheson, *An Inquiry Concerning the Original of our Ideas of Virtue or Moral Good*.

144. Edwards's moral theory, with its appeal to a heart transformed by a universal consent of all, is, I believe, clearly proto- Kantian. See Edwards, *A Dissertation on the Nature of True Virtue*, pp. 262, 273. On the antiutilitarian tendency of Edwards's moral thought, see Fiering, *Jonathan Edwards's Moral Thought and Its British Context*, pp. 346–56. Such proto-Kantian elements appear as well, I believe, in Shaftesbury, Butler, and Price. For Shaftesbury, see the remarkably Kantian passage on partial affections as inconsistencies in *An Inquiry Concerning Virtue and Merits*, pp. 40–41. For Butler, see p. 66, *Fifteen Sermons*. For Price, see pp. 160–161, *A Review of the Principal Questions in Morals*.

145. Thus, Kant's conception of practical reasoning may enable us critically to understand that utilitarian reasoning indeed corrupts liberal values, in the way Spragens has recently called "the irony of liberal reason"; see Spragens, *The Irony of Liberal Reason*. Spragens does not connect a Kantian account of practical reason to the criticism of utilitarian reasoning in politics, but many of his points can, I believe, be captured by such an account.

political theory transforms, in the way promised in chapter 3, our understanding of what our political tradition is or should be taken to be.

Kant's theory of the primacy of practical reason clarifies, in addition, two deep themes in the classic literature on conscience and universal toleration. These are its implicit rejection of a contemplative epistemological ideal of attunement to an evident order of being, and its morally motivated rejection of natural hierarchies of order and submission. Locke's and Bayle's argument for universal toleration is motivated by such a moral conception, which it both expresses and makes possible. Kant interprets these claims and arguments as expressive of the primacy of practical reason. On the one hand, practical reason allows the capacities of claim origination and revision; on the other, equal respect is shown for the capacity to exercise our twin moral powers of rationality and reasonableness. Thus, Kant, like Locke, Bayle, and Milton, sees equal respect as the justification of an inalienable right to conscience.[146] Failure to respect this right, among others, degrades, for Kant as for Bayle, the moral powers of our rational and reasonable wills, for it deprives us of the respect for our self-determination by reason, and thus of our moral freedom.

My proposal is to explicate the value of constitutional neutrality underlying religion clause jurisprudence in terms of a background inalienable right to conscience. In other words, the state must guarantee and secure to persons a greatest equal respect for the rational and reasonable capacities of persons themselves to originate, exercise, express, and change theories of life and how to live it well. Thus, the concerns of the religion clauses are instantiated at every stage in which the state may bear upon the process of forming such conceptions, the exercise and expression of such conceptions once achieved, and the changes and revisions in such conceptions.[147]

Two central interpretive issues are fundamental, on this view, to the jurisprudence of the religion clauses. The first issue is the kind of neutrality among beliefs and their expression that equal respect requires, and the second concerns what equal respect requires at the various stages of belief formation, expression, and revision. The first issue touches on the appropriate tests for state neutrality. The second issue enables us to understand the different, but coordinated purposes of the free exercise and antiestablishment clauses.

146. See, e.g., Kant, "An Answer to the Question: "What Is Enlightenment?"' Strikingly, Kant, like Madison, eschews "toleration" in favor of conscience, ibid., p. 58 (see note 136, above).
147. Analyses of these matters, which claim to eschew the Kantian ideal of the self-determination by reason, often, I believe, implicitly (and incoherently) appeal to some such ideal. See, e.g., Note, "Reinterpreting the Religion Clauses: Constitutional Construction and Conceptions of the Self."

Equal Respect and Neutrality

Equal respect for conscience requires that the state not confuse, as Locke and Bayle supposed that Augustinian intolerance did, true religious belief with the disparate ways in which people reasonably form their consciences. Such a confusion by the state corrupts the state's judgment of the proper scope of the right of reasonable judgment by question-begging assumptions of true sectarian belief. Bayle, though not a contractarian in his general political theory, proposed a strikingly contractarian way of drawing the distinction:

> I would ask him first to hold himself aloof from his own personal interest and the manners of his country and then to ask himself this question: If a certain custom were to be introduced into a country where it had not been in usage, would it be worthy of acceptance after a free and critical examination.[148]

Equal respect, on this formulation, is shown when a person considers what it would be like not to entertain his own current religious beliefs, and respects all forms of belief that could reasonably be adopted from such a position. The measure of the inalienable right to conscience, on this contractarian conception, is this right of reasonable judgment which can be surrendered neither to the state nor to any other person.

Even this contractarian conception of the right of reasonable judgment may be too strong. Locke and Bayle, for example, are clearly motivated by two related excesses in contemporary ideas about rational religious belief, both of which justified intolerance, one for Calvinists, the other for Catholics. The Calvinist appeal to the certitude of the "inner light," for example, justified heresy persecutions of those whose views lacked this light; the Catholic appeal to tradition justified repression of those who disagreed with the tradition. Both the appeal to inner light and the appeal to tradition require, however, an independent and public standard of reasonableness. But this, Locke and Bayle argue, is precisely lacking for religious controversy.[149] Accordingly, ideas of reasonable judgment may themselves be question-begging, and unworthy to be the measure of universal toleration.

The natural solution to this difficulty is not to measure toleration against the things believed or even their reasonableness, but against the rational competency of the believer. In short, is the believer's conscientious conception of a life well and humanely lived the expression of the normal capacities of rationality and reasonableness? Since the deeper value which this right to conscience serves is the exercise of our two highest moral powers (practical rationality and reasonableness),

148. Sandberg, ed., *The Great Contest of Faith and Reason: Selections from the Writings of Pierre Bayle*, pp. 45–46.
149. See Bayle, *Philosophique Commentaire*, pp. 433–43; and *Works of John Locke*, vol. 6, pp. 143–45, 297–300, 333–34, 418–20, 424–25, 536–37, 555–74.

equal respect must include all the ways in which persons exercise these twin powers of rationality and reasonableness in conceptions of a life well and ethically lived.

The good sense of this position is brought out by considering attempts to limit toleration to aspects of the things believed. The Supreme Court was very clear about the perils of this approach when, in *United States v. Ballard*, it rejected the truth of religious belief as a constitutionally valid criterion for state action. Such an enforceable state judgment of the falsity of religious belief would indulge in exactly the kind of inquiry that both philosophical principle and the political experience of intolerance condemn as an unacceptable measure of equal respect for persons. But, if judgments of true belief are for good reason forbidden as the measure of universal toleration, comparable judgments about the acceptability of things believed should be similarly suspicious. They too compromise the underlying value of independent expression of the twin moral powers in a way inconsistent with equal respect.

The classic exclusion from universal toleration for atheists is, I believe, wrong for this reason. As we have seen, the exclusion was justified by both Locke and Bayle because the substance of the thing believed (atheism) removed atheists from any just appeal to the inalienable right to conscience. Jefferson questioned this exclusion because he doubted the neutrality of the underlying conception of conscience. If ethics and religion are not linked in the simple way that Locke and Bayle supposed, then the motivation for universal toleration must encompass all belief systems, religious and nonreligious, expressive of our moral powers of rationality and reasonableness. In fact, the separability of ethics and religion is today, even more so than in Jefferson's day, a wholly reasonable position. Our heritage of both utilitarian and Kantian ethics maintains that our moral powers acknowledge uncompromisable ethical obligations independent of conceptions of God's will.[150] Indeed, as both Kant and Bayle note, we often determine what God's will is by our prior understanding of the demands of ethics.[151] The exclusion of atheists from universal toleration is, therefore, itself a violation of equal respect no different, in principle, from the question-begging contempt of Augustine for the Donatists.

150. For recent such utilitarian theories, see Hare, *Moral Thinking*; Brandt, *A Theory of the Good and the Right*. For neo-Kantian theories, see Gewirth, *Reason and Morality*; Rawls, *A Theory of Justice*; Richards, *A Theory of Reasons for Action*.
151. Thus, for Kant, the Bible should not be read to mean that God orders Abraham to slaughter his son; see pp. 174–75, Kant, *Religion Within the Limits of Reason Alone*. Kant believes, like Bayle, that biblical commands, read by Augustine to require persecution, cannot, because they are unethical, be read in that way. For Bayle, see pp. 367–72, *Philosophique Commentaire*. For an illuminating investigation of Kierkegaard's discussion of this Abraham example, see Outka, "Religious and Moral Duty: Notes on *Fear and Trembling*."

The other classic exclusion (of the intolerant) from universal toleration appears to raise sharper questions. Unlike atheists, whose moral
powers acknowledge principles of equal respect, the intolerant are
themselves committed to moral contempt for unbelievers: they would,
if in power, persecute those who now tolerate them. Their exclusion
from toleration is, it may be thought, exactly what they ethically
deserve and against which they have no just complaint. But the exclusion—whether in its historical form against Catholics or in its contemporary form against radicals of the left or right—confuses respect for
our moral powers with objection to things believed in precisely the way
that we have good reason to suspect.[152] The Augustinian argument for
persecution infers from wrong belief to corrupt conscience to insane
irrationality. The same vicious inference underlies the exclusion of the
intolerant from universal toleration. Their views are certainly morally
wrong, and their consciences may be corrupt. Nevertheless their views
are the exercise of their moral powers, and respect for them as persons
requires that we not confuse them with the insane or the childlike.[153]
   The scope of universal toleration is not, of course, coextensive with
the scope of the legitimacy of actions conscientiously motivated. The
principle of such toleration expresses one aspect of a deeper moral conception of respect for persons. As all the classical exponents of toleration make quite clear, that conception requires distinctions to be made
between protections of belief and action.[154] Thus,the respect for persons, which places such primacy on equal respect for our twin moral
powers, requires as well equal respect for various all-purpose general
or primary goods, including life and bodily security. For this reason,
the toleration of intolerant beliefs—required by respect for our powers
of moral independence—does not extend to harmful actions motivated
by prejudiced intolerance. The mere threat of such actions cannot,
however, compromise the right of conscience for at least two reasons.
First, the links between thought and action are complex, indirect, and
often tenuous. And second, the intolerance of conscience, allegedly
based on fear of actions motivated by its claims, often reflects a stereotypical hatred of the conscience itself and thus stifles the moral dialogue of the appeal to reasonable conscience most expressive of respect
for our moral powers (more on "clear and present" dangers in chapters
6 and 7).
   On preliminary examination, then, our model of equal respect for
conscience, as a background right, yields a conception of constitutional
neutrality with two strands. First, the state should show no concern

---

152. See, e.g., Marcuse, "Repressive Tolerance."
153. Cf. Rawls, *A Theory of Justice*, pp. 216–21
154. For Bayle, see pp. 425–19, *Philosophique Commentaire*; for Locke, see pp. 7–9, 33–
34, *Works of John Locke*, vol. 6; for Roger Williams, see pp. 108–9, 152, *The Bloudy
Tenent of Persecution*.

with the content of conscientious belief expressive of our moral powers, for such judgments suggest the kind of content-bias that is not consistent with respect for the right to conscience. Second, the state may appropriately regulate and protect general goods, even though this incidentally limits the expression of conscience. Roughly, we have arrived at the principle of Locke's first *Letter Concerning Toleration* and Kurland's more recent reformulation thereof: the state may not pursue religious purposes, but only secular ones. But this principle fails to distinguish the different points at which respect for the right to conscience applies. Such distinctions will yield, in turn, a more complex conception of the principles governing the religion clauses.

The Religion Clauses and Constitutional Neutrality

The concerns of the two religion clauses, free exercise and antiestablishment, are, I believe, coordinated by their basis in equal respect for our twin moral powers at three relevant stages: the formation, the expression, and the revision of conscience.[155] The free exercise clause centers on the expression of current conscientious belief; the antiestablishment clause focuses on state activity bearing on the formation and revision of conscience.

From this perspective, the moral basis of the free exercise clause, properly understood, is a negative liberty immunizing from state coercion the exercise of the conceptions of a life well and ethically lived and expressive of a mature person's rational and reasonable powers. The central exemplar of such a violation is compulsion to attend or not attend religious service on the basis of a state judgment of the truth, value, or reasonableness of one belief system over another. The principle of constitutional neutrality, for free exercise purposes, condemns such state coercion of expression of beliefs central to rational and reasonable conscience, an insult to our moral powers that Roger Williams called "Spirituall Rape."[156] The scope of its principle is sensitive, as we shall shortly see, to any such expression of contempt for independent conscience, including coercion of action which, on examination, rests only on such contempt.

In contrast, the moral basis of the antiestablishment clause is not the free exercise concern for the unjust coercion of the exercise and expression of our moral powers, but equal respect for the processes of forming and changing such conceptions. The constitutionally sensitive area, for establishment clause purposes, is state power as a religious teacher in contexts that bear upon belief formation and change. The forbidden role here is the endorsement of sectarian religious doctrines. Accordingly, the antiestablishment principle seeks to demarcate the relevant contexts in which the state is or is not illegitimately supporting

155. Cf. Note, "Toward a Uniform Valuation of the Religion Guarantees."
156. Williams, *The Bloudy Tenent of Persecution*, p. 182.

sectarian values: roughly put, in the Court's own terms, advancing a religious as opposed to a secular purpose.

Constitutional neutrality, for establishment clause purposes, falls at a rather different place and with a different emphasis than the neutrality concern of the free exercise clause. The constitutional peril, against which free exercise works, is state coercion of the specific content of any person's conscience, whatever its religious or other form. The antiestablishment worry is that the legitimate educational role of the state will be corrupted by the pressures of the sectarian conscience inconsistent with equal respect. These different concerns of the religion clause do not, in my judgment, place them in the kind of hostility that many commentators imagine when they call for exclusive emphasis on either anti-establishment or free exercise. The clauses protect, I believe, a common background right of the inalienable right to conscience at different points of its political peril. This unifying concern gives each clause a proper weight and significance, and suggests ways in which implicit conflict should be resolved.

The Constitutional Concept of Religion and the Scope of the Free Exercise Clause

The jurisprudence of the free exercise clause has tended to expand its scope. The constitutional concept of religion, whose free exercise is violated, has been broadly applied; its protections now encompass conscientious action as well as belief and worship. Both expansions are motivated by the gravitational pull of the background right of conscience. Properly understood, such expansions are not in conflict with establishment clause jurisprudence.

The tendency of free exercise jurisprudence to expand its conception of protected religion is required, for reasons already examined, by its background right of respect for conscience. Any attempt to limit the scope of constitutionally protectable religion to certain contents or institutions of belief would betray the underlying values of respect for the rational and reasonable conscience that both the history and practice of religion clause jurisprudence reflect. Respect for conscience cannot be limited, for example, to belief in a personal deity, for a religion such as Buddhism lacks such a belief.[157] Any vaguer characterization of the religious, which is what neutrality requires, includes everything and anything, including purely scientific beliefs about the causal structure of the world integrated into some larger rational and reason-

---

157. See Eliade, *A History of Religious Ideas*, pp. 72–106, 210–31. When two students of comparative religious ethics attempt to give a definition of "religion" that would encompass Theravada Buddhism, they appeal to a notion of "sacred authority," which, of course, begs the definitional question, since any central conception of a well-lived life would satisfy their conception of "sacred." See Little and Twiss, *Comparative Religious Ethics*, pp. 53–70.

able conception of one's ends.[158] Certainly, all of the classic exclusions from universal toleration are today unacceptable. They rest, as we have seen, on distinctions between or among kinds of conscience, secular or religious, which are today as unreasonably nonneutral as Augustine's distinctions were to Bayle. For the same reason, a sociological definition of religion,[159] whatever its explanatory value,[160] would not serve the normative purposes of the free exercise clause: it fails to give weight to respect for the person as an independent source of value. Finally, appeals to a contemporary common sense of the nature of "religion" fail to do interpretive justice to the history and philosophy of the religion claues.[161] Such constitutional conceptions of religion hopelessly track often unprincipled and ad hoc majoritarian intuitions of "proper" or "real" religion. Such majoritarian conceptions are, of course, often bitterly hostile to the moral independence of belief formation and voluntary association at the heart of the right to conscience as a background human and constitutional right. They cannot, therefore, be a just measure of constitutional protections motivated by the right to conscience.

For these reasons, the constitutional concept of religion, for free exercise purposes, has suggestively been elaborated in *Torcaso* and the conscientious objector cases to include all forms of conscientious belief that occupy the functional place in the person's life enjoyed by traditional theistic religious belief.[162] This form of functional test is the natural legal expression of my earlier argument that respect for conscience protects the exercise of a mature person's dual moral powers of rationality and reasonableness. Its pivotal role in the case law further justifies my claim that the right to conscience is a background constitutional right exerting a gravitational pull on the case law commensurate with its deeply rooted place in both the historical understanding and the political theory of the religion clauses.[163]

This gravitational pull to an expansive constitutional definition of

---

158. On the important connections between scientific and religious discourse, see Horton, "African Traditional Thought and Western Science"; also, Horton, "Tradition and Modernity Revisited."

159. See Dodge, "The Free Exercise of Religion: A Sociological Approach."

160. See Skorupski, *Symbol and Theory;* cf. Horton, "Levy-Bruhl, Durkheim and the Scientific Revolution."

161. See, e.g., Freeman, "The Misguided Search for the Constitutional Definition of 'Religion'"; Greenawalt, "Religion as a Concept in Constitutional Law."

162. *Torcaso v. Watkins,* 367 U.S. 488 (1961); *United States v. Seeger,* 380 U.S. 163 (1965); *Welsh v. United States,* 398 U.S. 333 (1970). *Gillette v. United States,* 401 U.S. 437 (1971) holds that the congressional refusal to exempt selective conscientious objectors (to some, not all wars) is constitutional. It does not question the idea that religious and nonreligious conscience stand equal before the law.

163. Cf. Note, "Toward a Constitutional Definition of Religion"; Boyan, "Defining Religion in Operational and Institutional Terms"; Note, "Defining Religion"; Hollingsworth, "Constitutional Religious Protection"; Konvitz, *Religious Liberty and Conscience.*

religion has, however, been resisted by the Burger Court because of its corresponding elaboration of free exercise protection beyond belief and worship to action. Since state burdens on religiously motivated actions of refusing to work on Saturday[164] or not sending one's children to school[165] are now violative of the free exercise clause, the Court is understandably concerned about endorsing any expansive constitutional concept of religion that would unleash such constitutional scrutiny for all forms of conscientiously motivated dissent. These cases establish the principle that state burdens on religiously motivated action are only consistent with religious free exercise when they pursue a compelling secular state purpose in a way least reasonably restrictive of the free exercise interest. If this principle were extended to all such burdens on conscience as such, religion clause jurisprudence would explosively curtail state power. For this reason, the Court's further expansion of such scrutiny beyond classic free exercise concerns of worship has been accompanied by a disclaimer that the constitutional concept of religion can encompass

> subjective evaluation and rejection of the contemporary secular values accepted by the majority, much as Thoreau rejected the social values of his time and isolated himself at Walden Pond. . . . Thoreau's choice was philosophical and personal rather than religious.[166]

Free exercise scrutiny does properly extend beyond expression of belief and worship to action, but in a way that does not justify the Court's deviation from an expansive view of religion.[167] As we earlier saw, a contractarian conception protects both conscience and life and property as all-purpose goods necessary for the diverse ways in which persons define and advance their rational and reasonable conceptions of their ends. This unifying conception gives a sense, as well, to the elaboration of free exercise to protect conscientiously motivated action abridged by the state not to protect all-purpose goods but to indulge a content-biased objection to conscience displaced to the sphere of

---

164. *Sherbert v. Verner*, 374 U.S. 298 (1963); *Thomas v. Review Board*, 450 U.S. 707 (1981).

165. *Wisconsin v. Yoder*, 406 U.S. 205 (1972). The extension of free exercise protection here, to a parent's decision not to send a child to school, is, of course, a much wider extension of such protection than in *Sherbert* and *Thomas*, cited earlier, since the latter involve burdens on the classic free exercise interest of attendance at the worship of one's choice. This expansion may explain the Court's corresponding desire to narrow the concept of protectable religion.

166. *Ibid.*, 406 U.S. at 216. But cf. *Thomas v. Review Board*, 450 U.S. 707, 713–16 (1981).

167. For a contrary view, see Weiss, "Privilege, Posture, and Protection of 'Religion' in the Law."

action. Indeed, respect for the inalienable right to conscience requires such scrutiny.

The inalienable right to conscience rests, I have suggested, on the primacy of practical reason. That right protects, accordingly, our moral autonomy in acknowledging the ethical principles that both define personal integrity and give shape indissolubly to the unity of belief and action that is one's life. The limitation of the right to conscience to belief alone disserves this ideal. It erects a wall between belief and action so that conscientious belief cannot shape and be shaped by the experiences and experiments of our lives and actions.[168] Such a sharp demarcation of belief from action suggests the contemplative model of rational attunement earlier rejected by the thinkers and advocates who shaped our traditions of respect for conscience, our highest-order interest in the independence of the moral powers that give sense and unity to our lives. Accordingly, the right to conscience protects the sphere of action when state intervention therein is not justified by the protection of all-purpose goods, but rather expresses contempt, indissolubly, for conscience and the way of life it actuates.

The Supreme Court's elaboration of free exercise scrutiny to encompass action is thus correct in principle, though controversial in application.[169] But its corresponding attempt to narrow the scope of protected religion is wrong. It is in tension with previous case law and inconsistent with equal respect for conscience, unhappily in the exact way (distinguishing among things believed) that should trigger the core concerns of both the historical understanding and the political theory of toleration. It is not an adequate answer to this argument to urge other constitutional arguments that could protect conscientiously motivated action from unjust coercion, for example, free speech or constitutional privacy.[170] On examination, as I shall argue later, these arguments depend for their interpretive force precisely on the background right of inalienable conscience denied its appropriate weight in religion clause jurisprudence.[171] If such arguments (constitutional privacy, for example) have been developed in part to fill the constitutional lacuna left by the Court's unprincipled narrowing of the constitutional concept of religion, that shows the Court's worry over unleashing a broader free exercise scrutiny to be baseless.[172] Its caution has given us

---

168. Cf. Dewey, *The Quest for Certainty.*
169. For criticism of *Wisconsin v. Yoder*, for example, see Richards, "The Individual, the Family, and the Constitution," pp. 40–45.
170. See Baker, "Scope of the First Amendment Freedom of Speech," pp. 1009–29; Choper, "Defining 'Religion' in the First Amendment," pp. 610–12, 591–92.
171. Cf. Marshall, "Solving the Free Exercise Dilemma"; Pepper, "*Reynolds, Yoder,* and Beyond: Alternatives for the Free Exercise Clause"; Note, "Toward a Constitutional Definition of Religion."
172. See, e.g., Clark, "Guidelines for the Free Exercise Clause"; Marcus, "The Forum of Conscience."

the worst of constitutional worlds: an unprincipled religion clause jurisprudence and a doctrinally incoherent constitutional privacy. The compromise of principle, in constitutional law, is political and intellectual
disaster.

The expansion of free exercise scrutiny does not, properly understood, conflict with the antiestablishment clause. The broader concept
of religion, for free exercise purposes, does not require a comparable
concept for establishment clause purposes. And the extension of free
exercise scrutiny into action does not violate the establishment clause,
as some critics suppose.

The argument that the free exercise and antiestablishment clauses
use a coextensive concept of religion is an appeal to textual wording:
the language of the religion clauses uses the word "religion" once, and
thus the same concept is used for both purposes—

> Congress shall make no law respecting an establishment of religion, or pro-
> hibiting the free exercise thereof.

On this view, a broader definition of religion for free exercise purposes
should be resisted because this would require a broader understanding
of an establishment of religion, with the consequence that much more
would violate the establishment clause than is usually supposed. The
argument that text requires the same concept of religion for both purposes is specious. It fallaciously imputes to one word one meaning,
when the word in question is ambiguous, essentially contestable, and
contextually modified by "establishment" and "free exercise," which
may pick out different strands of its complex meanings. In fact, both the
historical understanding and political theory of each of the religion
clauses bring out such different strands of meaning. The free exercise
clause focuses on the coercion of the specific form of one's rational and
reasonable conscience, which leads to a more general concern for any
coercion of conscience; the antiestablishment clause attacks the corruption of the state's educational role by sectarian conscience. The antiestablishment worry is not over regulations of conscience in general, but
over sectarian conscience using state power to unfair educational
advantage inconsistent with equal respect for conscience. Both clauses
share a common theme (protecting the background right of conscience), but their interest in this theme is different. Accordingly, there
is no good interpretive reason to straitjacket the free exercise concept
of religion to that of the antiestablishment clause. On examination, the
better reading of text, history, and political theory is to impute to them
different, though related, senses and concerns.[173]

This conception of the distinctive roles of each of the religion clauses

---

173. See Note, "Toward a Constitutional Definition of Religion"; cf. Tribe, *American
Constitutional Law*, pp. 812–18.

suggests that any attempt to reduce one clause to another fails to take seriously the different ways in which they bear upon protection of the background right of conscience at the stages of belief formation, expression, and revision. One such objection is that the elaboration of free exercise scrutiny to immunize Sabbatarians from legal requirements to work on Saturdays, as a condition of receiving unemployment benefits,[174] is itself a violation of the antiestablishment clause; such a constitutionally compelled exemption has a religious, not a secular purpose.[175] But, the argument fails to take seriously the different kinds of constitutional principles applicable at the stages of belief formation, expression, and revision.

Free exercise concerns are triggered by the coercion of conscience unjustified by the necessary promotion of a general all-purpose good; antiestablishment worries center on the corruption of the state's educational role, at stages of belief formation and revision, by an unfair sectarian advantage. It is, I believe, wrong to apply woodenly the principles relevant in one such context to another. For example, the Sabbatarian work requirement, which clearly burdens a central free exercise, is either supported by a secular interest that could easily accommodate the free exercise interests it burdens, or supported by an interest about whose secularity there is a certain lurking constitutional doubt.[176] If such an exemption gives expression to a religious purpose, it does so at the point of compulsion and in the interest of a fair-minded concern for free exercise interests. It does not do so at the stage of belief formation and revision where the antiestablishment principle has its proper home. The Sabbatarians are mature and committed believers, concerned to worship according to their conscience, and there is no reason to construe such exemptions as an encouragement to become a Sabbatarian. To the contrary, the exemptions, if anything, put Sabbatarians on a constitutionally fairer par with other religions. It is, therefore, a mistake to suppose that such exemptions, constitutionally compelled by the free exercise clause, are violations of the antiestablishment clause.

The Antiestablishment Clause

If some critics urge that the antiestablishment principle should prevail whenever it conflicts with free exercise, many more urge that the antiestablishment clause, properly understood, should yield to free

174. *Sherbert v. Verner*, 374 U.S. 398 (1963); *Thomas v. Review Board*, 450 U.S. 707 (1981).
175. See Kurland, "The Irrelevance of the Constitution," p. 16.
176. What is the *secular* status of requiring Sunday to be *everyone's* day of rest? See *McGowan v. Maryland*, 366 U.S. 420, 561 (1961) (Douglas, dissenting).

exercise.[177] This argument, like the converse one just examined, does not do justice to the powerful independent, though coordinate, purposes of each of the religion clauses. In particular, it fails to take seriously the distinctive force of the antiestablishment principle in the American constitutional tradition. I examine here both the history and political theory of the antiestablishment clause, and then focus on constitutional controversies over the establishment clause.

We earlier saw that the antiestablishment clause elaborates Lockean argument for universal toleration into a distinctively American hostility to established churches. Historically, this development reflects the extraordinary variety of religious groups and institutions in the American colonies (including several with no established churches), the principles of voluntarism internal to American religion, the widespread fear of an Anglican establishment, the corruption of an established church like Virginia's, and the effect of the Revolution in further discrediting Anglican establishments like Virginia's. The articulate expositors of such antiestablishment argument were Jefferson and Madison. They developed the standard contractarian arguments for the inalienable right to conscience and universal toleration, which are now used to support not only free exercise but antiestablishment as well.

These arguments of contractarian political theory disassociate religious teaching from state power. Jefferson condemned such state support ("forcing him to support this or that teacher of his own persuasion") because it usurped a choice of moral example that each person must make on one's own; he went on to condemn its degradation of religion:

> . . . withdrawing from the ministry those temporary rewards, which proceeding from an approbation of their personal conduct, are an additional incitement to earnest and unremitting labours for the instruction of mankind.[178]

Since conscience is an inalienable human right, the formation and revision of conscience in accord with religious teaching must be completely disassociated from state power (thus, Jefferson's "wall of separation," anticipated by Roger Williams, discussed earlier). Any attempt to associate state power with religious teaching, even a latitudinarian multiple establishment, would, Madison argued, put the state in the business of choosing among religious beliefs, exactly the degradation of equal lib-

---

177. See, e.g., Choper, "The Religion Clauses of the First Amendment"; Moore, "The Supreme Court and the Relationship Between the 'Establishment' and 'Free Exercise' Clauses"; Katz, *Religion and American Constitutions*; Kauper, *Religion and the Constitution*.
178. Boyd, ed., *Papers of Thomas Jefferson, 1777–1779*, vol. 2, p. 545.

erty of conscience at the root of Augustinian intolerance. Edmond Cahn put the point well: separation is the natural expression of the required equal respect.[179]

The tradition of historiography of the religion clauses, which either denies or distorts the interpretive importance of these arguments of Jefferson and Madison, combines badly argued history with an incoherent conception of constitutional interpretation.[180] We need to understand the background political theory that Jefferson's and Madison's arguments assumed, since this theory best articulates the background rights implicit in our constitutional tradition.

The immediate concern of Jefferson's Bill for Religious Freedom was the use of tax monies to support churchmen. For Jefferson and Madison, this state support was sectarian religious teaching by the state. In effect, the state endorsed adoption of one religious view or rejection of another. Such endorsement violated equal respect for the twin moral powers of persons to form such views on their own. For Jefferson and Madison, this principle extended, as their later records as presidents and private citizens attest, to any state support of religion that appeared so to endorse a religious point of view that it encouraged or discouraged belief adoption and change, including, for example, a presidential endorsement of a day of religious thanksgiving.[181]

This principle is not a historically contingent residuum of an anachronistic Madisonian political theory of the minimal state.[182] On this mistaken view of it, the antiestablishment clause is one of several substantive as well as procedural devices (federalism, the separation of powers) that separate and divide power to assure diverse political and religious groups least likely to dominate unjustly minorities through the state, which would be, in consequence, appropriately minimal. But contemporary conceptions of distributive justice, including the welfare state and the state role in supporting universal compulsory education, have so enriched our normative conceptions of legitimate state power that Madison's institutions are idle, indeed undesirable. In fact, however, both federalism and the separation of powers remain vital constitu-

179. Cahn, *Confronting Injustice*, pp. 186–87. Cf., in general, Pfeffer, *Church, State and Freedom*.

180. For a recent example of such revisionist historiography, see Cord, *Separation of Church and State*. Cord assumes a simplistic interpretive theory of Founders' intent like Berger's (see chapter 2), and thus fails to read history in light of abstract arguments of principle and background political theory which might explain, for example, why Justice Story's views, once a reasonable interpretation of those principles, no longer are.

181. For a useful review of their records, see Levy, *Judgments*, pp. 203–214. Madison, in fact, as president, proclaimed several days of fast and thanksgiving, but claimed the extenuating circumstance that he was chief executive during a war on national soil. In principle, he regarded all such acts as violative of the antiestablishment clause; see *ibid.*, p. 207. See, in general, Curry, *The First Freedoms*.

182. See, e.g., Giannella, "Religious Liberty, Nonestablishment, and Doctrinal Development: Part I," pp. 1383, 1389.

tional institutions.[183] Even if they were not, the guarantees of the antiestablishment clause, which are substantive, not procedural, speak to contemporary democratic concerns about moral independence in a mass society directly and vitally. To a large extent, the worries that actuated the antiestablishment clause remain our worries. The institutions of the welfare state have not changed our principles. They have, if anything, enlarged the scope of their application.

The rise of the welfare state has, of course, enormously expanded state services, many of which were traditionally among the charitable services sponsored by religious groups. It does not follow that all state support of such services, sponsored by a religious group, violates the antiestablishment clause. The role of religiously motivated charity in rendering many such services (for example, medical care) may enrich the humane quality of the service rendered. Certainly, the antiestablishment clause does not compel bureaucratic impersonality in the welfare services the state supports.[184] The concern of the antiestablishment clause is not with such services. It is with services that directly bear on the formation and revision of conscience in ways that compromise equal respect for rational and reasonable conscience.

The principle of the antiestablishment clause is, like that of the free exercise clause, a principle that limits state power to the pursuit of the all-purpose goods in keeping with equal respect for the diverse ways that our moral powers of rationality and reasonableness may define and pursue our ends. The specific concern of the antiestablishment clause is that, in contexts of belief formation and revision, the state not illegitimately (nonneutrally) endorse any one conception (whether religious or secular) from among the range of conceptions of a life well and humanely lived that express our twin moral powers of rationality and reasonableness. For this reason, the antiestablishment principle rejects as its criterion any such substantive conception, and requires that state power in the relevant contexts pursue the general goods consistent with rational and reasonable choice of any such conception. The antiestablishment principle, properly understood, distinguishes such general goods from such substantive conceptions. For this reason, state support of the general goods (medical care, and so on) sponsored by religious groups does not violate this principle.[185]

183. Indeed, we properly see the judiciary's supposition of an inconsistency between these institutions and modern conceptions of distributive justice as an interpretive blunder, a failure to understand what those institutions are and require. Among these now discredited and overruled decisions are *Carter v. Carter Coal*, 298 U.S. 238 (1936) (New Deal maximum hours/minimum wages legislation for coal industry held in excess of Congress's commerce clause powers, thus unconstitutionally trenching on powers of states) and *United States v. Butler*, 297 U.S. 1 (1936) (New Deal legislation, inducing farmers to limit productive acreage, violates reserved rights of states).
184. Cf. Giannella, "Religious Liberty, Nonestablishment, and Doctrinal Development: Part II," pp. 554–561.
185. See, e.g., *Bradfield v. Roberts*, 175 U.S. 291 (1899).

Rather, the natural focus of establishment clause jurisprudence has been to monitor the constitutional neutrality of state involvement with early schooling, either state aid to parochial schools or the content of education in the public schools. The concern is not that schools should refrain from imposing values, but that state support for schools should refrain from endorsing values in the constitutionally illegitimate way that triggers the central historical worry that tax monies would support religious teaching. Establishment clause jurisprudence in these and related areas has struggled to articulate tests of constitutional neutrality.

Education in Public Schools

The national commitment to state support of universal public education postdates the religion clauses. Jefferson, however, clearly urged such education, and designed its form in self-conscious consistency with his antiestablishment principles. Thus, the Bill for Religious Freedom is, in the words of one historian,

> the fourth and culminating item in a tight cluster of measures designed not simply to terminate the old religious establishment but to replace it with a positive alternative. The three draft laws (numbered 79, 80, and 81) that preceded the famous one that alone became law were bills "for the More General Diffusion of Knowledge," for "Amending the Constitution [and totally reorganizing the curriculum] of the College of William and Mary;" and "for Establishing a Public Library."[186]

With the termination of state funding of religious teaching in the Bill for Religious Freedom, Jefferson's proposal in the "Bill for the More General Diffusion of Knowledge" was for public education that steeped the young in secular republican morality. In express opposition to the use of the Bible as the reading primer employed theretofore in Virginia, Jefferson's plan required,

> At every of these schools, the books which shall be used . . . for instructing the children to read shall be such as will at the same time make them acquainted with Graecian, Roman, English, and American history.[187]

Jefferson's proposal for the College of William and Mary, and his later active role, with Madison, in planning the University of Virginia were

---

186. Isaac, *The Transformation of Virginia, 1740–1790*, pp.293–94,. See, for these bills, Boyd, ed., *Papers of Thomas Jefferson 1777–1779*, vol. 2, pp. 526–53.
187. Boyd, ed., *Papers of Thomas Jefferson 1777–1779*, vol. 2, p. 528.

to similar effect.[188] Antiestablishment values require that public support of education must limit itself to those programs of a general educational usefulness which any good education (religious or nonreligious) must offer. State support of public education must limit itself to imparting the general educational goods that develop our rational and reasonable powers, and avoid endorsing specific substantive conceptions that those powers should adopt.[189]

Clearly, drawing the distinction between general educational goods and substantive sectarian conceptions is historically controversial, may shift over time, and has been drawn in constitutionally nonneutral ways.[190] But if the line can sensibly be drawn, antiestablishment values require us to observe it. Three recent contexts of controversy show that acceptable lines can be drawn: release time, school prayer, and the debates over teaching Darwinian evolution.

We have noted that the interpretation of the background right of conscience may shift over time. For example, Jefferson and Madison extended the right to atheists and Catholics, whereas Locke and Bayle did not. Correspondingly, our constitutional community, in which this right enjoys a focal interpretive significance, has changed its conception of this abstract ideal over time to accommodate shifts in the rela-

188. See, for a general overview, Levy, *Judgments* pp. 209–14. For the College of William and Mary curriculum, Jefferson proposed abolition of both the school of theology with its professorships of religion and the school for teaching Indians. For the former, he substituted a professor of moral philosophy and another of civil and ecclesiastical history. For the latter, he proposed a missionary whose business was not to teach religion, but to engage in anthropological research and report to the university. For the University of Virginia, a similar curriculum was provided with no professor of divinity, such teaching being left to independent colleges supported by sects around the university. A university room was to be designated for religious services on condition that students used it in the mornings prior to class attendance. In fact, Jefferson, as rector of the university, refused to allow such rooms to be used for Sunday services, claiming that the previous plan had been superseded by one calling for students to attend services at one of the surrounding divinity schools. *Ibid.*, pp. 212–14. As rector, Madison only permitted the university to appoint a chaplain when he was paid by students themselves on a voluntary basis. *Ibid.*, p. 214.
189. Jefferson was not inconsistent in supporting federal aid to religious groups that proselytized the Indians. See Cord, *Separation of Church and State*, pp. 38–46. Jefferson—historically remarkable in extending universal toleration to Catholics and atheists—may have drawn the line at a preliterate culture which was also a potentially hostile and violent enemy. Aid to proselytizing religions, otherwise questionable, advanced secular purposes when these religions were one of the only historically feasible educators of the hostile culture in peaceful acculturation. Jefferson may have been wrong in entertaining such beliefs about what was fact, but—given such beliefs—he was not inconsistent in regarding such state aid as serving constitutionally neutral purposes.
190. For example, the dominance of the American public school during much of its history by the Protestant Bible was nonneutrally contemptuous of Catholics and Jews. See "Introduction," pp. vi–xvii, McCloskey, *The Bible in the Public Schools*.

tion of ethics and religion, developments in Bible interpretation and science, and the like. Consequently, the common sense of one historical period—for example, the neutral centrality of Bible reading in public schools to good moral education—in the eyes of the next generation is constitutionally illegitimate state support of sectarian religion.

Both release time for religious teaching in public schools[191] and school prayer in public schools[192] illustrate this underlying interpretive shift. Today, our powers of rational and reasonable conscience do not necessarily require for their development religious training or school prayer. The imposition by the public schools of either Bible reading or prayer generally is, therefore, an endorsement by the state of one substantive conception of the good and decent life, compromising the rational independence of conscience formation and revision required by equal respect.

The constitutional assessment of the battles over the science curriculum of public schools requires a working criterion of educational programs that secure general educational goods to encompass the diverse ways in which rational and reasonable conscience may be formed. The exclusion of Darwinian evolution from the public schools is not, by this criterion, a hard case, and was quite properly struck down by the Supreme Court as a violation of the anti-establishment clause.[193] Scientific method is, as I argued in the preceding chapter, a natural development of our capacities of epistemic rationality. One of the minimum epistemic responsibilities of good education is the cultivation of the epistemic rationality of students; and the teaching of good scientific method is one crucial organon for imparting and cultivating principles

191. See *McCollum v. Board of Education*, 333 U.S. 203 (1948) (release time for religious instruction on the site of the public school held violative of the antiestablishment clause). But cf. *Zorach v. Clauson*, 343 U.S. 306 (1952) (such release time for religious instruction away from the site of the public school not violative of the antiestablishment clause). The dissent in *Zorach* expresses, I believe, the better view, focusing on the fact that the release time was supported by the force of the compulsory education laws of the state. There would and should, in my judgment, be no objection to purely voluntary such programs unsupported by state force or endorsement. Cf. also *Grand Rapids School District v. Ball*, 53 U.S.L.W. 5006, 105 S.Ct. 3216, 466 U.S.—(1985) ("shared time" program of public school teachers teaching on premises of parochial schools and "community education" state program of parochial school teachers teaching on premises of parochial schools after hours held violative of anti-establishment clause).
192. See *Engel v. Vitale*, 370 U.S. 421 (1962) (use of state-composed "non-denominational" prayer in public schools held violative of antiestablishment clause); *Abington School Dist. v. Schempp*, 374 U.S. 203 (1963) (reading of selections from Bible and Lord's Prayer in public schools violative of antiestablishlment); *Wallace v. Jaffree*, 53 U.S.L.W. 4665, 105 S.Ct. 2479, 466 U.S.—(1985) (state authorization of one-minute period of silence in public schools "for meditation or voluntary prayer" held violative of anti-establishment clause). Cf. *Stone v. Graham*, 449 U.S. 1104(1980) (state statute requiring posting of Ten Commandments in public school classrooms violative of anti-establishment).
193. See *Epperson v. Arkansas*, 393 U.S. 97 (1968) (state statute forbidding teaching of evolution in public schools violative of antiestablishment clause).

of epistemic rationality. Scientific method is precisely that: a neutral method that, like any good critical technique, deepens our critical rationality, our capacity to follow out reason even against our preconceptions. The absolute bar on teaching Darwin in public schools was motivated by a sectarian religious view of Bible interpretation.[194] This interpretive perspective supposed Darwinian theory, one of the best-evidenced scientific theories of its kind,[195] to be inconsistent with the truth of and belief in the Bible, an interpretation itself disputed by many religious believers in the Bible.[196] A constitutional tradition, shaped by argument honoring Galileo's defense of empiricist rationality against the abuse of Bible interpretation, must find any state intervention on such grounds resonant with its historical understanding of central political evils of state nonneutrality.[197] Accordingly, such an exclusion from the science curriculum is a clear violation of the principle of the antiestablishment clause. A neutral educational good, training in scientific method, is distorted by a substantive sectarian belief.

More recent controversy is over compulsory inclusion of creationist science in the science curriculum together with teaching Darwinian evolution, and appears to raise a more interesting question than the wholesale exclusion of Darwin. The issue is not a sectarian exclusion of a neutral educational good, but a more equal dialogue among points of view on scientific truth, method, and inquiry. But this appearance is constitutionally illusory. The dialogue called for is not an intrascientific dispute relevant to the educational mission of a science curriculum. The federal judiciary has, accordingly, quite properly found such statutes violative of the antiestablishment clause.[198]

194. See, e.g., Hofstadter, *Anti-intellectualism in American Life*, pp. 81–136. See, in general, Sandeen, *The Roots of Fundamentalism;* Marsden, *Fundamentalism and American Culture;* Marsden, "Everyone's Own Interpreter—The Bible, Science, and Authority in Mid-Nineteenth-Century America"; Weber, "The Two-Edged Sword: The Fundamentalist Use of the Bible."
195. See, in general, Mayr, *The Growth of Biological Thought.*
196. See Marty, *Righteous Empire*, pp. 188–198, Weber, "The Two-Edged Sword: The Fundamentalist Use of the Bible," pp. 36–44; Fackre, *The Religious Right and Christian Faith;* Ong, *Darwin's Vision and Christian Perspectives.*
197. For example, Milton, whose *Areopagitica* is one of the central works shaping our traditions of free speech, cites Galileo, whom he visited, as a central example of the effects of the political evil of licensing and censorship. See p. 306, *Areopagitica,* in Patrick, ed., *The Prose of John Milton.* On Protestant identification of the persecution of Galileo with all they hated in "Popery," see p. 52, Bozeman, *Protestants in an Age of Science.* See, in general, on Galileo's view of commonsense rationality and the orthodox and proper limits of Bible interpretation, Drake, *Galileo.* See also de Santillana, *The Crime of Galileo.*
198. See *McLean v. Arkansas Board of Education,* 529 F. Supp. 1255 (E.D. Ark. 1982) (statute requiring balanced treatment to be given creation science and evolution science held violative of antiestablishment clause). Cf. *Daniel v. Waters,* 515 F.2d 485 (6th Cir. 1975) (statute requiring that evolution science may only be taught with disclaimer that theory and biblical account be given equal emphasis held violative of antiestablishment clause).

Creationist science is not science in the sense that is of interest to the educational mission of the public schools. It is not training in a neutral method of critical inquiry, expressive of our capacities of epistemic rationality, whose educational importance is training our capacities of critical rationality to follow reason wherever it leads, upsetting and challenging beliefs and preconceptions. Creationist science is science only of interest to a sectarian religious believer with absolute certitude about the truth of a certain view of Bible interpretation. Its point is to show how its view of the truth of the Bible *could* be rendered consistent with the scientific record.[199] But this kind of distortion of a neutral educational good by a substantive conception of sectarian religious belief is the same violation of the principle of the antiestablishment clause that motivated the exclusion of Darwinian evolution from the educational curriculum. As such, the inclusion of creationist science in a science curriculum is equally wrong constitutionally.

Believers in creationist science are not, of course, demented in any sense, nor are their beliefs necessarily irrational by the criteria for rational religious belief discussed in the previous chapter. They are rigorously committed to two central principles of American Protestantism of the nineteenth century: a Baconian conception of scientific method and a certain literal reading of and belief in the truth of the biblical narrative.[200] Scientific method has, of course, moved well beyond Baconian inductivism (if it ever adhered to it), and most Protestants now hold different views of Bible interpretation and how it relates to scientific findings.[201] Believers in creationist science are not necessarily irrational in taking a different view. They try, rather, to show how their commitment to faith and science is not ruled out by minimum epistemic criteria and might reasonably be defended as an integration of their will to believe, in James's sense, in science, ethics, and the Bible, endowing their personal lives with grace and their moral lives with rigor.

However, consistent with the antiestablishment clause, it is not the task of the state to endorse such intramural sectarian argument, nor is it the task of public education to relieve the tensions and perplexities to which a good education may give rise. Perhaps public education best realizes its virtues when it most fully imparts what a method of critical rationality, like science or philosophy, can and does mean to the widening autonomy of our moral powers. Perhaps, also, it best serves reli-

199. For an excellent analysis of the empirical claims of creationist science to this effect, see Kitcher, *Abusing Science: The Case Against Creationism*. See also Futuyama, *Science on Trial;* Godfrey, ed., *Scientists Confront Creationism;* Montagu, ed., *Science and Creationism*.
200. See, for the best general treatment, Bozeman, *Protestants in an Age of Science*.
201. Ibid., pp. 166–167. See works cited in notes 108 and 109, above. See also Neill, *The Interpretation of the New Testament, 1861–1961;* Barr, *The Bible in the Modern World;* Hutchison, *The Modernist Impulse in American Protestantism;* Richardson, "The Rise of Modern Biblical Scholarship and Recent Discussion of the Authority of the Bible."

gion if, as Pascal and Kierkegaard argue, understanding the critical limits of rationality and religion is the tension that nourishes a living
faith.[202] Surely, for Kierkegaard, established religion was the death of a
living faith.[203] So understood, the antiestablishment criterion (advancing a secular, not religious purpose) misdescribes its aim, which no
more sanctifies the secular than it attacks the religious. The issue,
rather, is the protection of moral independence of any kind (secular and
religious) in the direction of one's spiritual life.[204] Thus, the constitutional focus of public education on general educational goods is not
based on a philosophy of secularism as an ultimate or final good, but on
an ascetic educational discipline which makes possible the moral freedom that Western culture values in the personal integrity of religious
conscience and belief.[205]

Aid to Parochial Schools
Many constitutional commentators today question the Supreme Court's
constraints, grounded in the antiestablishment clause, on state aid to
parochial elementary and secondary schools.[206] The standard argument
is this. Education is a general good in a democratic society, and parochial schools provide education comparable to and sometimes better
than that offerred by public schools.[207] It should not therefore violate
the neutrality principles of the antiestablishment clause for the state to
give financial aid to religious schools at least in an amount that covers
that aspect of the education which is a general good (for example, training in basic epistemic skills).[208] The argument is not that state aid to the

202. See, in general, Pascal, *Pensees;* Kierkegaard, *Concluding Unscientific Postscript.*
203. See Kierkegaard, *Attack Upon "Christendom."*
204. The secular/religious test of antiestablishment neutrality wrongly suggests a dichot-
omy between the contemporary forms of our religious and secular lives. In fact, the secularization, which shapes both our religious and secular sensibilities, is fueled by peculiarly Western, antiontocratic religious concerns of respect for person. See van Leeuwen,
Christianity in World History.
205. See note 204, above; cf. Newman, *Foundations of Religious Tolerance,* pp. 83–84.
206. See, e.g., *Lemon v. Kurtzman,* 403 U.S. 602 (1971) (state statutes paying salaries of
teachers in nonpublic schools or reimbursing such schools for teachers' salaries, text-
books, and instructional materials held violative of antiestablishment clause). But cf. *Committee for Public Education. v. Regan,* 444 U.S. 646 (1980) (state reimbursement for test-
ing and reporting services required by state not violative of antiestablishment); *Mueller
v. Allen* 463 U.S. 388 (1983) (state statute allowing parents to deduct expenses for tui-
tion, etc. for sending children to such schools not violative of anti-establishment). In general, the Court has been much more hospitable to aid to higher education sponsored by
religious groups. See, e.g., *Tilton v. Richardson,* 403 U.S. 672 (1971) (federal construction grants to religious colleges held constitutional).
207. See, e.g., Coleman, Hoffer, and Kilgore, *High School Achievement: Public, Catholic,
and Private Schools Compared.*
208. See, e.g., Choper, "The Establishment Clause and Aid to Parochial Schools";
Nowak, "The Supreme Court, the Religion Clauses, and the Nationalization of Education"; Katz, *Religion and American Constitutions,* pp. 72–78; Kauper, *Religion and the
Constitution,* pp. 109–113.

religious classes in such schools could be squared with the Constitution. Rather, those aspects of the education, resonating in general educational goods, may justly be supported by the state.

The simplest answer to this argument is that it supposes a distinction that cannot constitutionally be drawn. The point of such early education is the infusion of all education with a religious shape and spirit; at this level, such education, is, in contrast to safety or health care, peculiarly sectarian in ideological purpose and effect. For this reason, any attempt by the state to distinguish various "secular" and "religious" components of the education rendered is unreal and would implicate the state in the demarcation and supervision of such components in an independently unconstitutional way.[209] The state not only would inextricably support religious teaching as such, but would do so by making ideologically nonneutral judgments on the character and shape of religious education (the secular versus religious component). Such accountability to state standards is, as Jefferson warned, not only a corruption of state power, but a degradation of both the integrity and independence of religious education itself. The argument of principle here is forthright. State support of sectarian religious teaching at the stage of belief formation and revision is at the heart of the values protected by the antiestablishment clause—and that is what state aid to parochial education is.

There is, however, another argument not so easily dismissed, one itself grounded in an appreciation of the distinctive role of the antiestablishment clause in religion clause jurisprudence.[210] This argument grants, indeed insists, that the antiestablishment clause is centrally concerned with the state imposition of sectarian values, inducing belief formation or revision. Aid to parochial education does not instantiate this evil, however, for parents who send children to parochial schools are often committed religious believers. Such aid would not induce them in any constitutionally suspicious way. To the contrary, the lack of aid to parochial schools burdens parents' free exercise rights, since sending their children to such schools is expressive of their central religious commitments. One commentator expressed this latter point even more starkly: the antiestablishment prohibition on aid to parochial schools

209. Cf. Freund, "Public Aid to Parochial Schools"; Giannella, "Religious Liberty, Nonestablishment, and Doctrinal Development: Part II," pp. 572–581. For a recent case in which these considerations are given great weight, see *Aguilar v. Felton*, 53 U.S.L.W. 5013, 105 S.Ct. 3232, 466 U.S.—(1985) (federal program paying salaries of public school teachers who teach remedial classes in parochial schools held violative of antiestablishment clause). Judge Friendly's opinion for the Second Circuit, affirmed by *Aguilar*, is even more explicit on these points. See *Felton v. Secretary, U.S. Department of Education*, 739 F.2d 48. (2d Cir. 1984)
210. See Schwarz, "No Imposition of Religion"; also his "The Nonestablishment Principle: A Reply to Professor Giannella."

evinces the incipient totalitarianism that children are the property of the state, thus violating natural parental rights and duties.[211]

This argument is, I believe, fallacious precisely in the point on which it insists: the moral unit of analysis is and must be the parent. This belies the morally sensitive issue that absorbs antiestablishment argument at the level of basic education; namely, that basic education is the psycho-social stage with the most pervasive impact on belief formation and revision by the child. The concern of the antiestablishment clause is not that parents impose values (religious or nonreligious) on their children, nor that parents themselves support religious schools with the intent that religious values will be imparted there. Indeed, the constitutional right of parents to send their children to such schools, according to state minimum education requirements, gives proper weight to the legitimate interest of parents in shaping the religious and moral life of their children.[212] But it is a non sequitur to infer from the degree of parental value imposition which is legitimate that the state may itself endorse, inconsistent with equal respect, such value imposition in a context at the heart of the historical understanding and political theory of antiestablishment.

Both the Lockean political theory so central to the religion clauses and the ideology of release from patriarchal bondage of the revolutionary period suggest that basic democratic ideals of respect for persons must restrain the extravagant abuse of paternalistic arguments by monarchist political theorists, for example, Robert Filmer.[213] Even natural parents, Locke insists, have duties of educating their children to rational independence, whereupon the child is emancipated from parental rule.[214] Children, for Locke, are neither the property of their parents nor of the state, both of whom are under moral obligations to them to assure the appropriate care and development of their moral powers. The rights and obligations of parents are not the measure of those of the state. Both are rooted in independent and often countervailing principles concerned to ensure a proper balance of respect for children and their developmental rights.[215]

The antiestablishment clause expresses one such independent principle: state support of basic education at the stage crucial for belief formation and revision must not support sectarian teaching of any kind.

---

211. See Murray, "Law or Prepossessions?", pp. 36–37

212. *Pierce v. Society of Sisters*, 268 U.S. 510 (1925) so holds.

213. The best general study is Fliegelman, *Prodigals and Pilgrims: The American Revolution against Patriarchal Authority, 1750–1800*. For pertinent discussion, see Richards, "The Individual, the Family, and the Constitution," pp. 11–31.

214. See pp. 321–336, Locke, *Second Treatise of Government*, in *Two Treatises of Government*. See, in general, Tarcov, *Locke's Education for Liberty*.

215. See, for general discussion, Richards, "The Individual, the Family, and the Constitution."

The presence of vulnerable children, already subject to parental value imposition, suggests, if anything, the gravest sort of violation of establishment clause neutrality by the public commitment of state resources to the endorsement of sectarian education. On contractarian principles, the state has a legitimate interest in, perhaps even a duty to make available, the kind of education that Jefferson supposed to be necessary for democratic self-rule. That responsibility requires that state support of education must observe constitutional neutrality. That parents want state support of religious education no more removes the taint of state endorsement from such support than a multiple establishment, for Jefferson, was constitutionally neutral because of "the forcing him to support this or that teacher of his own persuasion."[216] The interpretation of the issue as one of the free exercise rights of parents is the assimilation of antiestablishment to free exercise to which I have taken objection. Both clauses have their proper place and role in securing equal respect for the background right of conscience; neither can or should be reduced to the other.

Of Tax Exemptions, Legislative Prayer, and Creches

My argument has, in general, defended much of the recent religion clause jurisprudence of the Supreme Court, though sometimes with criticisms of its way of formulating, explicating, and limiting doctrinal development. However, the Court's work in other areas of establishment clause jurisprudence is not, I believe, consistent with the principles so far discussed. Education is understandably the most constitutionally sensitive area for establishment clause purposes. Perhaps it is enough that the Court's work in this area is defensible. But a court with the power of the Supreme Court should be held to the highest standards of arguments of principle. We should, therefore, be clear where, when, and why it has failed us and itself.

We may organize critical discussion around a common interpretive mistake in the appeal to history, which will tie together various points about the role of historiography and political theory in constitutional interpretation. This mistake is a form of Berger's abuse of history earlier examined, namely, the ascertainment of Founders' language or later applications of general language (usually achieved by counting up various relevant interpretive moments) and the supposition that such applications are interpretively binding for us. I have, of course, denied that Founders' applications should enjoy such authoritative interpretive force. In each case, rather, we must evaluate such applications in terms of the background principles and political theory they reflect and

---

216. Accordingly, it should be constitutionally irrelevant, in my judgment, that certain tax deductions applicable to parental expenses for parochial school education are initiated by the parent. For this reason, the majority opinion in *Mueller v. Allen*, 463 U.S. 388 (1983), which gives this consideration great weight in upholding the constitutionality of such deductions, is wrong.

assess independently how those principles apply to us. In some cases, Founders' applications should, on such grounds, not bind us. For example, Madison's presidential veto of the incorporation of a church, on antiestablishment grounds, reflects the then historical practice of particularized legislative incorporations, which raises constitutional problems of religious preference.[217] However, our current practice of general incorporation statutes for all forms of nonprofit corporations would not and should not raise establishment clause difficulties.[218] On examination, Madison's interpretive application, sound in his day, is demonstrably not sound in ours. Founders' applications, as such, do not bind us. We may now further see the point of that earlier denial in the Court's distorted interpretation of such applications in several areas of antiestablishment clause jurisprudence.

The interpretive line is roughly this. The Court reviews interpretive practice in the early constitutional period or later, and discovers what it usually calls an unbroken line of precedent to the effect, for example, that tax exemptions for religious groups,[219] or prayers in legislatures by chaplains paid by the state,[220] or state sponsorship of days of religious thanksgiving were acceptable.[221] The contrary views of Jefferson or Madison, expressed and acted on during their respective presidential tenures, are dismissed as inconsistent with larger patterns of interpretive practice; or such views, expressed at other points sometimes late in their lives as private citizens, are construed to deserve less interpretive weight than their actions as public servants. In effect, the argument is posed, sometimes quite starkly, as a totaling of interpretive moments. But this style of interpretation is incoherent. It offers no theory of why something counts as an interpretive moment, no conception of weight, and no idea of how these moments are to be cumulatively assessed. At its worst, the interpretive style degenerates into a kind of impressionistic grab bag of disconnected precedents. Indeed, the problem with this style is the absence of interpretation at all. No attempt is made to connect abstract arguments of principle with the historical context of application, and thus justice is not done to what our history means or should be taken to mean. In consequence, a kind of parroting of precedent substitutes for the interpretive dignity of doctrinal elaboration of arguments of constitutional principle.

The historical tradition of tax exemptions for religious groups, for example, dates from a period when our constitutional community

217. See Brant, "Madison: On the Separation of Church and State," p. 18.
218. Cf. Giannella, "Religious Liberty, Nonestablishment, and Doctrinal Development: Part II," p. 522.
219. *Walz v. Tax Commission of the City of New York*, 397 U.S. 664 (1970) (property tax exemptions for religious groups held constitutional).
220. *Marsh v. Chambers*, 463 U.S.703 (1983) (legislative prayer by chaplain paid by state held not violative of antiestablishment clause).
221. *Lynch v. Donnelly*, 465 U.S.668 (1984) (Christmas display of creche by city held not violative of antiestablishment clause).

regarded such institutions as the vehicles of general community goods: various welfare functions, and moral training. This historical tradition, which was the basic ground for the Court's upholding such exemptions, cannot be decisive today. Many of the historical welfare functions of religious groups are now transferred to the state; and as we have seen, religious and ethical thinking are sufficiently disjointed today that their nonneutral identity can no longer be constitutionally assumed. I do not, of course, question that those neutral services rendered by religions should, *pro tanto*, receive whatever exemptions are appropriate for services of that kind (for example, for hospitals). But a blanket exemption for religions is the clear equivalent today of a multiple establishment, that is, financial support for religious teaching as such, a public endorsement inconsistent with the kind of free choice of conscience formation and change that the establishment clause commands.[222] If state aid to parochial schools is the just subject of establishment clause scrutiny, tax deductions—which directly aid religions themselves—must, in principle, be constitutionally limited to their secular functions. The required showing of distinct secular functions, which this analysis would require, is no more than any comparable group must show, and no less than constitutional neutrality commands. The Supreme Court's attempt to read this requirement as an "entanglement" itself violative of antiestablishment is circular.[223] It assumes, in a striking non sequitur, that making such distinctions would be more violative of constitutional neutrality than the current system of tax exemptions. In effect, the degree to which the continued tax exemption of religions no longer reflects the reasonable grounds internal to that historical self-understanding is distortively suppressed by the Court's question-begging rhetoric of "entanglement."

The continuation of the tradition of prayers in the legislature by chaplains paid by the state reflects a similarly anachronistic retention of a practice without any principled historical self understanding. Prayers in the legislature made principled sense in a historical period that could plausibly identify, as Washington did in his Farewell Address, religion with republican morality.[224] But that practice lacks an interpretive sense worth following when that assumption is no longer reasonable. For the same reason that prayers in the public schools no longer reflect a principled conception of neutral educational goods, prayers by paid chaplains in the legislature publicly endorse a sectarian perspective. That endorsement is inconsistent with our public philosophy of constitutional neutrality, a philosophy that our legislative practice should, above all, respect. Such a context of state endorsement advocates forms of conscience formation and revision, among which the state—consistent with equal respect—should remain neutral. In con-

222. Cf. Hook, *Religion in a Free Society*, pp. 71–90.
223. *Walz v. Tax Commission of the City of New York*, 397 U.S. 664, 674 (1970).
224. See Stokes, *Church and State in the United States*, vol. 1, pp. 494–95.

trast, state-supported chaplains in the armed services should not be subject to comparable objection.[225] The circumstances of army life, which deprive service people of their normal liberties (including free exercise interests), justify the removal of unfair burdens on such liberties. Here state support does not unwarrantably endorse sectarian values but fairly accommodates various forms of conscience in a way unjustly prejudicial to none.

Finally, the tradition of state sponsorship of days of religious thanksgiving was, of course, historically controversial. Jefferson, as president, refused to endorse it; Madison was conscience-struck that he had not forthrightly resisted the practice.[226] In any event, the historical meaning this practice had for our constitutional community cannot reasonably survive the secularization of ethical values which has, as we have seen, shifted our conception of constitutional neutrality in so many other areas. Accordingly, the Court's 1984 endorsement, in a 5 to 4 opinion, of state sponsorship of a creche at Christmastime, on the ground of the historical practice of such state-sponsored religious thanksgivings, is interpretively anachronistic, all the more because it endorses a symbol offensive to many other religious groups.[227] The majority's remarkable characterization of the creche as a secular symbol begs the question in a way that might have been acceptable when Justice Story wrote of Protestant Christianity as our de facto established church.[228] Today, however, state display of a creche instantiates the central evil against which the establishment clause stands. As Madison commented,

> It degrades from the equal rank of Citizens all those whose opinions in Religion do not bend to those of the Legislative authority.[229]

The occasion of this scandalous opinion is the most blatant example, among those so far discussed, of the interpretive technique of cumulating interpretive moments. Chief Justice Warren Burger, writing for the majority, cumulates a historical record. He studiously avoids the interpretation of that record. Such interpretation requires making sense of the principles which that record reflects, an inquiry that would have disciplined the reasoning of the Court by the kind of argument of principle this opinion travesties. There can be no clearer example of how the disengagement of historiography from political theory unmoors constitutional argument from its interpretive responsibilities. Ad hoc

225. But cf. Giannella, "Religious Liberty, Nonestablishment, and Doctrinal Development: "Part II," p. 225.
226. Levy, *Judgments*, pp. 207–8.
227. *Lynch v. Donnelly*, 465 U.S. 668 (1984).
228. Whom the Court, remarkably, cites, 465 U.S. at 678.
229. *Memorial and Remonstrance Against Religious Assessment*, in Meyers, ed., *The Mind of the Founder*, pp. 10–11.

historiography is here the expressive vehicle of unreflective majoritarian religious conceptions, concealed by the ideology of Founders' intent which makes sense neither of that intent nor of its meaning for us.

The theme of this and the preceding chapter has been to establish the moral and constitutional primacy of religious toleration. The place of such toleration among moral and constitutional values reflects, I have argued, both a moral and constitutional argument. In chapter 4, the moral argument identified and explicated equal respect for the inalienable right to conscience as a central human right. This chapter has argued that this moral right is, in fact, a background constitutional right, in Dworkin's sense, underlying and making interpretive sense of the religion clauses of the First Amendment. Through this style of argument, I have tried to show how and why political theory has a central place in American constitutional interpretation.

But the primacy of religious toleration, among moral and constitutional values, can only be fully understood when the argument of these two chapters is shown to order and illuminate other significant moral and constitutional rights. Religious toleration will be seen to have the primacy that I believe it to have when we can see this model of analysis as the background conception implicit in much other moral and constitutional argument, which it both explains and clarifies. If this task can be met, a general political theory will, in a way some have denied possible, make the best interpretive sense of our constitutional traditions. In subsequent chapters, I propose reasons of both a normative and descriptive kind for believing that the primacy of religious toleration organizes our moral and constitutional thought about other important liberties of thought, speech, and action.

III / Free Speech

6 · A Theory of
Free Speech

In the previous two chapters, I developed an interpretive theory of the religion clauses based on a background right of conscience. In this and the next chapter I show how the structure of interpretive argument, as proposed for the jurisprudence of the religion clauses, affords both abstract and concrete clarification of the interpretation of the constitutional guarantees of free speech and press. It is more than a textual accident that the language of the First Amendment unites the protections of religious liberty with these and other guarantees:

> Congress shall make no law respecting an establishment of religion, or prohibiting the free exercise thereof; or abridging the freedom of speech or of the press; or the right of the people peaceably to assemble, and to petition the government for a redress of grievances.

Implicit in the theory of the primacy of religious toleration is the theory of the free speech and free press clauses. It is a matter of common principle that many of the applicable tests for free speech evolved from religion clause jurisprudence.[1] The point is not just that some early free

1. For example, the clear and present danger test, central to the jurisprudence of free speech, was inchoately stated in Jefferson's Bill for Religious Freedom, as follows: ". . . it is time enough for the rightful purposes of civil government for its civil officers to interfere when principles break out into overt acts against peace and good order," p. 546, Boyd, ed., *The Papers of Thomas Jefferson 1777–1779*. For historical links between arguments for liberty of conscience and free speech, see Levy, *Emergence of a Free Press*, pp.102–3, 163–166, 193–5, 285–6, 315–23.

speech cases are also understood by the Court as free exercise cases,[2] or that cases very like compulsory abridgment of free exercise are construed by the Court as free speech cases.[3] More fundamentally, the right to conscience, interpretively central to religion clause jurisprudence, is the background right that underlies the free speech guarantee as well.

I propose to defend this proposition according to the interpretive methodology of the previous chapters, first as a proposition of political and moral theory and then as an explanatory and critical principle of constitutional law. This chapter will develop a contractarian political theory of free speech and use it to clarify the historiography of the free speech and press clauses and the interpretation of the distinctive protection of subversive advocacy in American free speech jurisprudence. In the next chapter, this explanatory and critical perspective on free speech will be applied to several areas of ongoing controversy in the American constitutional law of free speech.

CONSCIENCE AND COMMUNICATIVE INTEGRITY

I have argued that a rights-based interpretation of treating persons as equals justified the inalienable right to conscience, namely, equal respect for this right of the interpretive independence of our twin moral powers of rationality and reasonableness. Correlatively, the free exercise and antiestablishment clauses afford a coordinated protection of this underlying right at the relevant stages of formation, expression, and change of conscience.

It is possible to imagine creatures, not human and/or not in the circumstances typical of human life, for whom equal respect for conscience would not justify concern for communication in its various forms. They might communicate telepathically through pure (nonlinguistic, in our sense) thought, not subject to any influence by a medium of communication. These pure intellects might value the right to conscience and free thought, and thus would recognize such constitutional protections as free exercise and antiestablishment. They would, how-

---

2. Such cases involve the right of unpopular religious minorities (such as Jehovah's Witnesses) to proselytize. See, e.g., *Lovell v. Griffin*, 303 U.S. 444 (1938); *Cox v. New Hampshire*, 312 U.S. 569 (1941). For more recent cases to similar effect, mixing free exercise and free speech analysis, see *Heffron v. International Society for Krishna Consciousness, Inc.*, 452 U.S. 640 (1981); *Schaumburg v. Citizens for a Better Environment*, 444 U.S. 620 (1980); *Widmar v. Vincent*, 454 U.S. 263 (1981).
3. Such cases, constitutionally striking down on free speech grounds compulsory affirmations of belief, also encroach on compulsory expression contrary to conscience, a value at the core of free exercise values. See, e.g., *Board of Education v. Barnette*, 319 U.S. 624 (1943); *Wooley v. Maynard*, 430 U.S. 705 (1977).

ever, see no corresponding point in a right to free speech. Their natures and situation would not give rise to the kind of connection between respect for persons and free speech that is the case with us.

For us, rationality itself flows from our capacities for speech and writing and from an appropriately supportive material and cultural environment for their cultivation and exercise.[4] Both practical and epistemic rationality are expressed through speech and writing, which make possible reflection about our ends, reasoning about our beliefs, and, in general, the imaginative constructions of reality that, in art, science, and religion, are literally our "ways of worldmaking."[5] The exercise of moral powers of rationality and reasonableness uses our capacities for speech and writing in precisely the inward way that such powers of telepathic intelligences, *ex hypothesi*, do not.

Moreover, in important causal ways whose nature has only recently come under sustained study,[6] the media through which we communicate (for example, phonetic script, books, and other print media) transform our capacity, both as individuals and as communities, to explore and innovate rational thought, including the forms and range of self-consciousness, experience, and imagination. Phonetic script may, for example, have made possible the critical self-consciousness called philosophy and much else in history, art, mathematics, and science that the Greek genius introduced into the foundations of the civilization we call Western.[7] And the printing press, as Elizabeth Eisenstein's important study attests,[8] made available knowledge preservation, comparison, and dissemination, which transformed the sense of cultural reality and identity of whole communities. Western culture, for example, changed its conception of the authority of ancients and moderns, and experienced cumulative and cooperative knowledge and thus came to view progress as a regulative cultural and social ideal. In consequence, the culture found new ways of reading its central texts (Bible criticism, for example), and enjoyed the widespread literacy so hospitable to the growth of democratic practice and theory.[9]

---

4. See, e.g., Bennett, *Rationality;* and his *Linguistic Behaviour.*
5. Goodman, *Ways of Worldmaking.* See also Putnam, *Reason, Truth and History.*
6. See, e.g., Goody, *Literacy in Traditional Societies;* and Goody, *The Domestication of the Savage Mind;* Havelock, *Preface to Plato;* and the following books of Walter Ong: *The Presence of the Word; Rhetoric, Romance, and Technology; Inferfaces of the Word; Ramus, Method and the Decay of Dialogue;* and his important review of the burgeoning literature in *Orality and Literacy.* Recent studies include Tedlock, *The Spoken Word and the Work of Interpretation;* Stock, *The Implications of Literacy;* and, on the relationship between oral and written cultures, Todorov, *The Conquest of America.*
7. The classic study to this effect is Havelock, *Preface to Plato.*
8. See Eisenstein, *The Printing Press as an Agent of Change.*
9. On literacy, see Lockridge, *Literacy in Colonial New England.* The metainterpretive diversity, to which such widespread literacy gave rise, made the very conception of Christianity itself essentially contestable. See, in general, Sykes, *The Identity of Christianity.*

The cultivation of writing or script as such does not have any natural egalitarian or democratic implications; on the contrary, the scribal cultures of ancient Babylonia and Egypt were important bulwarks of bureacratic and theocratic centralization and domination.[10] Indeed, even a widespread literacy, subject to tyrannical control and manipulation, may more profoundly enslave the human personality than any crude external domination by threat.

It is this truth that Milton had in mind when he laid the foundations of the modern constitutional principle of free speech and press in *Areopagitica*:[11] government control of the printing press (through licensing) unleashes new demons of intellectual tyranny against which anyone (like Milton),[12] passionately committed to the inalienable right of independent religious conscience, must construct a defense. It is precisely because Milton, a great literary artist, understood that our nature as rational creatures is so intertwined with speech and other media of communication that he appreciated as well that tyrannous domination of such speech and media works the most corruptive distortion of our spiritual integrity. Accordingly, for Milton, serious moral and political defense of equal respect for our inalienable right to conscience must ground a right to free speech. We may understand the nature and weight of this right to free speech by reference to the background right of conscience it serves.

The right to conscience rests, we have seen, on equal respect for persons, interpreted by reference to the highest-order twin moral powers of rationality and reasonableness: rationality in a person's self-conception of a life well lived, reasonableness in regulating such self-conceptions by an acknowledgment of the just claims of others. This right justifies the enforceable claim to noninterference in the basic freedoms of thought and reflection that dignify self-determination by the moral powers of one's rational and reasonable nature. The American constitutional guarantees, which protect this background constitutional right, command state neutrality among forms of conscience and thus preserve the ultimate moral sovereignty of persons both over themselves and their political community. The associated political theory is contractarian. Respect for persons, thus interpreted, requires that the moral sovereignty of the person is prior to the power of the state, that the rights protective of such sovereignty must be immune from any political bargaining, and that allegiance and political obligation can be dissolved when these central rights are in peril. State-supported religious intolerance is a grave political wrong because, through it, the state usurps

10. See Goody and Watt, "The Consequences of Literacy," pp. 27–68.
11. Milton, *Areopagitica: A Speech of Mr. John Milton for the Liberty of Unlic'd Printing,* p. 265.
12. Milton, *A Treatise of Civil Power in Ecclesiastical Causes,* pp. 448–74; Milton, *Considerations Touching the Likeliest Means to Remove Hirelings from the Church,* pp. 475–518.

the independent moral authority of the person, the very ethical independence against which the legitimacy of the state's claims must ultimately be assessed.

But the ethical independence, thus protected, is, as Milton clearly saw, imperiled not only by the classic forms of Augustinian contempt for the autonomy of rational and reasonable conscience condemned by the neutrality principles of the religion clauses. It is imperiled as well by comparably nonneutral state judgments about the worth of communications that usurp a person's control over the range of communications of facts and values central to the self-determination of rational and reasonable powers. In the same way that state imposition of judgments about the worth of religious beliefs chooses one such conception among others equally reasonable, comparable state judgments of the value of communications illegitimately prejudge the nature and weight of the communications relevant to the exercise of these powers. Often such illegitimate state judgments forbid the communications most critical of state policy or the social conventions reflected in such policy. In effect, such a political force, if unchecked, would forbid those communications most relevant to the independence of critical moral judgment essential to the dignity of a free conscience. The consequence would be the perversion of underlying political values: controversial communications, most legitimately critical of the authority of the state or the community, would receive least protection when they deserve most. The necessary prophylaxis against such abuse is the same withdrawal of state power from enforceable judgments of the truth or value or reasonableness of substantive beliefs that we saw in religion clause jurisprudence. In short, the state may not restrict communicative activity based on comparable judgments about the truth or value or reasonableness of the substance of communications central to the exercise of our twin moral powers and associated conceptions of a life well and humanely lived.

On this view, the nature and weight of the right to free speech, as a basic human right, is a further elaboration of the equal respect that grounds the inalienable right to conscience.[13] For the same reason that the conscience of every person stands equal before the law, the communicative integrity of the exercise of each person's rational and reasonable powers enjoys a comparable protection. Such protections aim to disperse control of belief formation to all persons in the society, and therefore to extend to every aspect of communication (including their media) through which persons as equals may express or realize their communicative integrity in conscience formation, exercise, and revision. The right to free speech, through the focus of a general contrac-

---

13. Cf. Rawls, "The Basic Liberties and Their Priority." My account puts a rather more central emphasis on the connection of free speech to conscience than does Rawls's account.

tarian theory, reveals its nature as a kind of extrapolation of the priority
of religious freedom in American constitutional law.

Such communicative integrity, consistent with its background right,
protects decisions whether, with whom, and how to communicate both
as speaker and as audience about the issues central to our dual moral
powers of rationality and reasonableness. The right to free speech
accordingly forbids state restrictions of these communicative decisions
based on judgments about the truth, worth, or reasonableness of the
substance of such communications. In effect, such judgments are remit-
ted to the communicative integrity of the moral powers of speakers and
audiences.

The values of such communicative integrity are in play both for
speakers and audiences.[14] For speakers (and writers and other communicators), the choice of an audience is often integral to what one
communicates and to the larger agenda of one's communicative purposes and ends. Writers, for example, self-consciously write for certain
kinds of real as well as imagined audiences. The power of their imagi-
nations is often measured by how their work creates new kinds of audiences and thus communicative communities.[15] Such creative aims
include fundamental changes in the terms of discourse of communicative communities. For example, an author may seek to redefine social
concepts of respect owed and due other persons, and attempts to construct, or dignify, new images of self.[16] For these reasons, the choice of
audience is a core decision of the communicative integrity of our constructive moral powers.

The right of an audience to choose a speaker enjoys no less dignity.
Audiences must have the right to control access to those communicators whose speech or work advances the exercise of their moral powers.
Through such participation in communicative communities, we often
not only better secure our existing aims for a good and humane life, but
transform our conception of what those aims properly are.

On this conception, the communicative integrity of speakers and
audiences should not, in a just society, be a scarce commodity. On the
contrary, respect for conscience, a primary political good of a society
committed to respect for persons, requires a coordinate scope for free
speech. It is not enough that all speakers or audiences be treated

14. Redish, in "The Value of Free Speech," makes this point ably. Cf., however, Baker's
otherwise convergent account, which gives weight to the communicative integrity of
speakers, but not to audiences; Baker, "Scope of the First Amendment Freedom of
Speech"; also his "Realizing Self-Realization." For response, see Redish, "Self-Realization, Democracy, and Freedom of Expression."
15. See Ong's "The Writer's Audience Is Always a Fiction," in Ong, *Interfaces of the
Word*, pp. 53–81.
16. See Richards, "Rights, Resistance, and the Demands of Self-Respect." Cf. Baker,
"The Process of Change and the Liberty Theory of the First Amendment."

equally, for equality is consistent with minimal amounts equally distributed. To be consistent with its background right and other rights of the person, the applicable principle governing the distribution of the right to free speech must be a right to a greatest equal liberty of both speakers and audiences, with a like liberty for all.[17]

This principle of a greatest equal liberty sharply distinguishes the justifiability of two grounds familiarly urged for the abridgment of free speech: first, audience offense at what is said; second, circumstances of diminished audience responsibility. The former is, in principle, an illegitimate ground for such abridgment; the latter is a legitimate ground.

State prohibitions of speech, on the sole ground that some or many in the audience find what is said or written offensive, abridge essential free speech interests. A speaker justly claims the protection of free speech when she seeks to confront an audience in the appropriate circumstances with her views on any issue central to the exercise of her and their moral powers. This right is in play when the content of the protected communication is disturbing and offensive to the consciences of its audience, for the communication then addresses often unexercised powers of critical moral independence, that is, reflection on basic values in living. The state may no more ratify audience judgments about the worthlessness of speech by imposing restrictions on behalf of the offended audience, than it may expressly impose such judgments on its own. In either case, the state assumes what, on contractarian grounds, it lacks: the power to make judgments that restrict persons' right themselves to decide and reflect upon the conceptions central to the integrity of their personal and moral lives. Independent reflection on such issues essentially dignifies the moral powers of each person. Each person must therefore retain the inalienable right to assess such questions on one's own, which one cannot, in principle, surrender to anyone.

The offense—against which such state abridgments of speech often are directed—reflects actual disturbance to peace of mind.[18] But as we saw in chapter 4, the political principles, expressive of equal respect for persons, are not utilitarian: they not only constrain the maximization of utility that utilitarian principles require, they independently limit what may count as a political good or evil to which a just polity may give weight. From this perspective, the disturbance to one's peace of mind, inflicted on one's conscience by antagonistic expressions of conscience, is not a political evil. Such disturbance is, rather, an unavoidable ingredient of the fair distribution of the general good of the reflective independence of the exercise of one's moral powers, a

17. See Rawls, *A Theory of Justice*, ch. 4.
18. The point that speech may be harmful and that some ground must thus be found for distinguishing these harms, which free speech protects, from other harms, which it does not, is sharply posed by Schauer, *Free Speech;* also his "Must Speech Be Special?"

reflective independence that (like good education) strains, stretches, and provokes as it dignifies.

From a contractarian perspective, speech enjoys a special value and status because it is linked to the reflective exercise of our highest-order moral powers of rationality and reasonableness. The self-determination of our exercise of these capacities is a general good, enabling a person to construct personal and ethical aims that guide all other choices in life; consequently, the self-determination of our communicative integrity is a general good as well. The frustrations of conscientious disagreement are not the deprivation of a general good, but a necessary ingredient of securing equal respect for such a general good. Consistent with equal respect, such frustration is justly resolved not by repression of speech, but by the exercise of one's moral powers in rebuttal.

From a contractarian perspective, there are general goods, things that persons would demand as general conditions of whatever else they want, which may appropriately qualify the scope of free speech (see chapter 7 on reputational integrity and privacy). Conscientious agreement is not such a general good, nor are the aggravations of disagreement an evil. It is the point of respect for conscience and communicative integrity that the self-determination of our moral powers be surrendered to the judgment of no other person. The appeal to the frustrations of conscientious disagreement, as a ground for speech abridgment, is thus itself a political evil.

There should, in principle, be no comparable objection to those restrictions of communications narrowly directed at the responsibility or fair capacity of audiences adequately to consider and weigh communications as an expression of their reflective moral powers. Such restrictions are not directed against the substance of what is communicated; instead they enhance the procedural safeguards that give fair play to the moral powers of speakers and audiences. In order to reflect its proper basis in such concerns for fair deliberative procedures, such restrictions must be narrowly limited to coercion, fraud, immediate provocation, mass hysteria, and the like: well-recognized forms of either deliberative incapacity or unfair manipulation.[19] In particular, such restrictions must be carefully scrutinized to ensure that they do not conceal covert and unjustified state judgments about the value of what is communicated. The mere fact, for example, that certain speech is deeply offensive to some audience cannot justify the abridgment of speech on the ground of provocation to violence. Such abridgment would enforce judgments of the worthlessness of speech when fair procedures of rebuttal often exist, and when, in keeping with the consti-

19. See Leader, "Free Speech and the Advocacy of Illegal Action in Law and Political Theory"; Scanlon, "A Theory of Free Expression," Cf. Scanlon, "Freedom of Expression and Categories of Expression."

tutional priority of free speech, justifiable police work should protect the speaker, not the offended sensibilities of the audience.[20]

For similar reasons, there should be no objection, in principle, to those state regulations of time, place, and manner of speech not aimed at the substance of what is said, but at the fair and neutral regulation of all communications.[21] Fair procedural rules enable different speakers to be heard, and ensure that audiences have a fairer chance to hear what is said. However, the justification of such regulations must not be abused to prejudice free speech rights in general or certain such rights in particular. An evenhanded prohibition of all speech in a public forum is not a just procedural regulation but a substantive infringement of the state's duty to ensure the greatest equal liberty of free speech rights. And regulations, presumptively directed at neutral regulations of the manner of speech, may illegitimately censor the substance of what is said and meant (see chapter 7).

The utility of fair procedural regulations of speech suggests a larger moral truth about why free speech is essential to the character of political and other argument in a constitutional democracy. Faithful to its background right to conscience, effective constitutional protection of the right of communicative integrity maintains the principle of proper procedure in argument about persons' common political and social life. Such arguments should display respect for constructive exchange among equals and for each person's deliberative rationality and reasonableness.[22] The ideal of a communicative community, constituted by this conception of fair deliberative procedure, motivates the potent force that a critical and enlightened public opinion must have in constitutional democracies.[23] It explains why the very integrity of democracies calls for fair deliberative procedures surrounding free speech. A working constitutional democracy can only express its internal ideals of a moral community of equal respect when its public culture affords an adequate basis for its citizens fairly to exercise the deliberative powers of independent critical thought essential to their sovereignty over themselves and their state. A properly working system of free speech both implements and expresses these background moral values.

Such a procedural ideal cannot be separated either from the substantive moral values that actuate it or from the kinds of substantive arguments of principle to which it appeals. In both cases, the substantive moral conception of equal respect for persons requires a certain con-

---

20. Justice Black makes precisely this point in his dissent in *Feiner v. New York*, 340 U.S. 315, 321 (1951).
21. See, e.g., Meiklejohn, *Political Freedom*, pp. 24–28.
22. Cf. Ackerman, *Social Justice in the Liberal State*.
23. On the historical emergence of such a public opinion, associated with ideas of religious and political self-rule, see, in general, Michael Walzer, *The Revolution of the Saints*.

ception of fair procedure in dialogue; it also dictates the arguments of principle so common in constitutional democracies.[24] Citizens of such democracies differ in various ways about what the best arguments of principle are, and about the nature and pursuit of substantive justice. Equal respect motivates not only a fair procedure of debate (leaving conscience free and observing civility in dialogue), but a dialogue of arguments of principle that themselves pull toward equality. Thus even the most profound disagreements of a democratic people are articulated in a way that reflects their common aspirations to constitute a community of equal respect.

THE HISTORIOGRAPHY OF FREE SPEECH AND PRESS CLAUSES

The historiography of the free speech and press clauses is much less disputed than that of the religion clauses. There is nothing comparable in the history of these clauses, for example, to the revisionist historiography of the religion clauses. The difference in treatment arises from the rather articulate history surrounding the religion clauses, including the relatively clear statement and application of principles of religion clause jurisprudence both before and after approval of the Bill of Rights. Proponents of various interpretive positions on religion clause jurisprudence naturally mine this extraordinarily abundant history, for it is quite possible that something like their current position is implicit in those articulate original sources. In contrast, the contemporary scope of free speech jurisprudence extends, so it is argued, so much more protectively than any reasonable conception of the original understanding that interpretive debates must use history sparingly, if at all.[25]

The focus of such use of history tends not to be the original under-

---

24. On these arguments of principle, see, in general, Dworkin's *Taking Rights Seriously*, *A Matter of Principle*, and *Law's Empire*.
25. The most authoritative and influential statement of how limited the conception of free speech was in 1791 is Levy, *Legacy of Suppression*. Levy argues that the understanding of free speech in 1791 extended, at most, to Blackstone's conception that free speech forbade state licensing, not to criminal prosecutions for speech already said or printed. The idea that free speech might apply to such criminal prosecutions after publication is, Levy argues, a conception that postdates 1791. Although Levy argues that the First Amendment forbids Congress to make any regulation of speech whatsoever, the common law of seditious libel—enforceable by state and federal courts—is unaffected. For Levy, the congressional Sedition Act of 1798 was unconstitutional, not qua sedition act but as any regulation of speech whatsoever; such conduct would be constitutionally punishable under applicable state or federal common law. For two recent attempts to question Levy's historiography on this point, see Mayton, "Seditious Libel and the Lost Guarantee of a Freedom of Expression"; Anderson, "The Origins of the Press Clause," But see Levy, "The *Legacy* Reexamined"; Of the Origins of the Free Press Clause"; and *Emergence of a Free Press*.

standing as of 1791, or the prior history of free speech in Britain and colonial America, but later constitutional controversy. That controversy was over the effort of the Federalist Party to repress opposition newspapers through the Sedition Act of 1798, which imposed criminal sanctions on criticism of the government. Both Madison and Jefferson argued that the Sedition Act was an unconstitutional violation of free speech and press; Jefferson, when later elected president, saw to it that all fines collected under the law were returned and all persons convicted under the law were pardoned.[26] Use of this constitutional controversy today does not impute the contemporary interpretation of free speech to 1791, though the argument to that effect is rather more plausible than Leonard Levy's classic discussion of the original understanding appears to allow.[27] Rather, the political understanding, generated by the conscientious arguments of principle made by constitutionalists of the stature of Madison and Jefferson, is taken to have fixed a core understanding of the meaning of free speech that later constitutional interpreters may justly take as authoritative.[28]

Once the unconstitutionality of the Sedition Act of 1798 is taken as the central exemplar of what a violation of free speech and press is, a natural interpretive elaboration of this historical understanding is the narrower or broader limitation of the scope of speech protection to political speech critical of the government. In the narrowest reading of this history, only political speech in electoral campaigns should be protected.[29] In its more expansive reading, the scope of political speech extends to almost any area of legitimate public concern.[30] The tendency is to use the history to narrow the scope of appropriate free speech concern: constitutional guarantees of free speech and press essentially forbid the authorities of the democratic state from cutting off political criticism of itself.[31] The essence of free speech and press is its checking function on government abuses.[32]

This selective appeal to a history, admittedly postdating the Bill of Rights, distorts the significant historical dynamic that has linked, since

26. See, for commentary on the collaboration of Jefferson and Madison on the Virginia and Kentucky Resolutions, Koch, *Jefferson and Madison: The Great Collaboration*, pp. 174–220. For Madison's *Report on the Virginia Resolutions*, see Meyers, ed., *The Mind of the Founder*, pp. 229–73; see, esp., pp. 267–9 (linking conscience and free speech).
27. See, in particular, Anderson, "The Origins of the Press Clause." But see Levy, "Of the Origins of the Free Press Clause."
28. See, for example, *New York Times Co. v. Sullivan*, 376 U.S. 254 (1964). For a seminal introduction of this history into the American constitutional jurisprudence of free speech, see Justice Holmes's dissent in *Abrams v. United States*, 250 U.S. 616 (1919).
29. See Bork, "Neutral Principles and some First Amendment Problems."
30. See Meiklejohn, *Political Freedom*; also his "The First Amendment Is an Absolute," pp. 255–57, 262–63.
31. See BeVier, "The First Amendment and Political Speech: An Inquiry into the Substance and Limits of Principle."
32. See Blasi, "The Checking Value in First Amendment Theory."

Milton, free speech to the background right of conscience it serves. It fails, for example, to give appropriate interpretive value to the rich historical material connecting the long evolution of indigenously American patterns of religious thought and experience to the cumulative power of the right to conscience as a chief American political ideal (see chapter 5). That history records a characteristically American emphasis on an "experimental religion"of a free conscience and a growing hostility to the established religious orders that trammeled the Great Awakening.[33] In particular, this hostility included opposition to the attempts of the established religious and political order to impose constraints on the mobility and advocacy of the itinerant ministers and preachers of the Great Awakening, or on religious groups such as the Baptists and others later.[34] The limitation of Protestant ideas of free conscience to belief and thought alone was implicitly eroded, as seminal American thinkers, for example Jonathan Edwards, defended the right of preachers and audiences—unlimited by religious and political authority—to seek out one another.[35] For Edwards, free speech is not a vehicle of political criticism or an expression of republican ideology: it is the natural elaboration of the kind of communicative integrity that makes authentic religion and ethics possible. Free speech simultaneously expresses and provokes a vital religious and moral conscience.[36]

We distort the historical meaning of free speech in the colonial period when we limit it to seditious libel or general political criticism. If anything, the rights of conscience and free speech were, for this age, the conditions of any justice in government: they emphasized the highest-order interests of persons in their religious and moral integrity. Such rights were increasingly associated with political criticism of British oppression because British rule threatened or was perceived to threaten these and other rights.[37] The historical point is not that free

33. The phrase and similar phrases recur throughout Jonathan Edwards's *Religious Affections*, his defense of the religious experience made possible by the Great Awakening. See, e.g., pp. 113, 181, 275, 303, 451, 452 in *Religious Affections*.
34. See, in general, McLoughlin, *New England Dissent, 1630–1833*.
35. The idea was that belief and thought, being involuntary, should be immune from punishment, but expression and advocacy, causing harms to others, were subject to regulation. For a statement of this idea, see p. 188, Bury, *A History of Freedom of Thought*.
36. For Edwards's powerful influence on American political thought, see pp. 64, 212, 235, 484–89, Cobb, *The Rise of Religious Liberty in America*. For pertinent historical data linking arguments for the right to conscience to arguments for free speech, see Levy, *Emergence of a Free Press.* pp. 102–3, 163–166, 193–195, 285–6, 315–23.
37. For pertinent historical materials on this point, see Blasi, "The Checking Function in First Amendment Theory"; and Anderson,"The Origins of the Press Clause." See also Pole, *The Gift of Government.* For the profound links of American political and religious dissent, see, in general, Heimert, *Religion and the American Mind: From the Great Awakening to the Revolution.* For an interesting psychological perspective on these data, see Greven, *The Protestant Temperament.*

speech is linked to politics, but that such speech gives expression to the moral claims of a free conscience, against which state authority and everything else must be tested and assessed.

On this conception, the rights of conscience and free speech protect the moral sovereignty of the person, the self-determination of our moral powers of rationality and reasonableness in conceptions of a life well and humanely lived. This idea of the moral sovereignty of all persons over themselves and the state is naturally consolidated in the principles of American constitutional democracy, giving, as they do, central place to the protection of the right of conscience and other rights. If respect for such rights is one of the justifications for constitutional government, such government (or, the political sphere associated with such government) cannot be the measure of such rights, which rather are the measure of its legitimacy and proper scope.

The scope of the right of free speech must therefore be as broad as its background right of conscience. The progressive enlargement in the scope of the protection of conscience, discussed in the preceding chapter, dictates a corresponding scope for free speech, extending to all the issues central to the independent exercise of one's rational and moral powers. For this reason, it is deeply wrong to limit free speech to the political;[38] such a limitation trivializes the latitudinarian protection the clause should guarantee to moral independence in forming, expressing, and changing values. Many of life's most important decisions occur outside the political sphere, and free speech should secure the fullest conditions of moral freedom in all areas of life. In so doing, we protect the conditions of democratic self-rule, but also the fundamental ideals of self-rule that actuate what is most reflectively precious in constitutional democracy itself, understood now as providing the legal guarantees for a cooperative community of free, rational, and equal persons.

This conception of free speech is not at all inconsistent with the full protection of political speech. It captures much of what free speech theorist Alexander Meiklejohn may have meant to say in his quasi-contractarian conception of free speech and self-government, particularly his generous construction of the scope of free speech (extending to anything of public interest).[39] Since democratic constitutionalism rests on ideals of the moral sovereignty of the people, Jefferson, Madison, and Meiklejohn were surely correct to identify seditious libel laws as central violations of free speech: the government restricts speech on the basis of constitutionally suspect state judgments about the dangerousness of what is said. Such state judgments are doubly suspicious in a constitutional democracy: the judgments of dangerousness are cor-

---

38. This point is ably made by Kent Greenawalt in "Speech and Crime," pp. 691–91, 731, 732–37.
39. See Meiklejohn, "The First Amendment is an Absolute." This interpretation of Meiklejohn was suggested to me by Bollinger's "Free Speech and Intellecctual Values."

rupted by self-interest,[40] and prohibition of speech manipulates democratic consent.[41] In short, precisely those controversial disagreements
over the justice or good sense of government policy (essentially protected by the right of the communicative integrity of speakers and audiences) are the perverse ground for speech abridgment. Free speech,
elaborating the background right to conscience, rightly identifies such
state restrictions as central violations of free speech. As Madison, Jefferson, and Meiklejohn also understood, however, free speech includes
in its scope issues well beyond such political controversies (see chapter
7).

A contractarian political theory, linking free speech to the right to
conscience it serves, offers a better moral theory of how free speech
should be abstractly understood, and enables us to do better justice to
the interpretation of our historical traditions. In contrast, the interpretive limitation of free speech to the political rests on selective and distorting history, bad political theory, and consequently unsound constitutional interpretation. We should be struck that political theory thus
assists us in assigning a truer, less distorting sense to the political history of our constitutional community. We better understand, for example, the close historical links of conscience and free speech that cul-
minate in the coordinate provisions of the First Amendment; we assign,
in keeping with this history, more interpretive sense to the early consensus on seditious libel as a violation of free speech. Historical understanding, political theory, and constitutional interpretation work, it
seems, in tandem.

JURISPRUDENCE OF FREE SPEECH:
SUBVERSIVE ADVOCACY

If our contractarian political theory of free speech clarifies our historical understanding of this right, it should assist in the explication and
criticism of the judicial interpretation of this right. The judicial interpretation of our constitutional law is certainly not the last word on correct interpretation, but it is usefully taken as the first word. We may
therefore understand the explanatory and critical power of the
interpretive approach here taken by focusing it on such judicial interpretation. I begin with the cornerstone of current free speech jurisprudence, subversive advocacy.

---

40. Jefferson makes this point quite clearly in the Bill for Religious Freedom, noting that
making the state the judge of the bad tendency of religion "at once destroys all religious
liberty, because he being of course judge of that tendency will make his opinions the rule
of judgment," p. 546, Boyd, ed., *The Papers of Thomas Jefferson, 1777–1779.*
41. See, in general, Yudof, *When Government Speaks.* Yudof denies, however, the contractarian basis of the point, pp. 108, 151–52.

No area of free speech jurisprudence is more central to the contemporary understanding of free speech than the Supreme Court's current free speech jurisprudence on subversive advocacy, speech acts advocating illegal acts of either the obstruction of government policy or the overthrow of the government. That jurisprudence interprets a historical self-consciousness not only of the constitutional debates of 1798 over the unconstitutionality of the Sedition Act, but of striking shifts within the Supreme Court on this question in the twentieth century. The history of these interpretive shifts is instructive, for the Court's current interpretation is acutely self-conscious of earlier missteps in articulating and applying sound principles of free speech jurisprudence in this area.

The clear and present danger test, used by the Court to identify when subversive advocacy may be restricted, was introduced into First Amendment jurisprudence by Justice Holmes. In three important cases involving criminal prosecutions brought under the Espionage Act of 1917, Holmes gave the test so weak an interpretation that any showing of the "dangerous" tendency of the material written or spoken justified speech abridgment.[42] The controlling analogy, for Holmes, is shouting fire in a crowded theater[43] or the law of criminal speech,[44] neither of which raises free speech problems. Each analogy is quite unsound. The context of shouting fire in a crowded theater is certainly not the deliberative context for the circulars, newspapers, or public political speeches criminalized in these cases. And the law of criminal speech (solicitation, conspiracy, accessorial liability) applies to private, often secret speech that no one, including the criminals, supposes to be the vehicle of moral or political criticism or ideological dissent.[45] Holmes, still invoking the same test, applied it quite differently in a fourth case brought under the 1918 amendments to the Espionage Act, *Abrams v. United States*.[46] Dissenting in that case, Holmes argued that the leaflets distributed could not constitutionally be criminalized, not simply because there was no requisite intent, but because the leaflets of such "poor and puny anonymities" did not pose the requisite clear and present danger of the evil of curtailing production for the war effort.[47] In a

42. *Schenck v. United States*, 249 U.S. 47 (1919) (conviction for sending document to conscriptees urging right under the Thirteenth Amendment to resist draft); *Frohwerk v. United States*, 249 U.S. 204 (1919) (conviction for newspaper publication of article that it was a mistake to send American troops to France); *Debs v. United States*, 249 U.S. 211 (1919) (conviction for public speech about growth and success of socialism in context in which speaker had independently endorsed an antiwar proclamation).
43. See *Schenck v. United States*, 249 U.S. 47, 51 (1919).
44. See *Frohwerk v. United States*, 249 U.S. 204, 206 (1919).
45. See, in general, Greenawalt, "Speech and Crime."
46. *Abrams v. United States*, 250 U.S. 616, 624 (1919) (conviction for distribution of leaflets to workers stating that their production was supporting war efforts against the Russian Revolution).
47. Ibid., 250 U.S. 624, at 629.

number of later dissents from similar prosecutions, Holmes, joined by
Justice Brandeis, urged a more demanding showing of clear and present
danger of the illegal act before advocacy of the illegal act could be subject to criminal penalty.[48] In one of these cases, *Whitney v. California*,
Brandeis urged that the clear and present danger of the illegal act must
be not only highly probable and the illegal act very harmful, but the
force of the speech act must be not rebuttable in the normal course of
further dialogue.[49]

The point of the Holmes and Brandeis dissents was to urge a stricter
interpretation of what counted as a clear and present danger, and moreover to insist that the test applied to all forms of subversive advocacy,
however criminalized.[50] That latter position was adopted by the
Supreme Court in *Dennis v. United States*, but the interpretation given
to the test arguably was weaker than the test urged by Brandeis in
Whitney. The advocacy in *Dennis* was the knowing advocacy of the duty
to overthrow the government of the United States by members of the
American Communist Party. In dissent, Justice Douglas, joined by Justice Black, pointed out the absurdly small probability that such advocacy would result in the overthrow of the government. The responsive
position of Chief Justice Frederick Vinson, writing for the Court, was
that it sufficed that the harm posed be sufficiently grave (the overthrow
of American constitutional democracy), so that even a quite small probability yielded high expected utility (the small probability multiplied
by so grave a harm equaled a large threat).[51]

The last act in this interpretive history is *Brandenburg v. Ohio*, in
which the Court established the governing form of the clear and present danger test today.[52] In striking down a criminal prosecution of a
member of the Ku Klux Klan for advocacy of unlawful violence, the
Court found that the advocacy failed to satisfy the clear and present
danger test: the acts of unlawful violence were not imminently highly
probable in the way the test required. The *per curiam* opinion, in a way
that can only be called disingenuous, cited *Dennis* as support for this
interpretation of clear and present danger. In fact, the governing inter-

48. See, e.g., *Gitlow v. New York*, 268 U.S. 652 (1925) (conviction under state criminal
anarchy statute for publication of manifesto calling for left-wing socialism of revolutionary mass action).
49. *Whitney v. California*, 274 U.S. 357 (1927) (conviction under state criminal syndi-
calism statute for membership in Communist Labor Party which, after defendant's membership and over her objections, had endorsed terrorist tactics).
50. In *Gitlow v. New York*, 268 U.S. 652 (1925), the Supreme Court, with Holmes and
Brandeis in dissent, held that the clear and present danger test only applied to statutes
against obstructing government policy in fact applied to subversive advocacy, not to statutes, like the criminal anarchy statute in *Gitlow*, directed by its express terms against
subversive advocacy.
51. *Dennis v. United States*, 341 U.S. 494 (1951); Douglas at 581; Black at 579.
52. *Brandenburg v. Ohio*, 395 U.S. 444 (1969).

pretation now required a high and imminent probability of the kind that Chief Justice Vinson denied; the Smith Act prohibitions in *Dennis* could no more satisfy this requirement than those in *Brandenburg*. In effect, the governing test to determine when subversive advocacy threatened a clear and present danger was now Justice Brandeis's conception in *Whitney*: high and imminent probability, grave harm, and speech not rebuttable in the normal course of exchange. The kind of context that might exemplify such an interpretation of clear and present danger would be Holmes's example of shouting fire in a crowded theater: some outburst of political advocacy in a nondeliberative, highly personal context unleashing imminent violent illegality. Later case law, applying this test, indicated that anything short of such a context will not satisfy the test. For example, the Supreme Court found no such context of imminent violence when a speaker expressed the intent to kill President Johnson if the speaker was compelled to carry a rifle in the military.[53]

The free speech jurisprudence on subversive advocacy raises two interpretive puzzles that a theory of free speech must address: first, why free speech covers such communications at all; and second, why the judiciary has evolved over time a progressively more speech-protective interpretation of when a clear and present danger of harm justifies the abridgment of such speech. What is it that the Supreme Court has learned in its historically self-conscious interpretive shift to a more speech-protective posture?

It is, after all, easy to construct a plausible utilitarian defense for not regarding subversive advocacy as protected at all by the First Amendment, or, failing that, a defense for a quite weak test of when a clear and present danger is sufficient to justify abridgment of such speech. The advocated acts in question are illegal and often violent, so that a greater utilitarian balance of good over harm will often be secured by abridging the speech likely to cause such harms. Free speech may, as Holmes believed, have independent utilitarian justification as a way of advancing truth, and this may lead us to give some additional utilitarian weight to the protection of speech even when it makes certain harms more probable.[54] But the balance of utilitarian advantage will not be systematically speech-protective. Certainly, if subversive advocacy is extended protection on some such grounds, the test of clear and present danger should be sufficiently elastic to allow the appropriate abridgment of speech that the utilitarian balance sometimes requires.

53. *Watts v. United States*, 394 U.S. 705 (1969). Cf. *Hess v. Indiana*, 414 U.S. 105 (1973) (statement by defendant, after campus antiwar demonstration, "We'll take the fucking street later [or again]," held too remote from illegal action advocated to satisfy clear and present danger test).
54. See Holmes's invocation of such utilitarian argument in his dissent in *Abrams v. United States*, 250 U.S. 616, 630 (1919).

Holmes may have had something like this in mind when he emphasized, in his seminal dissent in *Abrams*, that the defendants were "poor and puny anonymities":[55] persons, in context, highly unlikely to suceed in achieving their illegal aims. In contrast, circulars sent to draftees encouraging draft resistance,[56] a German-American newspaper of general circulation,[57] and the political address of a political figure of the stature of Eugene Debs[58]—all these may, for Holmes, have made the illegal harms sufficiently probable that speech abridgment was appropriate. On this reading, Holmes's shift in the early subversive advocacy cases from writing for the Court to dissent was not an interpretive shift, but a consistent expression of utilitarian principle.

Such a utilitarian rationale would also justify the view of the clear and present danger test taken by Chief Justice Vinson in *Dennis*. Indeed, Vinson's conception is pointedly aggregative in the way that typifies utilitarian reasoning. A certain quantity of speech is measured against a certain aggregate of subversive harm by a probability calculation: clear and present danger is met when the expected disutility of the speech is high, though the probability is quite low. It suffices that the subversive harm (the overthrow of American constitutional government) is so grave that even the smallest probability would yield a sufficiently large expected disutility. The focus is completely aggregative. The consequence, as Justices Douglas and Black argued in dissent, is that subversive advocacy of any sufficiently grave harm can as such be abridged; the danger need be neither clear, nor present.

But there is another, quite different theme in the free speech jurisprudence on subversive advocacy, a view that the Supreme Court endorsed in *Brandenburg*. This is the conception of clear and present danger articulated on distinctly nonutilitarian grounds by Justice Brandeis in *Whitney*: the idea that the danger advocated by the speaker must be imminently highly probable, very grave, and not rebuttable in the normal course of further dialogue. On this view, it is not enough that the advocated harm is very grave indeed, for it must independently be shown to the satisfaction of a constitutionally independent judiciary that the harm is imminently highly probable and not rebuttable in the course of exchange and dialogue. This test makes little utilitarian sense. It resonates to a different moral conception entirely, which Brandeis identified with the view that "[t]hose who won our independence believed that the final end of the State was to make men free to develop their faculties; and that in its government the deliberative forces should prevail over the arbitrary."[59] On Brandeis's view of it, the core values

55. Ibid.,250 U.S. 624, at 629.
56. *Schenck v. United States*, 249 U.S. 47 (1919).
57. *Frohwerk v. United States*, 249 U.S. 204 (1919).
58. *Debs v. United States*, 249 U.S. 211 (1919).
59. *Whitney v. California*, 274 U.S. 357, 375 (1927).

of free speech are the values of moral independence; for him, advocacy of a moral right to trespass would be protected even if there was an imminent danger of the trespass.[60] What is this conception, and how can it explain the Supreme Court's and most lawyers' view that Brandeis's argument in *Whitney* is the better conception, both of why subversive advocacy should be protected, and of the appropriate measure of its protection?

These mysteries are remarkably clarified by the contractarian conception here urged, in a way that powerfully supports its proper interpretive role in the explication and explanation of constitutional doctrine in the United States. We begin with our first puzzle: why protect subversive advocacy at all?

A contractarian conception gives central value to equal respect for conscience, grounding an inalienable right that can be surrendered to no one, and thus not to the state. A legal system, like that of the United States, which constitutionally entrenches this moral right as a background constitutional right in the First Amendment, requires that persons must be guaranteed a communicative integrity consistent with this background right. But the force of the right is that persons must retain the right independently to form, express, and revise their highest-order moral powers of rationality and reasonableness in a conception of a life well and humanely lived. Such a guarantee of moral independence secures, in effect, that persons are and remain the sovereign moral critics of their government, a status of the person required by the underlying contractarian conception that government is justifiable and that obedience is owed it only if it meets certain tests: respect for rights, free and rational consent through democratic procedures, and so on. Persons are accorded this sovereign right of independent moral judgment over their government only if their associated right of communicative integrity protects advocacy that a government or its policies are wrong, should be obstructed, even should be overthrown. Brandeis expressed this idea when he gave the highest degree of speech protection to advocacy of a moral right to trespass and when he wrote of free speech as an expression of the deliberative moral powers of a free people. On a contractarian conception, subversive advocacy is at the very core of what free speech protects: the moral sovereignty of the people requires that they, not the state, retain the ultimate power of moral judgment over their governments, including the claim of that government to obedience.[61]

It does not follow that such advocates have a corresponding moral or political right to act in the way they advocate, though they may. Shel-

---

60. Ibid., 274 U.S. at 378.
61. See, for an able statement of this view, Leader, "Free Speech and the Advocacy of Illegal Action in Law and Political Theory."

don Leader comments,

> questions about the proper way to remedy a breach of contract are distinct
> from questions about the rights of the parties to have knowledge of such a
> breach.[62]

Even if a government ought to be overthrown, it does not follow that
various forms of opposition are consistent with rights of innocent third
parties, are proportional to the aims to be achieved, are feasible, and
so on. Contractarian thought, since Locke, has carefully distinguished
the right to disobey and even to revolt from the question of whether
and how the right should be exercised.[63] It is thus wholly coherent with
the moral basis of free speech that the protection of subversive advocacy should not automatically extend to the acts advocated.

In thus demarcating the protection of speech from action, contractarian theory also casts light on the basis and proper interpretation of
the clear and present danger test. That test was expressly stated by Jefferson, in his articulation of the proper scope of religious liberty, as
follows:

> that to suffer the civil magistrate to intrude his powers into the field of opin-
> ion and to restrain the profession or propagation of principles on supposition
> of their ill tendency is a dangerous falacy [sic], which at once destroys all
> religious liberty, because he being of course judge of that tendency will
> make his opinions the rule of judgment, and approve or condemn the sen-
> timents of others only as they shall square with or differ from his own; that
> it is time enough for the rightful purposes of civil government for its officers
> to interfere when principles break out into overt acts against peace and good
> order.[64]

The contractarian basis of Jefferson's formulation underlies his reasons
for suspicion of state judgments of the dangerousness of speech and his
separation of protection of belief from action. It is no accident, but a
matter of deep common principle, that free speech jurisprudence has
reflectively gravitated to comparable tests: suspicion of government
restrictions on speech based on judgments about the dangerousness of
what is said, and the limitation of speech protection at the point "when
principles break out into overt acts."

62. Ibid., p. 424.
63. The distinctness of the questions is preserved in the practice of constitutional democracies shaped by such contractarian political theory, a practice in which forms of protest
and redress for the violated rights of aggrieved parties are often institutionalized in the
very structure of constitutional law itself. See, in general, Richards, "Rights, Resistance,
and the Demands of Self-Respect"; also, Richards, "Conscience, Human Rights, and the
Anarchist Challenge to the Obligation to Obey the Law."
64. Boyd ed., The Papers of Thomas Jefferson, 1777–1779, p. 546.

The appeal to overt acts—in religion clause and free speech jurisprudence, as well as in the prohibition on constructive treason in Article III of the Constitution—is the natural contractarian limit of the relevant political protection of the common right underlying these
guarantees, namely, the right of moral independence of the person over
state authority and its claims.[65] When Brandeis interpreted the clear
and present danger test so narrowly in *Whitney*, his argument was
implicitly contractarian: since free speech expresses the background
right of the independent exercise of our moral powers, that right can
only be abridged in contexts where its exercise does not appeal to our
moral powers. A clear and present danger, thus understood, is not a
substantial expected disutility of the speech, as it may have been for
Holmes and was for Vinson. On a contractarian conception, speech may
have the highest expected disutility and still be fully protected. The
point is not the abstract probability or the gravity of harms, but the kind
of context of the speech—the explosive imminence of harms, or the
diminished responsibility of audiences in which the rebuttability of the
speech is not in effect. In short, the focus of this interpretation is the
context of interpersonal communication, the ways in which, consistent
with equal respect for moral independence, persons may themselves
decide about and give weight to communications. This explains Brandeis's emphasis on rebuttability, on giving appropriate weight to the
dignity of the deliberative powers of persons in themselves rejecting
noxious and unsound doctrines and never surrendering this inalienable
right to the state. Aggregative considerations of level and probability
of harm are to have weight in this area only when they are not trumped
by the required respect for the background inalienable right of
conscience.

The interpretive shifts by the Supreme Court, in its understanding of
the free speech jurisprudence of subversive advocacy, is explained and
justified by this contractarian account, which thus explains why free
speech protects such advocacy and the present form of the clear and
present danger test in our constitutional law. It also helps interpret
Holmes's early suggestions, however later abused by him, that free
speech did not encompass shouting fire in a crowded theater or the law
of criminal speech.

---

65. Article III, section 3, reads, in pertinent part: "Treason against the United States,
shall consist only in levying War against them, or in adhering to their Enemies, giving
them Aid and Comfort. No Person shall be convicted of Treason unless on the Testimony
of two Witnesses to the same overt Act, or on Confession in open Court." For discussion
of the constitutional prohibition on constructive treason in this connection, see Mayton,
"Seditious Libel and the Lost Guarantee of a Freedom of Expression"; Fletcher, "The
Case for Treason." For the range of legal strategies to repress free speech in Britain and
the late development of seditious libel, see Hamburger, "The Development of the Law
of Seditious Libel and the Control of the Press."

Shouting fire in a crowded theater is such a paradigmatic example of what free speech does *not* protect because it is the kind of incendiary context in which our deliberative moral powers are not in play. Contractarian theory would no more extend protection to such communicative acts than it would to hypnotism.

Most of the law of criminal speech, no matter how unwise or undesirable, falls outside the protection of free speech, not because it satisfies clear and present danger, but because we view most examples of it as not expressive of the moral powers of speakers to relevant audiences,[66] and thus as not within the scope of free speech values expressive of the background inalienable right of conscience. Most such criminal speech secretively advances specific criminal aims and projects not supposed by the relevant criminals to advance facts or conceptions of value central to the exercise of our or their moral powers of critical independence. Indeed, the criminals typically well know that their projects are criminally and morally wrong, and bind themselves to one another in ways that precisely impair the fair and free exercise of reflective powers of rational and reasonable independence.[67] Accordingly, such speech does not, in principle, fall within the protection of free-speech, understood as the expression of the background right of conscience. For this reason, the issue of clear and present danger does not arise.

The law of criminal speech may fall within the protection of free speech, if the speech is the relevant kind of conscientious protest, for example, an expression of public and conscientious dissent against military service in an unjust war, linked to advocacy of illegal acts.[68] In such cases, the communications express the background right of conscience in a communicative context that does call for such protection.[69]

Holmes's examples of shouting fire or of criminal speech do not support the analogical argument that Holmes placed on them. There are good reasons for excluding such speech from constitutional protection, but these reasons have no bearing on subversive advocacy. To the contrary, the very reasons, which justify exclusion of such speech from protection, require the full protection of such advocacy.

Holmes's argument, if it can be called that, plays on the concept of

66. Cf. Greenawalt, "Speech and Crime."
67. See *ibid.*; see also Greenawalt, "Criminal Coercion and Freedom of Speech."
68. For a conspiracy prosecution that I believe falls in this area, see *United States v. Spock*, 416 F.2d 165 (1st Cir. 1969).
69. Thus, on my view, the historical uses of the law of criminal conspiracy against religious and labor dissent are forms of criminal speech that centrally violate free speech values, and critical distaste for the law of criminal conspiracy properly reflects this unhappy history of abuse. See, e.g., Sayre, "Criminal Conspiracy." To the extent the law of conspiracy remains open to such abuses, we should retain it only if, consistent with appropriate legal protections against such abuses, there is some reasonable showing of need for a law of conspiracy to attack inchoate criminality. In fact, such a need appears quite doubtful indeed. See, e.g., Johnson, "The Unnecessary Crime of Conspiracy."

danger. The analogy is that subversive advocacy is dangerous and thus not protected by free speech in the same way that shouting fire and criminal speech are dangerous and not protected. Holmes could not, even on his own utilitarian premises, hold to this line, however; thus he tried later to discriminate when subversive advocacy is and is not sufficiently harmful to be abridged. His effort was unsuccessful and has not prevailed because the impersonality of his lofty utilitarian detachment from "these poor and puny anonymities" fails, however benevolent his aims, to give weight to the introspective personalism of the Brandeisian conception of free speech in *Whitney* (an opinion that, to his credit, Holmes joined). For Brandeis, subversive advocacy as such is not constitutionally dangerous. It is a central expression of the communicative integrity that dignifies the moral powers of a free people who, in mastering their fears of dangerous speech, master themselves, and best express the moral sovereignty of a free, because self-governing, people.

7 · The Jurisprudence of Free Speech

Contractarian political theory happily explains why the deepest constitutional thinkers of various historical periods (Jefferson and Madison in the 1790s, Holmes and Brandeis in the 1920s) should have identified subversive advocacy as a focal issue of free speech concern. The exercise of critical moral independence (pointing to the wrongness of a government's policies, indeed the duty to overthrow it) is at the heart of the contractarian conception that the moral obligation to obey law is at hazard when the state fails to keep its power within the determinate constraints that respect rights and advance the public good.

The self-correcting reflection on our history by an independent judiciary has gravitated around arguments and legal tests required by contractarian theory. But if contractarian thought explicates this interpretive development with a certain beauty, the very critical role of such argument internal to this interpretive process gives us good reason to press the case for the comparable use of this political theory in other areas of free speech jurisprudence.

The interpretive methodology of chapter 6 indicates how we should proceed. That examination of subversive advocacy showed how a certain contractarian conception of subversive advocacy was in play in a long interpretive process stretching from the constitutional controversies of the 1790s over the Sedition Act of 1798, to Holmes's articulation and increasingly speech-protective applications of the clear and present danger test, to Brandeis's even more speech-protective conception, the use and dilution of the test in *Dennis,* and finally to the current speech-protective interpretation of the test in *Brandenburg v. Ohio.* But if contractarian theory may usefully characterize an interpretive process in this way, surely contractarian theory might also clarify the interpretive shifts in areas of free speech jurisprudence still in flux. The modern Supreme Court has reconsidered and recast almost every traditional doctrine of free speech jurisprudence in the United States— offense in the public forum as a ground for speech abridgment, and the scope of free speech protection of defamation and privacy, obscenity, commercial speech. Much of the Court's work is in an intermediate stage of the interpretive process, which is now in an advanced stage in the jurisprudence of subversive advocacy. In these intermediate areas the task of political theory may be as much critical as it is explanatory; the task is to determine where the Court's work reflects sound principles, where it has worked them out inadequately or imperfectly, and where the state of constitutional doctrine is unacceptable. A critical theory of free speech advanced understanding of why *Dennis* wrongly articulated and applied the clear and present danger test and why *Brandenburg* was the better view. Might it not also enable us to evaluate comparable mistakes, not yet judicially recognized as such, and help us to prepare constructive corrections?

My strategy in this chapter is to enhance understanding of the interpretive promise of contractarian theory by using it in the explanation and criticism of a range of current doctrines and controversies in free speech jurisprudence. The interpretive power of a constitutional theory may be judged along two axes: depth and breadth. The interpretive examination of the religion clauses aimed to clarify a range of particular issues and controversies in some depth. My intention at this point is neither finality nor completeness, but interpretive breadth. I use contractarian theory over a wide range of interpretive issues in the law of free speech not to resolve discussion, but to show how contractarian theory may advance interpretive discussion over a wide front of doctrines and controversies.

GROUP LIBEL AND OFFENSE IN THE PUBLIC FORUM

Free speech rests, I have argued, on a principle requiring a greatest equal liberty of communicative integrity of speakers and/or audiences, with an equal liberty for all. The political essence of this principle is a prohibition of restrictive state judgments of the worth, truth, or dangerousness of communications central to our moral powers of rationality and reasonableness. My proposal was to think of these concerns as one with the concerns of religion clause jurisprudence discussed in chapter 5, namely, that the state should not enforce or mandate certain kinds of judgments about the truth or value or reasonableness of substantive beliefs at the core of our conscience. Rather, the state should observe the equal liberty principle, acknowledging the moral powers of all persons to address these matters on their own by remitting such evaluative choices to individual reflective deliberation. The core of free speech concern is thus the protection of the broad range of communications of fact and value bearing on the exercise of our moral powers.

This measure of free speech protection must reflect the historical concerns of religion clause jurisprudence for a genuine form of equal respect. The judgment of what is a central concern, for free speech purposes, may be as nonneutrally inconsistent with equal respect as Locke's exclusions of Catholics and atheists from the scope of toleration. The same progressive expansion in the scope of conscience in religion clause jurisprudence is reflected in free speech jurisprudence. In both areas, we need constitutional protections that guarantee respect on fair terms for the moral powers of rationality and reasonableness of all persons. Traditional conceptions of the scope of protection of conscience or speech may, on reflection, express the contempt for new forms of conscience and communicative integrity that equal respect forbids. In these cases, the principle of equal respect itself requires that the vision of the scope of free speech must be redrawn to accommodate its underlying principle.

This principle has motivated the modern Court to identify new free speech issues, questioning and curtailing previous conceptions of the scope of free speech protection that distorted the underlying principle of equal respect. I focus here on two such contexts: group libel laws and state restrictions on offense in the public forum. In both cases, the Court has reflectively expanded the scope of speech protection because a fair interpretation of equal respect so requires. Indeed, content-neutrality, a central requirement of contemporary free jurisprudence, is an elaboration of such equal respect.[1] To a remarkable extent, all these developments are shaped by the articulate elaboration of the background right to conscience.

Group Libel

Consider the reasons for the probable unconstitutionality of group libel laws under current American law, that is, laws making it a criminal and/ or civil wrong to engage in defamation of racial, ethnic, or religious groups.[2] Such laws require a demonstration that claims made about cer-

---

1. Cf. Karst, "Equality as a Central Principle of the First Amendment."
2. Despite earlier views to the contrary (*Beauharnais v. Illinois*, 343 U.S. 250 [1952]), cases such as *Brandenburg v. Ohio*, 395 U.S. 444 (1969), which strike down subversive advocacy statutes applied to speech fomenting racial and religious hatred and bigotry, suggest that group libel statutes directed against the expression of false racial or religious stereotypes, as such, would be similarly unconstitutional. See also *Collin v. Smith*, 578 F.2d 1197 (1978), *cert.den.*, 439 U.S. 916 (1978), holding unconstitutional the attempts of Skokie, Illinois, a heavily Jewish community, to stop a pending march of the Nazi party in Skokie.

tain groups subject its members to a false disparagement of social esteem like the harm inflicted on a person by a libel of him as an individual.[3] But the analogy to individual libel is defective in ways of the gravest constitutional concern. Individual libel actions have two distinctive features: they require the publication of false facts, often known to be false or easily thus ascertainable; and belief in such false facts by the audience naturally disparages the reputation of the individual expressly written or spoken about. But the communications, restricted by group libel, express general conscientious views of speakers and audiences, whose nature and effect both depend on evaluative conceptions. Group libel actions, in contrast to individual libel actions, require the state to make abstract evaluative judgments about the value of what is said and about the legitimacy of the objection taken to the assertions. These state judgments about the nature and effect of communicative utterances place group libel laws at the heart of the values of free speech. In effect, a broad range of personal grievances at hearing conscientious views opposed to one's own (and rebuttable as such) triggers state prohibitions. Inevitably, such laws impose state restrictions in the core area of evaluative conceptions appealing to the moral powers of speakers and audiences on the basis of state judgments of the worth of such conceptions, thus usurping the sovereign moral judgment of the people.[4]

Both the state and individuals may address racial and religious prejudice in various ways. The state is not constitutionally powerless against actions motivated by racial or religious bigotry; for example, it may vigorously enforce antidiscrimination laws. And there is no constitutional impediment to the state's design of educational policy in ways that affirmatively combat racial, religious, and other stereotypically unjust hatreds. For example, consistent with its just role in securing a basic education in democratic values,[5] the state should appropriately discourage the teaching of racist doctrines and encourage contrary views to be imparted;[6] it also rightly supports racial and religious integration in the public schools as a paramount educational goal, thus combating the force of racial and religious isolation and stereotypic thinking and practice.[7] And the values of free expression expressly legitimate the constitutional role of private political groups organized to rebut racist speech in ways consistent with constitutional values [for example, the Anti-Defamation League of B'nai B'rith or the National Association

3. For a classic defense, see generally Riesman, "Democracy and Defamation: Control of Group Libel."
4. For a similar criticism of these laws, see Kalven, *The Negro and the First Amendment*, pp. 7–64.
5. See, e.g., Richards, "The Individual, The Family, and the Constitution," pp. 20–31.
6. See, e.g., *Bob Jones University v. United States*, 461 U.S. 574 (1983) (religious schools, engaging in racial discrimination, not properly tax exempt).
7. See *Brown v. Board of Education*, 347 U.S. 483 (1954).

for the Advancement of Colored People (NAACP)]. But the state's restriction of such speech by group libel laws is inconsistent with the place respect for conscience holds in our constitutional traditions. Such laws indulge the Augustinian contempt for the moral powers of persons condemned by constitutional principles of equal respect.

The point of the protection of such speech is not the familiar utilitarian bromide, invoked by Holmes in *Abrams*,[8] that such speech may be true or, in the long run, may lead to more truth. Because the speech is so uncontroversially false to the central conscientious conceptions of democratic majorities (and thus rebuttable by them), it is all the more urgent that equal respect forbids *state* prohibition of such speech. Persons, as already observed, are not propositions or the propositions that they believe. It is a vicious political fallacy of the right and the left to assume that our contempt for false evaluative opinions may justly be transferred to contempt for the persons who conscientiously hold and express such views. Such persons are not, as it were, beyond the civilizing community of humane discourse. To the contrary, equal respect demands the assumption that all persons have a highest-order interest in the freedom and rationality of their moral powers, that the protection of this interest is an inalienable human right (if anything is), and that the scope of both freedom of conscience and speech must protect this right to form, express, and revise conscience fully in its proper context of application. This essentially procedural right cannot justly be compromised by prohibitions directed at the beliefs formed, whether they are beliefs in intolerance or in atheism (for Locke and the seventeenth century) or the pseudoscience of twentieth-century racism.[9] Indeed, we most undercut, as a democratic community of equal respect, substantive ideologies of racial and other inequalities when our principles extend to exponents of such views the dignifying equal respect for their moral powers as persons. Our practice thus embraces them in the vital, moralizing experience of a community of equal respect that most piercingly displays the nature of its moral community when it respects the conscience of advocates of ideologies at war with equal respect.

The elaboration of the principles of the free speech jurisprudence of subversive advocacy to group libel reflects a common contractarian theme. Respect for moral independence must preserve a right of advocacy of claims regarded by the state and community as subversive of its central claims to authority and obedience. Subversive advocacy and group libel fall in this nucleus of political and moral subversion; they make claims that attack central ideas of the political and moral legitimacy of the state and community. A contractarian conception, accord-

8. *Abrams v. United States*, 250 U.S. 616, 624, 629–31 (1919) (Holmes, dissenting).
9. See, e.g., Gould, *The Mismeasure of Man;* Blum, *Pseudoscience and Mental Ability;* Block and Dworkin, eds., *The IQ Controversy.*

ing central place to the moral independence of the person in making such claims on one's own, must remit these questions to the judgment of each person. Otherwise, authority will not be appropriately tested against the source of its contractarian legitimacy, the moral sovereignty of each and every person subject to its putative claims to obedience.

Offense in the Public Forum

Consistent with the foregoing analysis, the judiciary has elaborated a general principle applicable to the constitutional assessment of free speech. The state may not abridge speech on a content-biased ground of its view of the dangerousness of what is said.[10]. Content-bias is a natural way of articulating a justiciable standard for deciding when a state restriction on speech violates the principle requiring a greatest equal liberty with a like liberty for all. The state may not infringe speech on grounds actuated by state distaste for what is said either by a general such prohibition on speech or by a prohibition of one speech but not another. Both kinds of prohibitions violate the required greatest equal respect for the communicative integrity of speakers and audiences in making such judgments on their own. No speech, equally applied, is as much a violation of this principle as some speech unequally applied.[11]

This principle has been reasonably extended by the judiciary to exacting constitutional scrutiny of putatively neutral regulations of speech that enforce state restrictions premised on the offensiveness of speech to a certain audience. For example, the Supreme Court has become increasingly critical of the use of breach of the peace statutes to justify the abridgment of controversial speech found offensive by audiences in public forums.[12] Often the offense taken by the audience was at the substantive claims made, for example, by black demonstrators against violations of their civil rights in the South. For the same reason that the state cannot constitutionally forbid such speech on the ground that it is subversive, it may not do so when it enforces such judgments on behalf of an offended audience. As I put the point earlier, such offense is not a contractarian evil, but an ingredient of the general good of the independence of our moral powers. From this perspective, state prohibition of such offense is itself a political evil, the usurpation of a central opportunity for the exercise of otherwise stagnant moral powers. For this reason, the Supreme Court has sharply restricted the use of breach of the peace statutes in this constitutionally sensitive area. The constitutional burden is placed on the state to protect controversial speakers from hostile audiences, rather than to protect audi-

10. See, e.g., *Chicago Police Department v. Mosley*, 408 U.S. 92 (1972); Karst, "Equality as a Central Principle in the First Amendment."
11. For a failure to understand that the principle applies to the former as well as the latter, see Redish, "The Content Distinction in First Amendment Analysis."
12. See, e.g., *Cox v. Louisiana*, 379 U.S. 536 (1965); *Edwards v. South Carolina*, 372 U.S. 229 (1963).

ences from the offensive speech that confronts their moral powers with fundamental criticism of their values.[13]

If these developments are elegantly explained by the contractarian theory of free speech of the preceding chapter, a related interpretive strand of the judicial reexamination of free speech jurisprudence is even more informatively contractarian. In exactly the way that contractarian principles uniquely require, free speech values are given greatest constitutional weight when they guarantee the fuller communicative integrity of expressions of the speaker's independent and critical conscience.

This interpretive theme powerfully motivates the Supreme Court's reexamination and recasting of conventional constitutional doctrines of unprotected or neutrally regulable speech. Unprotected speech is speech that the state may restrict, even in content-biased ways, without calling for the heavy justification of a clear and present danger. Under traditional doctrine, aspects of conduct,[14] of "fighting words,"[15] or of the manner[16] (not the substance) of speech were all examples of unprotected speech. State restrictions of such aspects of speech would not trigger, as subversive advocacy or group libel would, the heavy constitutional burden of justification of leading to highly imminent, highly probable, very grave harms not rebuttable in normal discourse. But each of these doctrines has, in recent case law, been recast. The scope of free speech has been dramatically extended to cover many such acts. Constitutional violations of free speech have been found in all the following state prohibitions: school children wearing arm bands in protest of the Vietnam War;[17] mutilation or defacement of the flag as an expression of political protest;[18] highly provocative words used in protest of war and educational policies;[19] and use of the statement "Fuck the Draft" to make a point of political protest.[20] All these regulations of speech, once regarded as constitutionally neutral, are now interpreted as content-biased restrictions at the heart of free speech values.

The contractarian theme in these developments is their heightened concern for the fuller communicative integrity of critical conscience.

13. For a striking example of the contrasting treatment of otherwise similar factual contexts, with *Edwards v. South Carolina*, 372 U.S. 229 (1963), cf. *Feiner v. New York*, 340 U.S. 315 (1951).
14. *United States v. O'Brien*, 391 U.S. 367 (1968). For useful commentary, see Ely, "Flag Desecration: A Case Study in the Roles of Categorization and Balancing in First Amendment Analysis."
15. *Chaplinsky v. New Hampshire*, 315 U.S. 568 (1942).
16. *Kovacs v. Cooper*, 336 U.S. 77 (1949)(loudness regulable).
17. *Tinker v. Des Moines School District*, 393 U.S. 503 (1969).
18. *Street v. New York*, 394 U.S. 576 (1969); *Spence v. Washington*, 418 U.S. 405 (1974).
19. *Gooding v. Wilson*, 405 U.S. 518 (1972) (war protest); *Rosenfeld v. New Jersey*, 408 U.S. 901 (1972) (protest to school board).
20. *Cohen v. California*, 403 U.S. 15 (1971).

All these cases cluster around: persons' decisions about how they may express their critical viewpoints, and governmental prohibitions grounded in offense at these communicative decisions. When the defendant wore a jacket with "Fuck the Draft" written on it in a court-house corridor to make a political point,[21] or when a black person burned an American flag in protest upon learning of the shooting of James Meredith in Mississippi,[22] they were, as Justice Harlan quite clearly emphasizes in both these opinions for the Court, giving expression to their moral disgust at an unjust war or racist terrorism. The associations of the injustice of war with obscenity or of a betrayed national promise with flag mutilation are not points that could have been made, proportionate with the critical moral disgust experienced, by a color-less assertion of the war's injustice or the nation's betrayals. Each communication best conveyed its symbolic point in the way each was expressed—that unjust violence in war is the true obscenity and that a nation degrades itself when it degrades its citizens. Such communicative integrity, grounded in the fuller expression of its background right of critical conscience, is not one that can be abridged on grounds of offense, which would sanitize authentic exercises of the moral powers of a free people.

DEFAMATION AND PRIVACY

The judiciary's reconstruction and recasting of free speech jurisprudence has included three other conventional categories of constitutionally unprotected speech: defamation and privacy, obscenity, and commercial speech. In each case, the Supreme Court has critically reexamined these categories in ways connected to its broader concern for the articulate elaboration of the background right of equal respect for conscience. We may therefore advance interpretive and critical discussion of these developments by assessing how they square with such equal respect. I begin with the interconnected free speech issues of legal restrictions on defamation and incursions into privacy, and then turn to obscenity and commercial speech.

On the contractarian account here proposed, the scope of free speech sweeps as broadly as the range of facts and values that bear upon the independent exercise of our moral powers of rationality and reasonableness. But the scope of free speech, thus understood, does not touch aspects of communication that do not trench upon these focal concerns,[23] and that themselves are aspects of general goods that must

21. Ibid.
22. *Street v. New York*, 394 U.S. 576 (1969).
23. Cf. Greenawalt, "Speech and Crime."

be accorded appropriate weight by principles of equal respect.[24] In particular, equal respect must accord appropriate weight to general goods defined by our interests in reputational integrity and control over information central to the autonomous self-definition of a personal life. Each such general good defines a correlative right of the person; and the right of communicative integrity, crucial to free speech, must accommodate such rights.

Students of the methodology of free speech notice at this point that all plausible theories of free speech must balance different values (reputational integrity, privacy, communicative integrity).[25] Such forms of balancing must, they argue, show that any plausible theory of free speech must appeal either to utilitarian aggregation as a way of weighing these conflicting values, or to irreducibly pluralistic values weighed up by a commonsense intuition of political wisdom. Nonutilitarian theories of free speech, like contractarian theory, are scouted because they cannot properly assess such balancings of values: they reject utilitarian aggregation as well as pluralistic intuitions not structured by arguments of principle. The examination of how contractarian theory does address these issues will either confirm the justice of these methodological criticisms or show, if they are not just, how they misconstrue the interpretive shape contractarian argument gives these issues.

The initial point worth making is that interests in reputational integrity and in the control of private information are not, from the perspective of contractarian theory, idiosyncratic tastes or preferences with no controlling significance or valence. Contractarian theory, as we have seen, emphasizes the highest-order interest of persons in the integrity of their moral powers, thus justifying an inalienable right of conscience and an associated right of communicative integrity. The very moral structure of this argument confers a comparable weight on interests of the person in giving self-respecting shape to a life guided by one's moral powers. Interests in reputation and in privacy are among such concerns, as things that free and rational persons would want as conditions of the self-respecting pursuit of whatever else they want. Contractarian theory thus itself justifies correlative rights worthy of political protection.

The conditions of our self-respect—a central value for contractarian theory—include control over the reputational images of self that our works or our lives reflect in the minds of those whose respect nurtures our own image of self (our capacity to experience self-respect). Persons live in communities, and the sense of self is shaped by how we are regarded.[26] A contractarian conception takes these facts seriously

24. These twin conditions are not, I believe, necessary conditions for exemption from free speech protection, though they are sufficient conditions. See ibid.
25. See, in general, Shiffrin, "Defamatory Non-Media Speech and First Amendment Methodology." Cf. Shiffrin, "Liberalism, Radicalism, and Legal Scholarship."
26. See, e.g., Mead, *Mind, Self, and Society.*

indeed when it imposes moral and political constraints on the ways in which communities may, consistent with equal respect, form such social conceptions. The claim to reputational integrity (as a general good) is one such constraint, restricting the formation of such social conceptions to those based on fair views of one's works, life, and ambitions. The place of this reputational interest in the life of persons is shown by the kind of degradation of self-respect that its frustration inflicts. Persons, who can robustly endure deprivation of such general goods as wealth or even health, experience a suicidal despair in the degradation of self worked by an unjust social contempt for their reputational integrity. For them, such an insult may mean the death of what is most intimately personal, most meaningful in their ambitions for their lives.[27] Contractarian theory, which stresses our constructive moral powers, naturally requires protection of those spiritual interests through which we project and define, as free and rational persons, the aspirations of the self.

If reputational integrity is such a general good of a just social life, the corresponding such general good of a just private life is the right to privacy, understood, for present purposes, as the right to control private information or experience.[28] This right is closely allied to the right of communicative integrity central to free speech, a point implicit in Justice Brandeis's consistent articulation and defense both of rights of privacy[29] and of the right to free speech.[30] The right of communicative integrity ensures that speakers and audiences may decide on their own whether or how to communicate. But the right to privacy allows persons to decide on their own *not* to communicate, to preserve from public life and scrutiny the informational resources of conscience and intimate personal life.[31] In both cases, the background right of conscience protects the deliberative exercise of our moral powers, which the state may no more compel than it may forbid. To protect one right (free speech) at the expense of the other (privacy) would betray their common background right. In effect, it would allow free speech to usurp the communicative resources of our private lives, impairing essential

27. For a range of related examples of suicide connected to the loss of standing, etc., see Baechler, *Suicides*, pp. 84–107.
28. See, e.g., Fried, *An Anatomy of Values*, p. 140; Miller, *The Assault on Privacy*, p. 25; Westin, *Privacy and Freedom*, p. 7; Parker, "A Definition of Privacy."
29. See Warren and Brandeis, "The Right to Privacy"; *Olmstead v. United States*, 277 U.S. 438, 471 (1928) (Brandeis, dissenting).
30. *Whitney v. California*, 274 U.S. 357, 375 (1927) (Brandeis, concurring).
31. Justice Brandeis commented in his *Olmstead* dissent:

"The makers of our Constitution undertook to secure conditions favorable to the pursuit of happiness. They recognized the significance of man's spiritual nature, of his feelings and of his intellect. They knew that only a part of the pain, pleasure and satisfactions of life are to be found in material things. They sought to protect Americans in their beliefs, their thoughts, their emotions and their sensations." (*Olmstead v. United States*, 277 U.S. 438, 478 [1928]).

control over our moral powers by a homogenizing public scrutiny that paralyzes the independence of mind and action that alone honors free speech as a human and constitutional right. Cognate concerns, rooted in respect for conscience, underlie the right to silence associated with other constitutional guarantees.[32]

Each of these general goods (reputational integrity and privacy) bears in different ways on free speech concerns. Equal respect therefore requires us to strike a correspondingly different balance.

The balance between communicative and reputational integrity should be accomplished by reference to (1) the incursion of a legal restriction into facts and values central to the independent exercise of our moral powers, and (2) the status of reputational integrity as a general good, and the need to protect it by such a restriction. The vindication of one form of reputational integrity, by such laws as the Sedition Act of 1798, conflicts directly with central free speech concerns in the service of the least defensible kind of reputational integrity. Such libel liability, arising from the moral and political criticism of public officials, enforces restrictive state judgments about the falsity, wrongness, or dangerousness of such speech, and thus about the more general political and moral standards implicit in such criticism. As suggested in chapter 6, such seditious libel laws encroach upon core free speech interests not because they inhibit political speech as such, but because they usurp the more abstract right of a sovereign people to make independent judgments in terms of the public standards of critical discourse essential to the exercise of their moral powers. Protection of this right is at the crux of free speech values because it enables the people to retain critical moral judgment over their rulers and themselves. In contrast, the reputational integrity of rulers, allegedly protected by seditious libel laws, is so inextricably connected to political and moral controversy over values and the interpretation of facts that it cannot fairly be regarded as the kind of general good of fair representation of relevant facts that reputational integrity, properly understood, protects. Even when such libel actions rest on misrepresentation of uncontroversial facts, public officials appear well able and positioned to rebut such views in the normal course of exchange; legal restrictions thus are not needed to protect their legitimate reputational interests adequately.

For these reasons, the Supreme Court has properly taken the unconstitutionality of laws analogous to the Sedition Act of 1798 as a fixed interpretive point in the jurisprudence of free speech. In *New York Times Co. v. Sullivan*,[33] for example, the Court struck down, on First Amendment grounds, the application of a state libel law to the publication by the *New York Times* of an advertisement, charging "an

32. See, e.g., Greenawalt, "Silence as a Moral and Constitutional Right."
33. *New York Times Co. v. Sullivan*, 376 U.S. 254 (1964).

unprecedented wave of terror"[34] against blacks engaged in nonviolent demonstrations in the South. In fact, the advertisement made several rather minor misstatements of fact (for example, that Martin Luther King had been arrested seven times, when he had been arrested four times). Under applicable state law, the newspaper was strictly liable (that is, without proof of intent, knowledge, or negligence) not only for the false claims but for their disparagement of the county police commissioner who was awarded a $500,000 judgment. The Court found that such strict liability for libel of a state official struck at the core of free speech values, and established a constitutional rule that such libel liability of a newspaper to a public official could only arise if the statement was known to be false, or was published in reckless disregard of its falsity. In later cases, the *Sullivan* rule was extended to a narrowly construed category of public figures who had voluntarily thrust themselves into public life and attention.[35] In *Gertz v. Robert Welch, Inc.*,[36] strict liability of media defendants (for example, newspapers of general circulation) for libels of persons neither state officials nor public figures was circumscribed in three ways: liability requires, at a constitutional minimum, negligent publication of a false statement; compensatory damages can be awarded only in the amount of actual injury inflicted; and punitive damages can only be awarded if the false statements were made either knowingly or recklessly. The Court in *Gertz* acknowledged two constitutionally relevant differences between media libels of private parties and those of state officials and public figures: the latter voluntarily expose themselves to the risks of such libels, and typically have much greater access to the media to rebut the false claims made about them. The *Gertz* rule nonetheless acknowledged that even libels of private parties raise free speech issues; many such libels touch on public issues, and a constitutional rule turning on public issues might be unworkable.[37] For this reason, the standards of liability for such private libels by media defendants are constitutionally restricted across the board to accommodate these lurking background constitutional interests.

The implicit premise of these cases is the just proposition that public

---

34. Ibid., 376 U.S. at 256.
35. See *Curtis Pub. Co. v. Butts* and *Associated Press v. Walker*, 388 U.S. 130 (1967). For examples of the narrowness of the category of public figures, see *Time, Inc. v. Firestone*, 424 U.S. 448 (1976)(wealthy socialite not a public figure); *Hutchinson v. Proxmire*, 443 U.S. 111 (1979)(federally funded scientist not public figure).
36. *Gertz v. Robert Welch, Inc.*, 418 U.S. 323 (1974).
37. The Supreme Court had briefly experimented with a rule that matters of public interest, not involving public figures or state officials, would trigger the *Sullivan* rule. See *Rosenbloom v. Metromedia, Inc.*, 403 U.S. 29 (1971). It abandoned the attempt as unworkable in *Gertz*. However, the Court recently revived a form of the *Rosenbloom* rule in a case not involving a media defendant. See *Dun & Bradstreet v. Greenmoss Builders*, 53 *U.S.L.W.* 4866, 105 S. Ct. 2939, 466 U.S.—(1985).

and private libels raise quite different issues both in terms of free speech interests and the right of reputational integrity, an interpretive fact supported by the historical dissension over the constitutionality of seditious libel laws and the contrasting historical consensus of private reputation as a basic human right of the person.[38] The real question is whether these cases go far enough in their balance of communicative and reputational integrity. Restrictions on public libels, as we have seen, cut at essential free speech concerns in reputational matters that either do not rise to the dignity of a general good or that may, in any event, be adequately preserved by available rebuttal in due course. Restrictions on private libels do not threaten core free speech interests, and do serve the general good of fair representation of the facts of one's life and work. Nonetheless, as the *Gertz* rule acknowledges, many such private libels may sufficiently touch on controversial moral and political issues that some form of constitutional rule must protect such background free speech interests consistent with this legitimate right of reputational integrity. A natural form of such a rule would be an enforceable right to reply to a judicially proved private libel; a newspaper, for example, would have to circulate a retraction and reply sufficient to expunge the false disparagement of one's reputation.[39] A limited compensatory remedy would apply in those cases in which the damage would not be expunged by such a full and fair retraction and rebuttal. Such a balance of communicative and reputational integrity would justly preserve reputational integrity in a way more consistent with free speech values of fair rebuttal. American constitutional law has, in my judgment, failed to accord this remedy a preferred place in the balance of rights of the person in this area.[40]

The proper balance of communicative integrity and the right to privacy, consistent with equal respect, is quite a different matter. As we have seen, the balance of these rights must turn on the degree to which restrictions on privacy incursions trench upon central free speech values, and the degree to which the privacy interests thus protected are general goods not otherwise adequately defended. Yet control over information and experience essential to the dignity of one's moral powers is, by definition, control over the essentially private sphere of one's mind, experience, and identity. Appropriate protection of this sphere of experience and information is not a restriction of legitimately public

38. That the conception of such a natural right was part of the cultural context of the First Amendment is clear, inter alia, from Hutcheson's inclusion in his list of natural rights of "a natural right to the simple character of probity and honesty," p. 298, Hutcheson, *A System of Moral Philosophy.* John Witherspoon, in the lectures a form of which Madison heard when a student at Princeton, tracks Hutcheson's list of natural rights, including, among them, a "right to character, that is to say, innocence, not fame." See p. 123, Witherspoon, *Lectures on Moral Philosophy.*
39. I agree here with the position on this issue of Franklyn S. Haiman. See pp. 43–60, Haiman, *Speech and Law in a Free Society.*
40. Cf. Ingber, "Defamation: A Conflict Between Reason and Decency."

facts and values essential to the exercise of those moral powers. To the contrary, the background right of conscience, which justifies a right of communicative integrity, supports a correlative right of privacy. That privacy right, itself grounded in control of interests central to moral independence, is not, unlike reputational integrity, adequately defended by rebuttal. Private information is true, and unlike the falsities of libel, cannot be expunged by rebuttal. The wrong of a violation of privacy rights is the exposure of the relevant private facts. Once violated, the wrong cannot be remedied.

Judicial interpretation in this area has failed to understand these distinctive normative issues. On the one hand, the Court has assimilated forms of privacy actions to libel, supposing that, once thrust into public attention, claims to privacy protection cannot constitutionally be allowed without proof of the culpable mental state required by the *Sullivan* rule.[41] On the other hand, the very truth of private information has led one justice of the Supreme Court to indicate that privacy actions, restricting publication of such private facts, must be constitutionally forbidden.[42] The idea is this. Libelous falsehoods enjoy no constitutional protection, and thus some restrictions on libel may appropriately be permitted as consistent with free speech. In contrast, since private facts are truths and truth is the central concern of free speech, such facts are central to free speech, and cannot constitutionally be restricted at all. Neither view is correct. Privacy actions are distinct from libel restriction in ways favorable to lesser constitutional concern for libel than for privacy. Private facts are not facts or values central to free speech interests, and the damage to privacy control, essential to moral independence itself, is irreparable in a way many libels are not.[43]

Restrictions on publications of private facts require some state judgment about what is properly private, and this, it may be suggested, is a kind of judgment itself distorted by controversial moral and political judgments suspect on free speech grounds.[44] But if these judgments are not to be made by the state subject to careful judicial scrutiny, they will effectively be delegated to the press. The press's interests in publication and disclosure are not likely to fairly reflect an appropriate

41. *Time, Inc. v. Hill*, 385 U.S. 374 (1967)("false light" privacy action, involving publicizing story of family held hostage by criminals, required *Sullivan* standards). There is doubt, however, whether this case survives *Gertz*, since *Gertz* and later cases narrow the category of public figures to those *voluntarily* thrust into the limelight, which the Hill family certainly was not.
42. *Cox Broadcasting Corp. v. Cohn*, 420 U.S. 469, 497 (1975) (Powell, concurring). *Cox* is a narrow holding that a broadcaster enjoyed a constitutional immunity from a privacy action for publication of true information released in official court records, here, the name of a rape victim.
43. Cf. Nimmer, "The Right to Speak from *Times* to *Time*: First Amendment Theory Applied to Libel and Misapplied to Privacy."
44. See, e.g., Haiman, *Speech and Law in a Free Society*, pp. 61–86; Zimmerman, "Requiem for a Heavyweight: A Farewell to Warren and Brandeis's Privacy Tort."

weight for overriding privacy interests, neither waived by an individual nor reasonably required to maintain the integrity of public discourse. The judicial review, adequate to determine when state restrictions violate communicative integrity, is equally adequate to make reflective judgments on the proper scope and weight of those basic privacy interests essential, in a mass society, to the dignity of a personal life.[45] The legitimate public interest in even a newsworthy fact does not, for example, always require that the identity of persons be disclosed, and the judiciary may properly require newspapers to observe such distinctions.[46] There is no good reason for the judiciary to suppose that free speech forbids such privacy actions. Rather, the judiciary best vindicates free speech when it gives appropriate weight to the full elaboration of the background right to conscience that defines the proper dignity and scope of that right in equal respect for persons.

My views on the balance of free speech and interests in reputational integrity and privacy are, as they should be, controversial. But the methodology of balancing is decisively neither utilitarian nor intuitionist in the way that critics of contractarian theories of free speech sometimes suppose they must be.

My methodology here is nonutilitarian in both its identification of general goods and its conception of how they should be balanced. General goods are not identified as one among other preferences, all neutrally totaled in accord with preference intensities, or the like. On the contrary, general goods are selected and given weight by an ideal of the person, which precisely justifies rights in reputational integrity and privacy as spiritual interests of the person central to freedom and rationality. And these various components of respect for the person (communicative integrity, reputational integrity, privacy) are not aggregated, but assessed in terms of how best to secure equal respect for persons. For example, one general good, reputational integrity protected by private libels, is given greatest protection when it is least controversially a general good and least violates the values of communicative integrity. Privacy is accorded greater protection when free speech interests are negligible, and when its defense is not otherwise possible. The adjustment of communicative integrity, reputational integrity, and privacy is thus made possible because a background contractarian theory determines when greater political weight should be justly given to one and lesser weight accorded another. The ingredients of self-respect are sufficiently different yet mutually complementary

---

45. One relevant kind of consideration, in identifying such legitimate privacy interests, is the kind of intimate personal life increasingly protected by the constitutional right to privacy (see chapters 8–9), and often threatened by forms of prejudice no longer enjoying the just support of law.

46. See, e.g., *Melvin v. Reid,* 112 Cal.App. 285, 297 P. 91 (1931) (married women identified by maiden name).

that we can reasonably adjust their relative values in the service of a suitably complex ideal of the person and in consideration of how equal respect is best realized overall. Aggregation is simply not in play.

Similarly, the balancing in question is not the intuitional adjustment of independent values. All the values in question express an integrated underlying ideal, and their coordination is guided by both the ideal and the mandate of a greatest equal respect overall.

Judgments of these kinds are not an algorithm of decision. Many controversial points appear both in the conception of general goods and in the kinds of trade-offs among them required by reflective deliberation on what equal respect means or should mean.[47] But the general form of the analysis guides reflection in ways neither utilitarian nor intuitional. Neither account corresponds to our interpretive practices in these areas or to the best critical reflection on what these practices should be. The methodology of free speech does indeed require balancing here and elsewhere (for example, free speech with rights of a fair criminal process,[48] or rights of national secrecy, properly defined).[49] Nevertheless, the balance is reflectively guided by principled argument about the meaning of equal respect for persons.

OBSCENITY

The Supreme Court's treatment of the free speech aspects of obscene materials is a paradoxical combination of an acute narrowing of what may constitutionally be regarded as obscene, and its retention, by a slight majority,[50] of the conventional doctrine that the obscene is unprotected speech. As unprotected speech, the obscene may be restricted by the state without a showing of a clear and present danger of some imminent harm. In this section, I argue that the proper interpretive view is no longer to restrict artificially what may count as obscene, but to acknowledge frankly that prohibitions on the access of consenting adults to such materials violate core free speech interests.[51]

The judicially avowed ground for the exclusion of obscene material from free speech protection is that "the lewd and obscene . . . are no

---

47. Thus, the account itself guides the way in which these trade-offs are identified and made in a way that critics do not, I believe, understand. For one such critic, see Hart, "Rawls on Liberty and Its Priority," pp. 223–47 of *Essays in Jurisprudence and Philosophy*. For a related strategy of response, see Rawls, "The Basic Liberties and Their Priority."

48. See, e.g., *Nebraska Press Ass'n v. Stuart*, 427 U.S. 539 (1976).

49. See, e.g., *New York Times Co. v. United States*, 403 U.S. 713 (1971).

50. See *Miller v. California*, 413 U.S. 15 (1973); *Paris Adult Theatre I v. Slaton*, 413 U.S. 49 (1973). Both cases were decided by a 5 to 4 majority.

51. See, in general, Richards, "Free Speech and Obscenity Law: Toward a Moral Theory of the First Amendment."

essential part of any exposition of ideas, and are of such slight social value as a step to truth that any benefit that may be derived from them is clearly outweighed by the social interest in order and morality.''[52] In effect, obscene speech is relegated to a class of clearly communicative employments of speech that the Court has held not to be "free speech" within the meaning of the First Amendment. Other members of the class are "fighting words," for example the epithets "damned racketeer" and "damned fascist";[53] libels;[54] and commercial uses of speech.[55]

However, contemporary interpretive strands in free speech jurisprudence have circumscribed and reexamined the forms of unprotected speech thus used by the Supreme Court. The scope of unprotected "fighting words" has been diminished by the principles that limit offense in the public forum as a ground for free speech abridgment; defamation is no longer exempt from free speech scrutiny; and commercial speech is now subjected to an exacting free speech analysis. If anything, the exclusion of obscene material from free speech protection is even more unprincipled than these now reexamined exclusions. We may see this point by considering the way in which the Court has effectively limited the scope of the obscene: to hard-core pornography.

The exclusion of such pornographic material from free speech protection familiarly rests on the ground that the material, while communicative, lacks the relevant kind of ratiocinative purpose. This exclusion does not have the sense it would have if the constitutionally obscene were limited to provocative obscenities; such a limitation would be arguably a regulation of manner (not substance) of speech. But the Court has not only included some such obscenities in free speech protection,[56] but its restriction on the pornographic is clearly directed at what is communicated. The tests of the constitutionally obscene thus require certain fairly specific kinds of pornographic depictions.[57] The point of the exclusion is the purpose and effect that a certain substantive message has: namely, that it lacks ratiocinative purpose and effect.[58]

This argument is constitutionally suspect in ways that a contractarian political theory of the First Amendment clarifies: it rests on essentially nonneutral assumptions inconsistent with the required equal respect

52. See *Roth v. United States*, 354 U.S.476, 485 (1957) (quoting with approval *Chaplinsky v. New Hampshire*, 315 U.S. 568, 571–72 [1942]).
53. *Chaplinsky v. New Hampshire*, 315 U.S. 568 (1942).
54. *Beauharnais v. Illinois*, 343 U.S. 250, 266 (1952).
55. *Breard v. Alexandria*, 341 U.S. 622 (1951).
56. *Cohen v. California*, 403 U.S. 15 (1971).
57. *Miller* limits the constitutional scope of the obscene to "representations or descriptions of ultimate sexual acts, normal or perverted, actual or simulated" or "of masturbation, excretory functions and lewd exhibition of the genitals," 413 U.S. at 25.
58. For a defense of this position, see Schauer, "Speech and 'Speech'—Obscenity and 'Obscenity.'"

for moral independence. A historical analogy—bearing on interpretive shifts in the scope of free speech protections—helps introduce my argument in support of this claim.

If one were trying to concoct a historical argument against the broad constitutional protection that the First Amendment gives art, one could invoke the clear distaste of at least some prominent representatives of the Puritan tradition for forms of art (the theater, for example).[59] In contrast to a Puritan masterpiece of sustained dialectic in high Ramist style as in Milton's *Paradise Lost*,[60] the theater, on this view, is not "protected speech" because it does not appeal in the proper way to the mind. We properly find a historical appeal of *this* kind transparently unacceptable. The scope of free speech cannot reasonably be limited to a historically narrow, crabbed, and excessively rationalistic conception of our rationality and reasonableness (including didactic poetry, excluding the theater). Such a limitation would introduce yet another kind of Augustinian contempt for the diverse ways people exercise their legitimate moral independence. Our understanding of how equal respect shapes the ambit of free speech is separated from Puritan understanding by an intervening revolution in sensibility and self-consciousness, perhaps motored by the growing literacy that the Puritans cherished and spearheaded.[61] This revolution celebrates the imaginative role of art, in Abrams's apt metaphor,[62] as a transforming lamp of self-consciousness; it also gives central place to the imagination among the constructive moral powers in a life fully and humanely lived.[63] Not to include the theater or art within the protections of the First Amendment fails to recognize the role of imagination in the rational and reasonable freedom of mind and of the person. Such an exclusion takes an invidiously nonneutral viewpoint on what rationality is, and thus fails today to be a just application of the principle of equal respect interpretively fundamental to the value of free speech.

The reasons why we find this historical appeal to Puritan understanding unacceptable reflect, on examination, such interpretive arguments of principle. But such arguments apply to the First Amendment status of pornographic communications as well: equal respect for rational and reasonable freedom must neutrally protect here as elsewhere the imaginative resources of our constructive moral powers. Pornography may not be art, but it is certainly a communicative expression whose aim and effect are imaginative, namely, the cultivation and stimulation of sexual

59. See, e.g., Wright, *The Cultural Life of the American Colonies, 1607–1763*, pp. 176–87.
60. On Milton's training in the logic of Ramus, see Hill, *Milton and the English Revolution*, pp.240–1. On Ramus, see Ong, *Ramus, Method, and the Decay of Dialogue*.
61. See, e.g., Ong, *Rhetoric, Romance, and Technology*, pp. 255–83 (1971).
62. See Abrams, *The Mirror and the Lamp*; see also Engell, *The Creative Imagination*.
63. For a recent philosophical treatment of this issue, see Wollheim, *The Thread of Life*.

imagination. As I now aim to show, there is today good reason to believe that content-based restrictions on these communications are as nonneutrally degrading of a just moral independence as are restrictions on art. Certainly, if pornographic communications were (as I argue) protected speech, the constitutional burden for clear and present dangers could not be met.[64]

From a contractarian perspective, prohibitions on access of consenting adults to pornographic materials are rendered centrally suspect by the nonneutral and now highly controversial moral judgments invoked both in identifying what is obscene and in justifying suppression. The currently applicable test for the constitutionally obscene is threefold:

(a) whether "the average person, applying contemporary community standards" would find that the work, taken as a whole, appeals to the prurient interest . . .; (b) whether the work depicts or describes, in a patently offensive way, sexual conduct specifically defined by the applicable state law; and (c) whether the work, taken as a whole, lacks serious literary, artistic, political, or scientific value.[65]

The operative notion of offense taken at certain depictions, which this test requires, expresses extremely controversial moral judgments that no longer command either general or critical moral consensus.

In America, and in Western culture more generally, there is substantial and growing disagreement regarding many questions of sexual and personal morality,[66] a few of which have already surfaced dramatically in major constitutional adjudications.[67] Part of this disagreement is over notions of proper sexual function, with serious arguments being proposed for major constitutional attacks on various statutes regulating sexual function.[68] The revaluation of the obscene is one aspect of this debate.[69] In this context, pornography can be seen as the unique medium of one vision of sexuality, a "pornotopia"—a view of sensual delight in the erotic celebration of the body.[70] In opposition to the Victorian view, which rigidly defines proper sexual function in a way analogous to ideas of excremental regularity and moderation,[71] pornogra-

64. See, in general, Williams, *Obscenity and Film Censorhip*, pp. 61–86; also, United States, *The Report of the Commission on Obscenity and Pornography*.
65. *Miller v. California*, 413 U.S. 15, 24 (1973) (quoting *Roth*, 354 U.S. at 489).
66. See, e.g., Bell, *Premarital Sex in a Changing Society*; Smith and Smith, eds., *Beyond Monogamy*; *Wolfenden Report: Report of the Committee on Homosexual Offenses and Prostitution*; Klaich, *Woman and Woman*.
67. See, e.g., *Roe v. Wade*, 410 U.S. 113 (1973) (abortion); *Griswold v. Connecticut*, 381 U.S. 479 (1965) (contraception); *People v. Onofre*, 51 N.Y. 2d 476 (1980), *cert.den.* 451 U.S. 987 (1981) (consensual sodomy).
68. See, e.g., Barnett, *Sexual Freedom and the Constitution*; Richards, *Sex, Drugs, Death and the Law*. Cf. *People v. Onofre*, 51 N.Y. 2d 476 (1980).
69. See Ellis, "The Revaluation of Obscenity," in Ellis, *On Life and Sex*, pp. 103–42.
70. See Marcus, *The Other Victorians*, pp. 216, 268–74.
71. See ibid., pp. 24–25, 233, 243; Ellis, *On Life and Sex*, pp. 21–25.

phy offers an alternative model of plastic variety and joyful excess in sexuality. In opposition to the Catholic dismissal of sexuality as an unfortunate and spiritually superficial concomitant of propagation,[72] pornography affords an alternative idea of the independent status of sexuality as a profound ecstasy that may sustain intimate bonding between persons.[73] Pornography, on this view of it, is a just vehicle for the liberation of starved and shriveled capacities of sexual imagination and experience in the service of moral powers engaged in the construction of more fulfilling and humane personal relationships.

Debate among feminists about whether subvarieties of pornography are or are not "degrading to women" confirms the degree to which the evaluation of pornographic images reflects deeper moral controversies about sexuality and gender.[74] On the one hand, certain pornographic images are pointed out as central symbols of the subjugation and powerlessness of women, from which women, as collective victims, may justly be protected.[75] On the other hand, the interpretation placed on these images (as degrading) is itself viewed as an expression and legitimation of a stereotypically and regressively sexist image of women— the childlike and dependent object of protection, unworthy of respect for elementary claims to an independent imaginative and sexual life.[76] In the absence of reliable evidence that such communicative material is a clear and present danger of harmful acts,[77] such interpretive disagreements manifest aspects of larger moral controversy over conceptions of sexuality and gender that divide feminists as they do the society at large. In this area, the judgments of "harm" are parasitic on larger moral objections to the images communicated. Such judgments of "dangerous" speech reflect exactly the kinds of interpretive disagreements over broader moral controversy about which the state must, on classical free speech grounds, remain neutral.

The contractarian conception of equal respect for persons requires that the scope of free speech be assessed in terms of facts and values relevant to the independent exercise of our moral powers of rationality and reasonableness, a protection of critical conscience that rules out those state restrictions aimed at "dangerous" speech, which usurp one's right of conscience to assess these questions on one's own. Both the advocacy of political and moral subversion are, on this conception, elaborations of the respect for the independent moral judgment of each

72. See Gardiner, "Moral Principles Toward a Definition of the Obscene," p. 564.
73. Cf. Sontag, *Styles of Radical Will*, pp. 35–73.
74. For a useful study of these arguments, see Berger, "Pornography, Feminism, and Censorship." For a feminist perspective, see Hunter and Law, "Brief *Amici Curiae* of Feminist Anti-Censorship Taskforce"; Burstyn, ed., *Women Against Censorship*.
75. See, in general, Lederer, ed., *Take Back the Night*.
76. See Hunter and Law, "Brief *Amici Curiae* of Feminist Anti-Censorship Taskforce"; Burstyn, ed., *Women Against Censorship*.
77. See note 64, above; see also Berger, "Pornography, Feminism, and Censorship," pp. 24–32.

person, who must stand as ultimate arbiter of conscience and of the legitimacy of the claims of state and community. Yet the restrictive decisions, fundamental to the identification and prohibition of obscene material, make such judgments. Indeed, they do so in an area of ongoing moral and political controversy over a rational private life, a reasonable and nonsexist ethics of sexual responsibility and fulfillment, and unjust state restrictions of aspects of intimate sexual and personal life. An age replete with diverse and often reasonable arguments of sexual and other liberations is also an age for which equal respect must encompass a broader community of independent conscience than may once have been regarded as natural or appropriate, in the same way and for the same reason that respect for conscience can no longer exclude Catholics, atheists, or artists.[78] We best keep faith with our constitutional traditions, as I argued in chapter 2, when we reasonably elaborate the background rights interpretively central to those traditions. The scope of free speech, thus understood, must encompass the choice of consenting adults to use "obscene" materials: the imaginative resources of our constructive moral powers today justly include both sexual imagination and its expression. Indeed, there is no extant restriction on speech in more unprincipled violation of the reflective values of the communicative integrity of a free people.

From this contractarian perspective, the prohibition of obscene materials is constitutionally of a piece with prohibitions of heresy[79] and blasphemy,[80] on the one hand, and restrictions on subversive advocacy and group libel on the other. The analogy to heresy and blasphemy prosecutions is the attempt to regulate intellectual and emotional life, the internal landscape of the mind that constitutional guarantees make the responsibility of each person alone. The analogy to subversive advocacy and group libel is the familiar objection to obscene material, that it corrupts moral values or that it degrades either those it depicts or those who use it. But such grounds for prohibition are, as we have seen, the kinds of controversial moral and political arguments that free speech remits to the deliberative judgment of each person. The offense taken at pornographic materials, the often unsupported inferences about their harms—these are, as I earlier suggested, the familiar arguments of dangerous belief and speech and advocacy, what Brandeis called the fears that a free people masters when it subjects these issues, through the First Amendment, to the deliberative exercise of its moral powers of argument and rebuttal.[81] There is much to be said about these matters, much to be learned from the criticism of their images

78. Cf. Greenawalt, "Speech and Crime," pp. 732–37.
79. "Heresy trials are foreign to our Constitution," *United States v. Ballard,* 322 U.S. 78, 86 (1944) (Douglas writing for the Court).
80. See, in general, Levy, *Treason Against God.*
81. See *Whitney v. California,* 274 U.S. 357, 375 (1927).

and their assumptions, much to be rebutted.[82] The First Amendment, which protects racist and anti-Semitic slurs, encompasses much that is false and immoral. Its point is that the dignity of a free people cannot yield to the state the issues of conscience that are each person's inalienable responsibility to defend and vindicate.

COMMERCIAL SPEECH

There are at least two reasons why prohibitions on commercial speech (that is, advertising) might not implicate the values of free speech. First, advertising does not state facts or values central to those protected by free speech. Second, the communicative context (speaker communication and audience reliance) does not lend itself to the usual free speech presumption that dangerous speech may be rebutted in the normal course of exchange. The Supreme Court has, however, recently elaborated the protection of free speech to advertising.[83] In this section, I show how a contractarian theory of free speech justifies this interpretive development.[84]

The first objection to such protection is made from two alternative perspectives. In the first place, free speech should be limited to the political, which excludes commercial speech.[85] Moreover, commercial speech neither expresses nor appeals to moral powers.[86]

The limitation of free speech to the political cannot be sustained as sound interpretation of the historical understanding or as good argument of principle (see chapter 6).

The rationale for this limitation is sometimes posed as a claim about the kind of argument of principle most naturally elaborated by an independent judiciary.[87] But the use of the political is either too unacceptably narrow,[88] or too uninformatively broad.[89] The more plausible, broad construction thus sweeps into the scope of free speech all ideas

---

82. See, e.g., Lederer, ed., *Take Back the Night.*
83. The leading case is *Virginia Pharmacy Board v. Virginia Consumer Council,* 425 U.S. 748 (1976). But cf. *Central Hudson Gas v. Public Service Commission,* 447 U.S. 557 (1980).
84. See also Redish, "The First Amendment in the Marketplace: Commercial Speech and the Values of Free Expression."
85. See, in general, BeVier, "The First Amendment and Political Speech: An Inquiry into the Substance and Limits of Principle."
86. For a statement of both arguments, see Jackson and Jeffries, "Commercial Speech: Economic Due Process and the First Amendment." For a statement of the latter argument, see Baker, "Commercial Speech: A Problem in the Theory of Freedom."
87. See, e.g., BeVier, "The First Amendment and Political Speech: An Inquiry into the Substance and Limits of Principle."
88. See, e.g., Bork, "Neutral Principles and Some First Amendment Problems."
89. See, e.g., Meiklejohn, "The First Amendment Is an Absolute."

and views of serious public debate, which easily degenerates into the conventional consensus on legitimate political debate. Such consensus is not a principled judgment on the political principles of free speech, but a centrist appeal to conventional political wisdom—the product of the accidents of the political process, its nonneutral mirroring of the shifting coalitions of majority tastes and preferences on various issues, its possible distortion by economic inequalities. Such a conception of the core values of free speech is a degradation of its moral foundations. Its measure of the scope of free speech is the conventional consensus that may least reflect the principle of equal respect for the independent conscience of the dissenter or the advocate of political or moral subversion. Such majoritarian consensus on the agenda of political debate is highly likely to suppress those subversive political and moral points of view essential to such dissent. In effect, the speech that most calls for free speech protection receives the least. This interpretive distortion is one we have historical reason to fear.[90] The long history of the suppression of left-wing "subversive advocacy,"[91] as well as the use of obscenity laws to suppress abortifacient and contraceptive information,[92] dissemination of sex manuals,[93] advocacy of contraception and population control,[94] and sexual imagination—were standardly justified by this seductive but constitutionally incoherent picture of free speech as political.

For this reason, there is a vicious circularity in the argument from the political. While the plausibility of the argument depends on its contractarian assumptions about protecting the sovereignty of the people, its use in the definition of the scope of the political betrays its moral foundations. This argument cannot therefore be accorded decisive weight in excluding advertising (or pornography, for that matter)[95] from free speech protection.

Another more self-consciously contractarian argument for such

90. On the recurrent American tendency to attack forms of basic moral and political criticism, see Hofstadter, *Anti-intellectualism in American Life*. Cf. Miller, *The Life of the Mind in America*.

91. On the way in which our history has not given fair play to basic political criticism by the left and its consequences for inadequate political alternatives today, see Lindblom, *Politics and Markets*.

92. The text of the substantive section of the Comstock Act Sec. 2, ch. 258, sec. 2, 17 Stat. 598, 599 (1873), *as amended*, 18 U.S.C. 1461 (1970), includes in its prohibitions of obscene matter "[N]o obscene, lewd, or lascivious book, . . . or any article or things designed or intended for the prevention of conception or procuring of abortion."

93. See, e.g., *United States v. Chesman*, 19 F. 497 (E.D. Mo. 1881).

94. See, e.g., *United States v. Bennett*, 24 F.Cas. 1093, No. 14,571 (C.C.S.D.N.Y. 1879); *Regina v. Bradlaugh*, 2 Q.B.D. 569 (1877), *rev'd on other grounds*, 3 Q.B.D. 607 (1878).

95. In fact, contemporary moral controversy over pornography (see discussion in the preceding section) would suggest that pornography restrictions must, even for purposes of the political theory of free speech, be regarded as political.

exclusion points out that advertising should not be constitutionally protected speech because it does not express the moral powers of speakers and audiences.[96] On this view, advertising reflects essentially economic interests of speakers and audiences, which control and shape both the substance and aims of the communication; in particular, this speech does not exercise our moral powers. But this interpretation of relevant contractarian principles fails to give appropriate weight to two relevant aspects of equal respect for communicative integrity.

First, equal respect must recognize the diverse ways that persons express their moral powers of rationality and reasonableness in conceptions of a life well and humanely lived. It is therefore inconsistent with equal respect to draw dichotomous distinctions between protected and unprotected speech which give constitutional effect to popular offense at the ways of life people conscientiously choose. The exclusion of advertising from free speech protection rests on such constitutionally unacceptable distinctions. Those who advertise goods may well believe in their products and in their utilities for consumers in ways that express, for them, conscientious conceptions mixed, as communicative acts often are, with other motives. Other communicators, whose speech is fully protected, often do so for combined personal and economic motives (writers, for example, often as much write to live as live to write). The supposition that advertising as such, in contrast to other kinds of speech, is not only alienated from our moral powers but controlled by malign economic interests is thus a constitutionally suspect substantive judgment;[97] it does not express one of the acceptable reasons for restricting advertising (for example, fraud), and it draws constitutionally unjust lines between kinds of speakers and speech. Such a ground for exclusion from free speech protection assumes that the ethics and economics of business people are antagonistic—that economic interests derail the moral autonomy of advertisers, and that advertisements play a suspect role in the moral life of the advertiser. Such judgments are, in principle, not the proper measure of free speech protection: they use dubious factual premises to mask constitutionally suspect judgments about the integrity of certain speakers, their speech, and the "proper" role of speech in a good and humane life. Equal respect forbids use of such nonneutral judgments by the state to abridge communicative integrity. In such multiply motivated cases as commercial speech, a contractarian theory of constitutional neutrality thus favors free speech protection of advertising.

Second, free speech protects the communicative integrity not only of speakers but of audiences as well. Advertising does make available to

96. The best statement of this position is Baker, "Commercial Speech: A Problem in the Theory of Freedom."
97. See, in general, Redish, "Self-Realization, Democracy, and Freedom of Expression: A Reply to Professor Baker."

consumers facts, interpretations of facts, and evaluative conceptions relevant to the exercise of their moral powers of rationality and reasonableness.[98] Advertising sets forth, for example, information about cheaper and better goods and services that may enable one to define and pursue personal as well as ethical aims. Indeed, the availability of more informative advertising may make the economic ideal of consumer sovereignty less fictive, and allow a deliberative reflection on competing values and costs and their connections to one's personal and ethical aims. It is very difficult to see on what contractarian ground such audience interests in communicative integrity can be accorded no weight other than the contempt, forbidden by equal respect, for the place of these communications in the structure of the lives of many decent and good people. Surely, the powers of rationality and reasonableness of many people, rarely exercised as speakers or writers, are cultivated in their role as audiences, and, in part, as audiences for advertising. A political theory of free speech, which accords fundamental weight to the conditions of deliberative self-rule of a free people, cannot justly omit such audience interests in communicative integrity.

Contractarian theory justifies a broad range of reasons that support the regulation of advertising. There are, for example, contractarian grounds for regulations of communication that forbid speech in contexts of coercion, fraud, mass hysteria, and the like; speech in such contexts neither expresses nor appeals to the deliberative moral powers of persons.[99] These grounds properly take a more extensive form, in the regulation of advertising, than they do and would for other kinds of speech. For example, fraudulent advertising is often uncontroversially false factually, and not tainted by the background moral, philosophical, and ideological controversies over facts and values central to other kinds of speech. There is thus no just constitutional impediment to prohibitions of, and even prophylactic measures against, fraud in advertising in the way that there is in attempts to restrict fraud in religion.[100] And advertising may be relied on by consumers to their immediate detriment in a way not naturally intermediated by the usual patterns of reflective rebuttal in other communicative areas. For this reason, our toleration of the false, the specious, the bad, and even the criminal in other areas of speech cannot be generalized to advertising. Even prohibitions of true advertising may be just if such prohibitions reflect a deliberative political judgment about not encouraging the use of a

98. See ibid.
99. Cf. pp. 182–241, Haiman, *Speech and Law in a Free Society*; Greenawalt, "Criminal Coercion and Freedom of Speech."
100. See *United States v. Ballard*, 322 U.S. 78 (1944). On the general issue of appropriate regulations of commercial speech in this area, see Reich, "Preventing Deception in Commercial Speech."

product dangerous to health.[101] Finally, amounts of advertising may be appropriately regulated to secure equality among speakers; otherwise, for reasons analogous to those in the case of political contributions, background economic inequalities might undermine equal respect itself. These grounds for special regulations or prohibitions of advertising do not justify the complete exemption of advertising from free speech scrutiny. They reflect the articulate application of free speech principles to this communicative context with certain consequences for certain good reasons sometimes not found in other areas of speech. But they point to other areas of truthful and nondeceptive advertising of goods and services neither harmful nor criminal in which classic free speech principles properly apply in the usual way.

Such classic free speech concerns arise when the ground for the state restriction on speech is a view of the dangerousness of the speech, which expresses an unjustified contempt for the moral powers of the person in making these judgments on his or her own. Prohibitions on true and nondeceptive advertising of goods and services (neither criminal nor harmful) are often grounded on these constitutionally questionable assumptions, rather than such reasonable purposes as ensuring equality. In many cases, state prohibitions have endorsed forms of information control by professional groups, who thus unfairly entrenched their domination of the consumers of their services in ways detrimental to good and reasonably priced professional care. This pattern of unjust domination of relevant communications, here supported by the state, is and should be at the heart of free speech concern and scrutiny. The Supreme Court has thus correctly invalidated state-enforced prohibitions of advertisements of prescription drugs[102] and advertisements by lawyers.[103] Its interpretive work, albeit not altogether consistently, properly extends free speech principles into an area of their proper application.[104]

101. See *Capital Broadcasting Co. v. Acting Attorney Gen.*, 405 U.S. 1000 (1972), *aff'g* 333 F.Supp. 582 (D.D.C. 1971) (upholding constitutionality of 15 U.S.C. Sec. 1335, which prohibits broadcast advertising of cigarettes)
102. *Virginia Pharmacy Board v. Virginia Consumer Council*, 425 U.S. 748 (1976). See also *Linmark Associates, Inc. v. Willingboro*, 431 U.S. 85 (1977) (ordinance forbidding posting of real estate "For Sale" and "Sold" signs, to forestall "white flight," unconstitutional abridgment of free speech).
103. *Bates v. State Bar of Arizona*, 433 U.S. 350 (1977). But cf. *Ohralik v. Ohio State Bar Ass'n*, 436 U.S. 447 (1978) (in-person lawyer solicitation of clients may be prohibited); *In Re Primus*, 436 U.S. 412 (1978) (lawyer solicitation of clients by letter may not be prohibited).
104. See, e.g., *Friedman v. Rogers*, 440 U.S. 1 (1979) (Texas law prohibiting practice of optometry under a trade name held constitutional). Justice Harry Blackmun's dissent in this case states, I believe, the better view. But cf. *Central Hudson Gas v. Public Service Commission*, 447 U.S. 557 (1980) (state ban on promotional advertising by an electrical utility held unconstitutional).

Such an elaboration of free speech principles is not properly
regarded, as its critics suppose,[105] as the unjust intervention of the judiciary into economic regulation that was centrally exemplified for lawyers by the now overruled *Lochner v. New York*.[106] The criticism
depends either on the idea that free speech must be political or on a
protection of the deliberative autonomy of a free people. But the political restriction of the scope of free speech is, for reasons already canvassed, wrong. And the idea that the deliberative rationality of a free
people is not advanced by advertising fails to give proper gravity to the
informational properties of advertising and its role in the deliberative
rationality of speakers and audiences. A contractarian conception of
free speech, properly understood, must insist that the lines of constitutional protection be wholly free of any bias against the diverse ways
that people exercise the full range of their communicative integrity. If
advertising contains some elements thus improperly regulated and others properly regulated by the state, the priority of communicative
integrity among constitutional values requires that the balance be
struck favorably to the protection of those elements involving legitimate free speech interests, reserving other elements for justifiable regulation and restriction. Contractarian theory thus both explains and justifies an important interpretive development in the conception of free
speech protection.

The proper elaboration of free speech principles often has economic
consequences. Unlicensed newspapers or newspapers protected by *Sullivan* and *Gertz* standards of defamation publish, for example, in certain
freer ways, forming the public opinion that shapes economic policy,
and the like. We do not regard such applications of free speech principles as questionable because they affect businesses, or shape economic policy by exposing it to freer criticism. To the contrary, that is
the point—the dispersion of control of information more broadly
throughout the society to independent agents of thought and deliberation. The prohibitions on advertising, rightly struck down by the
Supreme Court, controlled information in the constitutionally forbidden way. They allowed suspect professional judgments, degrading to
client autonomy, to cut off important information relevant to deliberative rationality. Certain benign redistributive and/or allocative economic effects may have, in consequence, occurred. But these are the
familiar kinds of consequence associated with a principled elaboration

105. See Jackson and Jeffries, "Commercial Speech: Economic Due Process and the First
Amendment."
106. *Lochner v. New York*, 198 U.S. 45 (1905) (New York statute forbidding baker to
permit his employees to work more than 60 hours per week held unconstitutional violation of personal liberties of contract and work). For repudiation of this approach, see,
e.g., *West Coast Hotel Co. v. Parrish*, 300 U.S. 379 (1937) (minimum wage regulation for
women held not unconstitutional violation of freedom of contract).

of the values of free speech, namely, a people more in control of the information that empowers as it dignifies.

The question of the free speech status of advertising is easily confused with another issue: appropriate attempts by the state to equalize the power of the speech of persons in the society. Some of those sympathetic to such policies of equalization may naturally support exemption of advertising from free speech protection because they suppose that prohibitions of advertising equalize free speech power in the relevant way. Yet the opposite is true. The Supreme Court's interpretive work, in striking down prohibitions of lawyer advertising, encouraged the better distribution of legal services to those in need of them. And other forms of state regulation of advertising, directed against fraudulent or manipulative advertising or toward ensuring equality among speakers, are quite consistent with free speech principles. Properly understood, the extension of these principles to commercial speech does not conflict with equalizing aims. Other doctrines of current First Amendment jurisprudence are, however, antagonistic to such equalizing aims. It is these, not the Court's quite just repudiation of the unprotected status of advertising, to which egalitarian critics should attend.

THE EQUALIZATION OF POWER AND FREE SPEECH

The system of free expression is the fair procedural way in which a democratic people shows equal respect for one another in the exercise of the moral powers fundamental to their status as sovereigns over themselves and the state. Since the background right of equal respect for moral independence enjoys such a priority among the goods regulated by contractarian principles, attempts to equalize the power of speech, particularly as it effects equal political liberties, should be regarded as a fuller realization of its principles of equal respect. In this section, I shall argue that the Supreme Court has failed to understand such principles of equal respect.

In *Buckley v. Valeo*,[107] the Court considered the constitutionality of the Federal Election Campaign Act of 1971 (as amended in 1974), which imposed, inter alia, limitations on both the amounts that could be contributed to presidential campaigns, and the amounts that could be spent on such campaigns by candidates and by independent groups on behalf of candidates. The crucial theme in the assessment of these two limitations was the Court's view of legitimate and illegimate state purposes. Anticorruption was a quite legitimate such purpose; equalizing political power was a constitutionally illegitimate state purpose. The Court thus legitimated the campaign limitations since they did not inhibit central free speech interests but did advance the constitution-

107. *Buckley v. Valeo*, 424 U.S. 1 (1976).

ally legitimate purpose of discouraging corruption. The Court, how-ever, struck down the expenditure limitations because they inhibited free speech interests and they did not reasonably pursue the anticor-ruption purpose (expenditures by "independent" groups, for example, were not coordinated with the candidate's campaign in a way that would encourage improper commitments by the candidate to them). The expenditure limits did reasonably pursue an equalizing purpose, but that purpose was constitutionally illegitimate.[108]

The pivotal premise of this case is that the aim of equalizing the power and impact of speakers on the democratic process is, in consti-tutional principle, illegitimate. A restriction on expenditures, trans-lated into a restriction on the communications that those expenditures support, is, on this view, a diminution of speech. This, so the argument goes, violates free speech values, for how can a lowering of speech activity by the state be consistent with the rich and robust communi-cative activity protected by the First Amendment from state inhibition and restriction? The judicial statement of the view is rhetorically dis-missive of equalizing aims for such reasons:

> . . . the concept that government may restrict the speech of some elements of our society in order to enhance the relative voice of others is wholly for-eign to the First Amendment, which was designed "to secure 'the widest possible dissemination of information from diverse and antagonistic sources.'"[109]

There is a sleight of hand in this inference from expenditure limits to less speech to a violation of free speech, namely, a blankly aggregative conception of the aims of free speech. More is better, no matter what the distributive effects and consequences, and any restraint on speech must therefore be condemned. But the Court's view is subject to three interconnected objections: first, the internal coherence of its own ratio-nale; second, its disregard of pertinent authority to the contrary; and third, its questionable political theory.

How, exactly, does a restriction on expenditures diminish diverse sources of speech? The idea makes sense only as applied to marginal

---

108. A case to similar effect is *First National Bank of Boston v. Bellotti,* 435 U.S. 765 (1978). In this case, the Supreme Court considered and invalidated, by a narrow 5 to 4 majority, a Massachusetts criminal law prohibiting certain expenditures by banks and business corporations for the purpose of influencing the vote on referendum proposals, in this case a proposed state constitutional amendment to authorize a graduated individ-ual income tax. Consistent with *Buckley,* any equalizing purpose of the statute was dis-allowed by the Court, since it inhibited speech activity in the way that the First Amend-ment putatively forbids. The constitutionally legitimate anticorruption purpose was not, in the Court's view, reasonably pursued by this legislation, in contrast to such a statute restricting corporate giving to candidate elections.
109. *Buckley,* 424 U.S. at 48–49, citing, with approval, *New York Times Co. v. Sullivan,* 376 U.S. at 266.

political parties that might require substantial support from a few donors before being able to muster sufficient general support from other donors so as not to be beholden to a few wealthy supporters. But this reasonable constitutional concern would be met by appropriate exemptions from the campaign financing law for such parties, who would thus be allowed and encouraged to establish their alternative perspectives and points of view. The restriction on expenditures does not diminish diversity in other electoral contexts. In fact, it requires that political support must be garnered from a broader and more diverse spectrum of the electorate, not from the much smaller groups of the wealthy and/or ideologically cohesive people who exercise a quite disproportionate power over electoral politics.

A second objection questions whether the fair regulation of speech and electoral politics is, as the Court supposes, "wholly foreign to the First Amendment." Many constitutionally acceptable constraints on free speech activity restrict the speech of some in order thus to secure a fairer forum for free speech (for example, neutral time, place, and manner regulations, or the fairness doctrine applicable to certain media).[110] Related constitutional doctrines mandate that the equality of voting rights may not be diluted by malapportionment[111] or distorted by irrelevant economic burdens on the right to vote.[112] The confluence of such established constitutional principles suggests that the Court's simplistic aggregative conception fails to do justice to the fabric of relevant constitutional principles.[113] Such doctrines suggest, if anything, that constitutional values of equality (integral to the rights of free speech and the vote) render unregulated electoral politics itself a distortion of background constitutional ideals.

The third objection concerns the Court's rejection of equalizing political and free speech power, which assumes that the First Amendment expresses a political theory hostile to such equalizing aims. In fact, however, the central values, guiding both religion clause and free speech jurisprudence, are the primacy of equal respect for our highest-order powers of rationality and reasonableness. This moral sovereignty of the person over herself and her state is the background theory that rights of religious freedom, free speech, voting, and much else, both preserve and express. Consistent with the equal respect of this back-

---

110. See, e.g., *Red Lion Broadcasting Co. v. FCC*, 395 U.S. 367 (1969).
111. See *Baker v. Carr*, 369 U.S. 186 (1962)(malapportionment of state legislature justiciable under the equal protection clause); *Reynolds v. Sims*, 377 U.S. 533 (1964) (state legislature apportionment must weight voters equally, with roughly the same numbers of voters per representative).
112. See *Harper v. Virginia Board of Elections*, 383 U.S. 663 (1966)(poll tax is unconstitutional economic burden on right to vote); *Kramer v. Union Free School District No. 15*, 395 U.S. 621 (1969) (right to vote in school district elections cannot be predicated, inter alia, on ownership of real property).
113. Cf. Nicholson, "Campaign Financing and Equal Protection."

ground theory, such rights are thought of as equal rights, as aspects of the greatest equal liberty of each, with a like liberty of all.

But the priority, enjoyed by these equal rights in our constitutional law, is imperiled by the degree to which economic and associated inequalities, perhaps justified on independent grounds of greater merit and contribution, undercut the background equality of equal respect. Economic and other inequalities, accorded for reasons relevant to the economic sphere alone, become, seductively, the measures of the basic respect accorded people as people; one's income becomes the measure of one's moral worth. From the perspective of democratic constitutionalism, the idea that greater income or wealth as such is a criterion of greater moral or political respect or weight should be a disgusting deviation from the proper moral order of democratic equality. If permitted, if left unregulated, this distortion of formal values of constitutional and political equality by economic inequality corrupts the internal ideals of equal respect that make democratic constitutionalism a defensible and legitimate form of government.[114]

For these reasons, attempts by the state to regulate electoral expenditures in the interest of equalizing political power should not, as the Supreme Court currently supposes, be regarded as antagonistic to the values of the First Amendment. On the contrary, the attempt to separate political from economic power, preserving the constitutionally compelled equality of the former from the inequalities of the latter, is required by the priority accorded equal respect for basic liberties of the person in a constitutional democracy. The diminution in speech activity from expenditure limits is not a content-biased restriction on speech condemned by free speech jurisprudence.[115] It is the wholly reasonable, indeed required, attempt to effect in modern circumstances the underlying constitutional ideal of equal respect. This ideal is not satisfied by an aggregate of speech activity whose reality, instead of the diversity of a free and equal people, is the economic power of the few exercised as greater political power and influence. Such political power is not only unequal, it is unequal in a way and in an area that morally degrades the sovereignty of one's equals under constitutional law. Limits on such expenditure advance the equal liberty that constitutional values require; they should be applied throughout American politics.[116] Both free speech and our common political life would be responsive on fairer terms to the people, who as moral equals stand equal before the law and maintain their sovereignty over our common political life.

There is no tension between free speech and such equalizing aims,

---

114. Cf., e.g., pp. 221–28, Rawls, *A Theory of Justice*; and pp. 72–79, Rawls, "The Basic Liberties and Their Priority."
115. Cf. Wright, "Politics and the Constitution: Is Money Speech?"; also his "Money and the Pollution of Politics: Is the First Amendment an Obstacle to Political Equality?"
116. Cf. Chevigny, "The Paradox of Campaign Finance."

as some of the most reflective legal thinkers on free speech today mistakenly suppose.[117] Both aims are rooted in the same conception of equal respect, motivated by the same concerns about the equality central to the priority of free speech in American constitutional law. Indeed, from such a contractarian perspective, we may see *Buckley*, rather than the recent commercial speech cases, as the free speech case that most clearly smacks of the discredited substantive economic due process of *Lochner v. New York*.[118] The blunder of *Lochner* was its holding that New York State's aim to equalize bargaining power between employers and employees in the baking industry was, in principle, constitutionally illegitimate. Today we properly recognize that such aims are consistent with a sound theory of distributive justice and with the theory of the Constitution. The essence of the blunder in *Buckley* is the blunder of *Lochner*: the holding that equalizing power is illegitimate. In fact, the mistake in *Buckley* is arguably more constitutionally egregious, for such equalizing of free speech power in electoral contexts is rooted in the egalitarian principles of the First Amendment itself. The specter of *Lochner* still haunts our law; we will exorcise it only when we have in place more articulate and more critical conceptions of our deepest ideals and thus recognize the authentic corruptions of those ideals. In this area, political theory is not only a useful device of explanation and explication; it is a moral need.

THE PUBLIC FORUM

The principles of free speech apply to a range of public communicative contexts. This section brings contractarian theory to bear on how the concept of a public forum should be understood and elaborated.

The classic principles of free speech jurisprudence were worked out for the communicative technologies (printing) and contexts of earlier historical periods. Our conception of the proper loci for free speech activity, for example, was shaped by the search of religious or political advocates for a communicative context in which they could reach relevant audiences. Since they often lacked access to mainstream newspapers or magazines, such advocates would confront audiences in pub-

117. See, e.g., Baker, "Scope of the First Amendment Freedom of Speech"; Redish, "The Value of Free Speech." Baker and Redish disagree over the correctness of *First National Bank of Boston*, with Baker attacking and Redish defending it. But both accept the legitimacy of *Buckley*. For an exchange between them, see Baker, "Realizing Self-Realization: Corporate Political Expenditures and Redish's 'The Value of Free Speech'"; Redish, "Self-Realization, Democracy, and Freedom of Expression: A Reply to Professor Baker." Both their theories, which are, I believe, implicitly contractarian, fail properly to interpret how equal respect must shape questions of the legitimacy of state equalizing of free speech power.

118. *Buckley v. Valeo*, 424 U.S. 1 (1976); *Lochner v. New York*, 198 U.S. 45 (1905).

lic parks[119] and even disseminated literature to homes.[120] In order to protect such offensive communications from state prohibition, the Supreme Court evolved its early formulations of content-neutrality as the operative free speech test. The Court insisted that such public places as streets could be regulated by the state only on neutral grounds of time, place, and manner.[121] Indeed, the Court suggested that certain public places (public parks, for example) had to be kept open to communicative activity; even a neutral prohibition of all communicative activity in these minimal public forums would violate free speech.[122] The doctrinal premise of the constitutional law of such classic public forums was that these guarantees ensured fair access of speakers and audiences to communicative contexts. In its desire to ensure such fair access, the Court extended its public forum principles even to the home, protecting the right of religious groups to engage in advocacy there. The right to refuse such access was the inalienable right of the homeowner; it could not be asserted by the state on her or his behalf.[123]

On a contractarian conception, the central role of free speech is the guarantee of a certain kind of critical moral independence, securing the moral sovereignty of free people over themselves and their government. An expansive conception of public forums is a natural elaboration of the principle of free speech, that is, the principle of a greatest equal liberty of the communicative integrity of speakers and/or audiences. The constitutional priority, thus accorded equal respect for communicative integrity, requires the state not only to avoid making the restrictive judgments of a content-biased kind earlier discussed, but to assure an abundant variety of communicative contexts beyond the minimal

---

119. See, e.g., *Lovell v. Griffin*, 303 U.S. 444 (1938); *Cox v. New Hampshire*, 312 U.S. 569 (1941); *Cantwell v. Connecticut*, 310 U.S. 296 (1940).
120. See, e.g., *Martin v. Struthers*, 319 U.S. 141 (1943).
121. Thus, permit systems were, respectively, disallowed and allowed depending on whether the Court was satisfied that the administration of the permits to parade were administered neutrally, without prejudice against certain religious or political groups. See *Lovell v. Griffin*, 303 U.S. 444 (1938) (disallowed); *Cox v. New Hampshire*, 312 U.S. 569 (1941) (allowed). Correspondingly, a criminal conviction for breach of the peace, applicable after the speech in question, was disallowed when the statute was applied in a way that bespoke state opposition to the advocacy in question. See *Cantwell v. Conneticut*, 310 U.S. 296 (1940). For a recent criticism of current jurisprudence of time, place, and manner restrictions, see Baker, "Unreasoned Reasonableness: Mandatory Parade Permits and Time, Place, and Manner Restrictions."
122. See, e.g., *Hague v. CIO*, 307 U.S. 496 (1939).
123. See *Martin v. Struthers*, 319 U.S. 141 (1943) (ordinance forbidding religious groups to distribute leaflets by ringing doorbells held unconstitutional); *Schaumburg v. Citizens for Better Environment*, 444 U.S. 620 (1980)(barring solicitations by charitable organizations at home unconstitutional). There is, of course, no constitutional objection to the application of a neutral trespass statute to such solicitors who have been put on specific notice by homeowners that they regard such solicitation as a trespass. Cf. *Rowan v. Post Office Dept.*, 397 U.S. 728 (1970)(person may constitutionally order the post office not to deliver certain sexually oriented mail).

public forums (parks and streets) of the historical understanding.[124] A state, constitutionally limited by free speech protections, must therefore itself ensure communicative contexts for moral independence to the greatest extent feasible consistent with legitimate state purposes. Since much of this criticism will be directed at the state and its policies, the scope of the guarantee includes state properties whose purposes are clearly consistent with free speech purposes (in particular, the state properties directly relevant to the substance of the criticism in question).[125] In doubtful cases, the priority of free speech values requires that the balance be resolved favorably to opening more forums to free speech.[126]

There are many cognate dimensions to the state's responsibility to shape its policies to comply with the priority of free speech principles in our law, for example, dispensing information relevant to the critical moral independence of its citizens[127] and maintaining the neutrality of government speech.[128] I focus here on the regulatory responsibilities of the modern state to assure the rich matrix of public forums required by free speech principles.

Classic principles of free speech assume that constitutional impediments on state interference suffice to guarantee diversity in communicative activity. In the modern context, however, serious students of American constitutional law argue that newspapers, for example, are themselves public forums.[129] In contrast to such traditional public for-

---

124. Cf. *Hague v. CIO*, 307 U.S. 496 (1939). See, in general, Kalven, "The Concept of the Public Forum."

125. See, e.g., *Brown v. Louisiana*, 383 U.S. 131 (1966) (segregated public library is sufficiently a public forum for a silent protest demonstration that First Amendment applies to protest). Cf. *Tinker v. Des Moines School District*, 393 U.S. 503 (1969) (public school classroom is appropriate forum for students to wear arm bands in protest of Vietnam war).

126. A number of Supreme Court cases fail properly to elaborate this presumption. See, e.g., *Adderly v. Florida*, 385 U.S. 39 (1966) (jails not public forum for protest); *Lehman v. Shaker Heights*, 418 U.S. 298 (1974) (public buses not public forum for paid political ads on buses); *Greer v. Spock*, 424 U.S. 828 (1976) (military bases not public forum for political speakers); *Hudgens v. NLRB*, 424 U.S. 507 (1976) (shopping centers not public forums).

127. See, e.g., *Richmond Newspapers, Inc. v. Virginia*, 448 U.S. 555 (1980) (absent articulated overriding interest to the contrary, criminal trials must be open to the public and press). One current manifestation of this argument is controversy over a special right of press access to prisons, not available to the public at large, in order adequately to preserve the press's checking functions in an area of state power isolated from public scrutiny. See, e.g., *Pell v. Procunier*, 417 U.S. 817 (1974); *Saxbe v. Washington Post Co.*, 417 U.S. 843 (1974); *Houchins v. KQED*, 438 U.S. 1 (1978). Since the press acts, for this purpose, as the instrument of informing experience for the public at large, the press is the free speech representative of the public at large and should be accorded protections for this role.

128. See Yudof, *When Government Speaks*; Kamenshine, "The First Amendment's Implied Political Establishment Clause"; Shiffrin, "Government Speech."

129. See, in general, Barron, "Access to the Press—A New First Amendment Right."

ums as public parks, however, the standard application of free speech principles does not here ensure fair access to these public forums. The state should therefore neutrally regulate the press, imposing access rights (such as the right to reply), meant to ensure fairer use of these public forums by the people at large. The opposing classic conception of the press, to which the Supreme Court has consistently adhered,[130] is that the press stands equal to any other speaker or writer before the law. Any access requirement, on this view, abridges the basic communicative integrity of the press as it would the integrity of any individual writer or speaker.

The problem with this view is its failure to take seriously the patterns of monopolization of the press that give these speakers and writers a disproportionate free speech power of a kind unavailable to other individuals.[131] The Supreme Court's rejection of statutorily compelled access rights not only fails to view these facts realistically; it wrongly analogizes rights to reply to a content-biased prohibition of speech.[132] In fact, such reply rights offer the fair rebuttal most consistent with underlying principles of equal respect for deliberative rationality. In the absence of clear evidence that such regulations have chilling effects on controversial news coverage, such access obligations and remedies would more broadly and equitably disperse free speech power in the direction of a greater equal liberty of communicative integrity for all.

In contrast, the Supreme Court has not experienced comparable difficulty in squaring forms of such access obligations and associated doctrines with free speech guarantees when considering new types of media not burdened with the salient place of the press in our constitutional history. Federal Communications Commission (FCC) access obligations, applicable to radio and television, have been regarded by the Court as neutral state regulations ensuring fairer use of a communications medium that, unlike the press, is a scarce resource to which everyone cannot have access.[133]

Radio and television are the most distinctive and massively influential media of communication in the modern era.[134] The proper regulatory treatment of them, consistent with First Amendment values, is perhaps the most urgent free speech issue of our electronic age, one compli-

130. See, e.g., *Miami Herald Pub. Co. v. Tornillo*, 418 U.S. 241 (1974).
131. See Barron, "Access to the Press—A New First Amendment Right."
132. *Miami Herald Pub. Co. v. Tornillo*, 418 U.S. 241 (1974).
133. *Red Lion Broadcasting Co. v. FCC*, 395 U.S. 367 (1969). But the Court has carefully qualified the scope of the access obligation even in this area, disallowing, for example, a constitutional challenge to CBS's refusal to allow all editorial advertisements when other commercial advertisements were allowed, *Columbia Broadcasting System v. Democratic Nat. Comm.*, 412 U.S. 94 (1973). Apparently, editorial discretion has significant constitutional weight, for the Court, even in a medium that it otherwise distinguishes from the press.
134. See, in general, Schmidt, *Freedom of the Press vs. Public Access*.

cated by the contemporary explosion of new communication technologies in cable, computers, video, telephones, and the like.[135] The characteristic American solution, in contrast to the British, has been to make radio and television a commercial medium, supported by advertising, with background FCC regulatory obligations (such as the fairness doctrine).[136] This unbalanced commitment of the medium to commerce has had the inevitable effect on programming that should have been anticipated, namely, that programming content has been cast to appeal to the lowest common denominator of a mass audience. The enormous promise of this medium, in deepening and broadening the deliberative discourse of a free people, has thus been squandered. If the aims of free speech are, as the Court ritually incants, "to secure 'the widest possible dissemination of information from diverse and antagonistic sources,'"[137] television programming must be judged, by any reasonable measure of achievement, a miserable travesty of the aims of free speech in a democratic society.

Much of the fault rests with the initial congressional decision to structure this medium in the way it did, rather than with the Supreme Court's struggles to square the congressional regulatory structure with the values of the First Amendment. Congressional commitment of the medium to advertising alone was an unbalanced failure to reserve some of the medium for the public discourse and culture essential to a free society; it is analogous, in constitutional principle, to any state requirement that an entire medium of communications (for example, print) must contain advertisements—as much an abuse of constitutional neutrality as the total prohibition of such advertisements. There is little that the judiciary can do to remedy such structural defects, which will remain until Congress adequately recognizes the national responsibility for public broadcasting on the British Broadcasting Corporation model of guaranteed independence. Nevertheless, what little the Court has done has been inconsistent and sometimes misguided. The special status of radio and television as public forums is, on the one hand, acknowledged; but the Court forbids the generous elaboration of access obligations that might assure a fairer use of these media consistent with central free speech values of airing "diverse and antagonistic sources."[138]

The Supreme Court's misguided treatment of the status of radio and television as public forums is exemplified by *FCC v. Pacifica Founda-*

---

135. For an illuminating general treatment, see Pool, *Technologies of Freedom.*
136. For pertinent history of the American regulatory pattern of federal licensing of radio and television as advertising media, subject to legal obligations of serving the public interest, a pattern set by the Federal Communications Act of 1934, see Schmidt, *Freedom of the Press vs. Public Access,* pp. 125–216; Pool, *Technologies of Freedom,* pp. 108–50.
137. *New York Times Co. v. Sullivan,* 376 U.S. at 266.
138. See, e.g., *Columbia Broadcasting System v. Democratic Nat. Comm.,* 412 U.S. 94 (1973). See note 133, above.

tion.[139] The Court in *Pacifica* rejected a constitutional challenge to FCC sanctions against the airing of a monologue by comedian George Carlin entitled "Filthy Words" containing various obscenities. The obscenities in question were not constitutionally obscene under applicable constitutional tests,[140] and the offense taken at the words would not have justified speech abridgment in a traditional public forum (the state would be enforcing content-biased distaste for what is said). The obscenities were in fact used in the monologue to make an ironic and caustically comic comment on unjust values reflected in popular obscenities; normally, such irony would be given heightened protection as the vigorous and critical dissent essential to free speech values.[141] The Court disallowed all these plausible constitutional analogies because, in its view, radio and television were not public forums. Rather, special features of the medium (the privacy of the home where such broadcasts could be heard, and the children exposed to them) justified FCC strictures on such offensive language at least during the times of the day when children might hear the material. The consequence of this decision, as Justice William Brennan pointed out in an eloquent dissent, is that the level of discourse on national television must be pitched at a level that would not offend children or their parents. In effect, the Court constitutionally endorsed the very tendency of this medium that conflicts with free speech values, namely, that speech in this medium cannot offend the lowest common denominator of majoritarian taste in the society.

It does not bode well for the judiciary's future treatment of new technologies of communication that it has so misunderstood the free speech concerns that surround the regulation of so powerful a medium of social control as radio and television. The Court's principled sensitivity to free speech values in traditional public forums is in striking contrast to its treatment of radio and television. The judiciary, which insists that the state may not make judgments for individuals about whether they want to hear the advocacy of a deviant religion on their doorstep, allows the state precisely to make such homogenizing judgments for radio and television programming. The state thus deprives each person of control over what he or his child will hear. If anything, such decisions by each person are more contextually deliberative than confrontations with religious advocates on one's doorstep. In contrast, the homogenizing impact of state judgments over radio and television is much more devastating than any comparable such judgments would be in restricting religious or political solicitations at one's home. The restrictions on

139. *FCC v. Pacifica Foundation,* 438 U.S. 726 (1978).
140. The speech does not depict a vivid pornographic or scatological scene in the way that the *Miller* tests require. See *Miller v. California,* 413 U.S. 15, 25 (1973).
141. Cf. *Cohen v. California,* 403 U.S. 15 (1971) ("Fuck the Draft" constitutionally protected speech).

offensive radio or television programming change the very nature of the communicative medium and the critical integrity of the meanings there expressed. In effect, the state manages the medium in the way most offensive to free speech values—only those views are heard that offend no one.

Critical reflection on the free speech jurisprudence of classic and contemporary public forums raises larger questions about how and why the judiciary has used and abused historical understandings in this area. Certain traditional conceptions of minimal public forums are properly maintained, and often sensitively elaborated in ways consistent with free speech principles.[142] But other familiar historical loci of free speech concern (the independence of the press, for example) are sometimes anachronistically protected from forms of state regulations quite consistent with the larger aims of free speech. New technologies of communication, which fall ambiguously between older historical models (a public forum subject to time, place, and manner regulations, and the press free from all regulation), are disastrously analogized now to one, now to the other, often in ways that travesty the free speech concerns appropriate to these new media. These blunders are the consequence of a sense of history unilluminated by the principled arguments of political theory, which should enable us to understand and apply our traditions sensibly and coherently.

Contractarian political theory reminds us that democratic constitutionalism is only as robust and as strong as the range and depth of the public forums in which a self-governing people exercises its powers of deliberative rationality. If public man has retreated, as Sennett argues,[143] to the privatized spaces of his home, then historical conceptions of the public forum and of the press may no longer be adequate to their underlying functions in the cultivation of the civic responsibilities of a democratic people. From this perspective, access obligations of the press are called for, and the new media of communication, to which we have access from our homes, must be as open, as diverse, and as free as the older public forums. Otherwise, the very conscience of a democratic people will be degraded by media that never confront them with the critical and offensive dissent that invigorates the minds and the morality of a free people. A public culture—thus stunted by a cramped repertoire of banal and stereotyped images—can sustain neither the range of imagination nor the intelligence required of a self-governing people.[144]

Critics of current free speech jurisprudence, concerned that the

142. See *Brown v. Louisiana*, 383 U.S. 131 (1966) (reading room of public library held to be public forum for purposes of silent protest of its policy of racial segregation).
143. See Sennett, *The Fall of Public Man.*
144. Cf. Dworkin, *A Matter of Principle*, pp. 221–33; Richards, "Human Rights and Moral Ideals: An Essay on the Moral Theory of Liberalism," pp. 483–86.

Supreme Court has brought advertising within the protection of free speech, are, I earlier suggested, wrong. The identification of urgent free speech concerns requires a probing use of political theory in criticizing background assumptions of the "natural" union of political and economic power, or of the role of new media in a mass society. We may thus face authentic free speech problems, for example, the distortion of equal respect by economic inequalities, and the scandal of powerful communicative media—radio and television—sanitized of serious discourse and sold to the highest commercial bidder. The First Amendment does not require, and we should not tolerate, either that economic inequalities distort the agenda of public discussion, or that the mass media mind of the nation is sold to commerce and never allowed to see or reflect on anything but the least controversial and most majoritarian images of itself.

CONCLUDING METHODOLOGICAL REMARKS

My examination of free speech jurisprudence, in the light of contractarian political theory, is both explanatory and critical. Major themes and particular structures of the constitutional law of free speech have, I believe, often been powerfully elucidated and organized by such conceptions. Indeed, many interpretive trends in the law are reasonably understood as attempts to articulate the principles required by such a conception. Religion clause and free speech jurisprudence are importantly connected, and the unity of their tests and themes bespeaks a deeper interpretive unity that political theory explains and guides. On the other hand, our examination also had critical and prescriptive aspects. Certain interpretive strands in free speech jurisprudence are worthy of criticism, and should be rethought. In certain areas (equalization of political power and the media), my theme was almost entirely critical.

This use of political theory, combining explanatory and critical aspects, should itself be interpreted historically, in the way we now see the current tests of subversive advocacy as the product of internal interpretive tensions over these questions within the judiciary and the larger interpretive community it reflects. We have learned, as a community, from the process of reflection upon our interpretive traditions over time. My critical use of contractarian theory is intended as a contribution to this kind of discourse in areas where our interpretive traditions are still deeply controversial, unstable, and fraught with self-doubt and divisions within the judiciary and the larger constitutional community. We invigorate our minds and our traditions by openness to this kind of critical exchange.

We have come a long way toward the aim of this book: the explication of religion clause and free speech jurisprudence on a certain interpretive model of the primacy of religious toleration. But both religious liberty and free speech are settled features of our law. Our examination so far provides good reasons for defending what many would already regard as uncontroversial and settled. The interpretive power of this approach should also be tested by its work in areas of intractable constitutional controversy. We therefore turn to another interpretive project: constitutional privacy.

IV / Constitutional Privacy

8 · A Theory of Constitutional Privacy

Controversy over the nature, provenance, and application of the constitutional right to privacy has followed in the wake of each of the Supreme Court's decisions extending that right to the use of contraceptives,[1] of obscene materials in the home,[2] and of abortion services.[3] Constitutional theorists have been among the critics of the Court's interpretive work in this area (for example, Ely, discussed in chapter 1). This chapter addresses the question of the interpretive legitimacy in principle of the constitutional right to privacy; the next chapter assesses various applications of the right (including the Court's controversial failure to apply the right to consensual homosexuality).[4] We have seen that contractarian political theory, rooted in the inalienable right to conscience as a background right, organizes and explicates much of the discourse of the First Amendment. It also reveals principled connections between this familiar range of discourse and another range of discourse (constitutional privacy). Contractarian theory

1. *Griswold v. Connecticut*, 381 U.S. 479 (1965); *Eisenstadt v. Baird*, 405 U.S. 438 (1972).
2. *Stanley v. Georgia*, 394 U.S. 557 (1969).
3. *Roe v. Wade*, 410 U.S. 113 (1973).
4. See *Doe v. Commonwealth's Attorney*, 403 F. Supp. 1199 (E.D. Va. 1975), *aff'd without opinion* 425 U.S. 901 (1976). But cf. *People v. Onofre*, 51 N.Y.2d 476 (1980), *cert. den.* 451 U.S. 987 (1981).

explains and justifies the general constitutional theme of toleration in various spheres—thought, speech, and action.

THE INTERPRETIVE LEGITIMACY OF THE RIGHT OF CONSTITUTIONAL PRIVACY

The conundrum of constitutional privacy is familiarly posed by critics of constitutional privacy in a twofold interrogatory. How can constitutional privacy, a right which is not textually rooted in any clause of the written constitution, be inferred with judicial fidelity to the interpretation of the terms of the Constitution? And assuming the right is textually based in some form, how can such textual inference by squared with basic premises of the political theory of democratic self-rule that sharply limit the scope of proper judicial invalidation of majority rule?

John Hart Ely most sharply poses the latter challenge.[5] He does not believe that the first prong of the conundrum, the interpretivist chal-·lenge to the judicial elaboration of constitutional privacy, is a decisive interpretive objection in principle to the judicial inference of the constitutional right to privacy. Ely concedes that the inference of the constitutional right to privacy in *Griswold v. Connecticut* "reveals strong interpretivist urges."[6] The Court thus struggles to relate the inference of the right to privacy of a married couple to use contraceptives to the First, Third, Fourth, and Fifth Amendments, making a special effort to acknowledge the Fourth Amendment by suggesting the methods the police would have to use to enforce the law (bugging the bedroom).[7] Ely also appears to concede that much of the text of the Constitution itself contemplated the inference of fundamental rights not specified in the Bill of Rights, for example, the privileges and immunities clause of the Fourteenth Amendment, adapted from the comparable clause of Article IV.[8] Therefore, an alternative interpretivist argument exists in support of a reasonable textual and historical inference of substantive rights such as constitutional privacy. For example, pursuant to Ely's assumption that various clauses of the Constitution contemplated unenumerated basic human rights that would be enforceable on a par with enumerated rights, we might give content to such rights by reference to the literature influential on and clearly expressive of the normative assumptions of the remarkably learned generation that wrote the United States Constitution and Bill of Rights. One such right—assumed by Founders—was what Hutcheson called "the natural right

---

5. Ely, *Democracy and Distrust*.
6. Ibid., p. 221 n. 4. Cf. Ely, "The Wages of Crying Wolf: A Comment on *Roe v. Wade*," pp. 928–30.
7. *Griswold v. Connecticut*, 381 U.S., 484, and 485–86.
8. Ely, *Democracy and Distrust*, pp. 22–30.

each one to enter into the matrimonial relation with any one who consents."⁹. Indeed, relevant historical materials suggest that the right may properly be more abstractly stated; for example, John Witherspoon, whose lectures Madison heard at Princeton, followed Hutcheson in listing as a basic human and natural right a "right to associate, if he so incline, with any person or persons, whom he can persuade (not force)—under this is contained the right to marriage."¹⁰ Such historical material, supplemented by relevant arguments of rights-based political theory like those assumed at the time, might reasonably support the interpretation that the constitutional text in question protects a basic human right of personal association, including intimate associations of which marriage is one central but nonexclusive example.¹¹ The inference of a constitutional right to privacy in *Griswold* would, on this alternative view, be construed as an interpretivist protection of a fundamental constitutional right (the marriage relationship) from state prohibitions lacking sufficient justification.¹²

Both these arguments are, in Ely's sense, interpretivist. Ely expressly endorses the former, because he regards it as sufficiently connected to interests in control of private information protected by various amendments of the Bill of Rights. He regards the elaboration of the constitutional right to privacy to the case of abortion as not supported by this argument because abortion services are not similarly limited to such enclaves of privacy as the bedroom or home. He rejects the second interpretivist explication of *Griswold* (and its possible implications for abortion) because it would involve filling out the Constitution's "more indeterminate phrases" with too controversial rights-based political theory.¹³ Ely thus rests his critical case against constitutional privacy on the second prong of the challenge to the interpretive legitimacy of constitutional privacy: textually and historically sustainable inferences

9. Hutcheson, *A System of Moral Philosophy*, p. 299. Accordingly, leading statesmen at the state conventions ratifying the Constitution, both those for and against adoption, assume that the Constitution could not interfere in the domestic sphere. Thus, Hamilton of New York denies that federal constitutional power does or could "penetrate the recesses of domestic life, and control, in all respects, the private conduct of individuals", Jonathan Elliot, *Debates in the Several State Conventions*, vol. 2, p. 268. And Patrick Henry of Virginia speaks of the core of our rights to liberty as the sphere where a person "enjoys the fruits of his labor, under his own fig-tree, with his wife and children around him, in peace and security", Jonathan Elliot, *id.*, vol. 3, p. 54. It is striking that the rhetoric of reserved rights both of leading proponents (Hamilton) and opponents (Henry) of adoption of the Constitution converges on this private sphere of domestic married life.
10. Witherspoon, *Lectures on Moral Philosophy*, p. 123.
11. See Karst, "The Freedom of Intimate Association."
12. These remarks only sketch what such an interpretivist account must do: explicate a political theory of why the historical understanding should properly be interpreted to identify marriage as a fundamental right, and explain why the purposes of the state prohibition were no longer adequate thus to burden a fundamental right. For a fuller account, see chapter 9.
13. Ely, *Democracy and Distrust*, pp. 221 n. 4, 56–60.

from at least the "more indeterminate phrases" of the written constitution should be rejected when they are inconsistent with the best political theory of constitutional democracy.

For Ely, this political theory maintains that a working democracy must secure fair representation to all relevant interests; judicial review of majoritarian legislation is justified if it secures on balance a fairer representation of interests than majority rule unqualified by judicial review. On this theory, the heart of justifiable judicial review is the form of equal protection review (suspect classification analysis) that invalidates legislation based on the kind of racist hatred that fails to accord fair democratic weight to the interests of racial minorities. Whatever the textual or historical warrant for constitutional privacy, the doctrine is not justifiably elaborated at least as an interpretation of the Constitution's "indeterminate phrases" when it does not secure fairer representation in the way democratic political theory requires. On this view, if it were not grounded in more determinate constitutional clauses, constitutional privacy would not properly be extended to contraceptive use, which protects not an insular minority but a large majority of contraceptive-using Americans. The abortion cases are, for Ely, wrong a fortiori: their only textual support is one of the "indeterminate phrases" of the Constitution and no insular minority is protected from unfair representation by extending to pregnant women an absolute right to terminate pregnancy during the first trimester. Rather, one may argue that quite an insular minority indeed (the unborn fetuses) is, by virtue of the abortion decisions, exposed to constitutionally invidious prejudice.[14]

Ely's form of argument is of interest in its frank redirection of interpretive debate over constitutional privacy from text and history to political theory. There is, as he concedes, much in the text and history of the Constitution that would support the general doctrine of constitutional privacy. The gravamen of his argument is that we must edit this text and history in the light of background political theory, accepting constitutional privacy in certain areas but not others. The theory naturally invites response in terms of an alternative political theory that is both a better account of constitutional legitimacy in general and a fuller justification of constitutional privacy in particular.

Three general forms of argument merit exploration as available ways to understand and justify constitutional privacy: first, the argument from shifting moral consensus; second, the harm principle, seminally stated by John Stuart Mill in *On Liberty*; and third, a contractarian argument elaborating themes earlier suggested in this book. I shall argue that the most promising strategy is an interpretation made available by contractarian political theory.

14. See Ely, "The Wages of Crying Wolf: A Comment on *Roe v. Wade*."

CHANGING MORAL CONSENSUS

The argument from changing moral consensus grounds privacy argument on putative shifts in the conventional moral values held in the society at large and thus regarded as the traditional basis for concepts of public morality. Since the values of the public morality supply the relevant standards enforced through the criminal law, any shift in conventional moral values in the direction of not regarding certain conduct as morally wrong would justify forms of decriminalization of that conduct. However, there is a lag between the shift in moral consensus and the associated decriminalization. Conventional social morality no longer regards certain conduct (for example, use of contraceptives) as wrong, and yet such conduct is still the object of criminal sanctions. Arguments of privacy arise in the interstices between shifts in moral consensus and unchanged criminal sanctions. Conduct is immunized from criminal sanction by invocation of a right to privacy when the moral basis for the criminal sanction is no longer supported by moral consensus.

Conventional moral views are the starting point of most serious reflection on ethical questions, including criticism of existing moral beliefs. When moral critics urge a more reasonable or humane way of thinking about ethics, often the very terms of their new discourse (for example, a conception of harms justly forbidden by law, or of the goods the deprivation of which is such a harm) are shaped by and shape such background conventional moral beliefs. Not unnaturally, critical moral argument determines what the moral consensus is or should be taken to be.[15] This way of thinking makes the argument from changing moral consensus trivially true almost by definition, which may account for the continuing attraction of the argument for many. Since the criminal law or its essential purposes rests on definitions of certain forms of moral wrongdoing, conduct that is, as we now see, not morally wrong should not be criminal. So far, so good.

But the argument from moral consensus is not confined to this trivially true interpretation. It is supposed to say something informative about the real basis for criminalization and the appropriate grounds for substantive shifts in the contraction or expansion of the scope of the criminal sanction, namely, criminal law should track changing moral consensus. As such, it misdescribes the phenomenon it purports to explain, and certainly renders incoherent any theory of constitutional privacy as a judicially enforceable right.

This informative interpretation of the argument from changing moral consensus appeals to a conception of conventional morality as the basis for criminal law. It fails to explain how changes in moral consensus

15. See, e.g., Dworkin, *Taking Rights Seriously*, pp. 240–58.

occur or how, normatively, we should assess their justifiability. It is by now a philosophical banality in decriminalization controversy in the recurrent forms of the Mill–Stephen[16] or Hart–Devlin[17] debates that the controversy centers on different interpretations of what public morality is and may properly demand through social convention. Serious arguments for decriminalization standardly controvert traditional moral conventions for failing to satisfy certain independently desirable criteria of rationality or critical morality. The standard answers of moral conservatives question the possibility of such internal moral reforms, given the inextricable web of moral conventions alleged by them to define the public morality; as Devlin quite clearly argued,[18] forms of decriminalization alleged to reflect a changing moral consensus may treasonably rend the very fabric of social unity. The argument from shifts in moral consensus fails to address the substance of such disagreements between advocates of and dissenters from proposed forms of decriminalization. Rather, the argument suppresses the issue in dispute (namely, the proper interpretation and assessment of conventional morality) in the name of the question-begging assertion that shifting moral consensus controls.

From the perspective of the traditional liberal concern for a program of decriminalization, the argument from shifting moral consensus fails to capture the dynamic of critical moral assessment fundamental to the explanation of shifts in moral consensus. Serious moral critics, liberal or not, do not regard conventional morality *simpliciter* as the measure of their moral criticism.[19] Rather, the premise of their criticism is that ethical arguments supply standards of assessment of conventional morality. From this perspective, the argument from shifting moral standards is especially dubious, for it proves too little (allowing moral reform only on the basis of moral consensus) or too much (requiring moral reform when, from the perspective of critical ethical thinking, the shift in moral consensus is morally corrupt, regressive, or atavistic).

If the informative form of the argument from shifting moral standards is a bad political theory of decriminalization, it is incoherent as a justification for judicial enforcement of decriminalization. The argument from shifting moral standards rests on the lag between shifts in moral consensus and decriminalization reflecting such shifts. But if there has been a massive shift in moral consensus (for example, regarding per-

---

16. See Mill, *On Liberty*; Stephen, *Liberty, Equality, Fraternity*.
17. See Hart, *Law, Liberty and Morality*; Devlin, *The Enforcement of Morals*, pp. 1–25.
18. See Devlin, *The Enforcement of Morals*, pp. 1–25.
19. The closest approximation to a purely conventional form of moral appraisal is some form of conventional rule-utilitarianism, of the kind that Stephen, for example, appears to assume; see his *Liberty, Equality, Fraternity*. However, such a perspective is still quite committed to the crucial relevance of utilitarian consequences in the moral assessment of actions and institutions, and thus convention, as such, has no controlling independent moral weight.

missible use of contraceptives), why do we need the intervention of a countermajoritarian judiciary? At most, judicial intervention may here accelerate the rate of legal change, but it does so at the real cost of diverting the issue from democratic politics, enervating the capacity of democratic majorities to use politics to achieve their rightful ends. Indeed, as a rationale for the right to constitutional privacy, the argument from shifting moral consensus counterintuitively justifies countermajoritarian judicial intervention when least needed, and fails to justify it when most called for. On the one hand, intervention is justified when the shift in moral consensus is widespread in large majorities; on the other, judicial intervention is withheld when its capacity for independent constitutional judgment may be most ethically required (the shift in moral consensus legitimating nonprocreational sex in its popular heterosexual forms has not consistently been extended to an isolated and stereotypically despised homosexual minority). On this theory, *Griswold v. Connecticut* would be correct (contraceptive use was popular); *Roe v. Wade* perhaps dubious (the shift in moral consensus at the time may have been unclear); *Doe v. Commonwealth's Attorney* correct (homosexuality was unpopular). Perhaps some of the Supreme Court's more startlingly inconsistent decisions may be explained in this way *(Naim v. Naim; Doe).*[20] Such an explanatory thesis, under which the Supreme Court tracks majoritarian moral consensus in order to preserve its institutional capital, hardly rises to the dignity of a political theory adequate to the classical role of the judiciary in vindicating arguments of constitutional principle.[21]

THE HARM PRINCIPLE

The argument based on the harm principle draws inspiration from its classic statement in a book of genius, John Stuart Mill's *On Liberty*. Mill's complex argument has two objectives, which have come to define two central planks in the political program of liberalism as a self-conscious political theory. The first is the primacy of freedom of expression as a political value; the second is a defense of a right of autonomy to act in certain areas without coercive state or social interference.[22] Mill's defense of a right of personal autonomy is, so it may be suggested, the basis of constitutional privacy.

Mill's argument for a right of personal autonomy rests on an extended and complex form of moral criticism of the degree to which a certain

20. *Naim v. Naim*, 350 U.S. 985 (1956)(dismissing on spurious jurisdictional grounds the appeal from a Virginia judgment dissolving a racially mixed marriage under the state's antimiscegenation statute, a statute later held squarely unconstitutional in *Loving v. Virginia*, 388 U.S. 1 [1967]).
21. See Gunther, "The Subtle Vices of the 'Passive Virtues.'"
22. Mill, *On Liberty*, chs. 2, 3–5.

form of conventional morality has unreflectingly been permitted to require both forms of state punishment through the criminal law and larger patterns of social condemnation enforced through informal mechanisms of social control. The form of conventional morality at issue shows this structure of argument: any form of conduct may be subject to state or social condemnation if an ordinary person, reflecting some statistical normalcy of sentiment and opinion of the society at large, would experience deep revulsion and offense at the thought of the action in question *simpliciter*. Mill argues that the Anglo-American conception of public morality, reflected in the work of temperance leagues and "purity" reformers, expresses this argument of conventional morality.

Mill's argument for the inadequacy of conventional morality as the measure of legal and social enforcement is the stark failure of the relevant standard (the offense taken by an ordinary person at the thought of the action in question) to advert to any impact of the conduct in question on any interests of persons. Forms of conduct are to be legally and socially condemned solely because an ordinary person would take offense at the thought of certain conduct, *without anything more*—in particular, without any required form of inquiry into the reasons why such conduct is condemned, the degree to which the conduct impedes or advances human interests, or the justifiability of requiring all persons similarly situated so to act. So understood, conventional morality mandates legal and social prohibitions that narrow the range of permissible actions to those simply of the most unquestioned popular prejudices based on crass stereotypes, elementary failures of moral and human imagination, and group ignorance and bigotry. If the achievement of democratic government leads, Mill suggests (following de Tocqueville),[23] to the unquestioned dominance of conventional morality so understood, the deepest values of the political theory of democracy will be betrayed. A tool intended to liberate human capacities for the enlightened pursuit of interests on terms fair to all will become an instrument for the crudest oppression of the varieties of the pursuit of happiness into Procrustean convention—rigid, unintelligent, wilful.

In order to obviate this betrayal of basic democratic values, Mill argues that conventional morality as such must be rejected as the basis for legal and social condemnation; in its place, he offers the harm principle. In contrast to the standard of conventional morality, which in principle allows anything to be the object of legal and social condemnation (depending on the feelings of offense of the ordinary person), the harm principle imposes determinate constraints on the degree to which legal and social condemnation may be applied to acts. For purposes of just criminalization, Mill's formulation limits the scope of the

23. See esp. de Tocqueville, *Democracy in America*, vol. 1, chs. 15–16.

criminal law, subject to a background theory of just distribution and of moral duties of fair contribution, in the following ways:

1. Acts may properly be made criminal only if they inflict concrete harms on assignable persons.
2. Except to protect children, incompetents, and "backward"[24] peoples, it is never proper to criminalize an act *solely* on the ground of preventing harm to the agent.
3. It is never proper to criminalize conduct solely because the mere thought of it gives offense to others.

The harm principle states, Mill argues, a form of reasoning that democratic majorities must observe in order to impose just criminal sanctions in the same way that justice in punishment requires that the definition and imposition of criminal sanctions must observe certain basic principles of legality, proportionality, concurrence of *actus reus* and *mens rea*, and the like.[25]

Mill's argument for the harm principle correctly seeks to dispel the superficial appeal of conventional morality as the most democratic way for a society to establish enforceable moral values:—the view that a society cannot more democratically decide these issues than by a kind of populist appeal to the felt values that unite democratic majorities as a people. Mill's provocative response is a deep political theory of the values fundamental to republican democracy. Populist moral romanticism (the basis of the appeal of conventional morality) does not express the critical values that make democracy a defensible form of government. Rather, such a conception of enforceable moral standards rests on an older, indeed ancient, idea of public tribal morality philosophically in tension with the values of equality and liberty of constitutional democracies (for example, the primacy of religious toleration and freedom of conscience).[26] The values distinctive of democracy, Mill argues, liberate human capacities for the enlightened pursuit of interests on terms fair to all, which the enforcement of the tribal conception of conventional morality frustrates in profoundly damaging ways. For this reason, an alternative conception of enforceable public morality (the harm principle) is required by democratic political theory.

Mill's arguments in *On Liberty* represent a great advance in political theory because they connect in a philosophically articulate way arguments for the priority of free speech and the harm principle to a plausible general theory of constitutional democracy. Nonetheless, the form of Mill's defense of liberalism suffers from the intractable internal

24. Mill, *On Liberty*, p. 10.
25. See, e.g., Richards, *The Moral Criticism of Law*, chs. 5–6.
26. I phrase Mill's argument in the terms used in this discussion. The express terms of his own argument are an appeal to "individuality"; see Mill, *On Liberty*, p. 55, and ch. 3.

tension between Mill's sympathy for rights-based arguments of principle and his doctrinal utilitarianism. Although Mill's harm principle places a constraint on the criminal law comparable to the one embodied in the French Declaration of Rights,[27] Mill did not justify the constraint on the basis of the human rights paradigm, as did the French Declaration. Rather, Mill appealed to a general utilitarian argument, derived from Jeremy Bentham, that failure to apply the harm principle reduces the aggregate surplus of pleasure over pain. Mill was less doctrinaire in his opposition to the language and thought of rights than Bentham, and some find in *On Liberty* rights-based arguments of personal autonomy. Although Mill did give great weight to preserving the capacity of persons to frame their own life plans independently, he appears—in accordance with his argument in *Utilitarianism*—to have incorporated this factor into the utilitarian framework of preferring "higher" to "lower" pleasures.[28] The argument of *On Liberty* is thus utilitarian: the greatest aggregate sum by which pleasure exceeds pain, taking into account the greater weight accorded by utilitarianism to higher pleasures, is secured by granting free speech and observing the harm principle as the measure of criminalization.

To the extent that the harm principle appears to be at least a good first approximation to a significant constraint of justice on permissible criminalization, there are grave objections to grounding this perception of justice on utilitarian argument.[29] The harm principle is not a necessary corollary of utilitarian tenets; quite the contrary. The basic desideratum of utilitarianism is to maximize the surplus of pleasure over pain. If certain plausible assumptions about human nature are

27. Several provisions of the Declaration of the Rights of Man and of Citizens, adopted by the French National Assembly in 1789, place express constraints on the scope of the criminal law. Specifically, persons were to have "the power of doing whatever does not injure another," Article IV, French Declaration of the Rights of Man and of Citizens. See also Articles V–XI. For text, see Paine, *Rights of Man*, p. 133.

28. See Mill, *Utilitarianism*, ch. 2.

29. For an elaboration of this criticism of Mill, see Richards, *Sex, Drugs, Death and the Law*, ch. 1. To the extent that scholars attempt to reconstruct Mill's argument on utilitarian grounds, they propose an interpretive structure not properly utilitarian but rather explicatory of central neo-Kantian values of the independence and integrity of the person. See, for example, Gray, *Mill on Liberty: a Defence;* and Berger's important study, *Happiness, Justice and Freedom.* When scholars tinker with utilitarian assumptions in order to yield anything as demanding as the harm principle, they confirm one's suspicions that, for them, the harm principle is a more secure moral judgment than any utilitarian rationale or assumption designed to justify it. Cf. the familiar utilitarian use of a dubious factual assumption, declining marginal utility, to justify beliefs in egalitarian distribution whose moral foundations are certainly more secure than our beliefs in diminishing marginal utility. See Richards, *A Theory of Reasons for Action*, pp. 114–15. If utilitarian arguments for the harm principle are thus dubious, as C. L. Ten suggests, we should explicate an alternative moral theory which will ground the harm principle more directly and securely and which, in any event, Mill appears to assume, albeit through a glass darkly. See Ten, *Mill on Liberty.*

made, however, utilitarianism would require the criminalization of certain conduct in violation of the harm principle. Assume, for example, that an overwhelming majority of people in a community takes personal satisfaction in their way of life and that their pleasure is appreciably heightened by the knowledge that conflicting ways of life are forbidden by the criminal law. Suppose that hatred of the nonconforming minority, legitimated by the application of criminal penalties, reinforces their pleasurable feelings of social solidarity, peace of mind, self-worth, and achievement in a way that toleration—with its invitation to self-doubt, ambivalence, and insecurity—could not. In such circumstances, the greater pleasure thus secured to the majority may not only outweigh the pain to the minority but, compared to the toleration required by the harm principle, results in a greater aggregate of pleasure. Utilitarianism would then call for criminalization in violation of the harm principle. From this perspective, James Fitzjames Stephen may be a more consistent utilitarian than Mill in seeing that a utilitarian analysis does not cohere with the stringent requirements of the harm principle.[30]

If the harm principle were only properly justified by utilitarian argument, this would pose special justificatory difficulties for constitutional privacy as a sound interpretation of the United States Constitution. The utilitarian cast that Mill gives his arguments is understandable in Great Britain, where Mill makes his argument to a parliament that enjoys constitutional supremacy. In the United States, however, arguments of this kind are made not only to legislatures but also to countermajoritarian courts empowered with judicial supremacy in the elaboration of a charter of human rights that constrains utilitarian aggregation. Arguments of utilitarian aggregation can hardly interpretively fit the structure of American constitutional law in general or the constitutional right to privacy in particular.[31] As it is, critics argue that the right to privacy is policy-based, legislative in character, and unsupported by neutral principles of justification.[32] If the rationale of constitutional privacy in these cases must be construed in utilitarian terms, such objections might be conclusive, and decriminalization arguments would be properly directed only to legislatures, not to courts.

Finally, even assuming that the harm principle were a justiciable standard justly enforced by countermajoritarian courts, the judicial interpretation of the application of the principle is subject to doubt and controversy in ways that do not advance critical understanding of the constitutional right to privacy in American constitutional law. In the first place, the utilitarian interpretation of the harm principle does not explain why the loci of American constitutional argument have been areas of *privacy*, rather than conduct in general that harms no one. Fur-

30. See Stephen, *Liberty, Equality, Fraternity*.
31. See, in general, Dworkin's *Taking Rights Seriously* and *A Matter of Principle*.
32. See, e.g., Ely, "The Wages of Crying Wolf: A Comment on *Roe v. Wade*."

ther, the interpretation of what counts as a "harm" in many cases may simply replicate the moral controversies over the proper scope of criminalization that the harm principle was supposed to clarify. Abortion may be a striking example. Advocates of the criminalization of abortion argue that it is not a victimless or complaintless crime: the unborn fetus is harmed in a straightforward sense—its life is terminated. Opponents of such criminalization respond that there is no harm to anyone (since there is no moral person killed) but only a great good to a woman, that of controlling her reproductive autonomy. The simple notion of "harm," perhaps very useful in some areas of decriminalization controversy, appears here only to carry the level of debate one step backward. The harm principle, often a useful starting point in decriminalization controversy, is not always the best ending point. In order to deepen analysis at crucial points, we must develop a plausible background theory that may interpret both why constitutional argument applies to certain areas of conduct and what "harm" should mean without collapsing into a utilitarianism that seems unable to capture either the force or the sense that the harm principle intuitively carries with it.

CONSCIENCE, PRIVACY, AND GENERAL GOODS

A contractarian perspective affords both a more plausible general political theory of these matters and a sounder interpretive account of the constitutional elaboration of the right to privacy. We may begin with the abstract statement of a contractarian perspective on privacy as a right of the person and on general goods as a constraint on state coercive power. In the next sections, this political theory is connected to constitutional interpretation.

Privacy as a Human Right

Contractarian thought takes seriously the ways community life shapes our self-conceptions, aspirations, and central aims (see chapter 7). Interests in reputational integrity and informational privacy are, in different ways, so associated with exercise of the right to conscience itself that they identify, from a contractarian perspective, general goods to which persons are entitled.

In the context of the discussion in chapter 7, the right to privacy was understood as the right to control private information about or experience of the self, a right violated, for example, by publication of private facts in which there is no legitimate public interest. That right was, I argued, closely allied to the communicative integrity central to free speech, reflecting, as Justice Brandeis saw, their common background right of conscience. If the right of communicative integrity protects decisions about whether or how to communicate, the right to privacy allows persons not to communicate, to preserve from public life essential resources of a life guided by personal conscience.

This moral ground of the right to privacy justifies more, however, than the informational interests narrowly in play in that earlier discussion. We can see this in the connections between privacy interests and the higher-order interests protected by the right to conscience itself. The objects of these latter interests are the conditions essential to independent exercise of the moral powers through which we assess our most basic self-conceptions of a life well and humanely lived. Control over informational privacy is in natural service of these interests because it is one of the resources (control of private information) essential to control over our moral powers, namely, protection from a homogenizing public scrutiny that paralyzes moral independence itself. These resources include not only informational privacy, but a cognate range of capacities for thought, emotion, and action integral to the self-image of a person exercising moral independence in the formation of intimate relationships. Respect for moral independence requires certain limits on the scope of state power and special protection of areas of crucial moral independence improperly subject to such state power. In particular, such areas of conduct must be removed from a public scrutiny peculiarly hostile to the just exercise of essential moral powers.

An analogy may clarify the nature of this private sphere. We regard religious belief, practice, and even action (when not violating compelling secular interests) as private matters, not because we associate religion with informational privacy (many religious activities take place in public). Rather, our commitment to the right to conscience associates integrity itself with the control of each person over the formation of the ultimate aims of moral powers, for example, an identity formed in personal relationship to an ethical God. Accordingly, we think of this relationship as not properly a matter of public interest and protect it from any public intrusion that compromises the moral independence expressed and often perfected in such relationships.

In a generic sense, we may say that the very idea of many classical constitutional rights against the state expresses, in principle, an enforceable distinction between a private sphere protected by such rights from public interest and the properly public sphere of legitimate state interest and action. Such rights, like religious liberty, often do not protect informational privacy interests as such. But we do naturally think of these rights as defining spheres of privacy, using the most abstract sense of privacy—freedom from unjust intrusion by other people.

On contractarian grounds, the scope of this private sphere includes those highly personal relationships and activities whose just moral independence requires special protection from a hostile public interest that compromises the range of thought, self-image, emotional vulnerabilities, sensitivities, and aspirations essential to the role of such relationships and activities in the formation of self expressive of one's moral powers. Intimate relationships—which give play to love, devotion, friendship as organizing themes in self-conceptions of permanent value in living—are among the essential resources of moral independence. Protection from hostile interest thus nurtures these intimate personal resources, a wholeness of emotion, intellect, and self-image guided by the self-determining moral powers of a free person.

Such conduct is properly called private not because it requires informational privacy (though it may), but because its centrality to moral independence requires—in the generic sense true of other rights— that it not be in the sphere of public concern. If the broadest sense of privacy includes the idea of a private sphere as such, violations of informational privacy are only one kind of peril to this private sphere. Another such peril may be posed by state intrusions into the most intimate decisions and associations of one's personal life, identity, and self-concept. Informational privacy and this properly private sphere of personal life thus elaborate different strands of the concept of privacy. Why, then, do we associate these rights as rights to "privacy" in a way we do not with other rights generically? The answer is this: both rights appear to be grounded in a similar moral justification: not just protection against state intrusion (true of many classical constitutional rights), but protection of the resources of our moral independence against specific perils of a homogenizing and hostile public scrutiny. This common ground of special concern explains the natural association of the two kinds of privacy argument.[33]

General Goods and Limits of State Power

Contractarian political theory extends special protection to certain interests of the person in conscience and privacy; it also imposes coordinate constraints on the frustration of those interests by the coercive power of the state. We must now explain the nature and justification of these constraints, which give a contractarian interpretation to the harm principle.

From a contractarian perspective, the conception of public morality, justly enforced through the criminal law, must be consistent with the required equal respect for conscience of all persons. On this view, the state is the larger political political community affording a just framework for a variegated range of subcommunities. As we earlier saw, this just framework includes guarantees of the inalienable right to conscience and communicative integrity, which secure state neutrality among the array of communicative and other communities that a person

---

33. On analogies between the two kinds of privacy, see Richards, *Sex, Drugs, Death and the Law*, pp. 33–34, 61–63. My thought here is indebted to correspondence with Judith DeCew and to two unpublished papers on privacy which she kindly made available to me. See also Richards, "Privacy."

may choose. The consequence of such state neutrality is moral independence exercised in commitment to particular moral, religious, or philosophical traditions. Since the point of these guarantees is to secure the moral independence of each and every person over oneself and the state, contractarian principles require that the scope of enforceable public morality—defining the moral standards of conduct enforceable at large—must not undermine this focal aim of contractarian government. Enforcement of public morality must thus achieve two ends: first, it should impose common standards of minimal decency necessary to ensure reasonable cooperation among persons; and second, it should define these standards in a way that respects the inalienable right to moral independence, exercised in commitment to diverse and often competing subcommunities. From this sort of contractarian perspective, an unjust enforcement at large of the ethical standards of one sectarian subcommunity—infringing on interests central to the just moral independence of others—is not an acceptable policy outcome of democratic politics, as it might be in spheres less central to integrity. In the areas of conscience and privacy, such a coercive imposition subjects to political bargaining and compromise an inalienable human right of each and every person reserved from the scope of state power: moral independence in choosing among these subcommunities. Such an affront to the just moral freedom of persons and communities undercuts the very legitimacy of state power. Appropriate principles must therefore constrain the scope of such state coercive power consistent with a contractarian equal respect.

The measure of equal respect for the independent exercise of our moral powers naturally gravitates to a conception of enforceable public morality limited by two constraints. Public power must be limited to the pursuit of the general goods that rational and reasonable people would want protected, as conditions of whatever else they want. And when the pursuit of such goods abridges essential moral interests (conscience, privacy), such a law must be both necessary and indispensable to secure such goods, and do so in the way least restrictive of such interests. Persons, empowered with moral sovereignty over ourselves and the state, can only surrender power over the interests essential to their moral independence to the extent indispensably necessary to secure goods consistent with retaining control of the diverse ways they might define and pursue ultimate personal and ethical ends. For this reason, when Locke defined the limits of state power in terms of "civil interests," he wrote of such interests as general goods:

> Civil interest I call life, liberty, health, and indolency of body; and the possession of outward things, such as money, lands, houses, furniture, and the like.[34]

34. Locke, *A Letter Concerning Toleration*, vol. 6, *Works of John Locke*, pp. 9, 10.

And he naturally appealed to such "civil interests" in defining when the state may and may not restrict or regulate conscience. The state may, for example, require that babies be washed if washing is understood to secure health interests, but it may not do so if the aim is not such an interest, for example in the case of compulsory baptism. The state may not stop a person from killing a calf in a religious ritual if no civil interest would be secured by such a prohibition, but it may forbid taking the life of a child in such a ritual.[35] The natural contractarian idea motivating this argument is that the necessary protection of general goods by the state is unobjectionable, because such protection is neutral among the diverse ways people may, consistent with their right to conscience, interpretively weight the pursuit of those goods in their vision of a good and decent life. But the state's pursuit of other aims not limited to these general goods would abridge the freedom of conscience. These aims (compulsory baptism, or prohibitions on killing animals in religious rituals) are reasonably authoritative only for those of one conscientious system of beliefs as opposed to another. Contractarian justice requires that the state remain neutral among such beliefs.

This contractarian constraint on state power was strikingly expressed by Locke in terms of a harm criterion. The state may not, for example, forbid killing a calf in one's religious rituals,

> for no injury is thereby done to any one, no prejudice to another man's goods.[36]

Jefferson stated the same point crisply:

> The legitimate powers of government extend to such acts only as are injurious to others. But it does no injury for my neighbor to say there are twenty gods, or no god. It neither picks my pocket nor breaks my leg.[37]

The harm principle, as a just constraint on state power, may thus be interpreted against the background of a contractarian theory of general goods, including a theory of distributive justice.[38] The criminal law may thus protect a general good, for example, life, since the deprivation of life, a general good, is the kind of harm that may be forbidden. Such a contractarian theory of harms, suitably developed and elaborated, provides the appropriate critical tool against which the enforcement of conventional morality may justly be assessed.[39]

35. Ibid., pp. 30–31, 33–34.
36. Ibid., p. 34.
37. Jefferson, *Notes on the State of Virginia*, p. 159.
38. See, in general, Rawls, *A Theory of Justice*; Richards, *A Theory of Reasons for Action*.
39. See, e.g., Feinberg, *Harm to Others*, which, I believe, implicitly assumes such a contractarian conception as the background for his account of the setback of interests which may, in his view, count as a harm. Feinberg's account of harms is, in my view, the general kind of account to which the kind of contractarian account, here proposed, would lead.

Nonetheless, the concept of injury or harm, implicit in contractarian views (Locke's, for example), often assumed the reigning moral consensus on issues of what counted, in the area of public morality, as a harm or injury that the state might forbid. Such public morality was often assumed to be a kind of general religious (more specifically, Protestant) morality. Both Locke[40] and Roger Williams[41] thus insisted that their arguments for toleration were quite consistent with the traditional scope of the state's power to uphold public morality.

But contractarian theory makes possible a more critical conception of when conventional morality is justly enforced by law. American constitutional law has evolved such a conception, one that coherently elaborates the internal contractarian ideals of American public law.

EQUAL RESPECT AND THE RELIGION CLAUSES

If contractarian political theory justifies special protection of certain private action on a par with its protection of conscience itself, it should not surprise us that the contractarian structures underlying constitutional principles of religious toleration and free speech should naturally clarify how and why the constitutional right of privacy was a just interpretive elaboration of constitutional principles. In this section, I characterize the interpretive dynamic in religion clause jurisprudence, which, in the next section, I use to clarify the naturalness and principled cogency of the elaboration of constitutional privacy.

American constitutionalism is marked, I argued in chapter 5, by the primacy of religious toleration characteristic of contractarian moral and political theory. Constitutional guarantees are thus crucially shaped by the background right of the inalienable right to conscience, namely, that the state must express the greatest equal respect for the highest-order interests of persons in the exercise of their twin moral powers of rationality and reasonableness. Respect for this background right explains the coordinated purposes of the free exercise and antiestablishment clauses of the First Amendment. The free exercise clause forbids state coercion of the expression of conscience inconsistent with this respect, and the antiestablishment clause insists on equal respect for the ways persons form and revise their consciences.

40. Thus, Locke insists that religious congregations would be punishable if they committed such public wrongs as to "pollute themselves in promiscuous uncleanness, or practise any other such heinous enormities," p. 33, *A Letter Concerning Toleration, The Works of John Locke,* vol. 6; cf. pp. 292, 535. Locke does note, however, that not all immoralities are justly punishable by law. Some, for example "[c]ovetousness, uncharitableness, idleness," are sinful wrongs but not punishable (p. 36); others ("lying and perjury") are only punishable by law in certain cases where we consider not the religious or ethical wrong to God, but "only the injury done unto men's neighbours, and to the commonwealth" (p. 37).
41. See, e.g., Williams, *The Bloudy Tenent of Persecution,* pp. 108–10, 152, 155.

Respect for the independent exercise of moral powers leads to a test for both the free exercise and antiestablishment neutrality of state action; the state restrictions (free exercise) or endorsements (antiestablishment) of conscience must be justified at the relevant points and in the proper way by general goods. Contractarian theory explains the basis for this interpretion of religion clause principles; it also clarifies how these principles have been elaborated in the modern world.

In our examination of the form these issues took in current free exercise jurisprudence (chapter 5), we noted three relevant shifts in critical understanding. First was the broader application of the right to conscience (including Catholics and atheists). Second, protection of conscience extends to actions as well as thoughts. And third, religion is no longer regarded as a proxy for the state's promotion of appropriately neutral purposes of public morality.[42] The justification for each of these three interpretive tendencies is discussed in the following sections.

Broadened Scope of Conscience

The Court's expansion in the scope of application of constitutionally protectable forms of conscience is justified by equal respect itself. Locke's exclusions of atheists and Catholics from religious toleration express the unjust contempt for moral independence that equal respect forbids. It would be anachronistic to retain these or other content-biased conceptions of conscience, as the measure of constitutional protections, when reasonable ethical independence cannot be measured in such ways.[43] Such sectarian limitations of the scope of protected conscience undermine the deeper moral and political respect for conscience as such, whose central place in contractarian thought and politics is the kind of dignifying ethical and religious self-determination that such independence makes possible.

Protection for Actions

The judicial elaboration of the protection of conscience to action as well as thought is not only historically more faithful to the harm principle invoked by Locke, Jefferson, and others, but is the sounder view

---

42. The Supreme Court has not, as noted in chapter 5, always consistently followed these interpretive tendencies in its free exercise jurisprudence. Thus, when the Court has expanded free exercise scrutiny into prohibitions of actions motivated by conscience, it has narrowed the conception of what may count as a religion for this purpose. See, e.g., *Wisconsin v. Yoder*, 406 U.S. 205 (1972).

43. For example, one scholar recently advocated limiting protected religion to beliefs in an afterlife. See Choper, "Defining 'Religion' in the First Amendment." But this view puts bizarre emphasis on a belief that the moral philosophers most influential on the eighteenth-century context of American constitutional ideals regarded as increasingly irrelevant to the nature and motive of ethical action. For the seventeenth-century background, see Walker, *The Decline of Hell*. For eighteenth-century views, see Shaftesbury, *An Inquiry Concerning Virtue or Merit*, pp. 1–67; also, Hutcheson, *An Inquiry Concerning the Original of Our Ideas of Virtue or Moral Good*, pp. 68–177.

of its internal ideals of equal respect for persons.[44] The distinctive shape of equal respect, as an emerging political ideal, was framed by an ideal of the primacy of practical reason, the self-determination of one's personal and ethical ends by reflective organization of the coherence of one's own ends and their larger ethical coherence with the aims of others (see chapter 4). But such practical self-determination integrates thought and action, so that respect for the independence of thought must radiate a corresponding independence for action, and conversely. The contrary view would extend toleration to thought but not to action, expressing the contemplative model of the mind so hospitable to degrading ideas of natural hierarchy. On this view, respect for religious and moral conscience is respect for capacities contemplative of some religious or moral order and our place in that hierarchical order; such respect is precisely not extended to our constructive moral powers, which make possible our moral independence (shaping thought and guiding actions in one integrated and often experimental process). Such a political mind-body dualism thus frustrates the internal ideal of moral independence that motivates equal respect. As the measure of political toleration, for example, it would guarantee the mind's moral independence, but the body and its actions would remain in fatalistic bondage to bigotry and intolerance.

The classic texts on toleration were, as noted in chapter 4, ambiguous about whether toleration extended only to thought (never to action), or to thought and nonharmful action. But the internal ideals of contractarian thought are historically oriented toward respect for practical rationality. It was therefore quite natural that contractarian thinkers should have used the harm principle as the measure of toleration, suggesting that toleration extends to action as well as thought. The point was not problematic for them because their conceptions of harm embraced the broad range of actions condemned by traditional conceptions of public morality.

Neutral Public Morality

A striking critical shift in the Supreme Court's thinking began around World War II, questioning the constitutional acceptability of religion as a suitable proxy for the state's promotion of appropriately neutral purposes of public morality. This kind of judgment must be understood in the perspective of the tradition it reflects and elaborates.

Skepticism about the necessity or inevitability of the link between morality and religion was not unknown to early advocates of toleration. In fact, forms of such skepticism pervaded almost all serious thought about and argument for the primacy of religious toleration both by Catholics (Italian humanists, Erasmus, Montaigne)[45] and Protestants

44. See, e.g., *Sherbert v. Verner*, 374 U.S. 398 (1963).
45. For pertinent commentary, see Lecler, *Toleration and the Reformation*, vol. 1, pp. 107–33; vol. 2, pp. 168–77.

(Bayle,[46] Locke,[47] Roger Williams,[48] Acontius, Castellio).[49] But the familiar and weak claim of these thinkers was that theological differences about the terms of theism did not track ethical differences, an idea consistent with the denial of the independence of religion and ethics as such.

This latter notion of the conceptual independence of ethical and religious concepts had been part of the Western philosophical tradition at least since Plato's *Euthyphro*. In the eighteenth century, Shaftesbury, Butler, and Hutcheson made the idea an important component of religious thought about the nature of God's goodness.[50] Even Madison's teacher, the orthodox Calvinist Witherspoon, assumed a form of the view, which indicates its pervasiveness during the period that gave birth to the philosophy of the religion clauses and their radical embodiment of the primacy of religious toleration.[51] Belief in the independence of ethics and religion cannot therefore reasonably be supposed to be unknown to the American constitutional tradition. On the contrary, Jefferson assumed the point in his formulation of the Act for Religious Freedom, "that our civil rights have no dependence on our religious opinions, more than our opinions in physics or geometry."[52]

Nonetheless, the dominant view, echoing Locke's and Bayle's exemption of atheists from full protection of their principles of toleration,[53] was that religion (more specifically, in nineteenth-century America, Protestantism) was the central vehicle for the moral values of constitutionalism. As noted earlier, Justice Story spoke of Protestant Christianity as the de facto established church of the republic, and identified its values with moral values as such.[54]

The Supreme Court's shift from this once dominant view now questions the link between ethics and religion and, a fortiori, between ethics and Protestant Christianity. In consequence, the use of religion as a neutral proxy for moral argument as such is questionable. This leads naturally, as we saw, to school prayer cases,[55] to battles over teaching

---

46. See Bayle, *Commentaire Philosophique*.
47. For Locke's latitudinarian conception of legitimate religious differences over moral questions, see Locke, *The Reasonableness of Christianity*.
48. See Williams, *The Bloudy Tenent of Persecution*.
49. For pertinent commentary, see Lecler, *Toleration and the Reformation*, vol. 1, pp. 336–60, 369–76. For relevant original texts, see Castellio, *Concerning Heretics*; Acontius, *Darkness Discovered (Satans Stratagems)*.
50. For the evolution of this idea and its impact on early American thought in the seventeenth and eighteenth centuries, see Fiering, *Moral Philosophy at Seventeenth Century Harvard*; Fiering, *Jonathan Edwards's Moral Thought and Its British Context*.
51. Witherspoon, *Lectures on Moral Philosophy*, pp. 85–86, 103–4; but cf. pp. 91–94.
52. Boyd, ed., *The Papers of Thomas Jefferson, 1777–1779*, vol. 2, pp. 545–46.
53. See, e.g., *A Letter Concerning Toleration, Works of John Locke*, vol. 6, p. 47; Bayle, *Philosophique Commentaire*, p. 431.
54. See excerpts from Story's *Commentaries on the Constitution of the United States*, pp. 128–30.
55. See, e.g., *Engel v. Vitale*, 370 U.S. 421 (1962).

Darwin in public schools,[56] and to more general constitutional concern that, consistent with neutrality values, the state not enforce at large an illegitimately nonneutral conception of ethical values.[57]

The idea of a neutral conception of enforceable public morality is, as we saw in chapter 5, itself the historical product of complex developments as much internal to religious ideals of respect for persons as to ethical, scientific, and other thinking.[58] The Supreme Court's gravitation to such a view reflects this historical trend and its own independent judgment of the natural elaboration of the underlying constitutional ideal of equal respect for persons. The imposition of sectarian interpretations of moral values on a dissenting conscience is in excess of the just power of the contractarian state, which limits its power to the necessary protection of general goods to allow full scope to the interpretive rationality and reasonableness of a free people. Indeed, the imposition of such sectarian interpretations impairs the moral independence of a free people in their right to interpret and organize general goods as the expression of their integral moral powers of rationality and reasonableness.

The Lockean assumption—that conventional conceptions of public morality are the measure of neutral harms regulable by the contractarian state—can no longer be sustained. The harm principle remains, as Locke saw, a natural constractarian constraint on the just scope of state power. But the interpretation of the principle, with its inherent ideal of respect for persons, requires careful scrutiny so that the values, in terms of which conventional morality construes harms, reflect the necessary protection of general goods. Reasonable disagreement may still occur over whether the law can be justified in terms of such general goods. Nevertheless, the nature of the ongoing controversy is framed by critical concepts not themselves reducible to moral consensus or conventional morality.

The limitation of state power to such general goods is hostile neither to religion nor to morality. It is rather the supreme procedural condi-

---

56. See, e.g., *Epperson v. Arkansas*, 393 U.S. 97 (1968).

57. An example is the nativist prohibitionism that foisted ideological Protestant perfectionism on Catholics and Jews. See Richards, *Sex, Drugs, Death and the Law*, ch. 4.

58. It is therefore a non sequitur to argue that, because our moral values are crucially shaped by religious ideals of respect for persons, our moral values should not be reexamined in light of such ideals. See, e.g., Mitchell, *Morality: Religious and Secular*, who confuses these questions, supposing that the important linkages between Western ethics and religion require us to enforce traditional religious views condemning voluntary euthanasia (pp. 129–31), suicide (p. 130), drug use (pp. 130–31), and abortion (p. 131). Mitchell is well aware, in fact, that values of Western liberalism are generated by the central weight our religious and ethical culture gives to a free conscience. See pp. 93–100, Mitchell, *Law, Morality, and Religion in a Secular Society*. He does not, however, connect this internal ideal, as much religious as political and ethical, to the kind of reexamination of conventional moral values and their just enforcement through law which this ideal, in fact, motivates.

tion that ensures that any imposition of values by the democratic state itself makes possible a religion and an ethics that validate the highest-order moral powers of rationality and reasonableness of a free people. A state, which thus limits its power to the protection of general goods, remits to the moral powers of its people the ways in which they will shape and weight such general goods. To this extent, such a constraint on state power itself makes possible the only kind of religion and ethics that respects the moral sovereignty of the people themselves, the ideal of the sovereign ethical dignity of the person against which the legitimacy of the contractarian state must be judged. Mill's harm principle expresses precisely this truth about the moral ideals of constitutional democracy, but we may now see that truth not as the consequence of utilitarianism, but of the long-standing contractarian ideals of democratic theory and practice and their natural elaboration.

All three developments in constitutional thought (expansion in the constitutional concept of religion for free exercise and other purposes, expansion of toleration values from thought to action, and closer scrutiny of religion as a neutral proxy for ethics) occur at different points of elaboration of the underlying moral ideal that I have called the background right of equal respect for moral independence. The force of that background right in our interpretive traditions is displayed in the way its reasonable elaboration actuates constitutional argument at each of these interconnected points.

PRIMACY OF TOLERATION AND CONSTITUTIONAL PRIVACY

The force of the background right of respect for moral independence is reflected as well in the natural development of the constitutional right to privacy. The same conception of toleration—embodied in the principled elaborations of religion clause jurisprudence already discussed—radiates in analogously principled ways to protect a constitutional right to privacy.

Contractarian political theory justifies a right of private life, the control a free person enjoys over personal relationships essential to personal and moral identity and integrity. That right is grounded in the same background right of moral independence which actuates the constitutional protections of the religion clauses: equal respect for the moral powers of human personality. The internal ideals of equal respect of the contractarian political theory of American constitutional law thus interpretively explain and validate, in a way Ely's political theory cannot, the basis of the historical understanding of marriage as a fundamental unenumerated right textually protected by the Constitution.

The elaboration of those ideals, in the ways we have already seen in religion clause jurisprudence, suggests why the principles underlying this historical understanding should coherently and sensibly have been elaborated today as the constitutional right to privacy. The same equal respect that motivated the expanded protection of conscience motivates the expanded protection of the essential moral powers of private life. First, the right to privacy protects, as does the right to conscience, a more general conception of essential moral powers (extending, as we shall see in chapter 9, beyond marriage). Second, the scope of the right to privacy inextricably embraces actions as well as beliefs and emotions; we can no more separate thought from action in the integrity of our personal lives than we can in our moral or religious lives. And third, this sphere of action may only be abridged on the showing of the kinds of neutral harms that justify the state's necessary protection of general goods; otherwise, a sectarian conception of personal life will be enforced by the state, debasing the essential moral powers of a just personal life. The ideals of equal respect, which led to analogous arguments in religion clause jurisprudence, justify similar interpretations of the constitutional right to privacy at these same three intersecting points of the underlying argument of principle.[59] That argument of principle is, of course, the working clear and clean of the meaning of equal respect itself. In both the areas of conscience and privacy, an enhanced public understanding of ways in which equal respect was at hazard dictated corresponding expansions of constitutional protections.

There is a unifying interpretive theme in the three areas of constitutional discourse examined in this book: religious liberty, free speech, and constitutional privacy. The abridgment of all such essential areas of moral independence, which often do not harm anyone in the constitutionally required way, is a generic form of content-biased hatred or intolerance, which internal constitutional ideals condemn in areas of conscience, speech, and action. The common structure of analysis in the jurisprudence of the religion clauses, free speech, and constitutional privacy is the equality of persons (their conscience, speech, and ways of life), only subject to state interference upon demonstration of a clear and present danger of neutrally understood harms. Its common theme is the primacy of universal toleration of conscience, speech, and ways of life.

The doctrine known as constitutional privacy arose in an area of personal relationships and activities essential to moral integrity, where state prohibitions could no longer satisfy the constitutional burden required for such impositions of value. As such, constitutional privacy is a wholly natural, indeed constitutionally required, development best understood as a principled constitutional argument working out the

---

59. Indeed, the Court's very reluctance to elaborate fully these interpretive tendencies in its religion clause jurisprudence (see note 42, above) may have made the elaboration of constitutional privacy all the more constitutionally compelled. See the discussion of this point in chapter 5.

enduring meaning of the primacy of toleration in our constitutional traditions.

The interpretive power of contractarian theory appears most eloquently in our discussion of the problem of constitutional privacy. In taking Ely's attack on constitutional privacy as the argument of political theory that it essentially is, we have answered his challenge by proposing an alternative conception of democratic political theory centered in the egalitarian and liberal ideals of the First Amendment itself. These ideals, construed in the light of this background political theory, explicate the jurisprudence of the religion clauses and of free speech; moreover, they encompass the right in our constitutional law known as constitutional privacy. Surely, our commitment in constitutional law to arguments of principle require that the background right of equal respect be fully and coherently articulated to accommodate the full scope of its background right. Constitutional privacy is the entirely just interpretive product of such arguments.

The application of this right in our law is a different, highly controversial question. Our argument so far indicates that the crucial point in applying constitutional privacy is the nature of the actions prohibited and the kinds of nonneutral arguments urged in support of such prohibitions. No part of the present argument appears to depend on the nature of the group who advocates certain claims. Religious groups in the United States were central vehicles of the moral independence that energized the abolitionist movement and many of the civil rights movements; their ethical aims were not therefore illegitimately nonneutral.[60] Prohibitionism in the United States may have been supported by many nonreligious groups, or antiabortion laws mainly by medical rather than religious groups;[61] their ethical aims may not be any the less nonneutral in nature today. Accordingly, we should use the tools of constitutional analysis not to examine the groups who advocate claims, but to scrutinize the claims advocated.

---

60. Cf. Neuhaus, *The Naked Public Square*; Diggins, *The Lost Soul of American Politics*, pp. 277–333.
61. See Mohr, *Abortion in America*.

9 · The Jurisprudence of Constitutional Privacy

The maintenance of a continuous yet vital constitutional tradition in the United States has required the Supreme Court to interpret relevant constitutional text in terms of abstract background rights (equal liberties of religion or speech, equal treatment, cruel and unusual punishment, and so on).[1] Continuity is ensured by the common appeal to an abstract intention in different historical periods; vitality, by the Court's duty to articulate reasonable changes in the scope of application of the common concept in light of each generation's best arguments of principle about basic liberties of the person,[2] or the demands of equality,[3] or unjustly disproportionate punishment.[4] We must now show how the elaboration and application of constitutional privacy under our law is a reasonable interpretation of the abstract rights of the person discussed in chapter 8.

1. Cf. Dworkin, *Taking Rights Seriously*, pp. 134–36.
2. On the Founders' quite narrow understanding of "free speech," see Levy, *Legacy of Suppression.* Yet contemporary case law quite properly views seditious libel prosecutions, not encompassed by that understanding, as at the core of the prohibitions of the free speech clause. See *New York Times Co. v. Sullivan,* 376 U.S. 254 (1964).
3. The contemporary constitutional conception of equal protection clearly interprets the idea more expansively than the conception of previous generations. See *Brown v. Board of Education,* 347 U.S. 483 (1954); *Frontiero v. Richardson,* 411 U.S. 677 (1973).
4. See, for example, *Furman v. Georgia,* 408 U.S. 238 (1972); *Gregg v. Georgia,* 428 U.S. 153 (1976).

PRIVACY AND CONTRACEPTION

The constitutional right to privacy was elaborated by the Supreme Court in terms of its traditional approach to the principled development of abstract background rights. Ely himself concedes[5] there is a sound historical and textual argument that the generation who drafted and approved the Constitution and Bill of Rights thought of these documents as protecting not only enumerated rights, but unenumerated basic human rights as well. Later judicial traditions certainly manifest such an understanding.[6] And we have already discussed some good historical reasons to believe both that one such assumed basic human right was the natural right to marriage,[7] and that this right was thought of as just one example of a more abstract right of personal relationships connected to the values of the religion and free speech clauses of the First Amendment.[8] Since these assumptions are appealed to by one or another of the clauses of the Fourteenth Amendment,[9] a comparable historical and textual argument suggests that such a right to marriage (and the more abstract background right it expresses) was among the unemumerated fundamental rights enforceable against the states under the Fourteenth Amendment.

Ely edits this text and history, because it appeals to one of the "more indeterminate phrases"[10] of the written constitution and a background rights-based political theory that he rejects in favor of his own conception of legitimate democratic political theory. Constitutional privacy is, he suggests, acceptable only to the extent that it is associated with informational privacy interests protected by specific amendments of

5. Ely expressly denies that either textual or historical argument belies the legitimacy of the Court's inference of the right; to the contrary, Ely argues that the best textual and historical inference is that the Ninth Amendment was intended to make clear that unenumerated rights such as constitutional privacy were to be enforceable against the federal government, in the same way that the privileges and immunities clause of Article IV contemplates a distinction between unenumerated fundamental and nonfundamental rights. See Ely, *Democracy and Distrust*, pp. 34–41, 22–30.

6. See *Corfield v. Coryell*, 6 F. Cas. 546 (C.C.E.D. Pa. 1823); see also Ely's discussion, *Democracy and Distrust*, pp. 28–30.

7. For example, Hutcheson's widely read and studied works list, among other fundamental rights, "the natural right each one has to enter into the matrimonial relation with any one who consents," p. 299, Hutcheson, *A System of Moral Philosophy*.

8. Striking evidence of this way of thinking appears in the lectures of John Witherspoon, a form of which James Madison heard and studied while a student at Princeton. Witherspoon, tracking Hutcheson's list of basic human rights, lists a "right to associate, if he so incline, with any person or persons, whom he can persuade (not force)—under this is contained the right to marriage," p. 123, Witherspoon, *Lectures on Moral Philosophy*.

9. Ely puts particular emphasis here on the privileges and immunities clause of the Fourteenth Amendment, which, he believes, incorporates the idea of unenumerated fundamental rights from the privileges and immunities clause of Article IV. See Ely, *Democracy and Distrust*, pp. 22–30. The Supreme Court, of course, has placed the inference of unenumerated rights on the due process clause of the Fourteenth Amendment. See, e.g., *Roe v. Wade*, 410 U.S. 113 (1973).

10. Ely, *Democracy and Distrust*, p. 221 n. 4.

the Bill of Rights. Any more generous inference of a constitutional right to privacy beyond this sphere, appealing to fundamental rights independent of informational privacy, must be rejected.

Ely's argument is only as strong as the interpretive power of the democratic political theory that motivates his rejection of the text and history supporting the more generous inference of the constitutional right to privacy. The cumulative force of arguments in chapters 1, 8, and 10 suggests that Ely's claim is neither a sound general political theory nor a useful interpretive theory of the United States Constitution. A contractarian political theory does better justice to the values of constitutional democracy, and interpretively clarifies the law of the First Amendment and its relationship to the right to constitutional privacy.

The contractarian concern for moral independence explains the place of both a right of informational privacy and a right to a private sphere of action (constitutional privacy) as constitutionally protected interests (chapter 8). In each case, resources central to the independent exercise of our moral powers are justly protected against a hostile and homogenizing public scrutiny. This common moral basis of both aspects of privacy indicates why the initial judicial inference of constitutional privacy identified an important analogy to associated informational privacy interests.[11] But it is a mistake to construe the analogy in any more substantive way as, for example, in Ely's limitation of constitutional privacy to areas of informational privacy. Ely is driven to that interpretation by his prior commitment to a political theory. Contractarian political theory enables us to identify the independent interpretive status of the constitutional right to privacy.

Contractarian theory thus makes interpretive sense of the historical assumption that marriage is an unenumerated fundamental constitutional right, and that it reflects a more abstract background right (the constitutional right of privacy) related to the rights protected by the First Amendment. The marriage relationship is a clear example of what the abstract right of constitutional privacy protects, namely, intimate personal relations through which we express and realize a wholeness of emotion, intellect, and self-image guided by the just play of the self-determining moral powers of a free person.[12] In such relations we achieve not only the complementary satisfaction of a broad range of interests of our personal lives, but we experience and cultivate the friendship, devotion, and love often essential to personal and moral

11. Constitutional privacy and informational privacy are conceptually distinct: the former is a substantive autonomy right of certain actions from criminal penalty, the latter essentially a right to control private information about oneself. But the rights have been linked by strong analogies that the judiciary has used in making inferences from one to the other; for example, the inference of constitutional privacy in *Griswold* notes that criminal enforcement of laws prohibiting contraception use would require egregious violation of informational privacy interests protected by the Fourth Amendment. *Griswold v. Connecticut*, 381 U.S. 479, 485–86 (1965). On such arguments of analogy connecting the rights, see Richards, *Sex, Drugs, Death and the Law*, pp. 33–34, 61–63.
12. Cf. Karst, "The Freedom of Intimate Association."

identity guided by desire for a life meaningfully, fully, and responsibly lived. The protection of the choices at the core of such private life is a guarantee, essential in mass society, of the most personal resources of moral independence.[13] The just independence of such choices, not their informational privacy, is the constitutional issue.

For these reasons, the Supreme Court properly elaborated a right to constitutional privacy originating in marriage relationships.[14] In consideration of the abstract nature of its background right of moral independence, there may be good reason in principle to extend the right beyond intimate relations in marriage to other spheres essential to the moral independence of one's personal life, for example, nonmarital use of contraceptives,[15] pornography in the home,[16] and abortion services.[17] In each case, the constitutional issue should be to determine whether the abstract background right is in play and whether its abridgment can be appropriately justified. The fact that such a right is in play does not conclude the latter question. The right to marriage has long been implicitly assumed to be a fundamental right guaranteed by the Constitution, but our law only elaborated its protection by the constitutional right to privacy when certain abridgments of marital choices came to be regarded as inadequately supported by the neutral justifications that internal constitutional ideals compelled. In other cases, our understanding that this background right is at issue comes into focus only when the power of critical argument rebuts the neutrality of the traditional justifications for abridgment. Before we turn to some of these cases (abortion and consensual homosexuality), let us look at the contraception cases, which arise in the heartland of the historical understanding of constitutional privacy, the right to marriage.

The contraception cases are, I believe, a clearly correct application of the principles of constitutional privacy. In the leading privacy case, *Griswold v. Connecticut*,[18] the state prohibition on the use of contraceptives in marriage limited the basic right of married couples to reg-

---

13. It is no accident that the most systematic modern totalitarian experiment in forms of domination self-consciously at war with the traditions of human rights essential to contractarian and constitutional thought should have proudly touted its "ethical" aims thus: "There is no such thing as a private individual in National Socialist Germany," p. 178, Bramstedt, *Dictatorship and Political Police*. See, in general, Richards, "Terror and the Law." The associated prohibitions on marriage (the Nuremberg laws, prohibiting miscegenation with Jews, etc.) signify precisely why the right to marriage is, in the contractarian tradition of respect for human rights, so much at the core of the respect it requires for the highest-order interests of persons in the intellectual and emotional integrity of their personal and ethical lives. See, e.g., Arendt, *The Origins of Totalitarianism*, pp. 288, 294, 394.
14. *Griswold v. Connecticut*, 381 U.S. 479 (1965).
15. *Eisenstadt v. Baird*, 405 U.S. 438 (1972).
16. *Stanley v. Georgia*, 394 U.S. 557 (1969).
17. *Roe v. Wade*, 410 U.S. 113 (1973).
18. *Griswold v. Connecticut*, 381 U.S. 479 (1965).

ulate the nature of their sexual lives and their procreative consequences in forming new intimate relations with offspring. The exercise
of this right is a deliberative, often highly conscientious choice by married couples not only about the way and context in which sexuality will
bond and express their intimate union, but of whether and when they
will bear offspring. Such control over sexuality has allowed couples to
choose the timing and number of children, which encourages more
responsive and responsible parenthood and permits integration of
reproduction with other personal and ethical aims.[19] It also permits the
experience of sexuality in marriage as a personal expression of the relationship to be an end in itself. Contraceptives have thus enormously
enhanced the rational dignity of women in separating and regulating
their sexual and procreative lives. Perhaps for the first time in human
history, women in general can have personally expressive sexual lives
and relationships, unburdened by self-conceptions of mandatory procreative function and duty.[20] In sum, the choice to use contraceptives
has been a key exercise of constructive moral powers in the rational and
reasonable redefinition of personal and moral relationships.

Since state prohibitions on use of contraceptives thus infringe essential moral powers of private life, they can only be justified by the constitutional burden of justification of the pursuit of neutral goods—
things all persons could reasonably accept as all-purpose conditions of
pursuing their aims, whatever they are. The prohibitions cannot satisfy
this burden. Such prohibitions do not protect the rights of other persons. To the contrary, legitimate state purposes of population control
may better be advanced through parental autonomy; parents may be
more responsible as parents and have more diversely fulfilled lives as
persons. And such prohibitions could not reasonably be supposed to
protect persons from self-destructive harms to neutral goods of the self,
in the way, for example, that just state paternalism might legitimately
be concerned to stem teenage suicides, and the like.[21] Contraceptive
use in marriage has secured for couples a deepened freedom and rationality of sexual expression in the bonding of their intimate lives and
greater control over their reproductive histories and other personal
aims. There is no neutrally understood harm to self here. Rather, there
is much good.

Any residual justification of these laws prohibiting contraception use
appears, on the requisite kind of constitutionally reflective examination, to be grounded either on ideals of the necessary link of sex and
procreation,[22] or the associated belief that sex without procreation is a

---

19. See, in general, Reed, *The Birth Control Movement and American Society*.
20. On Margaret Sanger's conception of the links of contraception and feminism, see
ibid., pp. 67–139.
21. See, e.g., Richards, *Sex, Drugs, Death and the Law*, pp. 225–27, 238–42.
22. See Augustine, *The City of God*, pp. 577–94.

kind of homicide.[23] Neither justification can satisfy the constitutionally neutral burden of justification required for laws that thus directly abridge fundamental rights of the person: such laws cannot be justified to the many reasonable persons who do not share this ideal or the associated view of nonprocreative sex as homicidal. Sexual love may be a general good, if it is a form of love that rational people often want as the condition of an emotional integrity that enables them to pursue whatever else they want.[24] But such love must be construed in terms consistent with the diverse interpretations and weights that rational and reasonable persons would give to this good consistent with the exercise of their moral independence. The ideal of the necessary link of sex and procreation is only one such interpretation among others. It cannot and should not enjoy the support of law. Correspondingly, that sex without procreation is homicidal rests on a larger interpretive context in which sexuality is endowed with natural moral obligations of procreation which, if unsatisfied, are a kind of killing. Yet the lurking picture of persons, otherwise born, thus killed, is an image compelling only to those who have already assented to the image in question. Such "persons," thus "killed," are not among the general goods that could fairly, on contractarian grounds, be submitted to the authority of the state. The underlying perceptions are simply not the broadly shared premises that leave the state neutral among competing sectarian interpretations of various goods. Rather, the enforcement of such perceptions through criminal prohibitions on contraception use enlists the state in the support of sectarian conscience in a core area of just moral independence. This usurpation of moral sovereignty is exactly what constitutional neutrality forbids.

Criminal prohibitions bearing on the right of constitutional privacy require a heavy burden of justification, which can in principle be met. There would, I assume, be no constitutional objection to the application of neutral criminal statutes to intrafamilial murders, or wife or husband beatings, or child abuse, no matter how rooted they are in intimate family life and sexuality; nor should there be any objection to rape laws applicable to married or unmarried sexual intimacies. In these cases, the constitutional burden of justification is met: countervailing rights of persons justify coercive interference into intimate relations. On the other hand, criminal prohibitions on the use of contraceptives could not meet this burden of justification: countervailing rights are

---

23. Thomas Aquinas elaborates Augustine's conception of the exclusive legitimacy of procreative sex in a striking way. Of the emission of semen apart from procreation in marriage, he wrote: "[A]fter the sin of homicide whereby a human nature already in existence is destroyed, this type of sin appears to take next place, for by it the generation of human nature is precluded." Thomas Aquinas, *On the Truth of the Catholic Faith: Summa Contra Gentiles*, pt. 2, ch. 122(9), p. 146.

24. See, e.g., Richards, *Sex, Drugs, Death and the Law*, pp. 49–57.

either too constitutionally nonneutral or controversial or speculative to satisfy the burden required to abridge such intimately personal sexual matters.

CONSTITUTIONAL PRIVACY AND ABORTION

The application of the constitutional right to privacy to abortion is controversial in a way that the contraception cases are not. For example, as we saw in the preceding chapter, John Stuart Mill's harm principle, which may clarify other areas of decriminalization controversy, appears, in the abortion context, only to replicate the underlying moral controversy in the form of whether killing a fetus is or is not a "harm." The harm principle, in Mill's intuitive form of it, may thus clarify why contraceptive use is improperly subject to criminal penalty. Contraceptive use does not harm third parties, and certainly does not harm the parties themselves; in Mill's terms, the harm principle must require that this conduct not be criminalized. But killing a fetus is arguably itself a harm, so that the harm principle does not straightforwardly justify the application of constitutional privacy to abortion services. If the harm principle is to do any work in justifying the abortion decisions, we must enlarge our understanding of the background moral theory that shapes the conception of what is and what is not properly regarded as a "harm." Abortion may thus be a useful test case for the explanatory and critical fertility of our alternative contractarian approach to understanding the nature and basis of the harm principle as fundamental to the justice of constitutional democracy.

Correspondingly, constitutional theorists[25] and federal judges,[26] who might be prepared to identify violations of constitutional neutrality in other areas of decriminalization controversy, have resisted the extension of such argument to the abortion context. For example, when the federal courts considered whether the 1977 Hyde Amendment (depriving women of Medicaid funding for most abortions) constitu-

---

25. Thus, Louis Henkin has argued that antiestablishment clause values should constitutionally condemn criminal prohibitions that rest only on religious, not secular, values (for example, prohibitions on obscene materials and of consensual adult homosexual relations). See Henkin, "Morals and the Constitution: The Sin of Obscenity." However, Henkin would not justify *Roe* on this ground (since the prolife view does not rest on a purely religious value), but on the ground of privacy as an autonomy right. See, e.g., Henkin, "Privacy and Autonomy." I am grateful to Louis Henkin for comments on an earlier draft of this chapter, which clarified his views for me. Laurence Tribe once defended the position that the prohibition of abortion rested on a forbidden religious view; see Tribe, "The Supreme Court, 1972 Term—Foreword: Toward a Model of Roles in the Due Process of Life and Law," pp. 21–25. However, for reasons similar to Henkin's views, he later withdrew the argument. Tribe, *American Constitutional Law*, p. 928.
26. For Judge Dooling, see *McRae v. Califano*, 491 F. Supp. at 741 (1980); for Justice Stewart, see *Harris v. McRae*, 448 U.S. 297, 319 (1980).

tuted a constitutionally forbidden establishment of religion, both Judge
Dooling for the lower federal court and Justice Potter Stewart for the
Supreme Court opined that abortion funding restrictions do not trench
upon antiestablishment values because they reflect "traditionalist" values toward abortion, not a sectarian religious view.[27] On this view, antiabortion arguments rest on a value of the protection of life—a general
good, not a sectarian aim. On this assumption, the only remaining
antiestablishment argument would be one focusing on the role that religious groups play in antiabortion political advocacy. But this would
contort ideals of constitutional neutrality into hostility to political advocacy by religious groups, prejudicing the very moral independence that
constitutional ideals centrally protect and that such groups have familiarly brought to bear on American political life (see chapter 8).

From the contractarian perspective on constitutional privacy, these
arguments about the neutrality of antiabortion views do not give proper
weight either to the nature of the interests that constitutional privacy
protects or the especially heavy burden of justification required when
they are abridged. On examination, the prohibition of abortion services
infringes essential moral powers of private life in the service of nonneutral values inconsistent with the constitutionally required equal
respect for general goods. Antiabortion laws violate principles of constitutional privacy, not because their political advocacy is today led by
certain religious groups but because the grounds for such laws are nonneutral in the constitutionally forbidden way in an area at the core of
the fundamental human right of intimate personal relationships. The
nature of this infringement can best be brought out first by analyzing
the kinds of arguments urged in support of antiabortion laws. When we
comprehend their precise nature and weight, we can understand their
lack of constitutional neutrality and why they unjustly burden moral
powers essential to a just private life. I do not claim that antiabortion
arguments are not moral arguments or that they lack weight. I maintain
that as moral arguments they are not of the weight required to justify
abridgments of the interests essentially protected by the constitutional
right to privacy.

Arguments for the Immorality of Abortion
Contemporary debates about the morality of abortion center on two
different kinds of queries. Is the fetus throughout pregnancy a moral
person, so that the usual proscription on homicide would fully apply?
Assuming the fetus is a person, is there any feature of the abortion situation that supports a justification or excuse for abortions?

Moral arguments of the second kind may justify abortion in certain
cases, but not in general. Abortion may be justified in order to save the
mother's life. Even here, however, the insistence by Catholic moral

27. See *Harris v. McRae*, 448 U.S. 297, 319 (1980).

theology that this is legitimate only when observing the "double effect" doctrine raises constitutional neutrality problems (many reasonable people extend the justification beyond double effect).[28] More general arguments of the second kind, showing that abortion is not wrong in general (self-defense, necessity), are often ethically problematic. The analogies drawn to ordinary self-defense or necessity principles, for example, are often weak.[29] Other arguments, designed for the abortion situation of imposing undue burdens on a woman to support life, focus on the extraordinary good samaritan obligations thus imposed on women, which are not consistent with the limited good samaritan obligations of Anglo-American law and morality.[30] But such arguments have force only in cases of nonculpably accidental pregnancies, which does not cover all abortions.[31] If these arguments were the only ones available to justify abortion, the prohibition on abortion might be sufficiently connected to uncontroversially neutral moral argument to be constitutionally neutral (except in the double effect context earlier discussed). However, antiabortion arguments depend on certain prior premises as well.

Such antiabortion arguments often rest on the truth of two logically independent assumptions, either of which would justify the prohibition on abortion services. First, the fetus is in all stages of pregnancy a moral person on a par with normal persons.[32] Second, having sex without intended procreational effect is always wrong. The latter assumption (which underlies anticontraception laws as well) is an unacceptably nonneutral argument that cannot be enforced on society at large. The constitutionally crucial ground for antiabortion views is the first one, the personhood of the fetus.

Apart from certain religious or other assumptions not reasonably shared at large, the claim that the fetus is a full moral person is unfounded. The claim of Catholic moral theory—which departs from its earlier Thomistic tradition and is not uniformly shared by Catholic theologians even today—rests on the potentiality principle of genetic individuality:[33] once a genetic individual exists, after fertilization or whenever, the individual is "life" and subject to the homicide proscrip-

---

28. See Sumner, *Abortion and Moral Theory,* pp. 115–23.
29. See Brody, *Abortion and the Sanctity of Human Life: A Philosophical View;* Feinberg, "Abortion," pp. 202–14; Davis, "Abortion and Self-Defense."
30. See Thompson, "A Defense of Abortion"; Regan, "Rewriting *Roe v. Wade.*"
31. See Feinberg, "Abortion," pp. 209–14. But see Myrna, "The Right to Abortion."
32. If the fetus at fertilization has a lesser moral status than that of a full person, the claims made on its behalf could not constitute claims of rights in the required sense. Cf. Quinn, "Abortion: Identity and Loss." However, even claims of a lesser moral status may be based on metaphysical assumptions that crucially confuse the conditions of moral personality with biological individuation, as Quinn may do.
33. McCartney, "Some Roman Catholic Concepts of Person and their Implications for the Ontological Status of the Unborn," pp. 313–23.

tion on killing persons.[34] But it simply does not reasonably follow, absent other implicit premises, that a *potential* person is a person or should ethically be treated as a person, when it lacks relevant characteristics of being a person—at a minimum, the capacity for self-consciousness, agency, and the like.[35]

The implicit premises, which naturally bridge the gap from potentiality to actuality, surely are specifically religious or metaphysical assumptions about the fetus. These assumptions include the following: at all points, the fetus has an individual soul; the soul requires baptism for release from original sin (so that death prior to birth has disastrous religious consequences for the inborn soul); fetal life is radically innocent; there is a moral obligation for sexual activity to lead to procreation (which leads to anticontraceptive policies as morally obligatory); pregnancy and birth are natural female burdens, a view historically associated with the Church's adoption of the potentiality view at the same time it adopted the doctrine of Immaculate Conception (celebrating and sanctifying a model of ideal maternity).[36] Many of those who regard abortion as immoral murder thus think and speak from a larger conception of natural processes both of sexuality and gender roles, and view abortion as an attack on and revolt against this natural order of sexuality and gender roles.[37] From the perspective of vital belief in these assumptions, abortion in the potentiality stage is as wrongful, perhaps more wrongful than ordinary homicide; the fetus is radically innocent and vulnerable, the woman murderously unnatural in her betrayal of her role as mother.

Outside the metaphysics of natural processes and divine will underlying these assumptions, the potentiality principle is simply fallacious. The many reasonable people, who neither believe in nor act on it, are guilty neither of logical nor of moral error. It does not follow, logically or morally, that a potential person is a person and must, logically or morally, be accorded the same level of coercive protection by the law.

Two ethical arguments may be urged against my challenge to the potentiality principle as a ground for coercive sanctions: the "slippery slope" argument about line drawing and the argument from prophylaxis against mistakes. Neither is valid.

The slippery slope argument rests on a fallacy about the concept of similarity: if A is similar to B, and B to C, and so on to Y and Z, then A is similar to Z. Since the early fetus is at one point similar to the fetus at a later point, and so on, the early fetus is so similar to the late fetus

34. See Callahan, *Abortion: Law, Choice and Morality*, pp. 409–41; Moraczewski, "Human Personhood," pp. 301–11.
35. See Feinberg, "Abortion," pp. 184–202; Bassen, "Present Sakes and Future Prospects."
36. See Bondeson et al., *Abortion and the Status of the Fetus*, pp. xvi–xvii.
37. For illuminating discussion, see Luker, *Abortion and the Politics of Motherhood*, pp. 159–75.

or newborn that the two should be assimilated; otherwise, we are on the slippery slope to genocide, infanticide, and senicide. But the concept of similarity is not transitive in this way. A continuum of similarities may yield dissimilarities between things at either end of the continuum; a criterion of dissimilarity may be formulated to sort out the cases without the slide down the slippery slope starting at all. True, some philosophers have denied that the neonate is a person and thus claim that infanticide does not violate anyone's natural right to life.[38] Their view is not an inevitable consequence of rejection of the potentiality principle; one may reasonably argue that the fetus's capacity for self-consciousness and agency occur in late pregnancy.[39] Second, their view is often associated with good consequentialist arguments justifying in contemporary circumstances a moral and political practice that forbids infanticide and indeed draws the line of permissible abortion on demand late in pregnancy.[40]

The argument from prophylaxis against mistakes rests on the superficially attractive claim that, when in doubt about the morality or immorality of the consequences of one's activity, guard against the possibility of being mistaken about morality by playing safe: by not doing the dubious deed. The implicit analogy is to the following case: on the verge of firing a gun at what looks like a target but which one believes to be a person, one plays safe and does not fire. But the analogy is fallacious. The supposed mistake in the abortion context is not that a thing known to be a person may look like something else (a target) but that a thing reasonably believed to be a target may be a metaphysical person, which is, morally, a totally different case. Moral people are not required to guide their moral conduct according to metaphysical assumptions they do not reasonably believe; if they did, the Hindu belief in reincarnation and practice of vegetarianism would morally impose vegetarianism on non-Hindus (animals are metaphysical persons in some stage of their reincarnation). Moral persons are not hostage in this way to beliefs they do not reasonably entertain.

Constitutional Neutrality and Antiabortion Laws

On examination, the potentiality principle cannot support the claim that all potential persons are persons. The linkage between potentiality and actuality is compelled neither by logic nor by ethics, but by background metaphysical and moral assumptions not shared by many reasonable religious and nonreligious people in society at large. An argu-

38. See Tooley, "Abortion and Infanticide"; Tooley, *Abortion and Infanticide*; Feinberg, "Abortion."
39. See Bassen, "Present Sakes and Future Prospects." Cf. Sumner, *Abortion and Moral Theory*; Brody, *Abortion and the Sanctity of Human Life: A Philosophical View*; Kluge, *The Practice of Death*.
40. See, e.g., Engelhardt, "Viability and the Use of the Fetus."

ment that requires such assumptions of one sectarian tradition (perhaps even internally incoherent within its own tradition)[41] is the kind of non-neutral value forbidden legal enforcement by constitutional ideals of toleration.

The potentiality principle may, however, be given a less ambitious metaphysical and moral interpretation, which may suggest to many a constitutionally neutral state purpose for antiabortion laws. On this interpretation, potential life is not a claim about moral personality, but a claim about values entitled to moral and political weight because of their symbolic reenforcement and protection of other values (including respect for persons). The lines of moral and legal protection are often drawn rather broadly beyond the protection of persons, properly understood, in order to afford ample symbolic and practical reenforcement of respect for persons. For example, suppose animals do not have rights, or that humans, in certain states of permanent brain inactivity and unconsciousness, are no longer moral persons. Moral and legal constraints might still protect animals from cruelty, or such permanently unconscious humans from termination of their lives, in order to surround core moral values of respect for persons with ample symbolic and practical protection. Correspondingly, the potentiality principle, on this interpretation, expresses an argument of similar moral weight: not that potential persons are persons with rights, but that protection of them affords important symbolic and practical protection of persons.

In the context of antiabortion laws, the analogy is, however, defective. The potentiality principle, on this interpretation of it, does justify an argument of moral weight like that accorded animals or the comatose. The argument for the constitutional right to privacy, developed in chapter 8, does not debar such arguments in general, but only when they compromise certain essential moral interests (conscience, privacy). If such arguments were given decisive force everywhere, there is no infringement of the most essential personal liberties that might not easily be justified. Prohibitions not only of abortion, but of contraception or pornography use, of many kinds of sexual relations in general, of much religious practice, of all conscientious dissent—could plausibly be justified by some symbolic or practical likelihood of protecting persons. Constitutional values of both religious liberty and free speech require, precisely for this reason, a more demanding burden of justification (thus, the clear and present danger test). And the argument about intrinsic contractarian limits on the scope of enforceable public morality denies controlling weight to these arguments for the same reason when rights to essential moral powers (conscience, privacy) are unjustly abridged by them. Instead, such abridgment is only justified if it is a necessary and indispensable protection of a general good. In the

41. See McCartney, "Some Roman Catholic Concepts of Person and their Implications for the Ontological Status of the Unborn."

abortion case, such rights are arguably in play, and a heavier burden of state justification may be required. If such privacy rights are in play (see the next section), the potentiality principle cannot satisfy *this* burden.

The theory of general goods, which expresses the kind of contractarian constraints imposed on abridgment of conscience and privacy, is a measure of the common goods so necessary to the lives of all rational people that each person could reasonably accept necessary protections of such goods by the criminal law even at the cost of essential interests in moral independence. The only interests that could have this status are those that all persons could reasonably acknowledge as not compromising the exercise of these moral powers, that is, the all-purpose interests that all could reasonably accept, no matter what the more particular aims and ends of their lives. The lives of nonpersons, whether potential persons or not, are not common goods of this kind. Whatever the moral weight of such claims, it is not the weight required of general goods: many persons could not reasonably accept, as a justification for abridgment of conscience or privacy, either such claims of value or the necessity to protect them. Since the theory of general goods identifies as such goods only those interests of persons whose necessary protection is acceptable to all reasonable persons at large, fetal life is not one of those interests. In view of the theory of harms made possible by the theory of general goods, we may now therefore understand why the termination of fetal life is not, for this purpose, a harm.

Abortion Choice as Privacy Right

So far, my argument has been hypothetical: if the abortion choice is protected by the constitutional right to privacy, the moral argument for prohibition of such choices cannot satisfy the required burden of constitutional neutrality. Our examination of the nature and proper weight of these arguments clarifies why the abortion choice is a privacy right.

The moral arguments for the prohibition of abortion cluster around certain traditional conceptions of the natural processes of sexuality and gender. On this view, abortion is an immoral revolt against this natural order of sexuality and gender roles. This rejection of abortion and (often) contraception arises from a conscientious and coherent conception of a good and decent life, embedded in a larger context of traditional expectations and class experience of proper gender roles.[42]

Once one takes seriously that fetal life is not a general good in the constitutionally required sense, the potentiality principle is not a constitutionally reasonable argument for regarding abortion as homicide, but a proxy for complex background assumptions often not reasonably believed in the society at large. This is not a neutral argument for protecting a general good, as it proclaims itself to be, but the enforcement

42. See Luker, *Abortion and the Politics of Motherhood*, pp. 159–75.

at large of the requirements of a now controversial, powerfully sectarian ideology about proper sexuality and gender roles.

From this perspective, the prohibitions on abortion encumber what many now reasonably regard as a highly conscientious choice by women regarding their bodies, their sexuality and gender, and the nature and place of pregnancy, birth, and child rearing in their personal and ethical lives.[43] The traditional condemnation of abortion fails, at a deep ethical level, to take seriously the moral independence of women as free and rational persons, lending the force of law to theological ideas of biological naturalness and gender hierarchy that degrade the constructive moral powers of women themselves to establish the meaning of their sexual and reproductive life histories. The underlying conception appears to be not discontinuous with the sexist idea that women's minds and bodies are not their own, but the property of others, namely, men or their masculine God, who may use them and their bodies for the greater good. The abortion choice is thus one of the choices essential to the just moral independence of women, centering their lives in a body image and aspirations expressive of their moral powers.[44] The abortion choice is clearly a just application of the constitutional right to privacy, because the right to the abortion choice protects women from the traditional degradation of their moral powers, reflected in the assumptions underlying antiabortion laws.

It is difficult to see the disagreements over sexuality and gender roles, which underlie the intractable controversy over the morality of abortion,[45] as anything but the kinds of antagonistic disagreements over the ways best to live a good and decent life that people of strong independent conscience will always entertain and advocate in a constitutional democracy. Properly understood, principles of constitutional neutrality secure the fullest possible scope for such forms of moral independence, affording the diverse range of visions and ways of living among which people may exercise their essential moral powers of choice and deliberation. Such internal ideals of constitutional neutrality require that this appropriate area of controversy must remain an appeal to moral powers, rather than an unjust coercive incursion on the proper play of those powers. The coercive imposition at large of one such moral view, tied to the premises internal to one form of conscience and not to general goods, compromises the very conditions of moral independence that actuate the larger constitutional conception of democratic toleration and civility. For example, a responsible politician, with a principled understanding of our constitutional traditions and the nature of the abortion issue, would not regard his tradition's own view about the immorality of abortion as decisive for the constitutionally legitimate

43. On the moral conscientiousness of an abortion decision for women, see Gilligan, *In a Different Voice*, pp. 70–71.
44. See Harrison, *Our Right to Choose*.
45. See, in general, Luker, *Abortion and the Politics of Motherhood*, esp. pp. 158–91.

enforcement of that view at large. To the contrary, he might insist that the power of his tradition is most fairly tested not by the usurpation of the rights of dissenting consciences, but by the moral eloquence of the larger humanity and charity that the way of life—embodying his view—expresses.[46] Constitutional neutrality does not enforce any ultimate vision of complete moral truth of either the good pursued or the evil avoided in a life well lived. It requires only the minimal procedural conditions of equal respect for the moral independence of each and every person in seeking such truth. The very integrity of this procedural minimum is that it takes so seriously the responsibility of each person for finding value in living. The sterile neutrality of its general goods is not thus the end of life. Indeed, the foundation of its minimal procedural conditions is what these conditions make possible: the competing visions of beauty and truth and good which must engross the imagination and intelligence of every free person absorbed in finding value in living.

The common belief that the prohibition of abortion rests on constitutionally neutral moral values is, I have suggested, wrong. My argument thus developed an alternative conception of the harm principle grounded in respect for the rational and reasonable independence of persons, a respect put at hazard by the tyrannous traditional morality that Mill anatomizes in *On Liberty*. Criminal laws, which rest on normative and other assumptions that many reasonable persons would not accept, debase moral independence. They make the lives of persons hostage to beliefs they do not and would not conscientiously or reasonably affirm, as much an insult to integrity as compulsion of belief or speech. The same considerations that debar the power of the state to homogenize religion or thought or speech require institutional respect for ways of life expressive of a just moral independence. Religious liberty, free speech, and constitutional privacy are thus linked by a common argument of constitutional principle. The harm principle, properly understood, specifies the terms of this just social contract among free persons committed to such political ideals. Just punishment of the exercise of essential moral powers must be limited, subject to background duties of justice and fair contribution, to forms of conduct that directly threaten the neutrally understood goods that all self-respecting persons demand, for example, security of life, bodily integrity, property, and the like.

PRIVACY AND SEXUAL AUTONOMY

The most undeveloped and least satisfactory area of the jurisprudence of constitutional privacy is the judicial treatment of the application of the right to constitutional privacy to consensual sexuality in general,

46. See Cuomo, "Religious Belief and Public Morality."

and consensual adult homosexuality in particular.[47] In this section, I analyze why constitutional privacy should protect sexual expression, and why state laws prohibiting oral and anal sex are unconstitutional.

Sexuality as Intimate Association

The best contemporary evidence about the nature and role of sexuality in the life of the person makes clear the rightful dignity, grounded in the traditional American commitment to an abstract right of privacy, of the right of persons to engage in forms of sexual expression central to the integrity of their intimate relations and personal lives.[48] In particular, criminalization of forms of oral and anal sex coercively abridges this fundamental right of three significant groups of persons: many heterosexual men and women, certain disabled people, and homosexual men and women.

The classic Kinsey and later sex studies revealed that large and growing numbers of heterosexual women and men regard forms of oral and anal sex as important options of sexual fulfillment central to their intimate relationships.[49] Indeed, professional therapies for sexual dysfunc-

---

47. See *Doe v. Commonwealth's Attorney*, 403 F. Supp. 1199 (E.D.Va. 1975), *aff'd without opinion* 425 U.S. 901 (1976). But cf. *People v. Onofre*, 51 N.Y.2d 476 (1980), *cert. den.* 451 U.S. 987 (1981).

48. The pervasive imaginative force of human sexuality in the life of the person, in contrast to the procreational periodicity of animal sexuality, is at the heart of Freud's central innovations in modern thought. See Freud, "'Civilized' Sexual Morality and Modern Nervous Illness," pp. 181, 187. For important confirmation of comparative ethology and anthropology, see Ford and Beach, *Patterns of Sexual Behavior*, pp. 199–267.

49. The early Kinsey studies found, for example, that 15 percent of high-school-educated men engaged in cunnilingus or experienced fellatio in marriage, and 45 percent of college-educated men engaged in cunnilingus and 43 percent experienced fellatio (Kinsey et al., *Sexual Behavior in the Human Male*, p. 371); 50 percent and 46 percent of high-school-educated women experienced cunnilingus or engaged in fellatio in marriage, respectively, and 58 percent and 52 percent of college-educated women, respectively (Kinsey et al., *Sexual Behavior in the Human Female*, p. 399). By 1974, 56 percent and 54 percent of high-school-educated men engaged in cunnilingus and fellatio, respectively, in their marriages; and 66 percent and 61 percent of college-educated men, respectively; 58 percent and 52 percent of high-school-educated women engaged in cunnilingus and fellatio, respectively, in marriage; and 72 percent of college-educated women engaged in both (Hunt, *Sexual Behavior in the 1970s*. p. 198). By 1983, the percentages of heterosexual couples reporting fellatio were as follows: 5 percent every time they have sex, 24 percent usually, 43 percent sometimes, 18 percent rarely, 10 percent never. The percentages reporting cunnilingus were 6 percent every time, 26 percent usually, 42 percent sometimes, 19 percent rarely, 7 percent never. (Blumstein and Schwartz, *American Couples*, p. 236). In the same study, heterosexual men who receive oral sex are happier with their relationships in general (pp. 231–33); women report no comparable increment (pp. 233–37). The Kinsey studies found heterosexual anal sex quite infrequent (Kinsey et al., *Sexual Behavior in the Human Male*, p. 579; Gebhard and Johnson, *The Kinsey Data*, pp. 304, 383). By 1974, half of the younger married respondents reported finding forms of it acceptable (Hunt, *Sexual Behavior in the 1970s*, pp. 199–200). Other, more informally gathered samples confirm all these trends in the data. See, e.g., Hite, *The Hite Report*; Pietropinto and Simenauer, *Beyond the Male Myth*; Tavris & S. Sadd, *Redbook Report on Female Sexuality*; Hite, *Hite Report on Male Sexuality*; Wolfe, *Cosmo Report*.

tion include, if the couple wishes, oral and anal sex techniques to enhance the mutual pleasure of the sexual experience.[50]

In working with persons whose sexual function is significantly altered by illness or disability, rehabilitation counselors, nurses, doctors, social workers, and others discuss and teach sexual techniques as part of patient education. In the absence of capacity for erection of the penis or in view of limitations in body movement, oral sex is a primary, sometimes exclusive way for many couples to experience continued sexual expression.[51] Such forms of disability include a broad range of conditions.[52]

Intimate relationships of homosexual women and men include oral sex as a primary option, and, for homosexual men, anal sex as well.[53]

Criminalization of all these forms of sexual expression abridges important, exclusive, or primary ways in which many persons in our society naturally feel and express sexual love for one another, voluntarily bond their lives in the intimate relations central to the integrity of their personal lives, and indeed sustain the sexual expression of these relationships. Increasing evidence supports the continuities in both the sexual experience and bonding that characterize the place these forms of sexual expression enjoy in the lives of diverse American couples today; such facts are attested to by the many careful studies that have followed in the wake of Kinsey's classic books.[54] It would blink reality, in this case facts bearing on fundamental constitutional rights, not to give these findings appropriate weight in elaborating the meaning of abstract background rights today in the constitutionally sensitive area of criminal coercion.

Our failure to understand the meaning these acts have in personal relationships will be clarified, as it was in the case of abortion, by scrutiny of the traditional moral arguments that justified prohibition of them. Once we see that these arguments do not rest on general goods, the nature of the privacy interests here abridged will come into sharper

50. See, in general, Barbach, *Women Discover Orgasm*; Kaplan, *The New Sex Therapy*; Masters and Johnson, *Human Sexual Inadequacy*; LoPiccolo and LoPiccolo, eds., *Handbook of Sex Therapy*.

51. See the references cited in note 50, above. See also Comfort, *More Joy*, pp. 210–13.

52. These disabilities include arthritis and other mobility problems (Diamond and Karlen, *Sexual Decisions*, p. 140; Boggs, *Living and Loving with Arthritis*); multiple sclerosis (Barrett, *Sexuality and Multiple Sclerosis*, pp. 20–22); spinal cord injury resulting in paraplegia and quadriplegia, and known side effects from medication (Mooney, Cole, and Chilgren, *Sexual Options for Paraplegics and Quadriplegics*, pp. 73–83; Woods, *Human Sexuality in Health and Illness*, pp. 358–59); diabetic disabilities (Kaufman, *Sexual Sabotage*, p. 134); cancer surgery in the vaginal area (Clark and Magrina, *Sexual Adjustment to Cancer Surgery in the Vaginal Area*, pp. 36–39; also brochure appendix, pp. 1–12); and cardiac disabilities (Hogan, *Human Sexuality*, p. 638; Cambre, *The Sensuous Heart*, p. 13).

53. See, e.g., Bell and Weinberg, *Homosexualities* pp. 106–15; Blumstein and Schwartz, *American Couples*, pp. 237–45.

54. For the continuities in the nature of sexual experience, see esp. Masters and Johnson, *Homosexuality in Perspective*. For continuities in both sexual experience and bonding, see Blumstein and Schwartz, *American Couples*.

focus. Indeed, we can crystallize critical understanding of truths that many of the people condemned have only recently come to understand for themselves. The attempt by law to isolate and criminally condemn such forms of sexual expression works a kind of spiritual violence on the moral integrity of the many persons for whom such acts authenticate the affection, attachment, and mutual love integral to their best conceptions of life lived well and humanely. On examination, this brutal and callous impersonal manipulation by the state of intimate personal life is the same constitutional evil as that condemned by the Supreme Court in disallowing the legitimacy of state control of contraceptive use in sexuality or state control of women's use of their bodies for procreation. Such coercive laws must satisfy a heavy burden of constitutional justification; they cannot do so.

Burden of Justification

Criminal prohibitions bearing on the right of constitutional privacy require a substantial burden of justification. That burden can in principle be met, for example, by neutral criminal statutes applicable to intrafamilial murders, or wife and husband beating, or child abuse, no matter how rooted in intimate family life and sexuality these acts may be. In such cases, the constitutional burden of justification is met: necessary protections of countervailing rights of persons justify coercive interference into intimate relations. On the other hand, criminal prohibitions on the use of contraceptives, abortion services or obscene materials in the home could not meet the burden of justification: arguments of countervailing rights are either too constitutionally nonneutral or controversial or speculative to satisfy the burden required to abridge such intimately personal sexual matters. Criminal prohibitions on forms of sexual expression satisfy this burden even less successfully.

The elaboration of the right to constitutional privacy in our law requires, for its intelligibility, a distinction between forms of reflective ethical argument that satisfy the constitutional burden required for its abridgment and other forms of argument that cannot meet this burden. I have suggested that the relevant ethical approach, on which the privacy cases implicitly depend, is the abstract ethical perspective fundamental both to Western conceptions of moral relations and specific to the commitment of American constitutionalism to respect for human rights. On this view, ethics treats other persons as one would oneself want to be treated, as a person with respect for one's basic demands for those liberties central to a free and self-governing person and moral agent.[55] Such equal respect for persons—which ensures the basic liberties to form different religious, philosophical, and political alle-

---

55. I have developed the ethical argument here deployed at greater length in its application both to consensual deviant sex and commercial sex in Richards, *Sex, Drugs, Death and the Law,* pp. 29–153.

giances—requires that the scope of the criminal law must itself express such respect for persons. Persons, thus respected for their powers of moral independence, will allow abridgment of those powers only to ensure necessary protections of the claims of persons for the neutral goods all would require to lead their lives as free persons, irrespective of other ideological differences in basic religious or other commitments. The state may justly enforce criminal statutes in areas of conscience and privacy only on the demanding terms of principles that, on fair terms to all, give necessary and indispensable protection to the interests of adult persons in life, bodily security and integrity, security in institutional relationships and claims arising therefrom, and the like. Such principles also justify needed protections of the rights of children to appropriate conditions of nurturance and development.

Such ethical principles dictate certain prohibitions and regulations of sexual conduct. For example, respect for the developmental rights of immature children requires that various rights, guaranteed to adults, not extend to children. Nor is there any objection to the reasonable and neutral regulation of obtrusive sexual solicitation as such or to forcible intercourse of any kind. In addition, forms of sexual expression would be limited by other ethical principles: principles of not killing, harming, or inflicting gratuitous cruelty (nonmaleficence);[56] principles of paternalism in narrowly defined circumstances;[57] and principles of fidelity.[58]

Statutes that absolutely forbid oral and anal intercouse cannot be justified by these principles. Such statutes are not limited to forcible or public forms of sexual intercourse or sexual intercourse by or with children; they extend to private, consensual acts between adults as well.

The argument that such laws are justified by their indirect effect of preventing homosexual intercourse by or with the underaged as absurdly fails to meet the required constitutional burden as the claim that absolute prohibitions on heterosexual intercourse could be thus justified. There is no reason to believe that homosexuals as a class are any more involved in offenses with the young than heterosexuals.[59] Nor is there any reliable evidence that such laws inhibit children from being

56. See Richards, *A Theory of Reasons for Action*, pp. 176–85.
57. See *ibid.*, pp. 192–95.
58. *Ibid.*, pp. 163–69.
59. See the classic Kinsey Institute study of sex offenders, Gebhard et al., *Sex Offenders;* and Hoffman, *The Gay World*, pp. 89–92. In general, seduction of the young appears to be more centered on heterosexual rather than homosexual relations. See Bell and Weinberg, *Homosexualities*, p. 230. The failure to note the distinction between homosexuality and pedophilia is deplored by the majority of homosexual people who "do not share, do not approve, and fear to be associated with pedophiliac interests," West, *Homosexuality*, p. 119. One recent study summarizes the pertinent empirical literature on sex offenders against children as follows: "these men are much more likely to have a heterosexual history and orientation than a homosexual one. Contrary to public belief, homosexual adult males rarely molest young male children." Geiser, *Hidden Victims: The Sexual Abuse of Children*, p. 75.

naturally homosexual who would otherwise be naturally heterosexual. Sexual preference is settled, largely irreversibly[60] and as a small minority preference,[61] in very early childhood well before laws of this kind have any effect.[62] If the aim of determining sexual preference by criminal penalty were legitimate (which is doubtful),[63] that interest could not constitutionally be secured by overbroad statutes that coercively violate the core privacy rights of exclusive homosexuals of all ages. So far from satisfying the constitutional burden of being a necessary and indispensable protection of a neutral good, such laws fail to meet even the much weaker constitutional threshhold of bare rationality; in fact, they irrationally pursue the state interest.

Other moral principles fail to justify absolute prohibitions on oral and anal sex. Such relations are not, for example, generally violent. Prohibitory statutes could thus not be justified by moral principles of nonmaleficence. There is no convincing evidence that these sexual acts as such harm the agent or correspond to any form of mental or physical disease or defect[64] so that paternalistic principles do not here come into proper play. And these statutes do not meet any just purpose the state might have in enforcing principles of fidelity. The acts often occur in ongoing and long-standing intimate relations, which they stabilize and enrich.

The failure of these laws to satisfy the constitutional burden required for abridgment of constitutional privacy is consistent with other Supreme Court cases. Like anticontraception laws, these laws coerce people to refrain from nonprocreative sex but do so even more unwarrantably since many disabled persons and many homosexual men and women find their exclusive or primary forms of sexual expression in these acts. The interest in autonomy in intimate relations is here at least as strong as that in the reproductive autonomy of abortion decisions or decisions to use obscene materials, and the evidence of harms to the

60. See Churchill, *Homosexual Behavior Among Males* pp. 283–91; Tripp, *The Homosexual Matrix*, p. 251; West, *Homosexuality*, p. 266.
61. Kinsey states that 4 percent of males are exclusively homosexual throughout their lives. Kinsey et al., *Sexual Behavior in the Human Male*, pp. 650–51.
62. See, for example, Money and Ehrhardt, *Man & Woman Boy & Girl*, pp. 153–201. One study hypothesizes that gender identity and sexual object choice coincide with the development of language, i.e., from 18 to 24 months of age. See Money, Hampson, and Hampson, "An Examination of Some Basic Sexual Concepts: The Evidence of Human Hermaphroditism." Cf. Bell, Weinberg, and Hammersmith, *Sexual Preference*.
63. See *Pierce v. Society of Sisters*, 268 U.S. 510 (1925) and *Meyer v. Nebraska*, 262 U.S. 390 (1923).
64. See *The Wolfenden Report*, pp. 31–33; Hooker, "The Adjustment of the Male Overt Homosexual." Both the American Psychiatric Association and the American Psychological Association no longer regard homosexuality as such a manifestation of psychological problems. Blumstein and Schwartz, *American Couples*, p. 44. For the ways in which criminalization fosters health problems in this area, see Note, "The Constitutionality of Laws Forbidding Private Homosexual Conduct," pp. 1631–33.

rights of concrete other persons even more controversial and speculative.

We may assume conventional morality does not give consistent value to privacy interests in sexual intimacy; presumably, conventional morality here gives a weight to symbolic and practical arguments, akin to the potentiality principle in the abortion area, that they do not enjoy when privacy interests are fully recognized. What could justify this? The failure to identify sexual intimacy as a privacy issue must be based on other moral reasons of great weight not yet examined. A critical assessment of these arguments confirms the justice of extending the constitutional right of privacy to these acts.

Residual Moral Arguments

One final moral argument has been used to justify a general prohibition on oral and anal sex—the argument invoked by the courts that have upheld the legitimacy, for example, of sodomy statutes, namely, "the promotion of morality and decency," interpreted as an appeal to traditional moral condemnation of certain acts.[65]

I have argued that a form of ethical argument is indeed necessary to the legitimacy of the criminal law in the United States. But the elaboration of the constitutional right to privacy consistent with fundamental principles of our constitutional law suggests that not every statement of "morality and decency," which surely could be invoked against all the privacy decisions, is of equal constitutional significance. In fact, all the privacy decisions reflect pervasive moral controversy within American society over which aspects of our collective moral traditions can and cannot justly be retained. Our moral practices as a community are not inextricably homogeneous. On critical reflection, we retain certain basic principles in them (for example, treating persons as equals), but we change lower order conventions that we come to believe are inconsistent with the reflective ethical core of our moral and constitutional values. The appeal to "morality and decency," without more, falsely begs the central issue in dispute, supposing precisely the kind of homogeneity in moral values that the general history of Western ethics and specific history of constitutional privacy belie. It is a valued and admirable distinction of Western ethics and law that they have changed, open to critical reflection on their own history (for example, of the primacy of toleration for conscience and the right of privacy) and to new empirical and normative perspectives that elaborate that history in principled ways.

The earlier argument proposed the kind of ethical principles to which controversies over proper criminalization appeal, consistent

65. See *Doe v. Commonwealth's Attorney*, 403 F. Supp. 1199, 1202 (E.D.Va. 1975), *aff'd without opinion* 425 U.S. 901 (1976); but cf. *People v. Onofre*, 51 N.Y.2d 476 (1980), *cert. den.* 451 U.S. 987 (1981).

with values of constitutional neutrality. It also demonstrated why the criminalization of acts of sexual expression cannot meet this burden of justification. I propose now to complete that argument by showing that the traditional moral conceptions underlying the criminalization of oral and anal sex reflect a history of false empirical and dubious moral beliefs that cannot constitutionally enjoy the force of law.

The traditional moral condemnation of oral and anal sex in our culture may be traced to a number of beliefs: (1) the notion that homosexual forms of such sexual expression undermine, particularly in men, desirable masculine character traits—for example, courage and self-control; (2) a general conception that sexuality has only one proper purpose (procreation) and any other form of sexual expression disengaged from procreation (including contraceptive use) is shamefully wrong; (3) an empirical belief that prohibitions of homosexual forms of such sexual expression combated pestilence, plague, and natural disaster;[66] (4) a theological understanding that relevant passages in the Old and New Testament condemned such acts; (5) various empirical beliefs about the inhumanly exceptional choice of sexual propensities, the evil consequences of their exercise to the agent and others (child molestation), their connections with other moral vices, and the like; and (6) a political conception that such acts constitute a willful heresy or treason against the stability of social institutions. None of these beliefs, discussed in the following paragraphs, can reasonably sustain, in terms of constitutional neutrality, the application of coercive sanctions to oral and anal sex as such.

(1) The view that male homosexuality necessarily involves the loss of desirable character traits[67] is without empirical foundation. Apart from sexual preference, exclusive homosexuals are indistinguishable from the general population.[68] If the traditional view rests on the idea that sexual relations between males involve the degradation of one or both parties to the status of a woman,[69] the view expresses intellectual confusion (sexual preference and gender identity are not correlated)[70] and

---

66. See Justinian, Novellae 77 and 141, reprinted in Bailey, Homosexuality and the Western Christian Tradition, pp. 73–75. The issuance of these imperial edicts seems to have been prompted by contemporary earthquakes, floods, and plagues, which Justinian, drawing an analogy to the Sodom and Gomorrah episode, supposed to be caused by homosexual practices; see pp. 76–77. Blackstone similarly cites the Sodom and Gomorrah episode, in support of the appropriateness of the death penalty for homosexual acts, indeed suggesting—since God there punished by fire—the special appropriateness of death by burning. Blackstone, Commentaries on the Laws of England, vol. 4, p. 216.

67. For the earliest statement of this view, see Plato, Laws, Book 8, 835d–842a.

68. See Bell and Weinberg, Homosexualities, pp. 195–231; Churchill, Homosexual Behavior Among Males, pp. 36–59.

69. In the ancient Greek and Roman world, for example, while homosexuality as such was not wrong, to allow oneself to be the passive partner (the "woman") was wrong. See Vanggaard, Phallos, pp. 87–99.

70. See, e.g., Simon and Gagnon, "Femininity in the Lesbian Community."

the unacceptable moral premise that the status of a woman is a degradation, an idea repugnant to contemporary constitutional law and ethics.[71]

(2) The general conception that sexuality has one exclusively legitimate function (procreation)[72] is almost certainly based on a misunderstanding of the unique features of human sexuality, its expression of higher cortical functions of imagination and bonding, and its independence from the reproductive cycle.[73] For humans, sexual relations are intrinsically valuable in the expression of love and bonding and the forms of intimate relations and personal lives they make possible.[74] The insistence that sex must be procreational, which denies this fact, is doubly wrong. From the perspective of individuals, it works a moral debasement of valuable resources of human nature for personal relationships; from the viewpoint of society, it unwisely cabins a natural way of meeting the increased concern for population control. Both these considerations justify the Supreme Court's rejection of the neutrality of anticontraception laws and apply as well to nonprocreational sex acts as such.[75]

(3) Empirical beliefs about the causal connection of oral and anal sex to natural disasters are, of course, without foundation, and would not be worthy of mention had they not been cited by influential Western legal authorities as the reason for condemning homosexuality as a capital offense, preferably punishable by burning.[76]

(4) Many interpretations of the Bible to the effect that homosexual relations are condemned are almost certainly erroneous.[77] Other forms of moral argument to the same effect, by prominent theologians,[78]

71. See, e.g., *Frontiero v. Richardson*, 411 U.S. 677 (1973); Mill, *The Subjection of Women*.
72. The classic statement is Augustine, *The City of God*, pp. 577–94. See, in general, Noonan, *Contraception*; Bullough, *Sexual Variance in Society and History*.
73. See Ford and Beach, *Patterns of Sexual Behavior*, pp. 199–267; Kaplan, *The New Sex Therapy*.
74. See Eibl-Eibesfeldt, *Love and Hate*, pp. 155–69; Masters and Johnson, *The Pleasure Bond*.
75. Certainly, the crude argument that if everyone were homosexual there would, disastrously, be an end of the human species, universalizes absurdly a principle no one seriously proposes; namely, that everyone should or must be homosexual, as if, contrary to all modern sex research, sexual preference is or could be chosen.
76. See Blackstone's comments cited in n. 66, above.
77. For example, the Sodom and Gomorrah episode, Gen. 19, is apparently not about homosexuality at all, but hospitality. See Bailey, *Homosexuality and the Western Christian Tradition*, pp. 1–28; McNeill, *The Church and the Homosexual*, pp. 42–50; Boswell, *Christianity, Social Tolerance, and Homosexuality*, pp. 91–105. Yet American courts cite this episode in support of the legitimacy of antisodomy laws, *Dawson v. Vance*, 329 F. Supp. 1320, 1322 (S.D. Tex. 1972). See *Doe v. Commonwealth's Attorney*, 403 F. Supp. 1199 (E.D.Va. 1975), *aff'd without opinion*, 425 U.S. 901 (1976), which points out that sodomy statutes have an "ancestry going back to Judaic and Christian law," Doe at 1202.
78. See Augustine, *City of God*. See also Thomas Aquinas, *On the Truth of the Catholic Faith: Summa Contra Gentiles*, pt. 2, ch. 122(9), p. 146.

reflect forms of the first two beliefs discussed here (loss of character and the procreative purpose of sex), which were absorbed from the surrounding culture and read into Western theology. Critical reflection on these two beliefs has led many religious people to question their continuing religious authority.[79] If these beliefs cannot sustain reflective scrutiny as neutral views fairly applicable to all persons, their religious origins cannot confer on them constitutional legitimacy. Indeed, the more powerful argument, based on constitutional neutrality, is to quite the opposite effect.[80]

(5) Traditional conceptions of the mysteriously anomalous, inhumanly exceptional, and harmful nature of homosexual preference to the agent and others cannot withstand empirical examination today. Homosexual preference appears to be an adaptation of natural human propensities to very early social circumstances of certain kinds, so that the preference is settled, largely irreversibly, at a quite early age.[81] The sexual acts that express this homosexual preference are a natural expression of human sexual competences and sensitivities, and do not reflect any form of damage, decline, or injury to self.[82] For homosexuals, these acts are at the core of intimate relationships as central to their integrity as are comparable intimate relationships of heterosexuals.[83] Aside from sexual preference, homosexuals are indistinguishable from the rest of the population, and they are no more likely to have sex with the underaged than are other groups.[84]

(6) The conception that homosexual forms of oral and anal sex are a form of heresy or treason is both an ancient and modern ground offered for its criminal condemnation.[85] There is no good reason to believe that the legitimacy of such forms of sexual expression destabilizes social cooperation. Homosexual relations are and will foreseeably remain the preference of small minorities of the population,[86] who are

---

79. See Bailey, *Homosexuality and the Western Christian Tradition;* Boswell, *Christianity, Social Tolerance, and Homosexuality;* and McNeill, *The Church and the Homosexual.*

80. Henkin, "Morals and the Constitution: The Sin of Obscenity."

81. See references at note 62, above.

82. See references at note 64, above.

83. See Blumstein and Schwartz, *American Couples,* pp. 44–45.

84. See references at notes 68 and 59, above.

85. Throughout the Middle Ages, homosexuals were prosecuted as heretics, and often burned at the stake. See Bailey, *Homosexuality and the Western Christian Tradition,* p. 135. "Buggery," one of the names for homosexual acts, derives from a corruption of the name of one heretical group alleged to engage in homosexual practices. See ibid., pp. 141, 148–49. For a modern use of the idea of treason in this context, see Devlin, *The Enforcement of Morals,* pp. 1–25. For rebuttal, see Hart, *Law, Liberty, and Morality;* Hart, "Social Solidarity and the Enforcement of Morals."

86. The original Kinsey estimate that about 4 percent of males are exclusively homosexual throughout their lives is confirmed by comparable European studies. See Gebhard, "Incidence of Overt Homosexuality in the United States and Western Europe," pp. 22–29. The incidence figure remains stable though many of the European countries do not apply the criminal penalty to consensual sex acts of the kind here under discussion. See Barnett, *Sexual Freedom and the Constitution,* p. 293.

as committed to principles of social cooperation and contribution as any other group in society at large. Indeed, the very accusation of heresy or treason brings out an important feature of the traditional moral condemnation in its contemporary vestments. It no longer rests on generally acceptable arguments of necessary protections of the rights of persons to neutral goods, but appeals to arguments internal to highly personal, often almost religious decisions about acceptable ways of belief and life-style. When a moral tradition in this way abandons certain of its essential grounds, it may justly retain its legitimacy for those internal to the tradition, all the more so because it remains more exclusively constitutive of their tradition. But if those essential grounds are constitutionally necessary for the tradition coercively to enforce its mandates through the criminal law, the abandonment of those grounds, must, *pari passu*, deprive the tradition of its constitutional legitimacy as a ground for coercive sanctions. The tradition now no longer expresses neutral ethical arguments that may fairly be imposed on all persons, but rather perspectives reasonably authoritative only for those who adhere to the tradition.

In exactly the same way suggested in our earlier examination of the contraception and abortion decisions, the enforcement of such perspectives is the functional equivalent of a heresy prosecution.[87] The grounds for prohibition are highly personal ideological or political views about which free persons reasonably disagree. The continuing force of the prohibitions rests not on protection of the rights of persons, but on fears and misunderstandings directed at the alien way of life of a small and traditionally condemned minority, as if, at bottom, the legitimacy of one's own way of life requires the illegitimacy of all others. Constitutional toleration, which forbids heresy prosecutions[88] and sharply circumscribes treason prosecutions,[89] must likewise be extended to criminal prohibitions that today have the political force of heresy and treason prosecutions.

In effect, our analysis of such criminal prohibitions reveals them as yet another form of those arguments of moral or political subversion which have recurrently stimulated our constitutional culture to a fuller understanding of its own internal contractarian ideals. Subversive conscience, speech, and ways of life are all of a piece, and all equally actuate the understanding and elaboration of our constitutional ideals of the moral sovereignty of each free person over oneself and the state. That sovereignty is accorded the respect it is due not when it is least

---

87. The English legal scholar Tony Honore observed of the contemporary status of the homosexual: "It is not primarily a matter of breaking rules but of dissenting attitudes. It resembles political or religious dissent, being an atheist in Catholic Ireland or a dissident in Soviet Russia." Honore, *Sex Law*, p. 89.

88. "Heresy trials are foreign to our Constitution," *United States v. Ballard*, 322 U.S. 78, 86 (1944) (Douglas, writing for the Court).

89. See United States Constitution, Article III, sec. 3.

controversial, but when it is most subversive. It is then that respect for the integrity of its thought, speech, and way of life most confirms our commitment as a democratic people to the equal respect against which the legitimacy of all power must be assessed.

The Harms of Criminalization

The argument just proposed makes possible for our legal and political culture the coherent progression of constitutional traditions consistent with contemporary empirical and normative insight. For example, the deep commitment of the Founders to the abstract background right of privacy (traditionally applied to marriage relations) should now reasonably be extended to forms of intimate personal relationships that have a comparable function and value in the lives of all persons. Indeed, laws criminalizing such intimate associations brutally and unethically work grievous harm in areas of personal intimacy at the very essence of ethical self-respect, which the right to constitutional privacy justly protects: health professionals are legally restricted from assisting people to achieve responsible sexual fulfillment, and the force of criminal law callously interferes in intimate relationships and personal aspirations essential to the moral powers through which we give meaning to life itself.

Consider the effects of these laws on the lives of exclusively homosexual men and women. On the basis of moral arguments that no longer rest on neutral purposes enforceable at large, such laws deny practicing homosexuals their just moral independence in building personal relationships with confidence and security in their most basic emotional propensities. Criminal penalties reenforce employment risks and social prejudice, which fragment emotions, physical expression, and self-image in the way most corrupting of the integrity essential to a free and morally responsible person. The deepest damage is the spiritual violence that these laws work on the human heart—on the imagination of, desire for, and achievement of a love that organizes and expresses the essentially human moral powers. Persons surrounded by false social stereotypes that are supported by law find it difficult to esteem their own emotional propensities, their natural expression, or their objects. Without such self-esteem, persons lack the moral resources of privacy even to frame the question of a personal love whose moral meaning engages their most responsible convictions of value in living. When law forbids exclusive homosexuals the option to express sexual love in the only ways they may find natural, it deprives them not only of love, an essential good of our socially companionate species, but of the moral independence essential to framing the only kind of life that can be, for them, a life with personal and moral value. Surely, this is a grievous harm to the spiritual lives of the good and innocent persons who deserve more from their constitutional traditions than such unjust contempt. The right to constitutional privacy is the precise remedy for this wrong.

BEYOND CONSTITUTIONAL PRIVACY

My remarks have been fairly abstract, and I would not want them to be taken to suggest that these principles easily resolve many hard cases or that decriminalization argument in general is coextensive with constitutional privacy. Certainly, the exploration of the meaning and appropriate institutional embodiment of the harm principle often requires legislative action and study of a kind inappropriate for courts (for example, in commercial sex, regulation of drug use, and certain decisions about death).[90] But there is significant overlap in the appeal to common principles, and the Supreme Court has correctly seen that these principles are of constitutional dimensions.

Some of these applications of the harm principle do not encroach on the right to intimate personal relationships, but on other rights associated with the right to conscience. The right to drug use, if it is a right, is a right associated with the control of consciousness and thus with the right of conscience itself, and should be understood accordingly. The right to die, if it is a right, is associated with the proper contractarian interpretation of the right to life itself and must be parsed in such an appropriate way.[91] My account is consistent with such accounts, although they would have to be developed in a somewhat different fashion than the right to privacy cases discussed here.

As we have found elsewhere, the interpretive work of the Supreme Court is in general sound, though in some areas it has failed to understand the proper scope of the principles it has elaborated. Contractarian political theory again appears to be a useful explanatory and critical tool of constitutional analysis. It clarifies our historical self-understanding, current interpretive traditions, and the ways in which the tradition has not coherently understood or elaborated its internal moral and political ideals.

90. See Richards, *Sex, Drugs, Death and the Law*, pp. 84–270.
91. See ibid., pp. 157–212, 215–70.

10 · Methodological Perspectives on Political Theory & Constitutional Interpretation

Our interpretive project is now complete. We used a political theory of constitutional law to explicate both our historical understanding and our current jurisprudence of central constitutional values of toleration in three areas: religious liberty, free speech, and constitutional privacy. My aim was to present an alternative interpretive approach to constitutional theory and law, one self-consciously guided by an articulate form of moral and political philosophy. My ambitions for this kind of theory were counterpoised to an alternative "clause-bound"[1] approach, which rejected the utility for constitutional law of this kind of general political and moral theory. We should now assess what this kind of interpretive project should mean for our conception of better and worse ways to formulate constitutional theory and thus to deliberate reflectively, as a free people, about the values essential to our conception of a just community.

Advocates of the "clause-bound" approach put their objection to general political theory in terms of certain abstract methodological objections to such theory and in terms of more concrete interpretive inadequacies. The former range of objections centered on the relations of theory and data in constitutional theory, and on examination, did not prove to be decisive objections to the use of general political theory in

1. See Schauer, "An Essay on Constitutional Language"; see also chapter 3 of this book.

constitutional interpretation. We are left with the alleged interpretive inadequacies of such general theories, namely, that such theories are nontextual; thus, Schauer remarks that clause-bound theories are superior to "free-wheeling" ones because "values specified in the text are more or less discrete."[2] But the point begs the interpretive question in dispute. It must be shown that a particular general theory does not account for text. The abstract arguments against general theories do not show this. They make general points about all theories, including "clause-bound" ones. No argument could show that general theories as such must betray text, because the claim is false. For the criticism to be made good, what is required is a detailed intertheoretical comparison of relative adequacy.

We are now in a position to offer such an intertheoretical comparison, drawing on the interpretive fruits of the approach to constitutional interpretation taken in this book. I begin with the examination of the issues discussed in the previous chapters, including the general question of the nature of interpretation in constitutional law. This discussion finally makes it possible to address the issue postponed in chapter 3, the proper role of judicial supremacy in American constitutional law. This discussion allows us to explore a range of constitutional law and doctrine not yet examined, in particular, federalism and separation of powers, and equal protection doctrine. I conclude with some general observations about the difficulties of forging constitutional theory in the style of this book in the context of the history and nature of the American law school, which has been the matrix for most serious constitutional theory in the United States.

INTERPRETING THE TEXT

A common interpretive argument against the use of general theories in constitutional interpretation is that such theories rest on the unfounded assumption that a unified theory of ethics or politics exists, which such theorists unwarrantably foist on the complexity of constitutional law. The implicit appeal here is to text, which allegedly cabins argument in ways that general theories disfigure. But we need to ask more searching questions about what the appeal to text means, or rather about the interpretive approach that such an appeal assumes and often fails critically to examine.

The governing interpretive assumption of the appeal to text is invariably some alternative and putatively better theory of textual interpretation than the position under criticism. Sometimes, the alternative theory is some version of positivist appeal, either to the historical denotations of the Founders or to the positivistic conventions of current

2. Ibid., p. 830.

interpretive practice. One latter such position is the appeal to horizontally clause-bound interpretation of discrete constitutional texts, a view
which recognizes:

> as more free-wheeling theories do not, that the values specified in the text
> are more or less discrete, and that they have a textual preeminence over
> values not so specified.[3]

But all of these alternative views are only as defensible as their underlying interpretive strategies, and many of these strategies are, as we saw
in chapters 2 and 3, unsatisfactory; they do no justice to either the complexity of our historical understanding or our interpretive practices of
constitutional law. The appeal to clause-bound interpretation is in no
better position.

The interpretive project of this book shows this in two interrelated
areas. First, a common interpretive strategy, made possible by the use
of general political theory (the primacy of toleration), advanced understanding of the interpretive practices surrounding two discrete kinds of
clauses: the religion clauses and the free speech and press clauses. Second, the same strategy gave a solid interpretive foundation to both the
inference and the application of the constitutional right to privacy.
Indeed, the general use of political theory, as a tool of constitutional
analysis, brought into critical focus the internal moral and political
ideals that guide constitutional interpretation. It is these ideals, not the
history or conventions imagined by those who appeal to text, which
give the best general and concrete sense to the activity of interpreting
the constitutional text.

Common Interpretive Structures

Our analysis of both the political theory and jurisprudence of the religion and free speech clauses brought out the utility of a general political theory in excavating and clarifying the common political ideals that
actuate both the coordinated interpretation and weight of the religion
clauses themselves, and the associated guarantees of free speech and
press (see chapters 4–7). The clarification is not only of certain
interpretive themes common to the history and jurisprudence of religious liberty and free speech, though that would be no insignificant
gain to our understanding of constitutional law and interpretation. It is
also a gain in the understanding of quite specific interpretive puzzles
over the applicable legal tests in religion clause and free speech
jurisprudence.

The great puzzle of religion clause jurisprudence traditionally concerns how to reconcile and coordinate the free exercise and antiestablishment clauses. As we saw in chapter 5, advocates tend to urge the

3. Ibid.

collapse of religion clause jurisprudence either into free exercise or into antiestablishment, as if the interpretive choice were necessarily a dichotomous choice of one or the other as the dominant paradigm for religion clause interpretation. But the quite abstract political theory of religion clause neutrality, there proposed, showed how each clause has an appropriate weight and scope at different points in the protection of the underlying political value or background right of equal respect for the inalienable right to conscience. A general theory thus gives an interpretive gravity to each clause and acknowledges their underlying ideals.

Correspondingly, the general political theory advanced historical self-understanding of the common interpretive structures of religion clause and free speech jurisprudence, and tightened our critical grasp on applicable legal tests for state abridgments of free speech in the United States (chapters 6 and 7). Indeed, these tasks proceeded in tandem. These common interpretive structures, focusing on religion clause and free speech neutrality, expressed the vital theme of equal respect for conscience, which these guarantees worked out at different stages but to similar effect. Applicable legal tests of content neutrality and associated prohibitions on content-bias reflect such common principles. And the idea that such abridgments of religious liberty or free speech could only be justified by a clear and present danger of certain harms was shown to rest on a remarkably clear historical self-understanding first suggested in articulations of religious liberty and naturally elaborated to free speech. The very stringency of the contemporary legal tests for a clear and present danger, not sensible on utilitarian grounds, were interpretively clarified and grounded in the common contractarian foundations of religious and speech liberties in American constitutional law. Advocacy of political and moral subversion is, on contractarian grounds, at the very heart of the critical moral independence that equal respect for conscience dignifies, as a protection of the ultimate moral sovereignty against which all power must be tested for its legitimacy. For this reason, constitutional guarantees, which express this conception, naturally have been progressively interpreted more fully to express this conception. My account clarifies the wide range of interpretive tendencies that reflect the pull of these background ideals, for example, the judiciary's reexamination and recasting of many conventional doctrines of speech or conduct unprotected by free speech values. In cases in which the law does not consistently uphold these principles, the political theory is a useful critical tool in diagnosing the tensions and incoherence that a body of law reflects, and in deciding how such conflicts should be resolved.

It is not plausible to say that such a constructive record of the utility of a general political theory in constitutional interpretation distorts text in any reasonable sense. To the contrary, its systematic character clarifies both macrointerpretive and microinterpretive structures, in a way that suggests, if anything, that its abstract and systematic character is the key to its explanatory and critical power.

An alternative clause-bound program will not do here, and probably will not do elsewhere for the following reason. It neither explains nor criticizes with any comparable power the coherent meanings of disparate constitutional texts and the larger structures in which they fit. The point is not limited to clauses situated in the same amendment. The same point applies equally to the tendency of clause-bound analysis to segregate the interpretive analysis of clauses in several different parts of the constitutional text. It would have us, for example, segregate the concepts implicit in the First Amendment from comparable concepts implicit in the treason requirements of Article III[4] and the *actus reus* requirements of the Eighth Amendment,[5] when all these concepts bear on a common political prohibition on crimes of thought. It would have us ignore the connections between control of the mind in the First Amendment, control of informational privacy in the Fourth Amendment, and control of the confession of guilt in the self-incrimination clauses of the Fifth Amendment, when these texts bespeak coherent principles.[6] And it would give no interpretation to the respect for persons implicit in the First Amendment and the kinds of respect implicit in many of the basic guarantees of constitutional criminal procedure, including the respect for deliberative rationality expressed by the notice and hearing requirements themselves.[7] These and other coherences among texts reveal an even more bleak intellectual barrenness in the clause-bound approach. It does not, as we shall shortly see, take seriously the larger historical meaning of a written constitution as an expression of a coherent political theory, and thus does not recognize how political theory internally bears on what we should expect from constitutional interpretation.

If the main reason offered for the clause-bound or other interpretive programs (antithetical to general political theory) is respect for text, the argument is not only question-begging. In the name of "text," the program ignores and distorts both historical self-understanding and interpretive traditions, and thus the meanings that the texts have. These alternative accounts are simply not the best description of the meanings of constitutional texts, which demonstrably reflect the inner coherence and coordination that, on purely a priori grounds, the clause-bound theory denies. On the basis of a theoretical examination made possible by general political theory, doctrines of religious liberty,

---

4. Cf., e.g., Mayton, "Seditious Libel and the Lost Guarantee of a Freedom of Expression."
5. See, e.g., Richards, *The Moral Criticism of Law*, pp. 199–209.
6. For a suggestive account, see Greenawalt, "Silence as a Moral and Constitutional Right."
7. Cf. Saphire, "Specifying Due Process Values: Toward a More Responsive Approach to Procedural Protection."

free speech, and constitutional privacy express a common structure of argument, the primacy of toleration. But clause-bound theory enjoins us from making this kind of clarifying interpretive inquiry. A moral dogma, misdescribed as an appeal to text, here deforms an interpretive hermeneutics. As I suggested in chapter 9, a powerful criticism may be made to similar effect about "textual" criticisms of the supposedly extratextual right, the constitutional right to privacy.

Interpretive Legitimacy of Constitutional Privacy

Controversy over the nature, provenance, and application of the constitutional right to privacy has marked all of the Supreme Court's decisions both extending and refusing to extend the right. Constitutional theorists have been critics of the Court's work in this area. Ely, as we noted, is an important secular critic of the abortion decision, and Schauer recently has joined the criticism on alleged interpretive grounds that the constitutional privacy decisions are not properly textual.[8] But Schauer's arguments against constitutional privacy are unsatisfactory, violating text, history, and background political theory, all of which support the interpretive legitimacy of the inference and elaboration of the constitutional right to privacy.

The inference and elaboration of the constitutional right to privacy is consistent with both text (the Ninth Amendment, Article IV's privileges and immunities clause, the privileges and immunities and due process clauses of the Fourteenth Amendment) and history (see chapter 9). It is also supported by good arguments of contractarian political theory: free and rational persons would preserve the dignity of a personal life from brutal and callous state manipulation ungrounded in the pursuit of neutral goods. The inference and application of the right to constitutional privacy is thus the principled elaboration of arguments central to the fabric of our law. It represents, so I have argued, the internal dynamic of arguments of principle in our law, their tendency to work out the integrity of the full and evenhanded elaboration of their background rights. Constitutional privacy is such an elaboration of equal respect (and thus of the primacy of toleration) in two ways. Equal respect protects the full range of our moral powers, with actions as well as thoughts motivated by such powers. And the abridgment of such powers cannot be based on sectarian religious or other argument, but only on neutral ethical argument fairly applicable at large. There is no interpretive lacuna here, no textual leap of faith, only the usual arguments of principle self-critically working clean and clear the enduring meanings that the text has and should be taken to have.

Arguments of these kinds explain the interpretive legitimacy of the right to constitutional privacy and can, as we saw, be used both to jus-

---

8. See Schauer, "Easy Cases," note 82. Cf. Ely, "The Wages of Crying Wolf: A Comment on *Roe v. Wade*".

tify and critically evaluate the Court's applications of the right. We can now therefore assess with some perspective how little there is in the so-called textual arguments against constitutional privacy as a general principle of our constitutional law. Ely recognizes that both the authority of text and history support constitutional privacy,[9] and then introduces arguments of political theory to delimit that authority. Schauer has no such excuse, for he wishes to resist the call of general political theory because it distorts the text. He is quite right about Ely, whose theory does distort the text and is an unacceptable political theory, independently considered.[10] But Schauer is wrong to claim, and he certainly does not show, that all general political theories distort text. On the contrary, the examination of constitutional privacy suggests an incoherence in clause-bound textualism. It is such views, attacking the interpretive legitimacy of constitutional privacy as such, that here make no sense of text, history, or political theory. This suggests that textualism, in this and related forms, itself rests on a political theory that interpretively distorts the fair construction of American constitutional law and doctrine. My diagnosis of such interpretive distortion is its failure forthrightly to recognize and discuss the central place of general political theory in constitutional interpretation.

Interpreting a Written Constitution
The inadequacies just discussed converge on a larger difficulty that these alternative interpretive strategies all reflect in their understanding of constitutional interpretation, namely, their positivistic search for constraints on interpretation. In the case of clause-bound theories, the appeal of "text," which more "free-wheeling" general theories putatively betray, is a conception of constraints on interpretation. But this conception of constraint is as controversial and as undefended as its underlying assumptions about interpretation. A more plausible and

9. Ely argues that the best textual and historical inference is that the Ninth Amendment was intended to make clear that unenumerated rights, such as constitutional privacy, were to be enforceable against the federal government, in the same way that the privileges and immunities clause of Article IV contemplated a distinction between unenumerated fundamental and nonfundamental rights. See Ely, *Democracy and Distrust*, pp. 34–41, 22–30. The privileges and immunities clause of the Fourteenth Amendment incorporates the idea of such unenumerated fundamental rights against the states from the privileges and immunities clause of Article IV. See ibid., 22–30. The Supreme Court, of course, has grounded the inference of constitutional privacy on the due process clause of the Fourteenth Amendment. See *Roe v. Wade*, 410 U.S. 113 (1973).
10. Ely's theory appears to be preference utilitarianism, which is not only inconsistent with much of the Constitution, as Ely acknowledges, but, as political theory, at least as dubious, if not more so, than the rights-based theories he dismisses. Cf. Brest, "The Fundamental Rights Controversy," pp. 1102–4. For a recent defense by Ely of his position, denying his commitment to utilitarianism, see Ely, "Professor Dworkin's External/Personal Preference Distinction." For Schauer's view, see Schauer, "An Essay on Constitutional Language."

defensible theory of interpretation, *pari passu*, deepens our understanding of what we properly seek in interpretive constraints.

There is a powerful moral and political intuition motivating the search for constraints in constitutional interpretation. It is the sense that power in constitutional government is determinately constrained by substantive and procedural guarantees. That intuition is, I believe, intensely contractarian. If the legitimacy of government depends on the government's observance of the terms of the contract of respect for rights, then the contract must constrain power, which subjects interpretation of the contract to correlative constraints consistent with this moral and political aim. But the way to articulate this intuition and the moral demand it reflects is not to invent positivistic fictions of Founders' denotations or current conventions or clear texts that do justice neither to the demand nor to the complexity of our interpretive practices. It is rather to articulate a conception of constraint directly responsive to the moral and political demand itself.

As I argued in chapters 2 and 3, we should understand our constitutional need for such constraints as itself reflective of the internal moral and political ideals that motivate the idea and practice of a written constitution, a tradition of which the United States Constitution is a kind of paradigm case. But those ideals are centrally expressed precisely by the equal respect for interpretive independence that guides and shapes the substantive law of religious liberty, free speech, and constitutional privacy. It guides as well the ways these and other constitutional guarantees are read and should be read.

The point is implicit in the interpretive methodology exemplified throughout this book. The proper interpretation of religion clause or free speech jurisprudence requires that we construe the historical self-understanding, interpretive traditions over time, and current jurisprudence in terms of certain background rights of equal respect. Our interpretations, by virtue of this approach, themselves express the equal respect that is constitutionally required. Such interpretive practices are, at every point, guided and constrained by these background rights, by the need to explain and criticize our history and traditions by reference to them, and by the kinds of equal respect they make incumbent on us. We have engaged in such arguments throughout this book, rejecting interpretations that fail to give proper weight to this or a coherent sense to that, or that leave too much unexplained or unexplicated, or that do not do justice to important interpretive moments in our history. Such arguments are not "free-wheeling." They are interpretations whose relevance, accuracy, weight, power, and plausibility can meet highly demanding standards of what counts as a better theoretical argument (in the sense discussed in chapter 3). If successful, such interpretations better explain both macrostructures and microstructures in a wider range of diverse data, appealing to simpler unifying conceptions, suggesting further interpretive strategies that promise equally fertile working hypotheses of interpretation in other areas. We are guided at every point by the range of data to be explained, by the interpretive principles implicit in those data, and by the larger conceptions that often organize and explain these principles, moving, as we have, between all three levels in the search for deeper explanatory and critical coherence.

The resulting sense of interpretive constraint is not a false and unreal search for the will of positivistic sovereigns, but an understanding of the patterns of principle and value that organize, explain, and critically guide a historically self-conscious moral, political, and legal tradition. Interpretive constraint is here itself the consequence of the background moral and political ideals that motivate the interpretation, requiring those constraints on state power whose observance dignifies the moral sovereignty of a free people. Since these ideals themselves require equal respect, the interpretive practice best accords with its internal rationale when interpretation itself reflects such respect in the way, as we have seen, that the constitutional jurisprudence of religious liberty, free speech, and constitutional privacy do so. Any other conception of interpretive constraint, including the various alternative interpretive strategies examined here and in chapters 2 and 3, is likely to betray the internal political ideals that actuate our historically self-conscious commitment to a written constitution. Such strategies dismiss other views as nontextual. Yet they themselves neither express nor elaborate the contractarian ideals of equal respect that made a written constitution the expression that it is of the ultimate respect for persons against which all state power must be tested and assessed. As such, they invoke a claim to a text on which they have no proper interpretive purchase.

THE SCOPE OF JUDICIAL REVIEW

This theory of interpretive constraints makes possible a fresh critical address to the central preoccupation of American constitutional theory, the justification of judicial review. That account in turn suggests fruitful interpretive strategies in other areas of constitutional doctrine.

I have taken interpretation, not judicial review, as the central subject of constitutional law in this book. The conception of interpretive constraints, which this approach has made possible, explains why our constitutional commitment to such constraints is associated with a commitment to judicial review and supremacy. These constraints impose a structure on the very idea of democratic legitimacy, namely, a constitutional democracy in which all citizens both understand and give weight to those limits on the power of the state to compromise the inalienable rights essential to a working community of self-governing and equal persons. The maintenance and vindication of the integrity of this public philosophy often requires, however, a disciplined and impartially just reflection on our history and traditions guided by a reflective use of arguments of political theory. For this reason, the interpretive integrity of the constraints themselves naturally calls for some institution of constitutional government with sufficient independence to undertake such disciplined reflection. In the United States, the text of the Constitution has been fairly read to identify this function with the judiciary.[11] Since such an interpretive function would be nugatory without any associated power, judiciary supremacy is, under our constitutional law, the power commensurate to this need. The idea is that overall such judicial supremacy will tend to secure a greater balance of fidelity to enduring constitutional values.

The approach taken in this book to interpretation suggests why judicial review is itself a sound interpretation of the American constitutional design. The approach also affords an invaluable critical perspective on judicial review itself. A judiciary, endowed with the power of judicial supremacy, does not need to be positivistically reminded that it is the ultimate arbiter of many issues of constitutional interpretation. It needs a critical perspective on better and worse constitutional interpretation, in terms of which it and all citizens may critically evaluate the interpretive contribution of the judiciary to the moral core of its mandated function and power, namely, maintenance and elaboration of the ideals of constitutional legitimacy.

It is fundamental to the contractarian foundations of American constitutional democracy that no political institutions can usurp the ultimate moral sovereignty of the people over themselves and their government. If the justification of judicial review and supremacy is the maintenance and elaboration of this ideal, certainly judicial performance must itself be subject to assessment in light of it. The interpretive reasons that justify the ultimate power of the judiciary in determining constitutional questions also require that the exercise of that power not be regarded as always interpretively correct. In chapter 3, I criticized conventionalist theories of constitutional interpretation because they elided the distinct questions of finality and correctness. A more adequate theory of constitutional interpretation must essentially preserve this distinction if it is to perform its proper work as a critical tool, in terms of which judicial mistake may be assessed and corrected. Contractarian theory both preserves and explains the distinction.

As we have seen, contractarian theory clarifies constitutional doc-

---

11. *Marbury v. Madison*, 5 U.S. (1 Cranch) 137 (1803). For pertinent discussion of the American debates over judicial review, see chapter 1. Strikingly, the very adoption of a Bill of Rights was motivated, in part, by the convincing argument of the more thoughtful anti-federalists that rights-based political morality, alleged by federalists to be implicit in the Constitution, can only be maintained by a Bill of Rights and associated institutions that keep the American people faithful to rights-based arguments of principle. See, e.g., pp. 79–81, *The Federal Farmer*, Storing, ed., *The Anti- Federalist*. Cf. Storing, *What the Anti-federalists Were For*, pp. 64–70.

trines elaborated by the judiciary, and on occasion affords a critical perspective on interpretive mistakes. On the one hand, contractarian theory gives the best justification that can be given for much of the work of the judiciary. For example, elaboration of much of the law of religious liberty, free speech, and constitutional privacy is, I have argued, the kind of principled explication of background constitutional ideals of equal respect that maintains the integrity of the public philosophy necessary to the legitimacy of constitutional government. On the other hand, such contractarian theory has given us on occasion sound interpretive reasons for believing that the judiciary's work in some area is wrong.

The tension between judicial supremacy and public arguments of judicial mistake is fundamental to the integrity of democratic constitutionalism. We gain in understanding the proper roles of each pole of the tension by virtue of a constitutional theory, like contractarian theory, which is both explanatory and critical. Judicial supremacy is thus working correctly when overall it tends to vindicate the best arguments of principle essential to our constitutional tradition. Public debate over constitutional issues is most reasonable when most engaged by comparable critical arguments against which the state (including judicial power) can be searchingly tested.

It is as much a corruption of our public philosophy for the judiciary to believe it is always right as for citizens to believe they bear no interpretive responsibility for the integrity of our constitutional traditions. Each corruption is encouraged by the kind of positivistic theory of constitutional interpretation currently dominant in American legal thought and practice. On the one hand, the judiciary misunderstands the critical demands on it, supposing, positivistically, that it is constitutional law. On the other, public debate over constitutional issues often collapses into a search for a shallow and uninformed populist (and positivistic) consensus. Our public philosophy will only be adequate to our constitutional tradition when the judiciary understands its role in preserving the moral sovereignty of the people and when the people dignify themselves and their law by holding the judiciary and themselves to this vision. These two complementary aims are facilitated by the conception of constitutional interpretation that a contractarian theory felicitously makes available.

REVIEW STANDARDS OVER FEDERALISM AND SEPARATION OF POWERS

If a contractarian theory of interpretation thus clarifies the place of judicial review and supremacy under the United States Constitution, it also may usefully advance discussion about the proper scope and standards of such review elsewhere. A theory should be judged by its fertility—its capacity to organize and explain the data we have (revealing such underlying simplicities as the primacy of toleration) and to point to new kinds of research problems and projects. Is the theory, for example, more interpretively fertile than comparable and competing theories in the field? The political theory here proposed suggests several interpretive research programs for the future that seem to me promising. In this section, I make some tentative, brief suggestions about proper standards of review for questions of federalism and separation of powers. The next section makes somewhat more elaborate interpretive suggestions about standards of review for equal protection.

Federalism

Structural features of our constitutionalism, such as federalism and the separation of powers, are often sharply demarcated by able constitutional theorists from the kinds of analysis appropriate to substantive guarantees like those of the First Amendment.[12] But the interpretive approach taken in this book suggests that these sharp divisions between substantive and procedural guarantees may be indefensible. Both kinds of guarantees may appeal to the same background political theory, which explains how they should be interpreted and determines the standards of judicial review appropriate to such questions.

Madison thus designs the federal system as an institutional solution to the two challenges to American democratic experiment: the creation of a stable republican government in a large territory, and the throttling of the political evil that had thwarted republican experiments elsewhere, namely, faction.[13] Faction, of which sectarian religious strife is a central case, is an evil that Madison does not believe we can, consistent with respect for liberty, uproot from human nature; but we can circumscribe its corruptive, even demonic impact on democratic politics viz., its tendency to blind members of groups to the rights and interests of outsiders. He elsewhere defends constitutional guarantees of the inalienable right to conscience (religion clauses of the First Amendment and the Virginia Bill for Religious Freedom) in order to protect essential liberties against abridgment by tyrannous factions (see chapter 5). Madison conceives the federal system as a division of federal and state power designed to serve similar ends. Essential liberties (including the moral independence of thought and association, protected by the religion clauses) are accorded procedural protection by the federal system's decentralization of properly state and local issues, thus enhancing the independence and importance of smaller associations. The structure of state representation in the federal government, empowered to deal with national issues, is so designed to filter the par-

12. See, e.g., Greenawalt, "Silence as a Moral and Constitutional Right," pp. 52–53.
13. See *The Federalist* No. 10 (Madison). For a useful history of the federal idea, in which American federalism has a central innovative role, see Davis, *The Federal Principle*.

tiality and invidiousness of faction into an impartial point of view more representative of fair concern with the public interest and human rights.[14] If the religion clauses expressly forbid the corruption of federal power by sectarian religious ambitions, the representative structure of the federal system was self-consciously designed to achieve similar ends. Both the structure of representation in Congress (covering larger territories and often dispersed populations) and its deliberative dynamics (some distance from constituents) would tend, on this view, to mitigate underlying tendencies of sectarian exclusivity and oppression of outsiders (failing to treat them as equals). The dispersion of constituents would presumably require each representative to consult interests and rights common to all, and the deliberative dynamics would further lead the representatives to focus on an appropriately fair-minded and national point of view. The representative principle, embodied in the structure of the federal system, thus turns the classical republican vice of a large territory into the republican virtue of taming the demons of faction, the betrayal by factionalized republics—unmediated by a well-working representative principle—of the basic democratic ideal of treating all persons as equals.[15]

If such concerns motivated the design of the federal system, surely the interpretation of the powers of Congress and the states in this system should reflect these concerns. Congress has thus itself been so structured not only fairly to represent the national interest, but also to give fair weight to state interests (for example, by state representation in the Senate). For this reason, its interpretive judgment on the scope of its powers may broadly be trusted, and the scope of judicial review should be therefore deferential.[16] On the other hand, state judgments on the scope of state power in such areas may not similarly be trusted. The national interest has no fair representation in the state political process that often may detrimentally affect national interests. The judi-

14. See, for useful elaborations, Adair, *Fame and the Founding Fathers*, pp. 75–106; Epstein, *The Political Theory of the Federalist*.

15. For the common anti-federalist argument, based in part on an interpretation of Montesquieu, that republics required a small territory, see Storing, *What the Anti-federalists Were For*, pp. 15–23. For Montesquieu, see Book VIII, sec. 16, *The Spirit of the Laws*, pp. 120–121. But cf. Book IX, secs. 1–3, *id.*, pp. 126–128 (confederation as solution to problem). At the state ratifying conventions, leading federalists made the point that classical republican experiments had been marred by faction and that the American discovery of the representative principle mitigated this evil at the same time as it called for a large territory. James Wilson of Pennsylvania is particularly clear on this point; see Jonathan Elliot, *Debates in the Several State Conventions*, vol. 2, pp. 421–424. See also Alexander Hamilton of New York, *id.*, vol. 2, pp. 253–4, 302, 307, 352–3; and James Madison of Virginia, *id.*, vol. 3, pp. 87, 256–8. The problem of size and democracy remains a central issue of democratic political theory and science. For an important contemporary study, see Dahl and Tufte, *Size and Democracy*.

16. See, in general, *McCulloch v. Maryland*, 17 U.S. (4 Wheat.) 316 (1819). Cf. Wechsler, "The Political Safeguards of Federalism: the Role of the States in the Composition and Selection of the National Government."

ciary should therefore elaborate constitutional tests for the legitimacy of such exercises of state power, assessing it by reference to the fairly representative decision appropriate to the issue and its impact.[17] Such different standards of judicial review of the interpretive judgments of Congress and the states thus turn on a conception of fair representation shaped, as we have seen, by the background substantive values (the theory of faction) that guided the design of the federal system. That theory informs, in different ways, both expressly substantive (First Amendment) and procedural (federalism) provisions of the Constitution.

Separation of Powers

A related kind of prophylaxis against partiality in public judgments informs the separation of powers as a pivotal feature of constitutional government. The doctrine known as separation of powers is rooted in diagnosis of a malady and a recommended cure. The malady is identified by a realistic republican tradition as the moral corruption of public power in republics by sectarian exclusivity.[18] The political cure is an institutional design, the separation of powers, keyed to restrain this corruption of judgment by procedural constraints on the scope of legislative, judicial, and executive power; the aim was to secure closer observance by each power of impartiality in treating persons as equals.[19] The structure of the separation of powers thus protects values of the rule of law in constitutional government, subjecting, as it does, all power to fairly applicable laws and constitutional principles. Our interpretive sense of the appropriate scope of legislative, executive, and judicial power should therefore be guided by such background principles. An executive assertion of coercive power, unsupported by a legislative judgment, threatens essential values of the rule of law;[20] and the executive's attempt to avoid appropriate judicial accountability for violations of law flouts the essential constitutional ideal of the equality of all before justly and constitutionally applicable laws.[21] Both abuses of power may justly be subjected to review by an independent judiciary concerned to maintain a structure of constitutional government committed to principles of the rule of law. The very interpretive shape and sense of the putatively procedural doctrine of separation of

17. See, e.g., *South Carolina State Highway Dept. v. Barnwell Brothers*, 303 U.S. 177 (1938); *Southern Pacific Co. v. Arizona*, 325 U.S. 761 (1945); *Bibb v. Navajo Freight Lines, Inc.*, 359 U.S. 520 (1959).
18. On the ethical roots of the separation of powers doctrine, see Pocock, *The Machiavellian Moment*, pp. 128, 288, 407–8, 420, 480–81; Skinner, *Machiavelli*, pp. 65–67. See also Gwyn, *The Meaning of the Separation of Powers*; Vile, *Constitutionalism and the Separation of Powers*.
19. See, e.g., *The Federalist* No. 51 (Madison).
20. See *Youngstown Sheet & Tube Co. v. Sawyer*, 343 U.S. 579 (1952).
21. See *United States v. Nixon*, 418 U.S. 683 (1974).

powers, including the standards of judicial review governing these matters, is thus crucially guided by the background substantive ideals and principles that nourish the doctrine as a pivotal structure of constitutional government.

EQUAL PROTECTION

The malign interpretive tendency of our law to demarcate substantive and procedural guarantees is motivated by a characteristic legal distaste for substance when procedure will avail. This tendency has been carried to its most overstated and strained extreme in the purely procedural interpretation of the equal protection clause of the Fourteenth Amendment in itself and as the model for constitutional legitimacy as such. The latter line is Ely's general position. Equal protection is not only regarded by him as properly a guarantee of fair representational procedure, as we have seen, but the legitimacy of other constitutional decisions is to be assessed on this model.[22] At this point, we need to look more closely at equal protection on its own interpretive turf. Ely's model of equal protection may be wrong precisely because he ignores the substantive values that actuate equal protection. If he is wrong here, the error of his more comprehensive account follows a fortiori. In order to see the mistake in his account of equal protection, we should connect equal protection to the substantive theory of toleration elaborated at length in this book.

While the equal protection clause is relatively late in our constitutional history, the underlying moral ideal of equality is not. I refer not only to the solemn aspirations of the Declaration of Independence, but to the invocations of the equality concept implicit in the Constitution and Bill of Rights as such. In this connnection, Ely has made much of the privileges and immunities clause of Article IV, but much should be made as well of the equality principle implicit in the First Amendment itself.[23] Madison, the chief architect of the First Amendment, clearly regarded values of religious freedom as a form of fundamental equal liberty. Consider the terms of his great *Remonstrance* with its expressed concern for

protecting every citizen in the enjoyment of his religion with the same equal hand that protects his person and property; by neither invading the equal rights of any sect, nor suffering any sect to invade those of others.[24]

22. Ely, *Democracy and Distrust.*
23. Ibid., pp. 83–88.
24. Madison, "Memorial and Remonstrance Against Religious Assessment", in Meyers, ed.,*The Mind of the Founder,* p. 10

This equality principle, in contrast to that implicit in the privileges and immunities clause of Article IV, does not lend itself to the interpretation of representational unfairness that Ely properly imputes to the clause in Article IV (and then overgeneralizes to equal protection jurisprudence, and finally to legitimate constitutional jurisprudence as such).

We should be quite clear on this point: it is neither a necessary nor sufficient condition of a violation of our constitutionally guaranteed equal liberties of conscience or speech that the violation be the product of representational unfairness in the Article IV sense. Such unfairness arises from the unequal burdens that a state law imposes on nonresidents, not themselves represented in the decision leading to the law in question.[25] The unfairness is the kind of burden imposed without the relevant opportunity to have a democratically appropriate voice and weight in a decision that thus affects one's life. But violations of equal liberties of conscience and speech are often the product of representationally fair procedures in this sense; all relevant persons have a fair voice in the decision to pass constitutionally nonneutral violations of conscience or speech. And representationally unfair procedures often do not threaten such constitutional equal liberties. It is not representational unfairness that is at issue in the kind of unjust inequality that Madison condemned as violations of equal liberties of conscience. It is rather the failure of the law in question, whatever its provenance, to maintain the inalienable right of the equal dignity of all consciences.

Such a failure to respect equal rights is simply not the same kind of political injustice as the failure to give all persons affected by state decisions appropriate democratic weight in the deliberative procedure leading to the decision. The wrong in such unequal respect is not the kind of procedural defect that the latter injustice exemplifies, for the latter injustice puts no constraint on the output other than certain kinds of inputs. In contrast, the principle of equal respect, central to the liberties of the First Amendment and related constitutional guarantees, forbids entirely a law that undermines the equal dignity of conscience and speech in the way forbidden by equal respect.

Two problems arise in supposing that this difference between the two kinds of injustice means that representational unfairness is acceptably procedural in a way that unequal respect is unacceptably a matter of substance. First, the very ground for our constitutional worries about representational unfairness, here and elsewhere, is itself guided by substantive considerations, often considerations of equal liberty itself. And second, the way in which equal respect for conscience and speech forbids content bias itself expresses a deeper procedural conception of the justice of constitutional democracy. Each point should be elaborated as a preface to my alternative interpretation of equal protection.

25. See *Baldwin v. Montana Fish and Game Commission*, 436 U.S. 371 (1978).

First, as Ely's critics have been at pains to emphasize, representational unfairness is itself a wrong against the background of certain substantive values that it preserves.[26] As suggested in chapter 1, if these substantive values are utilitarian, then we have the vicious circularity of an attack on substantive political theories that itself rests on an unexamined and probably even more controversial political theory. On the other hand, our concern for forms of representational unfairness is often actuated by a nonutilitarian concern for equal liberty itself. For example, a greater equal liberty in the political rights to vote and participate in government is as much subject to the mandates of equal respect as the rights of conscience, free speech, and privacy discussed at length in this book. Thus the reapportionment mandate, one person one vote,[27] reflects a concern for a greater equal weighting of the power of voting as a central equal liberty of political voice and participation in a community of free, rational, and equal persons.[28] Understanding representational unfairness as a constitutional value may thus require a background theory of equal respect, which guides our interpretation of how this value should be coordinated with other constitutional values of equal dignity. But the claim that representational unfairness is the exclusive value of constitutional legitimacy is then undercut; the very point and place of the value is guided by substantive values in which it is understood as one important value integrated with others of equal dignity.

Second, such constitutional guarantees of equal liberty of conscience and speech, properly understood, themselves express a procedural conception at a deeper level than that invoked by representational unfairness.[29] This procedural conception expresses the contractarian idea that state power and the use of state power must be conducted in ways that dignify, on fair terms, the twin moral powers of rationality and reasonableness of a free people. Both substantive and procedural guarantees of constitutional government are ways of so shaping the scope and uses of state power that it is conducted in the ways that express a vital community of equal respect. Our observance of the constitutional neutrality required by the First Amendment, for example, is procedural in this sense. We conduct the procedures of our common political life, the kinds of arguments we make and demands we exact, in ways that render each of us ultimately responsible for our personal and moral lives; we remit to each person deliberation over the ways their thought, speech, and lives will weight and order the general goods that our cooperation makes possible.[30] We thus rule out, as procedurally unfair, the state

26. See, e.g., Dworkin, "The Forum of Principle."
27. See, e.g., *Reynolds v. Sims*, 337 U.S. 533 (1964).
28. See Rawls, *A Theory of Justice*, pp. 222–23.
29. On these deeper conceptions of procedural justice, see ibid., pp. 83–90.
30. For elaboration of a similar conception of neutrality, see Stewart, "Regulation in a Liberal State: The Role of Non-Commodity Values." For a critical perspective, see Frug, "Why Neutrality?"

coercion or endorsement of constitutionally nonneutral substantive conceptions of what to think or say or how to live, because such state action fails to accord equal respect for persons.

The constitutional command of equal protection of the laws, in the Fourteenth Amendment, does not introduce any novel ideal into the fabric of our law, instead it builds on, consolidates, and elaborates familiar ideals of equal respect. These ideals, contra Ely, are not properly understood exclusively as ideals of representational fairness. Rather, both substantive and procedural guarantees of the Constitution and Bill of Rights express, on examination, background ideals of equal respect. It is therefore a historical and interpretive mistake to suppose that the equal protection clause can be circumscribed to forms of procedural unfairness. On the contrary, the equal protection clause takes all that is best in the egalitarian ideals of the Constitution and Bill of Rights, consolidates and elaborates them with the force and remedies of federal law, and decisively repudiates those compromises with these ideals in the Constitution that had permitted slavery to exist side-by-side with a Constitution of equal respect.[31] The equal protection clause, in short, decisively aligns constitutional ideals with equal respect.

The equal protection clause undoubtedly introduces new kinds of concerns into our constitutional dialogue, particularly, concerns for the force in our law of degrading prejudices as such—racial, ethnic, and (today) sexual. But some aspects of equal protection jurisprudence (in particular, the fundamental rights aspect of strict scrutiny under the equal protection clause) were already embodied in the equality principles of the First Amendment.[32] Constitutional arguments of a content-biased regulation of speech under the free speech clause may be made to precisely the same effect under this mode of equal protection scrutiny.[33] Ely argues that the novel concerns of the equal protection clause (which he characterizes as unfairness to unrepresented minorities) are the exclusive measure of constitutional legitimacy. A contractarian view, which gives central weight to the argument for religious toleration, illuminates and grounds other features of constitutional legitimacy, including, as we have seen, religious liberty, free speech, and constitutional privacy, and also aspects of equal protection jurisprudence (fundamental rights analysis) otherwise inexplicable. Ely may also be mistaken in his vision of the constitutionally novel concerns of the equal protection clause.

These concerns focus on the oppression of stigmatized minorities and are directed at the kind of stigma that thus oppressively enjoys the force of law.[34] These concerns are not new to our constitutional law.

---

31. See, in general, Pole, *The Pursuit of Equality in American History.*
32. On both fundamental rights and suspect classification analysis, see, "Developments in the Law—Equal Protection." See also Polyviou, *Equal Protection of the Laws.*
33. See, e.g., *Erznoznik v. Jacksonville,* 422 U.S. 205 (1975).
34. See, e.g., *Brown v. Board of Education,* 347 U.S. 483 (1954).

Further, to the extent they are new, they cannot be explained on the model of representational unfairness alone, which is only a symptom of the deeper moral evil condemned by equal respect itself.

Madison's theory of faction itself suggests such concerns. The Madisonian paradigm case of faction, sectarian religious groups,[35] displays an insightful understanding of the social psychology of intolerance, with its roots in the limitation of moral reasoning to one's reference group and the distorted perception and denigration of the claims of those outside one's group. Indeed, in light of our extensive examination of these questions in chapters 4 and 5, we may say that the central moral conception motivating the political tradition of respect for conscience that Madison elaborates was precisely the sense of how sectarian conscience had corrupted both ethics and religion. That corruption is a corruption (and was so understood by Jefferson and Madison) of our moral sense, our capacity to see the conscience, the speech, and the lives of others as consistent with a fair-minded respect for them as persons.

Recent accounts of the Madisonian theory of faction often distinguish it too sharply, in my judgment, from the kinds of degrading stereotypes central to the equal protection clause's concerns for suspect classifications.[36] The moral corruption of sectarian conscience, at the heart of Madison's worries about factions, is itself a kind of stereotyped thinking: the tendency to see others through the lenses of one's sectarian perceptions of a world divided into those that agree and disagree with these perceptions, as though civic virtue and vice track sectarian belief and disbelief. The arguments for toleration in Locke and Bayle, which American constitutional ideals elaborate, are acutely conscious of the political evil to which this kind of circular thinking leads, creating stereotypes of good and evil which remake moral reality in their own Manichaean image (see chapter 4). Such intolerance, both Locke and Bayle insist, itself creates moral disorder, oppression, and resistance, which it claims to combat.[37] The essence of the political wrong here is the stereotyped Augustinian contempt for the moral powers of those with whom one conscientiously disagrees, as if all such disagreement must reflect a wantonly irrational and even diabolic will. Such contempt itself creates the justification on which it feeds. But this kind of contempt, which is the political evil combated by both the substantive guarantees of the First Amendment and the procedural institutions shaped by the theory of faction, is continuous with the forms of contempt expressed by the stigma condemned by the equal protection

35. See Rossiter, ed., *The Federalist Papers*, No. 10, pp. 79, 81, 84; cf. No. 51, p. 324.
36. See, e.g., Cover, "The Origins of Judicial Activism in the Protection of Minorities," p. 1294.
37. See, e.g., *A Letter Concerning Toleration, The Works of John Locke*, vol. 6., pp. 6–9; Bayle, *Philosophique Commentaire*, pp. 415–19.

clause. Religious intolerance is, in this sense, the first suspect classification known to American law, and we best understand the equal protection clause when we connect it to the earlier historical perceptions that it assumes and elaborates.

Even if we grant the plausible claim that racial degradation (and the like) is a political evil distinct from the earlier concerns for religious persecution and unjust factions, the nature of that distinct evil is not precisely understood on the model of representational unfairness. Many decision procedures are representationally unfair in ways not necessarily actuated by the evil of stigmatizing prejudice (for example, malapportionment), which suggests that we identify this evil in a way independent of their representationally unfair expression. We need a more discriminating theory of the evil of stigma, and representational unfairness is not that theory.

The theory of equal respect affords the requisite moral discrimination indispensable to understanding the condemnation of such stigmatizing prejudices in our law and the connections of such condemnation to the earlier constitutional traditions on which it builds. Equal respect requires, as we have seen, a range of guarantees that validate our central capacities for moral independence. We identify substantive rights of conscience, free speech, and privacy, for example, by reference to the underlying capacities for moral independence in thought, speech, and action thus respected. Failure to respect such rights is, for this reason, a kind of contempt of or insult to such valued capacities. Yet another form of such contempt is to deny the existence of all such moral powers across the board. For example, the use of racial classifications to express such judgments of race-linked moral incapacities also violates equal respect. We identify these and other such classifications as constitutionally forbidden criteria of discrimination because we have come to understand the wider patterns of racial or other prejudice they reflect in the society at large, prejudices whose immoral force is the stereotyped and circular way they create the moral degradation on which they feed.[38] Such moral contempt deprives persons not only of the equal rights that are their due, but its denial of their moral status as persons independently insults their moral dignity.[39]

Both aspects of stricter scrutiny under the equal protection clause (fundamental rights and suspect classification analysis) thus express the requirements of equal respect at different points of its political threat. Fundamental rights analysis, on the model of the equal liberty principles of the First Amendment, ensures that the required equal respect

38. See, e.g., Patterson, *Slavery and Social Death.*
39. Political powerlessness is, in my judgment, not fundamental to this mode of analysis. For a recent attempt to make it fundamental, see Ackerman, "Beyond *Carolene Products.*" Many of Ackerman's proposals can, I believe, be accommodated by the alternative proposal here suggested. For example, as I suggest later, poverty may, on the analysis I propose, call for special scrutiny.

for basic rights is accorded. Suspect classification scrutiny strikes down laws or policies that explicitly or implicitly use stereotypes that deny the human dignity necessary for a creature to be capable of any rights at all.

A moral theory of equal respect thus explicates not only the independent and complementary importance of both aspects of more aggressive equal protection scrutiny. It also clarifies the gravitational pull such moral ideals exert on shaping the elaboration and application of these ideals to new areas of fundamental rights and suspect classes. We have already seen, for example, the natural impact of such ideals in properly justifying the legitimacy of campaign financing laws (chapter 7). The pull of background egalitarian ideals is most strongly felt when state practices bear on the equal liberties of the First Amendment: which they undermine, as unregulated campaign expenditures do, the equal power of voting rights; when they invidiously discriminate among the equal opportunity educational rights of children central to the values of the First Amendment, as unregulated school financing does;[40] when they crush basic self-respect through the experience of grinding and hopeless poverty, malnutrition, and neglect;[41] or when they nullify moral freedom by sexist stereotypes of dependence and incapacity.[42] The same process of reinterpreting basic political ideals discussed in chapter 2 applies, *mutatis mutandi*, here. As we achieve a fuller understanding of the economic and social institutions that crucially shape the distribution of basic resources of personal self-respect and moral independence, the interpretation of equal respect must and should vary accordingly. The American constitutional discourse of equality, set free by the First Amendment, and reinforced and extended by the equal protection clause, exerts a continuous gravitational pull on our constitutional conscience. We should understand this pressure to equality, this need always to justify inequality, as what it is: the natural elaboration of our deepest ideals of a community of equal respect.[43]

Finally, the residual requirement of equal protection jurisprudence is that all laws (not infringing fundamental rights or using suspect classifications) must have a fair rational basis for the classifications they use. This constitutional requirement suggests that even fair interest-group politics (fully consistent with fair representation) may nonetheless be inconsistent with background substantive values of the public interest and rights, which all legislation must serve.[44] That constitutional mandate, however judicially underenforced, is happily explained by a contractarian theory of equal respect, which requires that all public power

40. See Richards, *The Moral Criticism of Law*, pp. 138–61.
41. Cf. Michelman, "Foreword: On Protecting the Poor Through the Fourteenth Amendment."
42. Cf. Richards, *The Moral Criticism of Law*, pp.162–78.
43. See, in general, Rawls, *A Theory of Justice*.
44. See, for example, Sunstein, "Naked Preferences and the Constitution."

must be minimally justifiable in terms of the rational powers of a free people.

The attempt to construe our constitutional practices as a procedural ideal of representational fairness is then a profound interpretive mistake. This procedural ideal does justice neither to the values of the Constitution and Bill of Rights nor to the equal protection clause of the Fourteenth Amendment. Its attack on substantive values rests on substantive values; its proceduralism is a sham, clouding our understanding of the more complex values that actuate the coherent fabric of substantive and procedural principles characteristic of constitutional democracy. We need to think about why American legal theory appears so inadequate to its law.

INTERPRETATION, UNITY OF THEORY AND PRACTICE, AND THE AMERICAN LAW SCHOOL

This book has situated constitutional interpretation in the larger interpretive agenda, characteristic of Western thinking, of explicating our historical self-understanding as an increasingly literate community actuated by certain dominant ethical, religious, and political ideals. These ideals are thus a natural elaboration of the Augustinian introspection of Western philosophical psychology, its vision of God as a supremely free, rational, and ethical person working in history,[45] and a moral and political ideal of the respect due a person made in this God's image. The long historical development we have studied in this book may be understood as a struggle over the essential meaning of this absorbing ideal, and the inalienable right to conscience as its most profound expression. This right to conscience has come to characterize the core of the ethical motivations of equal respect: persons do not find their destinies in the unquestionable hierarchies of being in which they are fatally embedded, they achieve freedom through the dignifying construction of a way of life expressive of their integral moral powers of rationality and reasonableness. On this view of it, constitutional interpretation in the United States best understands itself when it addresses its interpretive task as one of the central humane studies of Western thought, bringing to bear on its task the complex tools of history, philosophy, and political theory.

For this reason, I objected to alternative approaches to constitutional theory that are inadequate to this interpretive task (chapters 1–3). Constitutional interpretation requires instead the use of articulate arguments of political theory in the explication of historical self-understanding. The quality of the moral and political theory we (as Americans) create is, if anything, enriched by the kind of historical recon-

45. Cf. de Rougemont, *Man's Western Quest.*

struction that legal interpretation demands. For example, an understanding of the complex historical foundations of the emergence of religious toleration as a political and constitutional tradition enriches philosophical explication of religious freedom abstractly conceived. Of course, this union of philosophical and historical understanding is not indispensable—philosophy and history may be brilliantly practiced apart from each other. And good moral reasoning does not as such track convention. But good legal interpretation requires that history and moral philosophy be practiced together. My point is that such an interpretive practice holds the promise of making us better legal interpreters as it makes us better historians and better philosophers.

My proposals may appear to err at the other extreme from the interpretive strategies earlier criticized and rejected. Constitutional interpretation must, I suggest, delve into the history and nature of the larger cultural and political traditions that constitutionalism expresses. Lawyers see this view as extreme because most constitutional theory is formulated in American law schools, where isolation from the larger dialogue of the university is self-justified on the ground of the lawyer's need to master the autonomous legal traditions of bench and bar. Both academic and practicing lawyers thus often gravitate to positivistic conventionalism, which in fact distorts the complexity of our interpretive practices and impoverishes the contribution of the American law school and legal profession to what the law school and profession have the preeminent educational and scholarly obligation to produce: a political theory of constitutional law.

Such isolation precludes the unique contribution that American lawyers could make to healing the tragic rifts of theory and practice that mar American public life: the ugly anti-intellectualism of public life, the stultifying and hermetic conversations of university elites. The task of legal practice in the United States is in all respects illuminated by a legal theory that seeks constructively to understand and critically to evaluate law by the use of the best available methods of critical historiography, moral philosophy, political theory and political science, normative and positive economics, and the like. And the sophistication of intellectual work of the most authentic integrity and seriousness might well be sharpened, illuminated, and even deepened if such work could see its problems as embedded, as they often are, in the very fabric of law itself.[46]

Our discussion of interpretation exemplifies this educational and political truth. The understanding of legal interpretation is enhanced by abstract inquiry into what interpretation is, and otherwise isolated

---

46. Perhaps, for example, philosophy of language might be less sterile if it took more seriously the complex interpretive practices of meaning in law. Cf. Baker and Hacker, *Language, Sense and Nonsense*, p. 274.

academic conversation about interpretation is keener when it confronts the interpretive task of law itself. Law, like music, is an interpretive art; its values are more feelingly experienced when its interpreters bring to bear on its texts humane learning. The positivistic assumptions of law are thus continuous with larger positivistic assumptions elsewhere,[47] an escape into history or convention that fails to enrich, and even distorts, interpretive understanding and performance. The vice of such assumptions is that they deny us the wholehearted engagement of our selves in the interpretations that enable us to make the best sense of our culture as we make the best sense of our lives. The inadequacies of our interpretive theories are thus at one with a badly lived, alienated praxis. The American law school, clearly deficient as it is in training in the skills of legal practice, is thus deficient for the same reason in its conception of legal theory. Its failure to sharpen intellectual understanding of the interpretive practices of law is of a piece with its unreal conception of what practice is and could be.

The consequences of such failure are, for all Americans, an unrealistic and corrupting division of the thought and practice of our essential public philosophy, democratic constitutionalism. It is difficult for me to believe that a people, so graced by this constitutional tradition, cannot be more adequate to its demands. If I am right in thinking that a more philosophical understanding of constitutionalism is an internal requirement of its integrity, that understanding may also be a moral need of the personal integrity of a people worthy of self-government. A better political theory of constitutional law might even assist in invigorating a unity of theory and practice that stretches and sharpens our minds as it calls upon a larger charity and toleration in our hearts.

47. See, e.g., Kerman, *Contemplating Music.*

Bibliography

BOOKS AND JOURNALS

Abrams, M. H. *The Mirror and the Lamp: Romantic Theory and the Critical Tradition.* New York: W. W. Norton, 1958.

Ackerman, Bruce A. *Social Justice in the Liberal State.* New Haven, Conn.: Yale University Press, 1980.

—————. "Beyond *Carolene Products.*" 98 *Harv. L. Rev.* 713 (1985).

Acontius, Jacobus. *Darkness Discovered (Satans Stratagems).* R. E. Field ed. Delmar, N.Y.: Scholars' Facsimiles & Reprints, 1978.

Adair, Douglass. *Fame and the Founding Fathers.* New York:W. W. Norton, 1974.

Adams, Dickinson W., ed. *Jefferson's Extracts from the Gospels: The Papers of Thomas Jefferson, Second Series.*Princeton, N.J.: Princeton University Press, 1983.

Agresto, John. *The Supreme Court and Constitutional Democracy.* Ithaca, N.Y.: Cornell University Press, 1984.

Ahlstrom, Sidney E. *A Religious History of the American People.* New Haven, Conn.: Yale University Press, 1972.

—————. "The Scottish Philosophy and American Theology." 24 *Church History* 257 (1955).

Albright, William F. *From the Stone Age to Christianity: Monotheism and the Historical Process.* Garden City, N.Y.: Doubleday Anchor, 1957.

Alexis, Gerhard T. "Jonathan Edwards and the Theocratic Ideal." 35 *Church History* 328 (1966).

Allport, Gordon W. *The Individual and His Religion.* New York: Macmillan, 1950.

Alter, Robert. *The Art of Biblical Narrative.* New York: Basic Books, 1981.

Anderson, David A. "The Origins of the Press Clause." 30 *U.C.L.A. L. Rev.* 455 (1983).

Antieau, Chester J.; Downey, Arthur T.; and Roberts, Edward C. *Freedom from Federal Establishment.* Milwaukee: Bruce Publishing, 1964.

Appleby, Joyce. "Commercial Farming and the 'Agrarian Myth' in the Early Republic." 68 *J. Am. Hist.* 833 (1982).

—————. "What Is Still American in the Political Philosophy of Thomas Jefferson?" 39 *Wm. & Mary Quar.* 287 (1982).

Aquinas, Saint Thomas. *On the Truth of the Catholic Faith: Summa Contra Gentiles.* Trans. Vernon Bourke. New York: Image, 1956.

————. *Summa Theologiae* 2a2ae. 8–16. Trans. Thomas Gilby. New York: McGraw-Hill, 1974.

Arendt, Hannah. *The Origins of Totalitarianism*. New York: Harcourt Brace Jovanovich, 1973.

Aries, Philippe. *The Hour of Our Death* Trans. Helen Weaver, New York: Knopf, 1981.

Augustine, Saint. *The City of God*. Trans. Henry Bettenson. Harmondsworth: Penguin, 1972.

————. *Confessions*. Trans. R. S. Fine-Coffin. Harmondsworth: Penguin, 1961.

————. *The Political and Social Ideas of St. Augustine*. Herbert A. Deane, ed. New York: Columbia University Press, 1963.

————. *The Political Writings of St. Augustine*. Henry Paolucci, ed. South Bend, Ind.: Regnery/Gateway, 1962.

————. *The Trinity*. Vol. 8 of *Augustine: Later Works* Trans. John Burnaby. Philadelphia: Westminster Press, 1955.

Austin, John. *The Province of Jurisprudence Determined*. H. L. A. Hart, ed. London: Weidenfeld & Nicolson, 1954.

Ayer, A. J. *Language, Truth and Logic*. London: Gollancz, 1936.

Baechler, Jean. *Suicides*. Trans. Barry Cooper. New York: Basic Books, 1979.

Bailey, Derrick S. *Homosexuality and the Western Christian Tradition*. New York: Longmans, Green, 1955.

Bailyn, Bernard. *The Ideological Origins of the American Revolution*. Cambridge, Mass.: Belknap Press of Harvard University Press, 1967.

Bainton, Roland H. *The Travail of Religious Liberty*. New York: Harper, 1951.

————. "The Bible in the Reformation." *The Cambridge History of the Bible.*, Vol. 3, S. L. Greenslade, ed., Cambridge: Cambridge University Press, 1963, 1–37.

Baker, C. Edwin. "Commercial Speech: A Problem in the Theory of Freedom." 62 *Iowa L. Rev.* 1 (1976.)

————. "The Process of Change and the Liberty Theory of the First Amendment." 55 *So. Calif. L. Rev.* 293 (1981).

————. "Realizing Self-Realization." 130 *U. Pa. L. Rev.* 646 (1982).

————. "Scope of the First Amendment Freedom of Speech." 25 *U.C.L.A. L. Rev.* 964 (1978).

————. "Unreasoned Reasonableness: Mandatory Parade Permits and Time, Place, and Manner Restrictions." 78 *Northwestern U. L. Rev.* 937 (1984).

Baker, G. P. & Hacker, P. M. S. *Language, Sense and Nonsense*. Oxford: Basil Blackwell, 1984.

Barbach, Lonnie. *Women Discover Orgasm*. New York: Free Press, 1980.

Barber, Benjamin. *Strong Democracy: Participatory Politics for a New Age*. Berkeley: University of California Press, 1984.

Barber, Sotirios A. *On What the Constitution Means*. Baltimore: Johns Hopkins University Press, 1984.

Barnett, Walter. *Sexual Freedom and the Constitution*. Albuquerque: University of New Mexico Press, 1973.

Barr, James. *The Bible in the Modern World*. London: SCM Press, 1973.

Barrett, Michael. *Sexuality and Multiple Sclerosis*. Toronto: Multiple Sclerosis Society of Canada, 1982.

Barron, Jerome A. "Access to the Press—A New First Amendment Right." 80
   Harv. L. Rev. 1641 (1967).
Barry, Brian. *The Liberal Theory of Justice.* Oxford: Clarendon Press, 1973.
Bassen, Paul. "Present Sakes and Future Prospects: The Status of Early Abor-
   tions." 11 *Phil. & Pub. Aff.* 314 (1982).
Bayle, Pierre. *Philosophique Commentaire sur ces paroles de Jesus Christ "Con-
   train-les d'entree."* Oeuvres Diverses de Mr. Pierre Bayle. Vol. 2. A la
   Haye: Chez P. Husson. et al., 1727, 357–560. The only English trans-
   lation of the entire text appears to be *A Philosophical Commentary on
   These Words of the Gospel Luke XIV.23, Compel them to come in, that my
   House may be full.* 2 vols. London: J. Darby, 1708.
Beard, Charles. *An Economic Interpretation of the Constitution of the United
   States.* New York: Macmillan, 1913.
————. *The Supreme Court and the Constitution.* New York: Paisley Press,
   1938.
Beccaria, Cesare. *On Crimes and Punishments.* Trans. Henry Paolucci, Indian-
   apolis-New York: Bobbs-Merrill, 1963.
Bell, Alan P., and Weinberg, Martin S. *Homosexualities: A Study of Diversity
   Among Men and Women.* New York: Simon & Schuster, 1978.
Bell, Alan P.; Weinberg, Martin S.; and Hammersmith, Sue K. *Sexual Prefer-
   ence.* New York: Simon & Schuster, 1978.
Bell, R. R. *Premarital Sex in a Changing Society.* Englewood Cliffs, N.J.: Pren-
   tice-Hall, 1966.
Bellah, Robert N., and Hammond, Phillip E. *Varieties of Civil Religion.* San
   Francisco: Harper & Row, 1980.
Benn, S. I. "Freedom, Autonomy and the Concept of a Person." 66 *Proceedings
   Aris. Soc.* 109 (1976).
Benn, S. I., and Mortimore, G. W. *Rationality and the Social Sciences.* London:
   Routledge & Kegan Paul, 1976.
Bennett, Jonathan. *Linguistic Behaviour.* Cambridge: Cambridge University
   Press, 1976.
————. *Rationality.* London: Routledge & Kegan Paul, 1964.
Bentham, Jeremy. "Anarchical Fallacies." *The Works of Jeremy Bentham.* Book
   II. Published under the superintendence of Bentham's executor John
   Bowring. Edinburgh, 1843, 491–529.
————. *The Limits of Jurisprudence Defined.* Charles W. Everett, ed. New
   York: Columbia University Press, 1945.
Bercovitch, Sacvan. *The Puritan Origins of the Self.* New Haven, Conn.: Yale
   University Press, 1975.
Berger, Fred R. *Happiness, Justice, and Freedom: The Moral and Political Phi-
   losophy of John Stuart Mill.* Berkeley: University of California Press,
   1984.
————. "Pornography, Feminism, and Censorship." Robert Baker and Fred-
   erick Elliston, eds., *Philosophy and Sex,* 2d. ed. Buffalo: Prometheus,
   1984, 327–351.
Berger, Raoul. *Congress v. the Supreme Court.* Cambridge, Mass.: Harvard Uni-
   versity Press, 1969.
————. *Death Penalties.* Cambridge, Mass.: Harvard University Press, 1982.
————. *Government by Judiciary.* Cambridge, Mass.: Harvard University
   Press, 1977.

Berman, Harold J. *Law and Revolution.* Cambridge, Mass.: Harvard University Press, 1983.

Bernstein, Richard J. *Beyond Objectivism and Relativism: Science, Hermeneutics, and Praxis.* Philadelphia: University of Pennsylvania Press, 1983.

BeVier, Lillian. "The First Amendment and Political Speech: An Inquiry into the Substance and Limits of Principle." 30 *Stan. L. Rev.* 299 (1978).

Bible (King James version). Genesis, 1 Corinthians. Chicago: Gideons, 1959.

Bickel, Alexander. *The Least Dangerous Branch.* Indianapolis-New York, Bobbs-Merrill, 1962.

———. *The Morality of Consent.* New Haven: Conn.: Yale University Press, 1975.

———. *The Supreme Court and the Idea of Progress.* New York: Harper, 1970.

———. "The Original Understanding and the Segregation Decision." 69 *Harv. L. Rev.* 1 (1955).

Bird, Wendell R. "Creation-Science and Evolution-Science in Public Schools." 9 *N. Ky. L. Rev.* 159 (1982).

———. "Freedom from Establishment and Unneutrality in Public School Instruction and Religious School Regulation." 2 *Harv. Jl. & Pub. Pol.* 125 (1979).

———. "Freedom of Religion and Science Instruction in Public Schools." 87 *Yale L. J.* 515 (1978).

Blackstone, William. *Commentaries on the Laws of England: Volume IV, Of Public Wrongs.* Boston: Beacon Press, 1962. (American ed. originally published 1771–2.)

Blasi, Vincent. "The Checking Function in First Amendment Theory." *American Bar Foundation Research Journal* 521 (1977).

Block, N. J. and Dworkin, Gerald, eds. *The IQ Controversy.* New York: Pantheon, 1976.

Blum, Jeffrey M. *Pseudoscience and Mental Ability.* New York: Monthly Review Press, 1978.

Blumenberg, Hans. *The Legitimacy of the Modern Age.* Trans. Robert M. Wallace Cambridge, Mass.: M.I.T. Press, 1983.

Blumstein, Philip, and Schwartz, Pepper. *American Couples: Money, Work, Sex.* New York: Morrow, 1983.

Boggs, Jo-An. *Living and Loving with Arthritis.* Honolulu: Arthritis Center of Hawaii, 1978.

Bolingbroke, Lord. *The Works of Lord Bolingbroke.* Vol. 3. London: Frank Cass, 1967.

Bollinger, Lee C. "Free Speech and Intellectual Values." 92 *Yale L. J.* 438 (1983).

Bondeson, William B. et al., eds. *Abortion and the Status of the Foetus.* Dordrecht: Reidel, 1983.

Bonner, Gerald. "Augustine as Biblical Scholar." *The Cambridge History of the Bible.* Vol. 1. P. R. Ackroyd, and C. F. Evans, eds. Cambridge: Cambridge University Press, 1970, 541–63.

Boorstin, Daniel J. *The Lost World of Thomas Jefferson.* New York: Holt, 1948. Reissued Chicago: University of Chicago Press, 1981.

Bork, Robert. "Neutral Principles and some First Amendment Problems." 47 *Indiana L. J.* 1 (1971).

Boswell, John. *Christianity, Social Tolerance and Homosexuality.* Chicago: University of Chicago Press, 1980.

Boudin, L. *Government by Judiciary.* New York: W. Godwin, 1932.

Bourke, Vernon J. *Will in Western Thought.* New York: Sheed & Ward, 1964.

Bouwsma, William J. *Venice and the Defense of Republican Liberty: Renaissance Values in the Age of the Counter Reformation.* Berkeley: University of California Press, 1968.

Bouyer, Louis. "Erasmus in Relation to the Medieval Biblical Tradition." *The Cambridge History of the Bible.* Vol. 2. G. W. H. Lampe, ed. Cambridge: Cambridge University Press, 1969, 492–505.

Boyan, A. Stephen, Jr. "Defining Religion in Operational and Institutional Terms." 116 *U. Pa. L. Rev.* 479 (1968).

Boyd, Julian P., ed. *The Papers of Thomas Jefferson, 1760– 1776.* Vol. 1. Princeton, N.J.: Princeton University Press, 1950.

————. *The Papers of Thomas Jefferson, 1777–1779.* Vol. 2. Princeton: Princeton University Press, 1950.

Bozeman, Theodore D. *Protestants in an Age of Science: The Baconian Ideal and Antebellum American Religious Thought.* Chapel Hill: University of North Carolina Press, 1977.

Bramstedt, E. K. *Dictatorship and the Political Police.* New York: Oxford University Press, 1945.

Brandt, Richard B. *A Theory of the Good and the Right.* Oxford: Clarendon Press, 1979.

Brant, Irving. *James Madison: The Virginia Revolutionist, 1751–1780.* Indianapolis-New York: Bobbs-Merrill, 1941.

————. "Madison: On the Separation of Church and State." 8 *Wm. & Mary Quar.* 3 (1951).

Brest, Paul. "The Fundamental Rights Controversy: The Essential Contradictions of Normative Constitutional Scholarship." 90 *Yale L. J.* 1063 (1981).

————. "Interpretation and Interest." 34 *Stan. L. Rev.* 765 (1982).

————. "The Misconceived Quest for the Original Understanding." 60 *B. U. L. Rev.* 204 (1980).

Brody, Baruch. *Abortion and the Sanctity of Human Life: A Philosophical View.* Cambridge, Mass.: M.I.T. Press, 1975.

Brown, Jerry W. *The Rise of Bible Criticism in America, 1800–1870: The New England Scholars.* Middletown, Conn.: Wesleyan University Press, 1969.

Brown, Peter. *Augustine of Hippo: A Biography.* London: Faber & Faber, 1967.

————. *The Making of Late Antiquity.* Cambridge, Mass.: Harvard University Press, 1978.

————. *Religion and Society in the Age of Saint Augustine.* New York: Harper & Row, 1972.

Bullough, Vern. *Sexual Variance in Society and History.* Chicago: University of Chicago Press, 1980.

Burnyeat, Myles, ed. *The Skeptical Tradition.* Berkeley: University of California Press, 1983.

Burstyn, Varda. ed. *Women Against Censorship.* Vancouver & Toronto: Douglas & McIntyre, 1985.

Bury, J. B. *A History of Freedom of Thought.* London: Oxford University Press, 1952.

Butler, Joseph. *Fifteen Sermons Preached at the Rolls Chapel.* W. R. Matthews, ed. London: G. Bell & Sons, 1969.

Butterfield, Herbert. *The Origins of History.* New York: Basic Books, 1981.

——. *The Whig Interpretation of History.* New York: W. W. Norton, 1965.

Cahn, Edmond. *Confronting Injustice.* Boston: Little, Brown, 1966.

Callahan, Daniel. *Abortion: Law, Choice and Morality.* New York: Macmillan, 1970.

Cambre, Suzanne. *The Sensuous Heart.* Atlanta: Pritchett & Hull, 1978.

Campbell, T. D. "Francis Hutcheson: 'Father' of the Scottish Enlightenment." *The Origins and Nature of the Scottish Enlightenment.* R. H. Campbell, and Andrew S. Skinner, eds. Edinburgh: John Donald Publishers, 1982, 167–85.

Cartwright, Nancy. *How the Laws of Physics Lie.* Oxford: Clarendon Press, 1983.

Cassirer, Ernst. *The Question of Jean Jacques Rousseau.* Trans. Peter Gay. Bloomington: Indiana University Press, 1963.

Castellio, Sebastian. *Concerning Heretics.* Trans. Roland H. Bainton. New York: Columbia University Press, 1935.

Cavell, Stanley. "The Availability of Wittgenstein's Later Philosophy." 71 *Phil. Rev.* 67 (1962).

Cherniak, Christopher. "Minimal Rationality." 90 *Mind* 161 (1981).

Chevigny, Paul G. "The Paradox of Campaign Finance." 56 *N.Y.U. L. Rev.* 206 (1981).

Choper, Jesse H. "Defining 'Religion' in the First Amendment." 1982 *U. Ill. L. Rev.* 579.

——. "The Establishment Clause and Aid to Parochial Schools." 56 *Calif. L. Rev.* 260 (1968).

——. "The Religion Clauses of the First Amendment: Reconciling the Conflict." 41 *U. Pitt. L. Rev.* 673 (1980).

——. "Religion in the Public Schools." 47 *Minn. L. Rev.* 329 (1963).

Churchill, Wainwright. *Homosexual Behavior Among Males.* New York: Hawthorn, 1967.

Clark, J. Morris. "Guidelines for the Free Exercise Clause." 83 *Harv. L. Rev.* 327 (1969).

Clark, M. Edward, and Magrina, Javier. *Sexual Adjustment to Cancer Surgery in the Vaginal Area.* Kansas City: University of Kansas Medical Center, 1983.

Cobb, Sanford H. *The Rise of Religious Liberty in America.* New York: Cooper Square Publishers, 1968.

Cochrane, Charles N. *Christianity and Classical Culture.* London: Oxford University Press, 1944.

Cohen, I. Bernard. *The Newtonian Revolution.* Cambridge: Cambridge University Press, 1980.

Cohen, Joshua, and Rogers, Joel. *On Democracy: Toward a Transformation of American Society.* Harmondsworth: Penguin, 1983.

Coleman, James S.; Hoffer, Thomas; and Kilgore, Sally. *High School Achievement: Public, Catholic, and Private Schools Compared.* New York: Basic Books, 1982.

Collingwood, R. G. *The Idea of History.* Oxford: Clarendon Press, 1946.

Colman, John. *John Locke's Moral Philosophy.* Edinburgh: Edinburgh University Press, 1983.

Comfort, Alex. *More Joy*. New York: Simon & Schuster, 1983.

Commager, Henry Steele. *The Empire of Reason: How Europe Imagined and America Realized the Enlightenment*. Garden City, N.Y.: Anchor Press/ Doubleday, 1977.

Cord, Robert L. *Separation of Church and State: Historical Fact and Current Fiction*. New York: Lambeth Press, 1982.

Cover, Robert M. *Justice Accused: Antislavery and the Judicial Process*. New Haven, Conn.: Yale University Press, 1975.

————. "Foreword: Nomos and Narrative." 97 *Harv. L. Rev.* 4 (1983).

————. "The Origins of Judicial Activism in the Protection of Minorities." 91 *Yale L. J.* 1287 (1982).

Cox, Harvey. *Religion in the Secular City: Toward a Postmodern Theology*. New York: Simon & Schuster, 1984.

————. *The Secular City: Urbanization and Secularization in Theological Perspective*. New York: Macmillan, 1965.

Crosskey, William Winslow. *Politics and the Constitution in the History of the United States*. 2 vols. Chicago: University of Chicago Press, 1953.

Cuomo, Mario M. "Religious Belief and Public Morality." 31 *New York Review of Books* 32 (October 25, 1984).

Curry, Thomas J. *The First Freedoms: Church and State in America to the Passage of the First Amendment*. New York: Oxford University Press, 1986.

Dahl, Robert A. *A Preface to Democratic Theory*. Chicago: University of Chicago Press, 1956.

Dahl, Robert A. and Tufte, Edward R., *Size and Democracy*. Stanford: Stanford University Press, 1973.

Daniels, Norman, ed. *Reading Rawls*. New York: Basic Books, 1974.

————. "Wide Reflective Equilibrium and Theory Acceptance in Ethics." 76 *J. Phil.* 256 (1979).

Danto, Arthur C. *Mysticism and Morality*. New York: Harper, 1973.

D'Arcy, Eric. *Conscience and its Right to Freedom*. London: Sheed & Ward, 1961.

Dargo, George. *Roots of the Republic: A New Pespective on Early American Constitutionalism*. New York: Praeger, 1974.

Davidson, Donald. "Belief and the Basis of Meaning." 27 *Synthese* 309 (1974).

Davis, Nancy. "Abortion and Self-Defense." 13 *Phil. & Pub. Aff.* 175 (1984).

Davis, S. Rufus. *The Federal Principle: A Journey Through Time in Quest of Meaning*. Berkeley: University of California Press, 1978.

Dean, Winton. *Handel and the Opera Seria*. Berkeley: University of California Press, 1969.

"Developments in the Law—Equal Protection." 82 *Harv. L. Rev.* 1065 (1969).

Devlin, Patrick. *The Enforcement of Morals*. London: Oxford University Press, 1965.

Dewey, John. *The Quest for Certainty*. New York: Perigee, 1980.

Diamond, Milton, and Karlen, Arlo. *Sexual Decisions*. Boston: Little, Brown, 1980.

Dickerson, Reed. *The Interpretation and Application of Statutes*. Boston: Little, Brown, 1975.

Diggins, John P. *The Lost Soul of American Politics*. New York: Basic Books, 1984.

Dodds, E. R., *Pagan and Christian in an Age of Anxiety*. New York: W. W. Norton, 1965.

Dodge, Joseph M., Jr. "The Free Exercise of Religion: A Sociological Approach." 67 *Mich. L. Rev.* 679 (1969).

Drake, Stillman. *Galileo.* New York: Hill & Wang, 1980.

Dunn, John. *Political Obligation in its Historical Context.* Cambridge: Cambridge University Press, 1980.

———. *The Political Thought of John Locke.* Cambridge: Cambridge University Press, 1969.

———. "From Applied Theology to Social Analysis." *Wealth and Virtue: The Shaping of Political Economy in the Scottish Enlightenment.* Istvan Hont, and Michael Ignatieff, eds. Cambridge: Cambridge University, 1983, 119–35.

Dunn, Mary M. *William Penn: Politics and Conscience.* Princeton, N.J.: Princeton University Press, 1967.

Dworkin, Ronald. *A Matter of Principle.* Cambridge, Mass.: Harvard University Press, 1985.

———.*Law's Empire.* Cambridge, Mass.: Harvard University Press, 1986.

———. *Taking Rights Seriously.* Cambridge, Mass.: Harvard University Press, 1977.

———. "Law as Interpretation." *The Politics of Interpretation.* W. J. T. Mitchell, ed. Chicago: University of Chicago Press, 1983, 249–313.

———. "The Forum of Principle." 56 *N.Y.U. L. Rev.* 469 (1981).

Eckenrode, H. J. *Separation of Church and State in Virginia.* New York: Da Capo Press, 1971.

Edwards, Jonathan. *Dissertation on the Nature of True Virtue. The Works of President Edwards.* Vol. 2. New York: Leavitt, Trow & Co., 1844, 262–304.

———. *Religious Affections. Works of Jonathan Edwards.* Vol. 2. John E. Smith, ed. New Haven, Conn.: Yale University Press, 1959.

Eibl-Eibesfeldt, Irenaus. *Love and Hate.* Trans. G. Strachan. New York: Holt, Rinehart & Winston, 1972.

Eisenstein, Elizabeth. *The Printing Press as an Agent of Change.* 2 vols. Cambridge: Cambridge University Press, 1979.

Eliade, Mircea. *A History of Religious Ideas. Volume 2: From Gautama Buddha to the Triumph of Christianity.* Trans. Willard R. Trask. Chicago: University of Chicago Press, 1982.

Elliot, Jonathan. *The Debates in the Several State Conventions on the Adoption of the Federal Constitution.* 4 vols., Washington, D.C.: Printed for the Editor, 1836.

Ellis, Brian. *Rational Belief Systems.* Totowa, N.J.: Rowman & Littlefield, 1979.

Ellis, Havelock. *On Life and Sex.* New York: New American Library, 1962.

Elster, Jon. *Sour Grapes: Studies in the Subversion of Rationality.* Cambridge: Cambridge University Press, 1983.

Ely, John Hart. *Democracy and Distrust: A Theory of Judicial Review.* Cambridge, Mass.: Harvard University Press, 1980.

———. "Flag Desecration: A Case Study in the Roles of Categorization and Balancing in First Amendment Analysis." 88 *Harv. L. Rev.* 1482 (1975).

———. "Professor Dworkin's External/Personal Preference Distinction", 1983 *Duke L. J.* 959.

———. "The Wages of Crying Wolf: A Comment on *Roe v. Wade.*" 82 *Yale L. J.* 920 (1974).

Engelhardt, H. Tristram, Jr. "Viability and the Use of the Foetus." *Abortion and the Status of the Foetus.* Dordrecht: Reidel, 1983,William B. Bondeson et al., eds. 183–208.

Engell, James. *The Creative Imagination: Enlightenment to Romanticism.* Cambridge, Mass.: Harvard University Press, 1981.

Epstein, David F. *The Political Theory of The Federalist.* Chicago: University of Chicago Press, 1984.

Evans-Pritchard, E. E. *Witchcraft, Oracles and Magic Among the Azande.* Oxford: Clarendon Press, 1937.

Fackre, Gabriel. *The Religious Right and Christian Faith.* Grand Rapids, Mich.: William B. Eerdmans, 1982.

Farrand, Max, ed. *Records of the Federal Convention.* 4 vols., New Haven, Conn.: Yale University Press, 1911.

Feinberg, Joel. *Harm to Others.* New York: Oxford University Press, 1984.

———. "Abortion." *Matters of Life and Death.* Tom Regan, ed. New York: Random House, 1980, 183–217.

Ferreira, M. Jamie. *Doubt and Religious Commitment: The Role of the Will in Newman's Thought.* Oxford: Clarendon Press, 1980.

Fiering, Norman. *Jonathan Edwards's Moral Thought and Its British Context.* Chapel Hill: University of North Carolina Press, 1981.

———. *Moral Philosophy at Seventeenth-Century Harvard.* Chapel Hill: University of North Carolina Press, 1981.

Fiss, Owen. "Objectivity and Interpretation." 34 *Stan. L. Rev.*739 (1982).

Fletcher, George P. "The Case for Treason." 41 *Maryland L. Rev.* 193 (1982).

Fliegelman, Jay. *Prodigals and Pilgrims: The American Revolution against Patriarchal Authority, 1750–1800.* Cambridge: Cambridge University Press, 1982.

Ford, Clellan S., and Beach, Frank A. *Patterns of Sexual Behavior.* New York: Harper, 1951.

Foucault, Michel. *Discipline and Punish: The Birth of the Prison.* Trans. Alan Sheridan. New York: Vintage, 1979.

Frankfurt, Harry. "Freedom of the Will and the Concept of a Person." 68 *J. Phil.* 5 (1971).

Frankfurter, Felix. *The Commerce Clause Under Marshall, Taney, and Waite.* Chicago: Quadrangle, 1964.

Franklin, Julian H. *John Locke and the Theory of Sovereignty.* Cambridge: Cambridge University Press, 1978.

Freeman, George C. "The Misguided Search for the Constitutional Definition of 'Religion.'" 71 *Georgetown. L. J.* 1519 (1983).

Freeman, Harrop A. "A Remonstrance for Conscience." 106 *U. Pa. L. Rev.* 806 (1958).

Freud, Sigmund. "'Civilized' Sexual Morality and Modern Nervous Illness" *The Complete Psychological Works of Sigmund Freud.* Vol. 9. Standard ed. 1908 London: Hogarth Press, 1959, 181–204.

Freund, Paul A. "Public Aid to Parochial Schools." 82 *Harv. L. Rev.* 1680 (1969).

Fried, Charles. *An Anatomy of Values.* Cambridge, Mass.: Harvard University Press, 1970.

Frug, Gerald. "Why Neutrality?" 92 *Yale L. J.* 1591 (1983).

Fuller, Lon L. *The Morality of Law.* New Haven, Conn.: Yale University Press, 1964.

————. "Positivism and Fidelity to Law—A Reply to Professor Hart." 71 *Harv. L. Rev.* 630 (1958).

Futuyma, Douglas J. *Science on Trial: The Case for Evolution.* New York: Pantheon, 1983.

Gadamer, Hans-Georg. *Truth and Method.* New York: Continuum, 1975.

Gallie, W. B. *Philosophy and the Historical Understanding.* 2d ed. New York: Schocken Books, 1968.

Gardiner, Harold C. "Moral Principles Toward a Definition of the Obscene." 20 *Law & Contemp. Prob.* 560 (1955).

Gay, Peter. *The Enlightenment: An Interpretation, Volume 1: The Rise of Paganism.* New York: W. W. Norton, 1966.

Gebhard, Paul. "Incidence of Overt Homosexuality in the United States and Western Europe." *National Institute of Mental Health Task Force on Homosexuality.* J. M. Livingood, ed. Washington, D.C.: U.S. Government Printing Office, 1972.

Gebhard, Paul H.; Gagnon, John H.; Pomeroy, Wardell B.; and Christenson, Cornelia V. *Sex Offenders.* New York: Bantam, 1965.

Gebhard, Paul H., and Johnson, Alan B. *The Kinsey Data.* Philadelphia: W. B. Saunders, 1979.

Geertz, Clifford. *The Interpretation of Cultures.* New York: Basic Books, 1973.

————. "From the Native's Point of View: On the Nature of Anthropological Understanding.", *Interpretive Social Science.* Paul Rabinow, and William M. Sullivan, eds. Berkeley: University of California Press, 1979, 225–41.

Geiser, Robert L. *Hidden Victims: The Sexual Abuse of Children.* Boston: Beacon Press, 1979.

Gewirth, Alan. *Reason and Morality.* Chicago: University of Chicago Press, 1978.

Giannella, Donald G. "Religious Liberty, Nonestablishment, and Doctrinal Development. Part I: The Religious Liberty Guarantee." 80 *Harv. L. Rev.* 1381 (1967), "Part II: The Nonestablishment Principle." 81 *Harv. L. Rev.* 513 (1968).

Gilligan, Carol. *In a Different Voice.* Cambridge, Mass.: Harvard University Press, 1982.

Gillispie, Charles C. *Genesis and Geology.* Cambridge, Mass.: Harvard University Press, 1951.

Gilson, Etienne. *God and Philosophy.* New Haven, Conn.: Yale University Press, 1941.

Glymour, Clark. *Theory and Evidence.* Princeton: Princeton University Press, 1980.

Godfrey, Laurie R., ed. *Scientists Confront Creationism.* New York: W. W. Norton, 1983.

Goldman, Alvin I. "Epistemics: The Regulative Theory of Cognition." 75 *J. Phil.* 509 (1978).

Goodman, Nelson. *Fact, Fiction, and Forecast.* 3rd ed. Indianapolis-New York: Bobbs-Merrill, 1973.

————. *Problems and Projects.* Indianapolis-New York: Bobbs-Merrill, 1972.

————. *Ways of Worldmaking.* Indianapolis: Hackett, 1978.

Goody, Jack. *The Domestication of the Savage Mind.* Cambridge: Cambridge University Press, 1977.

Goody, Jack, ed. *Literacy in Traditional Societies.* Cambridge: Cambridge University Press, 1968.

Goody, Jack, and Watt, Ian. "The Consequences of Literacy." *Literacy in Traditional Societies.* Jack Goody, ed. Cambridge: Cambridge University Press, 1968, 27–84.

Gould, Stephen Jay. *The Mismeasure of Man.* New York: W. W. Norton, 1981.

Grandy, G. "Reference, Meaning, and Belief." 70 *J. Phil.* 439 (1973).

Gray, John. *Mill on Liberty: A Defence.* London: Routledge & Kegan Paul, 1983.

Greenawalt, R. Kent. "Criminal Coercion and Freedom of Speech," 78 *Northwestern L. Rev.* 1081 (1984).

————. "Religion as a Concept in Constitutional Law." 72 *Calif. L. Rev.* 753 (1984).

————. "Silence as a Moral and Constitutional Right." 23 *Wm. & Mary L. Rev.* 15 (1981).

————. "Speech and Crime," *American Bar Foundation Research Journal* 645 (1980).

Greene, John C. *The Death of Adam: Evolution and Its Impact on Western Thought.* Ames, Iowa: Iowa State University Press, 1959.

Greenslade, S. L. "Heresy and Schism in the Later Roman Empire," *Schism, Heresy and Religious Protest.* Derek Baker, ed. Cambridge: Cambridge University Press, 1972, 1–20.

Greven, Philip. *The Protestant Temperament: Patterns of Child-Rearing, Religious Experience, and the Self in Early America.* New York: New American Library, 1977.

Gunther, Gerald. "The Subtle Vices of the 'Passive Virtues.'" 64 *Colum. L. Rev.* 1 (1964).

Gutting, Gary. *Religious Belief and Religious Skepticism.* Notre Dame: University of Notre Dame Press, 1982.

Gwyn, W. B. *The Meaning of the Separation of Powers.* The Hague: Martinus Nijhoff, 1965.

Hacking, Ian. *Representing and Intervening.* Cambridge: Cambridge University Press, 1983.

————. "The Logic of Pascal's Wager." 9 *Am. Phil. Quar.* 186 (1972).

Haiman, Franklyn S. *Speech and Law in a Free Society.* Chicago: University of Chicago Press, 1981.

Hamburger, Philip. "The Development of the Law of Seditious Libel and the Control of the Press", 37 *Stan. L. Rev.* 661 (1985).

Hamowy, Ronald. "Jefferson and the Scottish Enlightenment: A Critique of Gary Wills's *Inventing America: Jefferson's Declaration of Independence.*" 36 *Wm. & Mary Quar.* 503 (1979).

Hand, Learned. *The Bill of Rights.* New York: Atheneum, 1968.

Hanson, Donald W. *From Kingdom to Commonwealth: The Development of Civic Consciousness in English Political Thought.* Cambridge, Mass.: Harvard University Press, 1970.

Hare, R. M. *Moral Thinking: Its Levels, Method and Point.* Oxford: Clarendon Press, 1981.

Harman, Gilbert. *The Nature of Morality.* New York: Oxford University Press, 1977.

————. *Thought.* Princeton: Princeton University Press, 1973.

Harrison, Beverly W. *Our Right to Choose.* Boston: Beacon, 1983.

Hart, Henry, and Sachs, Albert. *The Legal Process.* Cambridge, Mass.: Harvard Law School, 1958.

Hart, Henry. "The Power of Congress to Limit the Jurisdiction of Federal Courts: An Exercise in Dialectic." 66 *Harv. L. Rev.* 1362 (1953).

Hart, H. L. A. *The Concept of Law.* Oxford: Clarendon Press, 1961.

———. *Essays on Bentham.* Oxford: Clarendon Press, 1982.

———. *Essays in Jurisprudence and Philosophy.* Oxford: Clarendon Press, 1983.

———. *Law, Liberty and Morality.* Stanford, Calif.: Stanford University Press, 1963.

———. "Between Utility and Rights." *The Idea of Freedom.* Alan Ryan, ed. Oxford: Oxford University Press, 1979, 77–98.

———. "Positivism and the Separation of Law and Morals." 71 *Harv. L. Rev.* 593 (1958).

———. "Social Solidarity and the Enforcement of Morals." 35 *U. Chi. L. Rev.* 1 (1967).

Hatch, Nathan O., and Noll, Mark A. *The Bible in America: Essays in Cultural History.* New York: Oxford University Press, 1982.

Havelock, Eric A. *Preface to Plato.* Cambridge, Mass.: Belknap Press of Harvard University Press, 1963.

Hay, Douglas et al., eds. *Albion's Fatal Tree: Crime and Society in England in the Eighteenth Century.* London: A. Lane, 1975.

Heimert, Alan. *Religion and the American Mind: From the Great Awakening to the Revolution.* Cambridge, Mass.: Harvard University Press, 1966.

Helm, Paul, ed. *Divine Commands and Morality.* Oxford: Oxford University Press, 1981.

Henkin, Louis. *Foreign Affairs and the Constitution.* New York: W. W. Norton, 1972.

———. "Morals and the Constitution: The Sin of Obscenity." 63 *Colum. L. Rev.* 391 (1961).

———. "Privacy and Autonomy", 74 *Colum. L. Rev.* 1410 (1974).

Hesse, Mary. *The Structure of Scientific Inference.* Berkeley: University of California Press, 1974.

Hill, Christopher. *Intellectual Origins of the English Revolution.* Oxford: Clarendon Press, 1965 (reissued, 1980, 1982).

———. *Milton and the English Revolution.* Harmondsworth: Penguin, 1977.

———. *The World Turned Upside Down.* Harmondsworth: Penguin, 1972.

Hirschfield, Robert A. *The Power of the Presidency.* 2d ed. New York: Atherton Press, 1968.

Hite, Shere. *The Hite Report.* New York: Macmillan, 1976.

Hoffman, Martin. *The Gay World.* New York: Bantam, 1968.

Hofstadter, Richard. *Anti-intellectualism in American Life.* New York: Knopf, 1964.

Hogan, Rosemarie M.. *Human Sexuality: A Nursing Perspective.* New York: Appleton-Century-Crofts, 1980.

Hollingsworth, William G. "Constitutional Religious Protection." 34 *Ohio St. L. J.* 15 (1972).

Hollis, Martin. *Models of Man.* Cambridge: Cambridge University Press, 1977.

Hollis, Martin, and Lukes, Steven, eds. *Rationality and Relativism.* Oxford: Basil Blackwell, 1982.

Holmes, Oliver Wendell. "The Path of the Law." *Collected Legal Papers.* New York: Harcourt, Brace, & Co., 1952, 167–202.

Honore, Tony. *Sex Law*. London: Duckworth, 1978.

Hook, Sidney. *Religion in a Free Society*. Lincoln: University of Nebraska Press, 1967.

Hooker, Evelyn. "The Adjustment of the Male Overt Homosexual." 21 *J. L. Projective Techniques* 18 (1957).

Hookway, Christopher, and Pettit, Philip. *Action and Interpretation*. Cambridge: Cambridge University Press, 1978.

Horton, Robin. "African Traditional Thought and Western Science." *Rationality*. Bryan R. Wilson, ed. New York: Harper, 1970, 131–71.

————. "Levy-Bruhl, Durkheim and the Scientific Revolution." *Modes of Thought*. R. Horton and R. Finnegan, eds. London: Faber & Faber, 1973, 249–305.

————. "Tradition and Modernity Revisited." *Rationality and Relativism*. Martin Hollis, and Steven Lukes, eds. Oxford: Basil Blackwell., 1982 201–60.

Horton, Robin, and Finnegan, Ruth, eds. *Modes of Thought*. London: Faber & Faber, 1973.

Horwich, Paul. *Probability and Evidence*. Cambridge: Cambridge University Press, 1982.

Howe, Mark DeWolfe. *The Garden and the Wilderness: Religion and Government in American Constitutional History*. Chicago: University of Chicago Press, 1965.

Hoy, David C. *The Critical Circle: Literature and History in Contemporary Hermeneutics*. Berkeley: University of California Press, 1978.

Hume, David. "Of the Original Contract." *Essays: Moral, Political and Literary*. Oxford: Oxford University Press, 1963, 452–73.

Hunt, Morton. *Sexual Behavior in the 1970s*. Chicago: Playboy Press, 1974.

Hunter, Nan, and Law, Sylvia. "Brief *Amici Curiae* of Feminist Anti-Censorship Taskforce." Submitted April 8, 1985, *American Booksellers Ass'n v. Hudnut* (7th Cir., No. 84–3147, decided 8/27/85, 54 *U.S.L.W.* 2143).

Hurst, James W. *Dealing with Statutes*. New York: Columbia University Press, 1982.

Hutcheson, Francis. *A System of Moral Philosophy* [1755]. 2 vols. in 1. New York: Augustus M. Kelley, 1968.

————. *Illustrations on the Moral Sense*. Bernard Peach, ed. Cambridge, Mass.: Belknap Press of Harvard University Press, 1971.

————. *An Inquiry Concerning the Original of Our Ideas of Virtue or Moral Good. British Moralists*. Vol. 1. L. A. Selby-Bigge, ed. New York: Dover, 1965, 68–177.

Hutchinson, W. T., and Rachal, W. M. E., ed. *Papers of Madison*. Vol. 1. Chicago: University of Chicago Press, 1962.

Hutchison, William R. *The Modernist Impulse in American Protestantism*. Cambridge, Mass.: Harvard University Press, 1976.

Hyman, Harold. *A More Perfect Union*. New York: Knopf, 1973.

Hyman, Harold, and Wiecek, William. *Equal Justice Under Law: Constitutional Development, 1835–1875*. New York: Harper & Row, 1982.

Ingber, Stanley. "Defamation: A Conflict Between Reason and Decency." 65 *Va. L. Rev.* 785 (1979).

Isaac, Rhys. *The Transformation of Virginia, 1740–1790*. Chapel Hill: University of North Carolina Press, 1982.

Jackson, Thomas H., and Jeffries, John C. "Commercial Speech: Economic Due Process and the First Amendment." 65 *Va. L. Rev.* 1 (1979).

Jacobson, Dan. *The Story of the Stories: The Chosen People and Its God.* New York: Harper & Row, 1982.

James, William. *The Varieties of Religious Experience.* New York: Collier, 1961.

————. "The Sentiment of Rationality." *Essays on Faith and Morals.* New York: New American Library, 1974, 63–110.

————. "The Will to Believe." *Essays on Faith and Morals.* New York: New American Library, 1974, 32–62.

Jammer, Max. *The Conceptual Development of Quantum Mechanics.* New York: McGraw-Hill, 1966.

Jefferson, Thomas. *Notes on the State of Virginia.* William Peden, ed. Chapel Hill: University of North Carolina Press, 1955.

Jenkins, John J., *Understanding Locke.* Edinburgh: Edinburgh University Press, 1983.

Johnson, Philip E. "The Unnecessary Crime of Conspiracy." 61 *Calif. L. Rev.* 1137 (1973).

Jordan, W. K. *The Development of Religious Toleration in England.* 4 vols. Cambridge, Mass.: Harvard University Press, 1932–40.

Kalven, Harry, Jr. *The Negro and the First Amendment.* Chicago: University of Chicago Press, 1965.

————. "The Concept of the Public Forum," 1965 *Supreme Court Review* 1.

Kamenshine, R. D., "The First Amendment's Implied Political Establishment Clause." 67 *Calif. L. Rev.* 1104 (1979).

Kames, Henry Home. *Essays on the Principles of Morality and Natural Reason* [1751]. R. Wellek, ed. New York: Garland Publishing, 1976.

Kant, Immanuel. *Critique of Practical Reason.* Trans. Lewis White Beck, Indianapolis-New York: Bobbs-Merrill, 1956.

————. *Foundations of the Metaphysics of Morals.* Trans. Lewis White Beck. New York: Liberal Arts Press, 1959.

————. *Religion within the Limits of Reason Alone.* Trans. Theodore M. Greene, and Hoyt H. Hudson. New York: Harper & Bros., 1960.

————. "An Answer to the Question: 'What Is Enlightenment?'" *Kant's Political Writings.* Hans Reiss, ed., trans. H. B. Nisbet. Cambridge: Cambridge University Press, 1977, 54–60.

————. "Concerning the Common Saying: 'This May be True in Theory, but It Does Not Apply in Practice.'" *Kant's Political Writings.* Hans Reiss, ed. Trans. H. B. Nisbet, Cambridge: Cambridge University Press,1970, 61–92.

Kaplan, Helen S. *The New Sex Therapy.* New York: Brunner/Mazel, 1974.

Karst, Kenneth I. "Equality as a Central Principle of the First Amendment." 43 *U. Chi. L. Rev.* 20 (1975).

————. "The Freedom of Intimate Association." 80 *Yale L. J.* 624 (1980).

Katz, Wilber G. *Religion and American Constitutions.* Evanston, Ill.: Northwestern University Press, 1964.

Kaufman, Sherwin A. *Sexual Sabotage.* New York: Macmillan, 1981.

Kauper, Paul G. *Religion and the Constitution.* Baton Rouge: Louisiana State University Press, 1964.

Kelsen, Hans. *General Theory of Law and State.* Trans. Anders Wedberg. Cambridge, Mass.: Harvard University Press, 1945.
————. *The Pure Theory of Law.* Trans. Max Knight. Berkeley: University of California Press, 1967.
Kenny, Anthony. *Faith and Reason.* New York: Columbia University Press, 1983.
Kerman, Joseph. *Contemplating Music: Challenges to Musicology.* Cambridge, Mass.: Harvard University Press, 1985.
Kierkegaard, Soren. *Attack Upon "Christendom."* Trans. Walter Lowrie. Boston: Beacon Press, 1956.
————. *Concluding Unscientific Postscript.* Trans. David F. Swenson, and Walter Lowrie. Princeton, N.J.: Princeton University Press, 1941.
Kimball, Roger. "Heidegger at Freiburg." 3 *New Criterion* 9–18 (June 1985).
Kinsey, Alfred C.; Pomeroy, Wardell B.; and Martin, Clyde E. *Sexual Behavior in the Human Male.* Philadelphia: W. B. Saunders, 1948.
Kinsey, Alfred C.; Pomeroy, Wardell B.; Martin, Clyde E.; and Gebhard, Paul H. *Sexual Behavior in the Human Female.* Philadelphia: W. B. Saunders, 1953.
Kitcher, Philip. *Abusing Science: The Case Against Creationism.* Cambridge, Mass.: M.I.T. Press, 1982.
Klaich, Dolores. *Woman and Woman: Attitudes Toward Lesbianism.* New York: William Morrow, 1974.
Kluge, E. W. *The Practice of Death.* New Haven, Conn.: Yale University Press, 1975.
Knox, R. A. *Enthusiasm: A Chapter in the History of Religion.* Oxford: Clarendon Press, 1950.
Koch, Adrienne. *Jefferson and Madison: The Great Collaboration.* New York: Knopf, 1950.
————. *The Philosophy of Thomas Jefferson.* Gloucester, Mass.: Peter Smith, 1957.
Konvitz, Milton R. *Religious Liberty and Conscience.* New York: Viking, 1968.
Kramnick, Isaac. "Republican Revisionism Revisited." 87 *Am. Hist. Rev.* 629 (1982).
Kuhn, Thomas S. *The Essential Tension.* Chicago: University of Chicago Press, 1977.
————. *The Structure of Scientific Revolutions.* 2d ed. Chicago: University of Chicago Press, 1970.
Kurland, Philip B. "Of Church and State and the Supreme Court." 29 *U. Chi. L. Rev.* 1 (1961).
————. "The Irrelevance of the Constitution." 24 *Vill. L. Rev.* 3 (1978–79).
————. "The Supreme Court, Compulsory Education, and the First Amendment's Religion Clauses." 75 *W. Va. L. Rev.* 213 (1973).
Labrousse, Elisabeth. *Bayle.* Trans. Denys Potts. Oxford: Oxford University Press, 1983.
Lakatos, Imre. "Falsification and the Methodology of Scientific Research Programmes." In Imre Lakatos and Alan Musgrave, *Criticism and the Growth of Knowledge.* Cambridge: Cambridge University Press, 1970, 91–196.
Laudan, Larry. *Progress and Its Problems.* Berkeley: University of California Press, 1977.
————. *Science and Values.* Berkeley: University of California Press, 1984.

Laycock, Douglas. "Taking Constitutions Seriously: A Theory of Judicial Review." 59 *Tex. L. Rev.* 343 (1981).

Leader, Sheldon L. "Free Speech and the Advocacy of Illegal Action in Law and Political Theory." 82 *Colum. L. Rev.* 412 (1982).

Lecler, Joseph. *Toleration and the Reformation.* 2 vols. Trans. W. L. Westow. New York: Association Press, 1960.

Lederer, Laura, ed. *Take Back the Night.* New York: William Morrow, 1980.

Levi, Isaac. *The Enterprise of Knowledge: An Essay on Knowledge, Credal Probability, and Chance.* Cambridge, Mass.: M.I.T. Press, 1980.

—————. *Gambling with Truth: An Essay on Induction and the Aims of Science.* Cambridge, Mass.: M.I.T. Press, 1967.

Levy, Leonard. *Emergence of a Free Press.* New York: Oxford University Press. 1985.

—————. *Judgments: Essays on American Constitutional History.* Chicago: Quadrangle Books, 1972.

—————. *Legacy of Suppression: Freedom of Speech and Press in Early American History.* Cambridge, Mass.: Belknap Press of Harvard University Press, 1964.

—————"The *Legacy* Reexamined." 37 *Stan. L. Rev.* 767 (1985).

—————"On the Origins of the Free Press Clause." 32 *UCLA L. Rev.* 177 (1984).

—————. *Treason Against God: A History of the Offense of Blasphemy.* New York: Shocken, 1981.

Lewis, David. "Radical Interpretation." 23 *Synthese* 331 (1974).

Lindblom, Charles E. *Politics and Markets.* New York: Basic Books, 1977.

Little, David, and Twiss, Sumner B. *Comparative Religious Ethics.* San Francisco: Harper & Row, 1978.

Locke, John. *An Essay Concerning Human Understanding.* 2 vols. Alexander C. Fraser, ed. New York: Dover, 1959.

—————. *A Letter Concerning Toleration; A Second Letter Concerning Toleration; A Third Letter for Toleration; A Fourth Letter for Toleration; The Works of John Locke.* Vol. 6. London: Thomas Davison, 1823, 1–574.

—————. *The Reasonableness of Christianity.* I. T. Ramsey, ed. Stanford: Stanford University Press, 1958.

—————. *Two Treatises of Government.* Peter Laslett, ed. Cambridge: Cambridge University Press, 1960.

Lockridge, Kenneth A. *Literacy in Colonial New England.* New York: W. W. Norton, 1974.

LoPiccolo, Joseph, and LoPiccolo, Leslie, eds. *Handbook of Sex Therapy.* New York: Plenum, 1978.

Lord, Albert B. *The Singer of Tales.* Cambridge, Mass.: Harvard University Press, 1960.

Lovejoy, Arthur O. *The Great Chain of Being.* Cambridge, Mass.: Harvard University Press, 1936.

Lovibond, Sabina. *Realism and Imagination in Ethics.* Oxford: Basil Blackwell, 1983.

Luker, Kristin. *Abortion and the Politics of Motherhood.* Berkeley: University of California Press, 1984.

McCarthy, Rockne; Oppewal, Donald; Peterson, Walfred; and Spykman, Gordon. *Society, State, and Schools.* Grand Rapids, Mich.: William B. Eerdmans, 1981.

McCartney, James J. "Some Roman Catholic Concepts of Person and their Implications for the Ontological Status of the Unborn." *Abortion and the Status of the Fetus.* W. B. Bondeson et al., eds. Dordrecht: Reidel, 1983, 313–23.

McCloskey, Robert G. *The Bible in the Public Schools.* New York: Da Capo Press, 1967.

MacCormick, Neil. *Legal Reasoning and Legal Theory.* Oxford: Clarendon Press, 1978.

MacIntyre, Alasdair. *After Virtue.* Notre Dame: University of Notre Dame Press, 1981.

Mackie, J. L. *The Miracle of Theism: Arguments for and against the Existence of God.* Oxford: Clarendon Press, 1982.

McLoughlin, William G. *Isaac Backus and the American Pietistic Tradition.* Boston: Little, Brown, 1967.

————. "Isaac Backus and the Separation of Church and State." 73 *Am. Hist. Rev.* 1392 (1968).

————. *New England Dissent, 1630–1833: The Baptists and the Separation of Church and State.* 2 vols. Cambridge, Mass.: Harvard University Press, 1971.

————. *Revivals, Awakenings, and Reform.* Chicago: University of Chicago Press, 1978.

McLoughlin, William G., ed. *Isaac Backus on Church, State and Calvinism: Pamphlets, 1754–1789.* Cambridge, Mass.: Belknap Press of Harvard University Press, 1968.

McManners, John. *Death and the Enlightenment.* Oxford: Clarendon Press, 1981.

MacMullen, Ramsay. *Christianizing the Roman Empire.* New Haven, Conn.: Yale University Press, 1984.

McNeill, John J. *The Church and the Homosexual.* Kansas City: Sheed, Andrews & McMeel, 1976.

MacPherson, C. B. *The Political Theory of Possessive Individualism.* Oxford: Clarendon Press, 1962.

Malone, Dumas. *Jefferson the Virginian (Volume 1 of Jefferson and His Time).* Boston: Little, Brown, 1948.

Marcus, Paul. "The Forum of Conscience." 1973 *Duke L. J.* 1216.

Marcus, Steven. *The Other Victorians: A Study of Sexuality and Pornography in Mid-Nineteenth-Century England.* New York: Basic Books, 1964.

Marcuse, Herbert. "Repressive Tolerance." In Robert P. Wolff; Barrington Moore, Jr.; and Herbert Marcuse, *A Critique of Pure Tolerance.* Boston: Beacon, 1965, 81–117.

Markus, R. A. "Christianity and Dissent in Roman North Africa: Changing Perspectives in Recent Work." *Schism, Heresy and Religious Protest.* Derek Baker, ed. Cambridge: Cambridge University Press, 1972, 21–36.

Marsden, George M. *Fundamentalism and American Culture: The Shaping of Twentieth Century Evangelicalism, 1870–1925.* New York: Oxford University Press, 1980.

————. "Everyone's Own Interpreter—The Bible, Science, and Authority in Mid-Nineteenth-Century America." *The Bible in America.* N. O. Hatch and M. A. Noll, eds. New York: Oxford University Press, 1982, 79–95.

Marshall, William P. "Solving the Free Exercise Dilemma." 67 *Minn. L. Rev.* 545 (1983).

Marty, Martin E. *The Infidel: Freethought and American Religion.* Cleveland: World Publishing, 1961.

————. *Righteous Empire: The Protestant Experience in America.* New York: Dial Press, 1970.

————. *Varieties of Unbelief.* Garden City, N.Y.: Anchor, 1966.

Masters, William H., and Johnson, Virginia. *Homosexuality in Perspective.* Boston: Little, Brown, 1979.

————. *Human Sexual Inadequacy.* Boston: Little, Brown, 1970.

————. *The Pleasure Bond.* Boston: Little Brown, 1975.

May, Henry F. *The Enlightenment in America.* New York: Oxford University Press, 1976.

Mayr, Ernst. *The Growth of Biological Thought.* Cambridge, Mass.: Belknap Press of Harvard University Press, 1982.

Mayton, William A. "Seditious Libel and the Lost Guarantee of a Freedom of Expression." 84 *Colum. L. Rev.* 91 (1984).

Mead, George H. *Mind, Self, and Society.* Vol. 1. Charles W. Morris, ed. Chicago: University of Chicago Press, 1962.

Mead, Sidney E. *The Lively Experiment: The Shaping of Christianity in America.* New York: Harper & Row, 1963.

Meiklejohn, Alexander. *Political Freedom.* New York: Oxford University Press, 1965.

————. "The First Amendment Is an Absolute." 1961 *Supreme Court Review* 245.

Merel, Gail. "The Protection of Individual Choice." 45 *U. Chi. L. Rev.* 805 (1978).

Merton, Robert K. *Science, Technology and Society in Seventeenth Century England.* New York: Howard Fertig, 1970.

Meyers, Marvin, ed. *The Mind of the Founder: Sources of the Political Thought of James Madison.* Rev. ed. Hanover-London: University Press of New England, 1981.

Michelman, Frank I. "Foreword: On Protecting the Poor Through the Fourteenth Amendment." 83 *Harv. L. Rev.* 7 (1969).

Mill, John Stuart. *On Liberty.* Alburey Castell, ed. New York: Appleton-Century-Crofts, 1947.

————. *The Subjection of Women.* In John Stuart Mill, and Harriet Taylor Mill. *Essays on Sex Equality.* Alice S. Rossi, ed. Chicago: University of Chicago Press, 1970, 125–242.

————. *Utilitarianism.* Oskar Piest, ed. Indianapolis-New York: Bobbs-Merrill 1957.

Miller, Arthur R. *The Assault on Privacy.* Ann Arbor: University of Michigan Press, 1971.

Miller, Charles A. *The Supreme Court and the Uses of History.* Cambridge, Mass.: Belknap Press of Harvard University Press, 1969.

Miller, Dickinson, S. "James's Doctrine of 'The Right to Believe.'" 6 *Phil. Rev.* 541 (1942).

————. " 'The Will to Believe' and the Duty to Doubt." 9 *Int'l Jl. Ethics* 169 (1899).

Miller, Perry. *Errand into the Wilderness.* Cambridge, Mass.: Belknap Press of Harvard University Press, 1956.

——————. *Jonathan Edwards*. New York: William Sloan Associates, 1949.

——————. *The Life of the Mind in America*. New York: Harcourt, Brace & World, 1965.

——————. *The New England Mind: From Colony to Province*. Cambridge, Mass.: Belknap Press of Harvard University Press, 1953.

——————. *The New England Mind: The Seventeenth Century*. Cambridge, Mass.: Belknap Press of Harvard University Press, 1939.

——————. *Orthodoxy in Massachusetts 1630–1650*. Cambridge, Mass.: Harvard University Press, 1933.

——————. *Roger Williams: His Contribution to the American Tradition*. New York: Atheneum, 1966.

——————. "Roger Williams: An Essay in Interpretation." *The Complete Writings of Roger Williams*. Vol. 7. Perry Miller, ed. New York: Russell & Russell, 1963, 1–25.

Milton, John. *Areopagitica: A Speech of Mr. John Milton for the Liberty of Unlic'd Printing. The Prose of John Milton*. J. Max Patrick, ed. Garden City, N.Y.: Anchor, 1967, 247–334.

——————. *Considerations Touching the Likeliest Means to Remove Hirelings from the Church. The Prose of John Milton*. J. Max Patrick, ed. Garden City, N.Y.: Anchor, 1967, 475–518.

——————. *Paradise Lost. The Complete Poetry of John Milton*. John T. Shawcross, ed. Garden City, N.Y.: Anchor, 1971, 250–517.

——————. *A Treatise of Civil Power in Ecclesiastical Causes. The Prose of John Milton*. J. Max Patrick, ed. Garden City, N.Y.: Anchor, 1967, 443–474.

Mitchell, Basil. *The Justification of Religious Belief.* New York: Oxford University Press, 1981.

——————. *Law, Morality, and Religion in a Secular Society*. London: Oxford University Press, 1970.

——————. *Morality: Religious and Secular*. Oxford: Clarendon Press, 1980.

Mohr, James C. *Abortion in America*. Oxford: Oxford University Press, 1978.

Monaghan, Henry. "Our Perfect Constitution." 56 *N.Y.U. L. Rev.* 353 (1981).

Money, John, and Ehrhardt, A. *Man & Woman Boy & Girl*. Baltimore: Johns Hopkins University Press, 1972.

Money, J.; Hampson, J. G., and Hampson, J. L. "An Examination of Some Basic Sexual Concepts: The Evidence of Human Hermaphroditism." 97 *Bull. Johns Hopkins Hosp.* 301 (1955).

Montagu, Ashley, ed. *Science and Creationism*. Oxford: Oxford University Press, 1984.

Montesquieu, Baron de. *The Spirit of the Laws*. Thomas Nugent trans. New York: Hafner, 1949.

Mooney, Thomas O.; Cole, Theodore M.; and Chilgren, Richard A. *Sexual Options for Paraplegics and Quadriplegics*. Boston: Little, Brown, 1975.

Moore, John Norton. "The Supreme Court and the Relationship Between the 'Establishment' and 'Free Exercise' Clauses." 42 *Texas L. Rev.* 142 (1963).

Moore, Michael S. "Moral Reality." 1982 *Wis. L. Rev.* 1061.

——————. "A Natural Law Theory of Interpretation." 58 *So. Calif. L. Rev.* 279 (1985).

——————. "The Semantics of Judging." 54 *So. Calif. L. Rev.* 151 (1981).

Moraczewski, Albert S. "Human Personhood: A Study of Person-alized Biology." *Abortion and the Status of the Foetus.*W. B. Bondeson, et al., eds. Dordrecht: Reidel, 1983, 301–11.

Morgan, Edmund S. *Roger Williams: The Church and the State.* New York: Harcourt, Brace & World, 1967.

Morgan, Richard E. *The Supreme Court and Religion.* New York: Free Press, 1972.

Murray, John Courtney. "Law or Prepossessions?" 14 *Law & Contemp. Prob.* 23 (1949).

Muzzey, David Saville. *Ethics as a Religion.* New York: Frederick Ungar Publishing Co., 1951.

Myrna, Frances. "The Right to Abortion." *Ethics for Modern Life.* 2d ed. Raziel Abelson, and Marie Friquegnon, eds. New York: St. Martin's Press, 1980, 103–16.

Needham, Joseph. *Science in Traditional China.* Cambridge, Mass.: Harvard University Press, 1981.

Neill, Stephen. *The Interpretation of the New Testament, 1861– 1961.* New York: Oxford University Press, 1966.

Nell, Onora. *Acting on Principle.* New York: Columbia University Press, 1975.

Nelson, William E. *The Roots of American Bureaucracy, 1830–1900.* Cambridge, Mass.: Harvard University Press, 1982.

Neuhaus, Richard J. *The Naked Public Square: Religion and Democracy in America.* Grand Rapids, Mich.: William B. Eerdmans, 1984.

Newman, Jay. *Foundations of Religious Tolerance.* Toronto: University of Toronto Press, 1982.

Newman, John Henry. *Grammar of Assent.* Garden City, N.Y.: Image, 1955.

Newton-Smith, W. H., *The Rationality of Science.* Boston: Routledge & Kegan Paul, 1981.

———. "Relativism and the Possibility of Interpretation." *Rationality and Relativism.* M. Hollis, and S. Lukes, eds. Oxford: Basil Blackwell, 1982, 106–22.

Nicholson, Marlene A. "Campaign Financing and Equal Protection." 26 *Stan. L. Rev.* 815 (1974).

Nickles, Thomas, ed. *Scientific Discovery, Logic, and Rationality.* Dordrecht: Reidel, 1980.

Nielsen, Kai. *Ethics Without God.* Buffalo, N.Y.: Prometheus Books, 1973.

Nimmer, Melville R. "The Right to Speak from *Times* to *Time*: First Amendment Theory Applied to Libel and Misapplied to Privacy." 56 *Calif. L. Rev.* 935 (1968).

Noonan, John T., Jr. *Contraception: A History of Its Treatment by the Catholic Theologians and Canonists.* Cambridge, Mass.: Harvard University Press, 1966.

Note. "The Constitutionality of Laws Forbidding Private Homosexual Conduct." 72 *Mich. L. Rev.* 1613 (1974).

———. "Defining Religion." 32 *U. Chi. L. Rev.* 533 (1965).

———. "Reinterpreting the Religion Clauses: Constitutional Construction and Conceptions of the Self." 97 *Harv. L. Rev.* 1468 (1984).

———. "Toward a Constitutional Definition of Religion." 91 *Harv. L. Rev.* 1056 (1978).

———. "Toward a Uniform Valuation of the Religion Guarantees." 77 *Yale L. J.* 77 (1970).

Nowak, John E. "The Supreme Court, the Religion Clauses, and the National-
    ization of Education." 70 *Northwestern U. L. Rev.* 883 (1976).
Nozick, Robert. *Anarchy, State and Utopia.* New York: Basic Books, 1974.
O'Neill, J. M. *Religion and Education Under the Constitution.* New York: Harper
    & Bros., 1949.
Ong, Walter J. *Darwin's Vision and Christian Perspectives.* New York: Macmil-
    lan, 1960.
————. *Interfaces of the Word.* Ithaca, N.Y.: Cornell University Press, 1977.
————. *Orality and Literacy.* London: Methuen, 1982.
————. *The Presence of the Word.* New Haven, Conn.: Yale University Press,
    1967.
————. *Ramus, Method, and the Decay of Dialogue.* Cambridge, Mass.: Har-
    vard University Press, 1958.
————. *Rhetoric, Romance, and Technology.* Ithaca, N.Y.: Cornell University
    Press, 1971.
O'Shaughnessy, Brian. *The Will: A Dual Aspect Theory.* 2 vols. Cambridge:
    Cambridge University Press, 1980.
Outka, Gene. "Religious and Moral Duty: Notes on *Fear and Trembling.*" *Reli-
    gion and Morality.* G. Outka, and J. P. Reeder, Jr., eds. Garden City,
    N.Y.: Anchor, 1973, 204–54.
Outka, Gene, and Reeder, John P., Jr., eds. *Religion and Morality.* Garden City,
    N.Y.: Anchor, 1973.
Paine, Thomas. *Rights of Man.* Henry Collins, ed. Harmondsworth: Penguin,
    1976.
Pais, Abraham. *'Subtle is the Lord . . .': The Science and the Life of Albert Ein-
    stein.* Oxford: Oxford University Press, 1982.
Parker, Richard B. "A Definition of Privacy." 27 *Rutgers L. Rev.* 275 (1974).
Pascal, Blaise. *Pensees.* Trans. A. J. Krailsheimer. Harmondsworth: Penguin,
    1966.
Patterson, Orlando. *Slavery and Social Death.* Cambridge, Mass.: Harvard Uni-
    versity Press, 1982.
Peacocke, Christopher. *Holistic Explanation: Action, Space, Interpretation.*
    Oxford: Clarendon Press, 1979.
Pepper, Stephen. "*Reynolds, Yoder,* and Beyond: Alternatives for the Free
    Exercise Clause." 2 *Utah L. Rev.* 310 (1981).
Perry, Michael J. *The Constitution, the Courts, and Human Rights.* New Haven,
    Conn.: Yale University Press, 1982.
Perry, Ralph Barton. *Puritanism and Democracy.* New York: Vanguard Press,
    1944.
Pfeffer, Leo. *Church, State and Freedom.* rev. ed. Boston: Beacon Press, 1967.
Pietropinto, Anthony, and Simenauer, Jacqueline. *Beyond the Male Myth.* New
    York: N.Y. Times Books, 1977.
Plantinga, Alvin. *God and Other Minds: A Study of the Rational Justification of
    Belief in God.* Ithaca, N.Y.: Cornell University Press, 1967.
Plato. *Euthyphro. Plato: The Collected Dialogues.* Edith Hamilton, and Hunting-
    ton Cairns, eds. Trans. Lane Cooper, New York: Pantheon, 1961, 169–
    85.
————. *Laws, Plato: The Collected Dialogues.* Edith Hamilton, and Hunting-
    ton Cairns, eds. Trans. A. E. Taylor. New York: Pantheon, 1961, 1225–
    1513.

Plumb, J. H. *The Death of the Past.* Boston: Houghton Mifflin, 1971.

Pocock, J. G. A. *The Ancient Constitution and the Feudal Law: English Historical Thought in the Seventeenth Century.* Cambridge: Cambridge University Press, 1957.

————. *The Machiavellian Moment: Florentine Political Thought and the Atlantic Republican Tradition.* Princeton, N.J.: Princeton University Press, 1975.

————. *Politics, Language and Time.* New York: Atheneum, 1973.

Polanyi, Michael. *Personal Knowledge: Towards a Post-Critical Philosophy.* New York: Harper & Row, 1964.

Pole, J. R. *The Gift of Government: Political Responsibility from the English Restoration to American Independence.* Athens: University of Georgia Press, 1983.

————. *Political Representation in England and the Origins of the American Republic.* London: Macmillan, 1966.

————. *The Pursuit of Equality in American History.* Berkeley: University of California Press, 1978.

Polyviou, Polyvios G. *The Equal Protection of the Laws.* London: Duckworth, 1980.

Pool, Ithiel de Sola. *Technologies of Freedom.* Cambridge, Mass.: Belknap Press of Harvard University Press, 1983.

Popkin, Richard H. *The High Road to Pyrrhonism.* San Diego : Austin Hill Press, 1980.

————. *The History of Scepticism from Erasmus to Descartes.* Assen: Van Gorcum, 1960.

————. *The History of Scepticism from Erasmus to Spinoza.* Berkeley: University of California Press, 1979.

Porter, Dale H. *The Emergence of the Past.* Chicago: University of Chicago Press, 1981.

Powell, H. Jefferson. "The Original Understanding of Original Intent." 98 *Harv. L. Rev.* 885 (1985).

Price, Richard. *A Review of the Principal Questions in Morals.* D. D. Raphael, ed. Oxford: Clarendon Press, 1974.

Prichard, H. A., *Moral Obligation: Essays and Lectures.* Oxford: Clarendon Press, 1949.

Putnam, Hilary. *Reason, Truth and History.* Cambridge: Cambridge University Press, 1981.

Quine, W. V. *Word and Object.* Cambridge, Mass.: M.I.T. Press, 1960.

————. "Epistemology Naturalized." *Ontological Relativity and Other Essays.* New York: Columbia University Press, 1969, 69–90.

Quine, W. V. O., and Ullian, J. S. *The Web of Belief.* 2d ed. New York: Random House, 1978.

Quinn, Philip L. *Divine Commands and Moral Requirements.* Oxford: Clarendon Press, 1978.

Quinn, Warren. "Abortion: Identity and Loss." 13 *Phil. & Pub. Aff.* 24 (1984).

Rabinow, Paul, and Sullivan, William M., eds. *Interpretive Social Science: A Reader.* Berkeley: University of California Press, 1979.

Rawls, John. *A Theory of Justice.* Cambridge, Mass.: Harvard University Press, 1971.

————. "The Basic Liberties and Their Priority." *The Tanner Lectures on*

328   BIBLIOGRAPHY

Human Values. Vol. 3. S. McMurrin, ed. Cambridge: Cambridge University Press, 1981, 3–87.
————. "Fairness to Goodness." 84 *Phil. Rev.* 536 (1975).
————. "Kantian Constructivism in Moral Theory." 77 *J. Phil.* 515 (1980).
————. "Reply to Alexander and Musgrave." 88 *Quar. J. Ec.* 633 (1974).
————. "Social Unity and Primary Goods." *Utilitarianism and Beyond.* Amartya Sen, and Bernard Williams, eds. Cambridge: Cambridge University Press, 1982, 159–85.
Raz, Joseph. *The Authority of Law.* Oxford: Clarendon Press, 1979.
————. *The Concept of a Legal System.* Oxford: Clarendon Press, 1970.
————. *Practical Reason and Norms.* London: Hutchinson, 1975.
Redish, Martin H. "The Content Distinction in First Amendment Analysis." 34 *Stan. L. Rev.* 113 (1981).
————. "The First Amendment in the Marketplace: Commercial Speech and the Values of Free Expression." 39 *Geo. Wash. L Rev.* 429 (1971).
————. "Self-Realization, Democracy, and Freedom of Expression." 130 *U. Pa. L. Rev.* 678 (1982).
————. "The Value of Free Speech." 130 *U. Pa. L. Rev.* 591 (1982).
Reed, James. *The Birth Control Movement and American Society.* Princeton, N.J.: Princeton University Press, 1978.
Regan, D. H. "Rewriting *Roe v. Wade.*" 77 *Mich L. Rev.* 1569 (1979).
Reich, Robert B. "Preventing Deception in Commercial Speech." 54 *N.Y.U. L. Rev.* 775 (1979).
Reid, Thomas. *Essays on the Active Powers of the Human Mind.* B. Brody, ed. Cambridge, Mass.: M.I.T. Press, 1969.
Rex, Walter. *Essays on Pierre Bayle and Religious Controversy.* The Hague: Martinus Nijhoff, 1965.
Richards, David A. J. *The Moral Criticism of Law.* Encino, Calif.: Dickenson-Wadsworth, 1977.
————. *Sex, Drugs, Death and the Law: An Essay on Decriminalization and Human Rights.* Totowa, N.J.: Rowman & Littlefield, 1982.
————. *A Theory of Reasons for Action.* Oxford: Clarendon Press, 1971.
————. "The Aims of Constitutional Theory." 8 *U. Day. L. Rev.* 723 (1983).
————. "Conscience, Human Rights, and the Anarchist Challenge to the Obligation to Obey the Law." 18 *Ga. L. Rev.* 771 (1984).
————. "Constitutional Interpretation, History, and the Death Penalty: A Book Review." 71 *Calif. L. Rev.* 1372 (1983).
————. "Free Speech and Obscenity Law: Toward a Moral Theory of the First Amendment." 123 *U. Pa. L. Rev.* 45 (1974).
————. "Human Rights and Moral Ideals: An Essay on the Moral Theory of Liberalism." 5 *Soc. Theory & Prac.* 461 (1980).
————. "The Individual, the Family, and the Constitution." 55 *N.Y.U. L. Rev.* 1 (1980).
————. "Moral Philosophy and the Search for Fundamental Values in Constitutional Law." 42 *Ohio L. J.* 319 (1981).
————. "Prescriptivism, Constructivism, and Rights." *Hare and Hounds.* D. Seanor, and N. Fotion, eds. forthcoming, Oxford University Press.
————. "Privacy." *Collier's Encyclopedia.* Vol. 19, pp. 393–95, New York: Macmillan, 1986.
————. "Rights and Autonomy." 92 *Ethics* 3 (1981).

————. "Rights, Resistance, and the Demands of Self-Respect." 32 *Emory L. J.* 405 (1983).

————. "Terror and the Law." 5 *Human Rts. Quar.* 171 (1983).

————"The Theory of Adjudication and the Task of the Great Judge." 1 *Cardozo L. Rev.* 171 (1979).

Richardson, Alan. "The Rise of Modern Biblical Scholarship and Recent Discussion of the Authority of the Bible." *The Cambridge History of the Bible.* Vol. 3. S. L. Greenslade, ed. Cambridge: Cambridge University Press, 1963, 294–338.

Riesman, David. "Democracy and Defamation: Control of Group Libel." 42 *Colum. L. Rev.* 727 (1942).

Rig Veda. Trans. Wendy Doniger O'Flaherty. Harmondsworth: Penguin, 1981.

Riley, Patrick. *Will and Political Legitimacy.* Cambridge, Mass.: Harvard University Press, 1982.

Rorty, Richard. *Philosophy and the Mirror of Nature.* Princeton, N.J.: Princeton University Press, 1982.

Ross, W. D. *The Right and the Good.* Oxford: Clarendon Press, 1930.

Rossiter, Clinton, ed. *The Federalist Papers* (Alexander Hamilton, James Madison, and John Jay) New York: Mentor, 1961.

Rougemont, Denis de. *Man's Western Quest: The Principles of Civilization.* Trans. Montgomery Belgion. Westport, Conn.: Greenwood, 1973.

Rousseau, Jean Jacques. *The Social Contract and Discourses.* Trans. G. D. H. Cole. New York: Dutton, 1950.

Ryan, Alan. "Locke and the Dictatorship of the Bourgeoisie." 13 *Political Studies* 219 (1965).

Sager, Lawrence G. "Rights Skepticism and Process-Based Responses." 56 *N.Y.U. L. Rev.* 417 (1981).

Sandberg, Karl C. *At the Crossroads of Faith and Reason: An Essay on Pierre Bayle.* Tucson: University of Arizona Press, 1966.

Sandberg, Karl C. ed. *The Great Contest of Faith and Reason: Selections from the Writings of Pierre Bayle.* New York: Frederick Ungar, 1963.

Sandeen, Ernest R. *The Roots of Fundamentalism: British and American Millenarianism, 1800–1930.* Chicago: University of Chicago Press, 1970.

Sandel, Michael J. *Liberalism and the Limits of Justice.* Cambridge: Cambridge University Press, 1982.

Sandmel, Samuel. *The Genius of Paul.* New York: Schocken, 1970.

Santayana, George. *Reason in Common Sense* (Volume 1 of The Life of Reason.) New York: Dover, 1980.

————. *Reason in Religion* (Volume 3 of The Life of Reason.) New York: Dover, 1982.

Santillana, Giorgio de. *The Crime of Galileo.* Chicago: University of Chicago Press, 1955.

Saphire, Richard B. "Specifying Due Process Values: Toward a More Responsive Approach to Procedural Protection." 127 *U. Pa. L. Rev.* 111 (1978).

Sayre, Francis. "Criminal Conspiracy." 35 *Harv. L. Rev.* 393 (1922).

Scanlon, T. M. "Contractualism and Utilitarianism." *Utilitarianism and Beyond.* Amartya Sen, and Bernard Williams, eds. Cambridge: Cambridge University Press, 1982, 103–28.

————. "Freedom of Expression and Categories of Expression." 40 *U. Pitt. L. Rev.* 519 (1979).

————. "Preference and Urgency." 72 *J. of Phil.* 655 (1975).

————. "A Theory of Free Expression." 1 *Phil. & Pub. Aff.* 204 (1972).

Schaff, Philip. *Church and State in the United States. Papers of the American Historical Association.* Vol. 2, no. 4. New York: G. P. Putnam's Sons, 1888.

Schauer, Frederick. "Easy Cases." 58 *So. Calif. L. Rev.* 399 (1985).

————. "An Essay on Constitutional Language." 29 *U.C.L.A. L. Rev.* 797 (1982).

————. *Free Speech: A Philosophical Inquiry.* Cambridge: Cambridge University Press, 1982.

————. "Must Speech Be Special?" 78 *Northwestern U. L. Rev.* 1284 (1983).

————. "Speech and 'Speech'—Obscenity and 'Obscenity.'" 67 *Georgetown L. J.* 899 (1979).

Scheffler, Israel. *Science and Subjectivity.* 2d ed. Indianapolis: Hacket, 1982.

Schmidt, Benno C., Jr. *Freedom of the Press vs. Public Access.* New York: Praeger, 1976.

Schneidau, Herbert N. *Sacred Discontent: The Bible and Western Tradition.* Baton Rouge: Louisiana State University Press, 1976.

Schwarz, Alan. "No Imposition of Religion." 77 *Yale L. J.* 692 (1968).

————. "The Nonestablishment Principle: A Reply to Professor Giannella." 81 *Harv. L. Rev.* 1465 (1968).

Seaton, A. A. *The Theory of Toleration under the Later Stuarts.* Cambridge: Cambridge University Press, 1911.

Selby-Bigge, L. A., ed. *British Moralists.* 2 vols., New York: Dover, 1965.

Sen, Amartya. *Poverty and Famines: An Essay on Entitlement and Deprivation.* Oxford: Clarendon Press, 1981.

Sennett, Richards. *The Fall of Public Man.* New York: Vintage, 1978.

Shaftesbury, Third Earl of (Anthony Ashley Cooper). *An Inquiry Concerning Virtue or Merit. British Moralists.* Vol. 1. L. A. Selby-Bigge, ed. New York: Dover, 1965, 1–67.

Shakespeare, William. *Troilus and Cressida. Shakespeare: Complete Works.* W. J. Craig, ed. London: Oxford University Press, 1966, 667–700.

Shapere, Dudley. "The Character of Scientific Change." *Scientific Discovery, Logic, and Rationality.* Thomas Nickles, ed. Dordrecht: Reidel, 1980, 61–101.

————. "Meaning and Scientific Change." *Mind and Cosmos: Essays in Contemporary Science and Philosophy.* R. Colodny, ed. Pittsburgh: University of Pittsburgh Press, 1966, 41–85.

Shapiro, Barbara J. *Probability and Certainty in Seventeenth-Century England.* Princeton, N.J.: Princeton University Press, 1983.

Shiffrin, Steven. "Defamatory Non-Media Speech and First Amendment Methodology." 25 *U.C.L.A. L. Rev.* 915 (1978).

————. "Government Speech." 27 *U.C.L.A. L. Rev.* 565 (1980).

————. "Liberalism, Radicalism, and Legal Scholarship." 30 *U.C.L.A. L. Rev.* 1103 (1983).

Simmons, A. John. "Inalienable Rights and Locke's *Treatises.*" 12 *Phil. & Pub. Aff.* 175 (1983).

Simon, W., and Gagnon, J. H. "Femininity in the Lesbian Community." *Sexual Deviance and Sexual Deviants.* E. Goode, and R. Troiden, eds. New York: Morrow, 1974, 256–67.

Skinner, Quentin. *Machiavelli*. New York: Hill and Wang, 1981.

————. "Meaning and Understanding in the History of Ideas." 8 *History and Theory* 1 (1969).

Skorupski, John. *Symbol and Theory: A Philosophical Study of Theories of Religion in Social Anthropology*. Cambridge: Cambridge University Press, 1976.

Smith, James R., and Smith, Lynn G., eds. *Beyond Monogamy: Recent Studies of Sexual Alternatives in Marriage*. Baltimore: Johns Hopkins University Press, 1974.

Sontag, Susan. *Styles of Radical Will*. New York: Dell, 1969.

Soper, Philip. *A Theory of Law*. Cambridge, Mass.: Harvard University Press, 1984.

Spragens,Thomas A., Jr. *The Irony of Liberal Reason*. Chicago: University of Chicago Press, 1981.

Stannard, David E. *The Puritan Way of Death*. New York: Oxford University Press, 1977.

Stephen, James Fitzjames. *Liberty, Equality, Fraternity*. R. J. White, ed. Cambridge: Cambridge University Press, 1967.

Stern, Robert. "That Commerce Which Concerns More States Than One." 47 *Harv. L. Rev.* 1335 (1943).

Stevenson, Charles L. *Ethics and Language*. New Haven, Conn.: Yale University Press, 1944.

Stewart, Dugald. *The Philosophy of the Active and Moral Powers of Man*. James Walker, ed. Philadelphia: J. H. Butler, 1878.

Stewart, Richard B. "Regulation in a Liberal State: The Role of Non-Commodity Values." 92 *Yale L. J.* 1537 (1983).

Stock, Brian. *The Implications of Literacy*. Princeton. N.J.: Princeton University Press, 1983.

Stokes, Anson Phelps. *Church and State in the United States*. 3 vols. New York: Harper & Brothers, 1950.

Storing, Herbert J., ed. *The Anti-federalist*. Murray Dry abridgement (*The Complete Anti-federalist*, 7 vols.).Chicago: University of Chicago Press, 1985.

Storing, Herbert J. *What the Anti-federalists Were For*. Chicago: University of Chicago Press, 1981.

Story, Joseph. *Commentaries on the Constitution of the United States*. [Cambridge: Brown Stattuck and Co., 1833]. In Philip Schaff, *Church and State in the United States* in *Papers of the American Historical Association*. Vol. 2, no. 4. New York: G. P. Putnam's Sons, 1888, 128–30.

Stove, David. *Popper and After: Four Modern Irrationalists*. Oxford: Pergamon Press, 1982.

Sullivan, William M. *Reconstructing Public Philosophy*. Berkeley: University of California Press, 1982.

Sumner, L. W. *Abortion and Moral Theory*. Princeton, N.J.: Princeton University Press, 1981.

Sunstein, Cass R. "Naked Preferences and the Constitution." 84 *Colum. L. Rev.* 1689 (1984).

Swinburne, Richard. *The Existence of God*. Oxford: Clarendon Press, 1979.

Sykes, Norman. "The Religion of Protestants." *The Cambridge History of the Bible*. Vol. 3. S. L. Greenslade, ed. Cambridge: Cambridge University Press, 1963, 175–98.

Sykes, Stephen. *The Identity of Christianity.* London: SPCK, 1984.

Taine, H. A. *L'Ancien Regime.* Paris: Hachette, 1896.

Tarcov, Nathan. *Locke's Education for Liberty.* Chicago: University of Chicago Press, 1984.

Tavris, Carol, and Sadd, Susan. *The Redbook Report on Female Sexuality.* New York: Delacorte, 1975.

Taylor, Charles. "The Concept of a Person." C. Taylor, *Human Agency and Language: Philosophical Papers,* vol. 1. Cambridge: Cambridge University Press, 1985, 97–114.

————. "The Diversity of Goods." C. Taylor, *Philosophy and the Human Sciences: Philosophical Papers,* vol. 2. Cambridge: Cambridge University Press, 1985, 230–247.

————. "Interpretation and the Sciences of Man." C. Taylor, *Philosophy and the Human Sciences: Philosophical Papers,* vol. 2. Cambridge: Cambridge University Press, 1985, 15–57.

————. "Rationality." C. Taylor, *Philosophy and the Human Sciences: Philosophical Papers,* vol. 2. Cambridge: Cambridge University Press, 1985, 134–151.

————. 'Self-Interpreting Animals." C. Taylor, *Human Agency and Language: Philosophical Papers,* vol. 1. Cambridge: Cambridge University Press, 1985 45–76.

————. "What Is Human Agency?" C. Taylor, *Human Agency and Language: Philosophical Papers,* vol. 1. Cambridge: Cambridge University Press, 1985, 15–44.

Tedlock, Dennis. *The Spoken Word and the Work of Interpretation.* Philadelphia: University of Pennsylvania Press, 1983.

Ten, C. L. *Mill on Liberty.* Oxford: Clarendon Press, 1980.

Thayer, James B. "The Origin and Scope of the American Doctrine of Constitutional Law." 7 *Harv. L. Rev.* 129 (1893).

Thompson, John B., and Held, David. *Habermas: Critical Debates.* Cambridge, Mass.: M.I.T. Press, 1982.

Thompson, Judith J. "A Defense of Abortion." 1 *Phil. & Pub. Aff.* 47 (1971).

Tierney, Brian. *Religion and the Growth of Constitutional Thought, 1150–1650.* Cambridge: Cambridge University Press, 1982.

Tocqueville, Alexis de. Democracy in America. 2 vols. Phillips Bradley, ed. New York: Vintage, 1945.

Todorov, Tzvetan. *The Conquest of America,* Richard Howard, trans. New York: Harper Colophon, 1985.

Tooley, Michael. *Abortion and Infanticide.* Oxford: Clarendon Press, 1983.

————. "Abortion and Infanticide." 2 *Phil. & Pub. Aff.* 37 (1972).

Tribe, Laurence H. *American Constitutional Law.* Mineola, N.Y.: Foundation Press, 1978.

————. "The Supreme Court, 1972 Term—Foreword: Toward a Model of Roles in the Due Process of Life and Law." 87 *Harv. L. Rev.* 1 (1973).

Trilling, Lionel. *Sincerity and Authenticity.* Cambridge, Mass.: Harvard University Press, 1971.

Tripp, C. A. *The Homosexual Matrix.* New York: McGraw-Hill, 1975.

Tully, James, *A Discourse on Property: John Locke and his Adversaries.* Cambridge: Cambridge University Press, 1980.

Tushnet, Mark. "Following the Rules Laid Down." 96 *Harv. L. Rev.* 781 (1983).

United States. *Report of the Commission on Obscenity and Pornography.* Washington, D.C.: U.S. Government Printing Office, 1970.

van Fraassen, Bas C. *The Scientific Image.* Oxford: Clarendon Press, 1980.

Vanggaard, Thorkil. *Phallos.* New York: International Universities Press, 1972.

van Leeuwen, Arend Th. *Christianity in World History.* Trans. H. H. Hoskins, New York: Charles Scribner's Sons, 1964.

Van Leeuwen, Henry G. *The Problem of Certainty in English Thought, 1630–1690.* The Hague: Martinus Nijhoff, 1970.

Veblen, Thorstein. *The Theory of the Leisure Class.* New York: Mentor, 1953.

Vile, M. J. C. *Constitutionalism and the Separation of Powers.* Oxford: Clarendon Press, 1967.

Walker, D. P. *The Decline of Hell: Seventeenth-Century Discussions of Eternal Torment.* Chicago: University of Chicago Press, 1964.

Walzer, Michael. *Exodus and Revolution.* New York: Basic Books, 1985.

―――――. *The Revolution of the Saints: A Study in the Origins of Radical Politics.* Cambridge, Mass.: Harvard University Press, 1965.

Warnock, G. J. *Morality and Language.* Oxford: Basil Blackwell, 1983.

Warren, Samuel D., and Brandeis, Louis D. "The Right to Privacy." 4 *Harv. L. Rev.* 193 (1890).

Weber, Timothy P. "The Two-Edged Sword: The Fundamentalist Use of the Bible." *The Bible in America.* N. O. Hatch, and M. A. Noll, eds. New York: Oxford University Press, 1982, 101–17.

Wechsler, Herbert. "The Political Safeguards of Federalism: The Role of the States in the Composition and Selection of the National Government." 54 *Colum. L. Rev.* 543 (1954).

―――――. "Toward Neutral Principles of Constitutional Law." 73 *Harv.L.Rev.* 1 (1959).

Weiss, Jonathan. "Privilege, Posture, and Protection of 'Religion' in the Law." 73 *Yale L. J.* 593 (1964).

West, D. J. *Homosexuality.* Chicago: Aldine, 1968.

Westin, Alan F. *Privacy and Freedom.* New York: Atheneum, 1967.

White, Morton. *The Philosophy of the American Revolution.* New York: Oxford University Press, 1978.

―――――. *Science and Sentiment in America.* New York: Oxford University Press, 1972.

White, Robert W. *Ego and Reality in Psychoanalytic Theory.* New York: International Universities Press, 1963.

Whitehead, John W., and Conlan, John. "The Establishment of the Religion of Secular Humanism and Its First Amendment Implications." 10 *Tex. Tech. L. Rev.* 1 (1978).

Williams, Bernard. *Descartes: The Project of Pure Inquiry.* Harmondsworth: Penguin, 1978.

―――――. *Ethics and the Limits of Philosophy.* Cambridge, Mass.: Harvard University Press, 1985.

―――――. *Moral Luck.* Cambridge: Cambridge University Press, 1981.

―――――. *Problems of the Self.* Cambridge: Cambridge University Press, 1973.

―――――. ed. *Obscenity and Film Censorship.* Cambridge: Cambridge University Press, 1981.

―――――. "A Critique of Utilitarianism." In J. J. C. Smart, and Bernard Williams, *Utilitarianism For and Against.* Cambridge: Cambridge University Press, 1973, 77–150.

Williams, Elisha. *The Essential Rights and Liberties of Protestants, A Seasonable Plea for the Liberty of Conscience and the Right of private Judgment, In Matters of Religion, Without any Controul from human Authority.* Boston: Kneeland & Green, 1744.

Williams, Roger. *The Bloudy Tenent of Persecution. The Complete Writings of Roger Williams.* Vol. 3. Samuel L. Caldwell, ed. New York: Russell & Russell, 1963.

Wills, Garry. *Explaining America: The Federalist.* Garden City, N.Y.: Doubleday, 1981.

———. *Inventing America: Jefferson's Declaration of Independence.* Garden City, N.Y.: Doubleday, 1978.

Winters, Barbara. "Believing at Will." 76 *J. Phil.* 243 (1979).

Witherspoon, John. *Lectures on Moral Philosophy.* Jack Scott, ed. East Brunswick, N.J.; Associated University Presses, 1982.

Wolfe, Linda. *The Cosmo Report.* New York: Arbor House, 1981.

Wolfenden Report: Report of the Committee on Homosexual Offenses and Prostitution. New York: Stein and Day, 1963.

Wolff, Robert Paul. *Understanding Rawls.* Princeton, N.J.: Princeton University Press, 1977.

Wollheim, Richard. *The Thread of Life.* Cambridge, Mass.: Oxford University Press, 1984.

Wood, Gordon S. *The Creation of the American Republic, 1776–1787.* New York: W. W. Norton, 1969.

Wood, Neal. *John Locke and Agrarian Capitalism.* Berkeley: University of California Press, 1984.

Wood, Neal. *The Politics of Locke's Philosophy.* Berkeley: University of California Press, 1983.

Woodhouse, A. S. P., ed. *Puritanism and Liberty.* London: J. M. Dent & Sons, 1974.

Woods, Nancy Fugate. *Human Sexuality in Health and Illness.* 2d ed. St. Louis: C.V. Mosby, 1979.

Wright, J. Skelly. "Money and the Pollution of Politics: Is the First Amendment an Obstacle to Political Equality?" 82 *Colum. L. Rev.* 609 (1982).

———. "Politics and the Constitution: Is Money Speech?" 85 *Yale L. J.* 1001 (1976).

Wright, Louis B. *The Cultural Life of the American Colonies, 1607–1763.* New York: Harper & Row, 1957.

Yolton, John W. *Locke: An Introduction.* Oxford: Basil Blackwell, 1985.

Yudof, Mark G. *When Government Speaks.* Berkeley: University of California Press, 1983.

Zimmerman, Diane L. "Requiem for a Heavyweight: A Farewell to Warren and Brandeis's Privacy Tort." 68 *Cornell L. Rev.* 291 (1983).

LEGAL CASES

Abington School Dist. v. Schempp, 374 U.S. 203 (1963).
Abrams v. United States, 250 U.S. 616 (1919).
Adderly v. Florida, 385 U.S. 39 (1966).
Aguilar v. Felton, 53 USLW 5013, 105 S. Ct. 3232, 466 U.S.—(1985).

Associated Press v. Walker, 388 U.S. 130 (1967).

Baker v. Carr, 369 U.S. 186 (1962).

Baldwin v. Montana Fish and Game Commission, 436 U.S. 371 (1978).

Bates v. State Bar of Arizona, 433 U.S. 350 (1977).

Beauharnais v. Illinois, 343 U.S. 250 (1952).

Bibb v. Navajo Freight Lines, Inc., 359 U.S. 520 (1959).

Board of Education v. Barnette, 319 U.S. 624 (1943).

Bob Jones University v. United States, 461 U.S. 574 (1983).

Bradfield v. Robert, 175 U.S. 291 (1899).

Brandenburg v. Ohio, 395 U.S. 444 (1969).

Breard v. Alexandria, 341 U.S. 622 (1951).

Brown v. Board of Education, 347 U.S. 483 (1954).

Brown v. Louisiana, 383 U.S. 131 (1966).

Buckley v. Valeo, 424 U.S. 1 (1976).

Cantwell v. Connecticut, 310 U.S. 296 (1940).

Capital Broadcasting Co. v. Acting Attorney Gen., 405 U.S. 1000, *aff'g* 333 F. Supp. 582 (D.D.C. 1971).

Carter v. Carter Coal, 298 U.S. 238 (1936).

Central Hudson Gas v. Public Service Commission, 447 U.S. 557 (1980).

Chaplinsky v. New Hampshire, 315 U.S. 568 (1942).

Chicago Police Department v. Mosley, 408 U.S. 92 (1972).

Cohen v. California, 403 U.S. 15 (1971).

Coker v. Georgia, 433 U.S. 584 (1977).

Collin v. Smith, 578 F.2d 1197 (1978), *cert.den.*, 439 U.S. 916 (1978).

Columbia Broadcasting System v. Democratic Nat. Comm., 412 U.S. 94 (1973).

Committee for Public Education v. Regan, 444 U.S. 646 (1980).

Corfield v. Coryell, 6 F. Cas. 546 (C.C.E.D. Pa. 1823).

Cox Broadcasting Corp. v. Cohn, 420 U.S. 469 (1975).

Cox v. Louisiana, 379 U.S. 536 (1965).

Cox v. New Hampshire, 312 U.S. 569 (1941).

Curtis Pub. Co. v. Butts, 388 U.S. 130 (1967).

Daniel v. Waters, 515 F.2d 485 (6th Cir. 1975).

Dawson v. Vance, 329 F. Supp. 1320 (S.D. Tex. 1972).

Debs v. United States, 249 U.S. 211 (1919).

DeFunis v. Odegaard, 416 U.S. 312 (1974).

Dennis v. United States, 341 U.S. 494 (1951).

Doe v. Commonwealth's Attorney, 403 F. Supp. 1199 (E.D. Va. 1975), *aff'd without opinion* 425 U.S. 901 (1976).

Dun & Bradstreet v. Greenmoss Builders, 53 U.S.L.W. 4866, 105 S. Ct. 2939, 466 U.S.—(1985).

Edwards v. South Carolina, 372 U.S. 229 (1963).

Eisenstadt v. Baird, 405 U.S. 438 (1972).

Engel v. Vitale, 370 U.S. 421 (1962).

Epperson v. Arkansas, 393 U.S. 97 (1968).

Erznoznik v. Jacksonville, 422 U.S. 205 (1975).

Everson v. Board of Education, 330 U.S. 1 (1947).

FCC v. Pacifica Foundation, 438 U.S. 726 (1978).

Feiner v. New York, 340 U.S. 315 (1951).

Felton v. Secretary, U. S. Department of Education, 739 F.2d 48 (2d Cir. 1984) *aff'd sub nom. Aguilar v. Felton*, 53 USLW 5013, 105 S.Ct. 3232, 466 U.S.—(1985).

First National Bank of Boston v. Bellotti, 435 U.S. 765 (1978).

Fowler v. North Carolina, 428 U.S. 904 (1976) including *Brief for Petitioner*
    (No. 73–7031).

Friedman v. Rogers, 440 U.S. 1 (1979).

Frohwerk v. United States, 249 U.S. 204 (1919).

Frontiero v. Richardson, 411 U.S. 677 (1973).

Fullilove v. Klutznick, 448 U.S. 448 (1980).

Furman v. Georgia, 408 U.S. 238 (1972).

Gayle v. Browder, 352 U.S. 903 (1956).

Gertz v. Robert Welch, Inc., 418 U.S. 323 (1974).

Gibbons v. Ogden, 22 U.S. (9 Wheat.) 1 (1824).

Gillette v. United States, 401 U.S. 437 (1970).

Gitlow v. New York, 268 U.S. 652 (1925).

Gooding v. Wilson, 405 U.S. 518 (1972).

Grand Rapids School District v. Ball, 53 USLW 5006, 105 S.Ct. 3216, 466
    U.S.—(1985).

Greer v. Spock, 424 U.S. 828 (1976).

Gregg v. Georgia, 428 U.S. 153 (1976).

Griswold v. Connecticut, 381 U.S. 479 (1965).

Hague v. CIO, 307 U.S. 496 (1939).

Harper v. Virginia Board of Elections, 383 U.S. 663 (1966).

Harris v. McCrae, 448 U.S. 297 (1980).

Heffron v. International Society for Krishna Consciousness, Inc., 452 U.S. 640
    (1981).

Hess v. Indiana, 414 U.S. 105 (1973).

Holmes v. City of Atlanta, 350 U.S. 879 (1955).

Home Building & Loan Association v. Blaisdell, 290 U.S. 398 (1934).

Houchins v. KQED, 438 U.S. 1 (1978).

Hudgens v. NLRB, 424 U.S. 507 (1976).

Hutchinson v. Proxmire, 443 U.S. 111 (1979).

In Re Primus, 436 U.S. 412 (1978).

Kovacs v. Cooper, 336 U.S. 77 (1949).

Kramer v. Union Free School District No. 15, 395 U.S. 621 (1969).

Lehman v. Shaker Heights, 418 U.S. 298 (1974).

Lemon v. Kurtzman, 403 U.S. 602 (1971).

Linmark Associates, Inc. v. Willingboro, 431 U.S. 85 (1977).

Lochner v. New York, 198 U.S. 45 (1905).

Lovell v. Griffin, 303 U.S. 444 (1938).

Lovett v. United States, 328 U.S. 303 (1946)

Loving v. Virginia, 388 U.S. 1 (1967).

Lynch v. Donnelly, 465 U.S. 668 (1984).

McCollum v. Board of Education, 333 U.S. 203 (1948).

McCrae v. Califano, 491 F. Supp. 630 (1980).

McCulloch v. Maryland, 17 U.S. (4 Wheat.) 316 (1819).

McGowan v. Maryland, 366 U.S. 420 (1961).

McLean v. Arkansas Board of Education, 529 F. Supp. 1255 (E.D. Ark. 1982).

MacPherson v. Buick Motor Company, 217 N.Y. 382, 111 N.E. 1050 (1916).

Marbury v. Madison, 5 U.S. (1 Cranch) 137 (1803).

Marsh v. Chambers, 463 U.S. 703 (1983).

Martin v. Struthers, 319 U.S. 141 (1943).

Mayor of Baltimore v. Dawson, 350 U.S. 877 (1955).
Melvin v. Reid, 112 Cal.App. 285, 297 P. 91 (1931).
Meyer v. Nebraska, 262 U.S. 390 (1923).
Miami Herald Pub. Co. v. Tornillo, 418 U.S. 241 (1974).
Miller v. California, 413 U.S. 15 (1973).
Mueller v. Allen, 463 U.S. 388 (1983).
Naim v. Naim, 350 U.S. 985 (1956).
Nebraska Press Ass'n v. Stuart, 427 U.S. 539 (1976).
New York Times Co. v. Sullivan, 376 U.S. 254 (1964).
New York Times Co. v. United States, 403 U.S. 713 (1971).
Ohralik v. Ohio State Bar Ass'n, 436 U.S. 447 (1978).
Olmstead v. United States, 277 U.S. 438 (1928).
Paris Adult Theatre I v. Slaton, 413 U.S. 49 (1973).
Pell v. Procunier, 417 U.S. 817 (1974).
People v. Onofre, 51 N.Y.2d 476 (1980), *cert. den.,* 451 U.S. 987 (1981).
Pierce v. Society of Sisters, 268 U.S. 510 (1925).
Plessy v. Ferguson, 163 U.S. 537 (1896).
Prize Cases, 67 U.S. (2 Black) 635 (1863).
Red Lion Broadcasting Co. v. FCC, 395 U.S. 367 (1969).
Regina v. Bradlaugh, 2 Q.B.D. 569 (1877), *rev'd on other grounds,* 3 Q.B.D.
    607 (1878).
Reynolds v. Sims, 377 U.S. 533 (1964).
Reynolds v. United States, 98 U.S. 145 (1878).
Richmond Newspapers, Inc. v. Virginia, 448 U.S. 555 (1980).
Roe v. Wade, 410 U.S. 113 (1973).
Rosenbloom v. Metromedia, Inc., 403 U.S. 29 (1971).
Rosenfeld v. New Jersey, 408 U.S. 901 (1972).
Roth v. United States, 354 U.S. 476 (1957).
Rowan v. Post Office Dept., 397 U.S. 728 (1970).
Saxbe v. Washington Post Co., 417 U.S. 843 (1974).
Schaumburg v. Citizens for a Better Environment, 444 U.S. 620 (1980).
Schenck v. United States, 249 U.S. 47 (1919).
Sherbert v. Verner, 374 U.S. 398 (1963).
South Carolina State Highway Dept. v. Barnwell Brothers, 303 U.S. 177 (1938).
Southern Pacific Co. v. Arizona, 325 U.S. 761 (1945).
Spence v. Washington, 418 U.S. 405 (1974).
Stanley v. Georgia, 394 U.S. 557 (1969).
Stone v. Graham, 449 U.S. 1104 (1980).
Street v. New York, 394 U.S. 576 (1969).
Thomas v. Review Board, 450 U.S. 707 (1981).
Tilton v. Richardson, 403 U.S. 672 (1971).
Time, Inc. v. Firestone, 424 U.S. 448 (1976).
Time, Inc. v. Hill, 385 U.S. 374 (1967).
Tinker v. Des Moines School District, 393 U.S. 503 (1969).
Torcaso v. Watkins, 367 U.S. 488 (1960).
United States v. Ballard, 322 U.S. 78 (1944).
United States v. Bennett, 24 F.Cas. 1093, No. 14,571 (C.C.S.D.N.Y. 1879).
United States v. Brown, 381 U.S. 437 (1965).
United States v. Butler, 297 U.S. 1 (1936).
United States v. Chesman, 19 F. 497 (E.D. Mo. 1881).

United States v. Darby, 312 U.S. 100 (1941).
United States v. Lee, 102 U.S. 1051 (1982).
United States v. Nixon, 418 U.S. 683 (1974).
United States v. O'Brien, 391 U.S. 367 (1968).
United States v. Seeger, 380 U.S. 163 (1955).
United States v. Spock, 416 F.2d 165 (1st Cir. 1969).
United Steelworkers v. Weber, 443 U.S. 193 (1979).
University of California Regents v. Bakke, 438 U.S. 265 (1978).
Virginia Pharmacy Board v. Virginia Consumer Council, 425 U.S. 748 (1976).
Wallace v. Jaffree, 53 USLW 4665, 105 S.Ct. 2479, 466 U.S.—(1985).
Walz v. Tax Commission of the City of New York, 397 U.S. 664 (1970).
Watts v. United States, 394 U.S. 705 (1969).
Welsh v. United States, 398 U.S. 333 (1970).
West Coast Hotel Co. v. Parrish, 300 U.S. 379 (1937).
Whitney v. California, 274 U.S. 357 (1927).
Widmar v. Vincent, 454 U.S. 263 (1981).
Williams v. Florida, 399 U.S. 78 (1970).
Wisconsin v. Yoder, 406 U.S. 205 (1972).
Wooley v. Maynard, 430 U.S. 705 (1977).
Youngstown Sheet & Tube Co. v. Sawyer, 343 U.S. 579 (1952).
Zorach v. Clauson, 343 U.S. 306 (1952).

STATUTES

Comstock Act Sec. 2, ch. 258, sec. 2, 17 Stat. 598, 599 (1873),
    as amended, 18 U.S.C. 1461 (1970).

Index